# ASEAN and the Responsibility to Protect

This book adopts a sociolegal and interdisciplinary approach to examine how the Responsibility to Protect (R2P) has been understood within the Association of Southeast Asian Nations (ASEAN).

Historically, the international community has struggled to effectively address humanitarian crises worldwide. The concept of the 'Responsibility to Protect' (R2P) has emerged over the past two decades as a principle that could guide states' efforts to prevent and respond to humanitarian crises. However, R2P's interpretation varies across different regions, and it remains to be established whether it can successfully achieve its goals. This book adopts an interdisciplinary approach to analyse how R2P has been perceived and applied within the Association of Southeast Asian Nations (ASEAN) and China. In particular, it explores ASEAN's, ASEAN member states', and China's understanding and implementation of R2P, paying special attention to the 1999 East Timor crisis, the Rohingya crisis, and the West Papua conflict. The book assesses whether R2P has influenced the actions of ASEAN, its member states, and China. At a broader level, the book also explores regional approaches to international law, shedding light on Southeast Asian states' perspectives on this aspect of global governance.

This book will be of much interest to students of Responsibility to Protect, Asian politics, human rights, international law, and International Relations in general.

**Thida Chanthima Neth** holds a PhD in Public International Law from City University, London, UK, and is Strategic Advisor at the Asian Vision Institute, Cambodia.

**Global Politics and the Responsibility to Protect**

Series Editors:

Alex J. Bellamy

*University of Queensland*

Sara E. Davies

*Griffith University*

and

Monica Serrano

*The City University of New York.*

The aim of this book series is to gather the best new thinking about the Responsibility to Protect into a core set of volumes that provides a definitive account of the principle, its implementation, and its role in crises, that reflects a plurality of views and regional perspectives.

**Covid-19 and Atrocity Prevention in East Asia**
*Edited by Mely Caballero-Anthony and Noel M. Morada*

**Advocacy Networks and the Responsibility to Protect**
The Politics of Norm Circulation
*Sarka Kolmasova*

**Regional Approaches to the Responsibility to Protect**
Lessons from Europe and West Africa
*Jochem Rietveld*

**Strengthening the Responsibility to Protect**
A Transitional Cosmopolitan Approach
*Richard Illingworth*

**Reconstructing the Responsibility to Protect**
From Humanitarian Intervention to Human Security
*Michael J. Butler*

**ASEAN and the Responsibility to Protect**
An Ambivalent Relationship
*Thida Chanthima Neth*

For more information about this series, please visit: https://www.routledge.com/Global-Politics-and-the-Responsibility-to-Protect/book-series/GPRP

# ASEAN and the Responsibility to Protect

## An Ambivalent Relationship

**Thida Chanthima Neth**

Routledge
Taylor & Francis Group
LONDON AND NEW YORK

First published 2025
by Routledge
4 Park Square, Milton Park, Abingdon, Oxon OX14 4RN

and by Routledge
605 Third Avenue, New York, NY 10158

*Routledge is an imprint of the Taylor & Francis Group, an informa business*



*British Library Cataloguing-in-Publication Data*
A catalogue record for this book is available from the British Library

*Library of Congress Cataloging-in-Publication Data*
Names: Neth, Thida Chanthima, author.
Title: ASEAN and the responsibility to protect : an ambivalent relationship / Thida Chanthima Neth. Other titles: Association of Southeast Asian Nations and the responsibility to protect
Description: Abingdon, Oxon [UK] ; New York, NY : Routledge, 2025. | Series: Global politics and the responsibility to protect | Includes bibliographical references and index.
Identifiers: LCCN 2024030166 (print) | LCCN 2024030167 (ebook) | ISBN 9781032566931 (hardback) | ISBN 9781032566962 (paperback) | ISBN 9781003436799 (ebook)
Subjects: LCSH: Responsibility to protect (International law) | Responsibility to protect (International law)—Southeast Asia. | Responsibility to protect (International law)—China. | ASEAN.
Classification: LCC KZ4082 .N48 2025 (print) | LCC KZ4082 (ebook) | DDC 341.4/80959—dc23/eng/20240909
LC record available at https://lccn.loc.gov/2024030166
LC ebook record available at https://lccn.loc.gov/2024030167

ISBN: 978-1-032-56693-1 (hbk)
ISBN: 978-1-032-56696-2 (pbk)
ISBN: 978-1-003-43679-9 (ebk)

DOI: 10.4324/9781003436799

Typeset in Times New Roman
by Apex CoVantage, LLC

**I would like to dedicate this book to my father. His unwavering support is one of the most cherished things in my life.**

**To my family and friends, thank you for your continuous support.**

# Contents

# Abbreviations

| | |
|---|---|
| AHRD | ASEAN Human Rights Declaration |
| AICHR | ASEAN Intergovernmental Commission on Human Rights |
| AMM | ASEAN Foreign Ministerial Meetings |
| APODETI | Timorese Democratic People's Union |
| APSC | ASEAN Political-Security Community |
| ARSA | Arakan Rohingya Salvation Army |
| ASDT | Timorese Social Democratic Association |
| ASEAN | Association of the Southeast Asia Nation |
| EU | European Union |
| FRY | Federal Republic of Yugoslavia |
| FRETILIN | Revolutionary Front for Independent East Timor |
| GA | United Nations General Assembly |
| HI | Humanitarian Intervention |
| HRW | Human Rights Watch |
| ICJ | International Court of Justice |
| ICISS | International Commission on Intervention and State Sovereignty |
| INTERFET | International Force East Timor |
| KLA | Kosovo Liberation Army |
| NATO | North Atlantic Treaty Organization |
| NGOs | Non-governmental Organisations |
| OPM | *Organisasi Papua Merdeka* |
| P-5 | Permanent Members of the United Nations Security Council |
| RPF | Rwandan Patriotic Front |
| R2P | Responsibility to Protect |
| SC | United Nations Security Council |
| TAC | Treaty of Amity and Cooperation |
| TNI | Tentara Nasional Indonesia |
| UDHR | Universal Declaration of Human Rights |
| UDT | Democratic Union of Timor |
| UN | United Nations |
| UNAMIR | United Nations Assistance Mission for Rwanda |
| UNPROFOR | United Nations Protection Force |
| UNTEA | United Nations Temporary Executive Authority |
| VAP | Vientiane Action Programme |
| ZOPFAN | Declaration on a Zone of Peace, Freedom and Neutrality |

# Cases, Statutes, Treaties, and Other Instruments

**Association of Southeast Asian Nations**

ASEAN Human Rights Declaration (18 November 2012)
ASEAN Intergovernmental Commission on Human Rights (Terms of Reference) (2009)
ASEAN Political-Security Community Blueprint (2009)
ASEAN Security Community Plan of Action (14 June 2012)
Bangkok Declaration, Bangkok (2 April 1993)
Charter of the Association of Southeast Asian Nations (2008)
Declaration of ASEAN Concord II (Bali Concord II) (11 May 2012)
Kuala Lumpur Declaration on the Establishment of the ASEAN Charter, Kuala Lumpur (12 December 2005)
The ASEAN Declaration, Bangkok (8 August 1967)
The Declaration of ASEAN Concord, Bali, Indonesia (24 February 1976)
The Declaration on a Zone of Peace, Freedom and Neutrality, Kuala Lumpur (27 November 1971)
Vientiane Action Programme (2004)

**International Court of Justice**

*Application of the Convention on the Prevention and Punishment of the Crime of Genocide (Bosnia and Herzegovina v. Serbia and Montenegro)* Judgement, I.C.J. Reports 2007.
*Military and Paramilitary Activities in and against Nicaragua (Nicaragua v. United States of America)*, Merits, Judgement, I.C.J. Report 1986.
*Reparation for Injuries Suffered in the Service of the United Nations*, Advisory Opinion: I.C.J. Reports 1949.

**Organization of Islamic Cooperation**

Declaration of the Contact Group on Rohingya Muslims of Myanmar (19 September 2017)

Resolutions on Muslim Communities and Muslim Minorities in the Non-OIC Member States Adopted to the 45th Session of the Council of Foreign Ministers, Resolution No.4/45-MM (5–6 May 2018)

Resolution on the Situation of the Rohingya Muslim Minority in Myanmar Present to the Extraordinary Session of the OIC Council of Foreign Ministers on the Situation of the Rohingya Muslim in Myanmar (9 January 2017)

**United Nations General Assembly**

Resolution 1514 (XV), A/RES/1514 (14 December 1960)
Resolution 2504 (XXIV) A/RES/2504 (19 November 1969)
Resolution 3485 (XXX), A/RES/3485(XXX) (12 December 1975)
Resolution 31/53, A/RES/31/53 (1 December 1975)
World Summit Outcome Document, A/RES/60/1 (24 October 2005)
Resolution 66/230, A/RES/66/230 (3 April 2012)
Resolution 72/248, A/RES/72/248 (24 December 2017)
Resolution 73/264, A/RES/73/264 (22 December 2018)
Resolution 74/246, A/RES/74/246 (27 December 2019)

**United Nations Human Rights Council**

Resolution 34/22, A/HRC/RES/34/22 (3 April 2017)
Resolution, S-27/1, A/HRC/RES/S-27–1 (8 December 2017)

**United Nations Security Council**

Resolution 384, S/RES/384 (22 December 1975)
Resolution 389, S/RES/389 (22 April 1975)
Resolution 743, S/RES/743 (21 February 1992)
Resolution 819, S/RES/819 (16 April 1993)
Resolution 824, S/RES/824 (6 May 1993)
Resolution 872, S/RES/872 (5 October 1993)
Resolution 1160, S/RES/1160 (31 March 1998)
Resolution1199, S/RES/1199 (23 September 1998)
Resolution 1203, S/RES/1203 (24 October 1998)
Resolution1236, S/RES/1236 (7 May 1999)
Resolution 1239, S/RES/1239 (14 May 1999)
Resolution 1244, S/RES/1244 (10 June 1999)
Resolution 1246, S/RES/1246 (11 June 1999)
Resolution 1257, S/RES/1257 (3 August 1999)
Resolution 1264, S/RES/1264 (15 September 1999)
Resolution 1272, S/RES/1272 (25 October 1999)
Resolution 1970, S/RES/1970 (26 February 2011)
Resolution 1973, S/RES/1973 (17 March 2011)
Resolution 2669, S/RES/2669 (21 December 2022)
Draft Resolution S/2011/612 (4 October 2011)

**Others**

Charter of the United Nations (26 June 1945)
Constitution of the People's Republic of China (1982)
Convention on the Prevention and Punishment of the Crime of Genocide (1948)
The Commonwealth, The Kampala Communiqué (23–25 November 2007)
The North Atlantic Treaty, Washington D.C (4 April 1949)
The Organisation of African Unity Charter (25 May 1963)
The Rome Statute of the International Criminal Court (1998)
The *Panchsheel* Agreement or the Five Principles of Peaceful Coexistence (1954)
The United States National Security Strategy (October 2022)
Vienna Declaration and Programme of Action, Adopted by the World Conference on Human Rights in Vienna (25 June 1993)

**United Nations reports and sessions**

A Publication of the United Nations Department of Political Affairs, Trusteeship and Decolonization: Issue on East Timor [1976] Vol.1, No.7, August.
'East Timor 1999: Crimes against Humanity': A Report commissioned by the United Nations Office of the High Commissioner for Human Rights (2003), July.
The Office of the United Nations High Commissioner for Human Rights (2022), Assessment of human rights concerns in Xinjiang Uyghur Autonomous Region, People's Republic of China, 31 August.
United Nations General Assembly (1969), Report of the Secretary-General Regarding the Act of Self-Determination in West Irian, (1969) A/7723, 6 November.
——(1975), 30th Session, 4th Committee, Trusteeship (Including Non-Self-Governing Territories) A/C.4/SR.2188, 11 December.
—— (1975), 30th Session, 4th Committee, Trusteeship (including Non-Self-Governing Territories), 2180th Meeting, A/C.4/SR.2180, 3 December.
—— (1975), 30th Session, Agenda item 88, 'Question of Territories under Portuguese Administration', Report of the Fourth Committee, A/10426, 11 December.
—— (1999), 'People of East Timor Reject Proposed Special Autonomy, Express Wish to Begin Transition to Independence, Secretary-General Informs Security Council', SG/SM/7119, 3 September.
—— (1999), Transcript of Press Conference of Secretary-General Kofi Annan at Headquarters, SG/SM/7124, 10 September.
—— (2004), *'A more secure world: our shared responsibility' Report of the High-Level Panel on Threats, Challenges and Change,* A/59/565, 2 December.
—— (2005), Fifty-ninth Session, 89th Plenary Meeting, A/59/PV.89, 8 April.
—— (2005), Sixtieth Session, 22nd Plenary Meeting, A/60/PV.22, 23 September.
——(1999), Report of the Secretary-General, 'Question of East Timor' S/1999/513, 5 December.
—— (2009), Report of the Secretary-General '*Implementing the responsibility to protect'*, A/63/677, 12 January.
——(2011), Letter dated 9 November 2011 from the Permanent Representative of Brazil to the United Nations addressed to the Secretary-General, A/66/551-S/2011/701, 11 November.

—— (2011), '*Report of the International Law Commission'*, A/66/10.
—— (2012), Report of the Secretary-General '*Responsibility to protect: timely and decisive response'*, A/66/874- S/2012/578, 25 July.
—— (2016), Report of the Secretary-General '*Mobilizing collective action: the next decade of responsibility to protect'* A/70/999-S/2016/620, 22 July.
—— (2018), 'Third Committee Approves 13 Drafts on Persons with Disabilities, Ageing, Human Trafficking amid Protracted Votes on Human Rights in Syria, Myanmar', GA/SHC/4254, 16 November.
—— (2006), Sixtieth Session, 98th Plenary Meeting, A/60/PV.98, 7 September.
—— (2007), Sixty-second Session, 12th Plenary Meeting, A/62/PV.12, 1 October.
United Nations Human Rights Council (2008), National Report of China to the Human Rights Council as part of the Universal Periodic Review, A/HRC/WG.6/4/CHN/1, (2–13 February).
—— (2011), '*Report of the Independent International Commission of Inquiry on the Syrian Arab Republic*', A/HRC/S-17/2/Add.1, 23 November.
—— (2018), '*Report of the independent international fact-finding mission on Myanmar'* A/HRC/39/64, 12 September.
—— (2023), Seventy-eighth session Third Committee, 'Situation of Rohingya Muslims and other minorities in Myanmar', A/C.3/78/L.40/Rev.1, 8 November 2023.
United Nations Group of Friends of the Responsibility to Protect (2016), Statement by the Group of Friends of the Responsibility to Protect in Geneva at the Informal Interactive Dialogue with the Under-Secretary-General Mr. Adama Dieng, Special Adviser to the Secretary-General on the Prevention of Genocide, 3 March.
—— (2019), Statement delivered on behalf of the Group of Friends of R2P on Item 2 at the 41st session of the Human Rights Council, 25 June.
United Nations Secretary-General (2000), Millennium Report of the Secretary-General '*We the Peoples—The Role of the United Nations in the 21st Century'*.
—— (2005), Secretary-General's message to ceremony marking the 10th anniversary of the Srebrenica massacre (delivered by Mark Malloch Brown, Chef de Cabinet)', 11 July.
—— (2011), 'Secretary-General's remarks at Breakfast Roundtable with Foreign Ministers on "The Responsibility to Protect: Responding to Imminent Threats of Mass Atrocities"', 23 September.
United Nations Security Council (1975), 1864th Meeting, S/PV.1864, 15 December.
—— (1976), The Situation in East Timor, 1909th Meeting, 14 April.
—— (1999), Letter Dated 28 July 1999 From the Secretary-General Addressed to the President of the Security Council, S/1999/830, 28 July.
—— (1999), 4043rd Meeting, S/PV.4043, 11 September.
—— (1999), Report of the Security Council Mission to Jakarta and Dili, 8 to 12 September, S/1999/976, 14 September.
—— (2004), 5040th Meeting, S/PV/.5040, 18 September.
—— (2008), 5898th Meeting, S/PV.5898, 27 May.
—— (2017), Statement by the President of the Security Council, S/PRST/2017/22, 6 November.

—— (2021), Statement by the President of the Security Council, S/PRST/2021/5, 10 March.

United Nations Security Council Press Release (1999), 'Security Council Rejects Demand for Cessation of Use of Force Against Federal Republic of Yugoslavia', SC/6659, 26 March.

—— (1999), 'Security Council hears 52 speakers in open debate on situation in East Timor', SC/6724, 11 September.

—— (2016), 'Security Council Fails to Adopt Two of the Draft Resolutions on Syria, Despite Appeals for Action Preventing Impending Humanitarian Catastrophe in Aleppo', SC/12545, 8 October.

—— (2022), 'Security Council Demands Security Council Demands Immediate End to Violence in Myanmar, Urges Restraint, Release of Arbitrarily Detained Prisoners, Adopting Resolution 2669', SC/15159, 21 December.

**Association of Southeast Asian Nations Reports and Statements**

ASEAN (1976), Joint Communique of the Ninth ASEAN Ministerial Meeting, 24–26 June.

—— (1979), Joint Statement The Special ASEAN Foreign Ministerial Meeting On the Current Political Development in The Southeast Asia Region, Bangkok, 12 January.

—— (2001) Address by Rodolfo C. Severino, Secretary-General of the Association of Southeast Asia Nations, at the International Law Conference on ASEAN Legal Systems and Regional Integration, 'The ASEAN Way and the Rule of Law'.

—— (2009), Chairman's Statement of the 14th ASEAN Summit "ASEAN Charter for the ASEAN Peoples', 28 February-1 March.

—— (2009), Joint Co-Chairmen's Statement of the 17th ASEAN-EU Ministerial Meeting (AEMM), Phnom Penh, Cambodia, 27–28 May.

—— (2009), Joint Communiqué of the 42nd ASEAN Foreign Minister Meeting "Acting Together to Cope with Global Challenges" Phuket, Thailand, 20 July.

—— (2009), Chairman's Statement of the 15th ASEAN Summit— "Enhancing Connectivity, Empowering People', 23–25 October.

—— (2012, Statement of ASEAN Foreign Ministers on the Recent Developments in the Rakhine State, Myanmar, 17 August.

—— (2012), Chairman's Statement of the 21st ASEAN Summit, 18 November.

—— (2017), Chairman's Statement of the 30th ASEAN Summit, 30 April.

—— (2017), Chairman's Statement on the Humanitarian Situation in Rakhine State, 24 September.

—— (2018), Chairman's Statement of the 32nd ASEAN Summit, Singapore, 28 April.

—— (2018), Joint Communique of the 51st ASEAN Foreign Ministerial Meeting, 2 August.

—— (2018), Chairman's Statement of the 33rd ASEAN Summit, 13 November.

—— (2019), Chairman's Statement of the 34th ASEAN Summit, 23 June.

—— (2019), Joint Communique of the 52nd ASEAN Foreign Ministerial Meeting, 31 July.
—— (2019), Chairman's Statement of the 35th ASEAN Summit, 3 November.
—— (2020), Chairman's Statement of the 36th ASEAN Summit, 26 June.
—— (2020), Joint Communique of the 53rd ASEAN Foreign Ministerial Meeting, 9 September.
—— (2020), Chairman's Statement of the 37th ASEAN Summit, 12 November.
—— (2021), Joint Communique of the 54th ASEAN Foreign Ministerial Meeting, 2 August.
—— (2021), Chairman's Statement of the 38th and 39th ASEAN Summit, 28 October.
—— (2021), Chair's Statement on the Informal Ministerial Meeting (IAMM), 2 March.
—— (2021), Chairman's Statement on the ASEAN Leaders' Meeting, 24 April.
—— (2022), Joint Communique of the 55th ASEAN Foreign Ministerial Meeting, 3 August.
—— (2022), Chairman's Statement of the 40th and 41st ASEAN Summit, 11 November.
—— (2023), Chairman's Statement of the 42nd ASEAN Summit, 11 May.
—— (2023), Joint Communique of the 56th ASEAN Foreign Ministerial Meeting, 11–12 July.
—— (2023), Chairman's Statement of the 43rd ASEAN Summit, 5 September.

**Non-governmental Organisations and Governments' Reports/ Statements**

Asian Human Rights Commission (2013), *The Neglected Genocide: Human rights abuses against Papuans in the Central Highlands,* 1977–1978'.
Amnesty International (1999), *East Timor: Demand for Justice*, ASA/21/191/1999, 27 October.
—— (2004), *Myanmar: The Rohingya Minority: Fundamental Rights Denied,* ASA 16/005/2004.
ASEAN Parliamentarians for Human Rights (2015), *Disenfranchisement and Desperation in Myanmar's Rakhine State: Drivers of a Regional Crisis,* October.
Asia Pacific Centre for the Responsibility to Protect (2015), Detailed conference report on "*The Responsibility to Protect at 10: Progress, Challenges and Opportunities in the Asia Pacific*", 26–27 February.
Government of Indonesia (2006), Statement by H.E. Dr. N. Hassan Wirajuda, Minister of Foreign Ministry of the Republic of Indonesia, Keynote Speech at the 2nd Roundtable Discussion on Human Rights in ASEAN: Challenges and Opportunities for Human Rights in a Caring and Sharing Community', 18 December.
—— (2009), Statement by H.E. Dr. R. M. Marty M. Natalegawa Ambassador, Permanent Representative of the Republic of Indonesia to the United Nations "Integrated and coordinated implementation of and follow-up to the outcomes

of the major United Nations conferences and summits in the economic, social and related field" and "Follow-up to the outcome of the Millennium Summit", 23 July.

—— (2014), Statement by the Deputy Permanent Representative of the Republic of Indonesia to the United Nations at the Informal Interactive Dialogue on the Report of the Secretary-General on "Fulfilling our collective responsibility: international assistance and the responsibility to protect", 8 September.

—— (2015), Statement by H.E. Mr. Muhammad Anshor Chargé d'affaires ad interim Permanent Mission of the Republic of Indonesia to the United Nations at the 'Informal interactive Dialogue on the responsibility of states to protect their populations by preventing genocide, war crimes, ethnic cleansing, and crimes against humanity', 8 September.

Government of Laos (2016), Statement by H.E. Dr. Khamlien Pholsena, Vice Minister of Planning and Investment of the Lao People's Democratic Republic at the Annual Ministerial Meeting on Least Developed Countries (LDCs), 24 December.

—— (2018), Statement by H.E. Dr Khiane Phansourivong, Permanent Representative of the Lao People's Democratic Republic to the United Nations at the Third Committee of the 73rd Session of the United Nations General Assembly, Agenda item 28, 2 October.

Government of Malaysia (2005), Statement by the Honourable Abdullah Ahmad Badawi, Prime Minister of Malaysia and Head of the Malaysian Delegation to the High-Level Plenary Meeting of the 60th Session of the United Nations General Assembly, 14 September.

—— (2012), Statement by H.E. Ambassador Hussein Haniff, Permanent Representative of Malaysia to the United Nations on 'Responsibility to Protect' at the Interactive Dialogue at CR4 of the United Nations, 5 September.

—— (2014), Statement by H.E. Ambassador Hussein Haniff, Permanent Representative of Malaysia to the United Nations on 'Fulfilling our Responsibility: International Assistance and the Responsibility to Protect' at the Interactive Dialogue of the General Assembly of the United Nations, 8 September.

—— (2015), Malaysia's Statement at the United Nations General Assembly Informal Interactive Dialogue on the Responsibility to Protect: "A vital and enduring commitment: Implementing the responsibility to protect", 8 September.

—— (2017), Statement by the Malaysian Minister of Foreign Affairs at the OIC Contact Group on the Rohingya Muslim Minority in Myanmar, 19 September.

Government of Myanmar (1947), The Constitution of the Union of Burma, 4 January.

—— (1982), Burma Citizenship Law, 15 October.

—— (2005), Statement by His Excellency U Nyan Win, Minister for Foreign Affairs and Chairman of the Delegation of the Union of Myanmar at the High-Level Plenary Meeting of the 60th Session of the United Nations General Assembly, 13 June.

—— (2013), 'Final Report of Inquiry Commission on Sectarian Violence in Rakhine State', 8 July.

—— (2014), Intervention by His Excellency Mr. Kyaw Tin, Permanent Representative of the Republic of the Union of Myanmar to the United Nations General Assembly Informal Interactive Dialogue on the Report of the Secretary-General on the Responsibility to Protect, 8 September.

—— (2015), Statement by His Excellency Mr. Kyaw Tin, Permanent Representative of the Republic of the Union of Myanmar to the United Nations at the 'Informal Dialogue on the Responsibility of States to Protect Their Populations by Preventing Genocide, War Crimes, Ethnic Cleansing and Crimes Against Humanity', 8 September.

—— (2017), Statement by Myanmar at the General Assembly Informal Interactive Dialogue on the Responsibility to Protect: "Implementing the Responsibility to Protect: Accountability for Prevention", 6 September.

—— (2018), Statement by Statement by Ambassador U Hau Do Suan, Permanent Representative of Myanmar to the United Nations at the United Nations High-level Conference of Heads of Counter-Terrorism Agencies of Member States, 28–29 June.

Government of the Philippines (2014), The Philippines' Statement to the 'Responsibility to Protect: 6th Annual Interactive Dialogue on the Secretary-General's Report, 8 September.

—— (2015), The Philippines' Statement at United Nations General Assembly interactive dialogue on the Responsibility to Protect: "A vital and enduring commitment: Implementing the responsibility to protect", 8 September.

—— (2016), The Philippines' Statement at United Nations General Assembly interactive dialogue on the Responsibility to Protect "Implementing the Responsibility to Protect: Accountability for Prevention", 6 September.

—— (2021), The Philippines' Statement for the Special Session of the Human Rights Council on the Human Rights Implications of the Crisis in Myanmar, 12 February.

Government of Singapore (2009), Statement by Ambassador Vanu Gopala Menon, Permanent Representative of Singapore to the United Nations, at the Interactive Dialogue on the Responsibility to Protect, 24 July.

—— (2012), Statement by Ambassador Albert Chua, Permanent Representative of Singapore to the United Nations at the General Assembly Interactive Dialogue on the Responsibility to Protect: 'Responsibility to Protect: Timely and Decisive Response', 5 September.

—— (2015), Statement by Ambassador Karen Tan, Permanent Representative of Singapore to the United Nations at the General Assembly Interactive Dialogue on the Responsibility to Protect 'A vital and enduring commitment: Implementing the responsibility to protect', 8 September.

—— (2016), Statement by Ambassador Burhan Gafoor, Permanent Representative of Singapore to the United Nations at the General Assembly Interactive Dialogue on the Responsibility to Protect 'Mobilizing Collective Action: the next decade of the Responsibility to Protect', 6 September.

Government of Thailand (2005), Statement by H.E. Dr Kantathi Suphamongkhon at the General Debate of the 69th Session of the UN General Assembly, 18 September.

—— (2013), Statement by His Excellency Mr. Chayapan Bamrungphon, Ambassador and Deputy Permanent Representative of Thailand to the United Nations, Thailand's Intervention at the 'Informal Interactive Dialogue on Responsibility of States to Protect Their Populations by Preventing Genocide, War Crimes, Ethnic Cleansing and Crimes Against Humanity through appropriate means and measures', 11 September.

—— (2015), Thailand's Statement at the United Nations General Assembly Informal Interactive Dialogue on the Responsibility to Protect: "A vital and enduring commitment: Implementing the responsibility to protect", 8 September.

—— (2016), Thailand's Statement at the United Nations General Assembly Informal Interactive Dialogue on the Responsibility to Protect "Mobilizing Collective Action: The Next Decade of Responsibility to Protect", 6 September.

—— (2017), Thailand's Statement at the United Nations General Assembly Informal Interactive Dialogue on the Responsibility to Protect "Implementing the Responsibility to Protect: Accountability for Prevention", 6 September.

Government of Vietnam (2009), Statement by H.E. Ambassador Bui The Giang, Deputy Permanent Representative of Viet Nam, at the GA's Plenary Meeting on Responsibility to Protect, 24 July.

—— (2012), Statement by Ambassador Pham Vinh Quang, Deputy Permanent Representative of the Socialist Republic of Vietnam at the United Nations General Assembly interactive dialogue on Responsibility to Protect: "Responsibility to Protect: Timely and Decisive Response", 5 September.

Human Rights Watch (1991), Asia Watch, *East Timor: The November 12 Massacre and its Aftermath*, Vol.3, No.6, 12 December.

—— (1995), *The Fall of Srebrenica and the Failure of UN Peacekeeping*, Volume 7, No.13, 15 October.

—— (2012), *The Government Could Have Stopped This": Sectarian Violence and Ensuing Abuses in Burma's Arakan State*, 1 August.

International Commission on Intervention and State Sovereignty (ICISS)(2001), *The Responsibility to Protect: Report of the International Commission on Intervention and State Sovereignty* (Ottawa: International Development Research Centre).

International Crisis Group (2016), *Myanmar: A New Muslim Insurgency in Rakhine State*, 283 Asia Group Report, 15 December.

People's Republic of China (2005), Statement at the Informal Interactive R2P Dialogue.

—— (2009), Statement by Ambassador Liu Zhenmin at the Plenary Session of the General Assembly on the Question of "Responsibility to Protect", 8 September.

—— (2011), Statement at the UN General Assembly Informal Interactive Dialogue on R2P "The Role of Regional and Sub-Regional Arrangements in Upholding the Responsibility to Protect", 12 July.

—— (2013), Statement at the UN General Assembly informal interactive dialogue on "The Responsibility to Protect, State Responsibility and Prevention", 11 September.

—— (2014), Statement at the UN General Assembly informal interactive dialogue on the Responsibility to Protect: "Fulfilling our collective responsibility: International assistance and the responsibility to protect," 8 September.

—— (2015), Statement at the UN General Assembly informal interactive dialogue on the Responsibility to Protect: "A vital and enduring commitment: Implementing the responsibility to protect," 8 September.

—— (2016), Statement at the UN General Assembly Thematic Panel Discussion, "From Commitment to Implementation: Ten Years of the Responsibility to Protect", 26 February.

—— (2017), Statement at the UN General Assembly informal interactive dialogue on the Responsibility to Protect: "Implementing the Responsibility to Protect: Accountability for Prevention," 6 September.

Report of the High-Level Advisory Panel on the Responsibility to Protect in Southeast Asia (2014), *Mainstreaming the Responsibility to Protect in Southeast Asia: Pathway Towards a Caring ASEAN Community*, 9 September.

The Independent International Commission on Kosovo (2000), *The Kosovo Report: Conflict, International Response, Lessons Learned* (Oxford University Press).

The New York Agreement (1962)

United Nations (1976), A Publication of the United Nations Department of Political Affairs, Trusteeship and Decolonization: Issue on East Timor [1976] Vol.1, No.7, August.

# 1 Introduction

## 1.1 The Context

Prior to the Cold War, the issue of human rights played a very limited role in both international law and relations. Traditionally, as Antonio Cassesse had stated, 'individuals were mere "appendices" of the State to which they belonged, simple pawns in its hands, to be used, protected or sacrificed according to what State interests dictated'.[1] That began to change with the end of the Cold War. The post-Cold War era has brought several fundamental changes into the international community as we see today. Due to globalisation, the world has become economically and socially intertwined, closer than ever before, which means that events in one part of the world can have profound implications for another.[2] Furthermore, States are no longer the only influential actors in the international community given the steady rise of international and regional organisations which began after World War II. In this changing setting, one of the main novelties brought by the end of the Cold War was the international community's growing concern with human rights, crucially facilitated by the collapse of the Soviet Union and the parallel rise of liberal democracies. Among other things, the latter sought to advance on the international plane 'the notion of equal autonomy of and respect for the individual' in which they firmly believe.[3] The perception of State sovereignty was inevitably affected by this new focus on individual rights. Pre-Cold War, sovereignty was understood in the traditional Westphalian concept, which entails that:

> the State is sovereign in that it must answer to no higher authority in the international sphere. It alone defines and protects the right of individuals and groups.[4]

However, the growing concern with the human rights of individuals living within States tore apart the veil that had been used traditionally to protect the rigid concept of Westphalian sovereignty.[5] As the concept of absolute sovereignty continued to erode, States no longer had free rein over the treatment of their people. The standards enshrined in the Universal Declaration of Human Rights began to acquire new emphasis and value.

DOI: 10.4324/9781003436799-1

Another parallel development that occurred in the past few decades is the increase in intra-state conflicts that have gradually come to outnumber the more traditional inter-state wars.[6] The international community was, and continues to be, not well equipped to deal with this type of conflict because the relevant provisions of the central legal instrument of the United Nations (UN), namely the UN Charter, are only responsive to inter-state conflicts.[7] Quite importantly, intra-state conflicts tend to lead to mass atrocity situations affecting and displacing the civilian population. According to a recent Report of the UN Secretary-General, in 2014 the numbers of deaths caused by atrocity crimes exceeded 100,000, its highest level since 1994 due to the increased targeting of civilians.[8] The report also highlighted that atrocity crimes contributed significantly to the global crisis of forced displacement, with 21.3 million refugees and more than 40.8 million internally displaced persons counted as of 2016.[9] Given these numbers, the ability of the international community to respond effectively to atrocity crimes becomes extremely important.

In the early and mid-1990s, the international community failed to respond to the well-known humanitarian crises in Rwanda and Srebrenica. In 1994, the international community failed to protect innocent civilians during the Rwandan civil war, which resulted in the 'one hundred days of genocide' of the Tutsi population.[10] Sadly, the same can be said about the genocide in Srebrenica. In 1995, the world saw the genocide of more than 8,000 Bosniaks by the Bosnian Serb army.[11] By contrast, the international community took action in relation to the humanitarian crisis, which erupted in Kosovo in the late 1990s. On this occasion, the North Atlantic Treaty Organization (NATO) launched an unprecedented bombing campaign to protect the Kosovar Albanians against the armed forces of the Federal Republic of Yugoslavia (FRY).[12] With the United Nations Security Council (SC) gridlocked, several failed rounds of negotiations and the atrocities on the ground escalating to ethnic cleansing, NATO commenced Operation Allied Force, which ultimately brought an end to the conflict. But was this military intervention legal? To answer this question, one must refer to the concept of humanitarian intervention.

For this book, humanitarian intervention is understood as

> the threat or use of force across state borders by a state (or group of states) aimed at preventing or ending widespread and grave violations of the fundamental human rights of individuals other than its own citizens, without the permission of the state within whose territory force is applied.[13]

Put simply, in international law there is no legal basis for humanitarian intervention. Indeed, this concept is riddled with both legal and political controversies. Legally, it conflicts with two important provisions of the UN Charter, namely Article 2(4) and 2(7). Article 2(4) states that 'All Members shall refrain in their international relations from the threat or use of force against the territorial integrity or political independence of any state'.[14] Article 2(7), instead, states 'Nothing contained in the present Charter shall authorize the United Nations to intervene in matters which are essentially in the domestic jurisdiction of any state'.[15] Politically, a key concern surrounding humanitarian intervention is that it cannot be guaranteed that interventions of these kinds would always be led exclusively by humanitarian motives. Thus, intervenors could claim a right to carry out an intervention on humanitarian grounds, while, in reality, through this intervention they could be pursuing their own self-interests or, even, an imperialistic agenda.[16] Another difficult question is who should have the right to intervene in humanitarian crises in another State?[17] Individual States? Or groups of States only, possibly under the auspices of a regional organisation or the SC?

The importance of each of these questions became apparent in relation to the NATO intervention in Kosovo. Legally speaking, the NATO military intervention was widely seen as illegal since it was in direct violation of the UN Charter, notably Articles 2(4) and 2(7) that were mentioned earlier. As argued by Nigel White, not only did NATO violate the two Articles of the UN Charter, but the organisation also stepped outside the parameters of the Charter when it failed to secure authorisation from the SC.[18] On the other hand, several authors, including Bruno Simma and Antonio Cassese, acknowledged the illegal character of the intervention but also referred to it as *legitimate*, since it was aimed at halting mass atrocities at a time when no other viable alternative was considered available.[19] The legal and political debates surrounding the NATO intervention left the international community facing a fundamental question: if Operation Allied Force represents a violation of international law, are we supposed to just stand by and watch another Rwanda and Srebrenica? The essence of this dilemma was perfectly captured by the words of former Secretary-General of the UN, Kofi Annan:

> if humanitarian intervention is, indeed, an unacceptable assault on sovereignty, how should we respond to a Rwanda, to a Srebrenica- to gross and systematic violations of human rights that offend every precept of our common humanity?[20]

This dilemma revealed powerfully the need for a different approach to responding to mass atrocities. In particular, the criticisms moved against NATO's intervention paved the way for a shift from an individual right to intervene—represented by the classic concept of humanitarian intervention—to a collective responsibility to protect, a new idea reflected in the concept of 'Responsibility to Protect' (R2P).[21] R2P was first envisioned as a concept in the Report of the International Commission on Intervention and State Sovereignty (ICISS).[22] R2P was revolutionary in the way in which it re-characterised 'the right to intervene' as a 'responsibility to protect'. Conceptually, the issue was no longer about the 'right' of any State to intervene but, rather, the 'responsibility' of all States to protect their own populations from mass atrocities.[23] Furthermore, sovereignty could no longer be used as a shield to protect States' actions; instead, the concept of sovereignty would carry with it a primary responsibility of States to protect their peoples from atrocities.

The introduction of this new perception of sovereignty departs from the traditional Westphalian way of thinking. In this way, R2P transformed both the concept of sovereignty and the concept of non-intervention, that is, a corollary principle of sovereignty. Rather than seeing intervention as an illegal interference in the domestic affairs of a sovereign State, R2P redefined it as sharing or overtaking the responsibility of a State to protect its people from mass atrocities when the State is unable or unwilling to do so.

As is discussed in the following chapter, in an effort to simplify the core concepts of R2P, in 2009 the then-UN Secretary-General, Ban Ki-moon, published a report outlining the three-pillar structure of R2P.[24] Pillar I outlines the primary responsibility of States in protecting their populations from genocide, war crimes, ethnic cleansing, and crimes against humanity.[25] Pillar II outlines the responsibility that the international community has in encouraging and assisting States in meeting their Pillar I responsibilities.[26] Finally, Pillar III outlines the responsibility of the international community, through the UN, to respond collectively to humanitarian crises in a timely and decisive manner.[27]

This book accepts that R2P promises to provide a better response to humanitarian crises than humanitarian intervention does. Unlike the concept of humanitarian intervention, R2P's principles are legally in accordance with the UN Charter. As mentioned earlier, R2P has reconciled the traditional concept of sovereignty and responsibility. Of course, sovereignty should be respected but only if the State is upholding its primary responsibility to protect its people. In a situation where the State is either unable or unwilling to do so, its sovereignty is then forfeited to the international community and is no longer protected by the UN Charter, namely Article 2(7). So, if an intervention occurs, it will not be in violation of the UN Charter since it would be as a result of the international community (with authorisation from the SC) taking over its responsibility to protect people from the State in question. Furthermore, because R2P operates within the UN Charter framework, it is politically more acceptable.

For these reasons, this book suggests that efforts should be made to further promote R2P as a key guiding principle of international action in situations of mass atrocities. However, R2P cannot be said, today, to have become very well established in international law. Conceptually, the fundamental idea of R2P is generally accepted by the international community. By contrast, the precise meaning and scope of R2P, as well as how it should be applied in practice, remain a subject of debate among States. This is not surprising given the implications that any attempt to redefine the principles of sovereignty and non-intervention can have on international law and affairs. This book recognises the potential of R2P to provide a more structured and effective answer to mass atrocities (in addition to the need to provide such answers), but also takes note of the ongoing disagreement among States as to its exact meaning and scope. Accordingly, this book posits that it is extremely important to examine the nature and degree of this 'disagreement' and that doing so could, in turn, contribute to promoting a more universal understanding of R2P. In particular, this book focuses on the approach to R2P taken in one particular region of the world, that is, Southeast Asia. Specifically, it considers the relationship between R2P, the Association of Southeast Asian Nations (ASEAN), and China. There are four fundamental reasons as to why I have chosen to examine ASEAN's approach to R2P. Firstly, ASEAN is becoming an increasingly important actor in international affairs and has arguably been the most successful regional organisation among developing countries.[28] ASEAN has become a worldwide trading hub with partnerships with the European Union (EU), China, Japan, South Korea and India.[29] ASEAN is also the United States' (US) fourth largest trading partner.[30] Unsurprisingly, ASEAN's growing economic and political importance has been recognised by great powers such as the US and China.[31] A recent article in the Economist pointed out that there is competition between the US and China over the hegemony of the region since the combined economies of the Southeast Asia countries would be the fourth biggest in the world and the region is home to 700 million people—more than the EU, Latin America or Middle East combined.[32] Going forward, Southeast Asia will become an even more important region of the world, making it all the more important to look at how international norms are seen, interpreted, and implemented in this part of the globe.[33] Secondly, ASEAN has traditionally taken a very conservative approach to the principles of sovereignty and non-intervention. As is explained in Chapter 3, ASEAN States had a long history of colonialism and external interferences, which contributed to reinforcing their commitments to a Westphalian type of sovereignty.[34] Indeed, since its creation, ASEAN has repeatedly reiterated its firm support for the concepts of sovereignty and non-interference.[35] Evidently, this conservative position is at odds with the fundamental principles of R2P that were discussed earlier, making it particularly interesting to examine the extent of the relevant clash between these two approaches to sovereignty. Thirdly, ASEAN is made up of quite a diverse group of States. Although, as mentioned earlier, these States have taken a conservative approach to the principles of sovereignty and non-intervention, the degree of conservatism varies greatly among them. For example, Myanmar, the Philippines, Malaysia, Cambodia, Laos, Singapore, and Vietnam are parties to the Convention on the Prevention and Punishment of the Crime of Genocide (1948), while Indonesia, Thailand, and Brunei are not.[36] Furthermore, among ASEAN States only Cambodia and the Philippines are parties to the Rome Statute of the International Criminal Court.[37] Fourthly, and on a more personal level, I come from Cambodia, which is one of the ASEAN States. Therefore, I have a personal attachment to this region of the world, and I am particularly interested in exploring ASEAN's position on a vital question such as that of atrocity crimes. Additionally, I also made the decision to include China in my analyses. Whilst China is not a member of ASEAN, as is discussed later in the book, China's approach to R2P and implementations of the concepts of sovereignty and non-interference largely mirror that of ASEAN and its member states. Therefore, by also examining China, it would give us a fuller picture of how this region of the world approaches questions of international law that are pertinent to humanitarian crises and has the potential to replace the current status quo of Western hegemony of international law.

## 1.2 The Research Questions and the Theoretical Framework of the Book

The central research question of this book is 'How do ASEAN and China approach R2P?' This central question is then divided into three subsections, namely what the ASEAN/China conceptual approach to R2P is, how has ASEAN/China practically engaged with R2P, and what does the correlation between ASEAN and China on R2P translate into. A broader question that is indirectly addressed by this study is that of the implications of regional approaches to international law. This is a growing area of interest under international law which sets, broadly, the theoretical framework of this book. The assumption of 'universal' international law suggests that the latter is 'universal', that is to say, that principles of international law are perceived in the same way all over the world.[38] In reality, international laws are approached in different ways by different States in different regions of the world in a way that better suits their preferences.[39] This is especially so now that the world order is no longer based on a unipolar structure but, rather, a multipolar one with power diffusing among several States.[40] Following this new distribution of geopolitical power, non-Western States such as Russia, China, India, Brazil, and South Africa have become more assertive powers.[41] With their increased importance and relevance on the international stage, these non-Western States, collectively and individually, are making themselves heard and seeking to impose their views and interpretations of international law in the international community to challenge the status quo of Eurocentrism.[42] The Eastern States have also become more assertive in offering their own interpretations of international law in order to prevent history from repeating itself.[43] Notably, China has been a champion in the Southeast Asia region for representing an alternative interpretation of international law that, in accordance with ASEAN States' preferences, places the highest importance on the principles of sovereignty and non-intervention.[44]

Against this background, regional approaches to international law originated as a specific methodology within the umbrella of contemporary comparative international law with the aim of identifying, analysing and explaining differences and similarities between the approaches taken by different actors on questions of international law.[45] Crucial authors have contributed to the rise of this approach to the study of international law, including Anthea Roberts,[46] William Burke-White,[47] Xue Hanqin,[48] Lauri Malksoo,[49] Onuma Yasuaki,[50] B.S. Chimni[51], and Congyan Cai.[52] In light of the changes in the geopolitical order mentioned earlier, these authors have suggested that different interpretations of international law must be taken into account instead of simply taking for granted the universal validity of Western interpretations. This approach to international law is, therefore, better suited to provide a genuine universal representation of international law that is based on worldwide views rather than just on the view representative of one region of the world. Seen from this perspective, considering and examining regional approaches to questions of international law actually enrich rather than weaken the universality of international law.

In accordance with this approach, I specifically choose to focus on the approach to R2P of one particular region of the world, namely Southeast Asia. As discussed in the book, this means that it is particularly important to examine how this region of the world approaches the principles of international law that are vital for the interpretation and implementation of R2P, namely State sovereignty, non-interference, use of force, and human rights. The gaps between how Western and ASEAN States/China interpret these principles are noteworthy. For example, while Western States have gradually moved away from the Westphalian concept of sovereignty, Eastern States have been wary of this change of perspective. These differences are particularly acute regarding humanitarian crises. For example, referring to NATO's intervention in Kosovo, it was the threat of veto by Russia and China that prevented the US, the UK, and France from obtaining a Security Council authorisation to intervene militarily. In these situations, regional approaches to humanitarian crises can, therefore, vary substantially.

Despite this, the importance of regional organisations in responding to mass atrocities and implementing R2P has been acknowledged by the ICISS Report, the World Summit Outcome Document (2005), and the Report of the Secretary-General 'The role of regional and subregional arrangements in implementing the responsibility to protect' (2011).[53] In fact, some have also suggested that regional actors could be better suited than international actors in implementing R2P.[54] This is so for four reasons. Firstly, given that mass atrocities are a threat to the peace, security, stability, and economy of a region, States within that region are more willing to act being the most affected ones.[55] Secondly, the SC does not always have the political will to respond to mass atrocities as is discussed in the Rwanda and Srebrenica cries in the following chapter.[56] Thirdly, regional actors would generally be more welcomed by local parties because of their intimate knowledge of the cultural, political, social, and geographical terrain.[57] Finally, non-Western States would always see an intervention led by Western States as a form of neo-colonial imperialism.[58] For all these reasons, my book seeks to examine ASEAN, ASEAN States', and China's approaches to R2P also with a view to highlighting the differences with the West and in the hope of fostering a stronger genuine universal approach to the relevant principles of international law.

## 1.3 Book Outline

This book is structured as follows. Chapter 2 discusses the emergence of R2P in international law. The chapter starts with the examination of the International Commission on Intervention and State Sovereignty's report 'The Responsibility to Protect'. Following on from that, it explores the gradual move of R2P from the political to the legal space starting with its institutionalisation at the UN 2005 World Summit. This chapter also seeks to highlight both the conceptual and practical controversies associated with R2P. Chapter 3 introduces ASEAN as the regional organisation placed at the centre of this book. The chapter, first, offers an overview of ASEAN's history, institutional structure and decision making-mechanisms. Crucially, this chapter also discusses the key principles guiding the conduct of the organisation in international relations. After having provided an overview of ASEAN in Chapter 3, the book turns to analyse, in Chapter 4, how ASEAN approaches R2P *conceptually*. This chapter considers both ASEAN and ASEAN States' positions on the three Pillars of R2P. Special attention is paid to individual States' engagement with the discussions held during the General Assembly Informal Interactive Dialogues on R2P that took place between 2009 and 2017. These are meetings where individual members of the UN discussed their positions and opinions on R2P seeking to identify the flaws and challenges faced by R2P. Accordingly, this chapter divides ASEAN States on the basis of their level of support for R2P, describing them as wary supporters, R2P-neutrals, or opposers.

The second part of the book, composed of Chapters 5, 6, and 7, focuses on ASEAN's practical responses to three humanitarian crises. Chapter 5 analyses ASEAN's position during a humanitarian crisis, which occurred before the formal emergence of R2P in international law, namely the 1999 East Timor crisis. ASEAN and its member states' reactions are analysed in detail, while also considering the reaction of the international community. Chapter 6, rather, focuses on ASEAN and ASEAN States' responses to a very recent mass atrocity situation, namely the Rohingya crisis in Myanmar. Crucially, and in contrast with the previous case study, this humanitarian crisis occurred after the emergence of R2P in international law. Considering the broad support, at the *conceptual* level, of ASEAN States for R2P, it will be interesting to see whether this conceptual support would ultimately translate into action or whether a similar behaviour to the one seen in the case of East Timor ended up characterising also ASEAN's response towards Myanmar. Chapter 7 focuses on ASEAN and ASEAN States' responses to the West Papua crisis that still occurs today in order to see whether their conceptual endorsements would translate into action, or not. Chapter 8 focuses on China's perceptions and engagements of R2P, which is then compared to ASEAN and the ASEAN States in order to analyse the extent of their similarities. Chapter 9 draws some final conclusions as to ASEAN's overall approach to R2P and about how their holding similar attitudes as China would express how this region's stance on R2P could affect the future development of this concept as a guiding principle of international law.

## Notes

1 Antonio Cassese, *International Law* (2nd edition, Oxford University Press, 2005) p. 376.
2 Aidan Hehir, *Humanitarian Intervention: An Introduction* (Palgrave Macmillan, 2010) p. 5.
3 David P. Forsythe, *Human Rights in International Relations* (3rd edition, Cambridge University Press, 2012) p. 22.
4 Robert Gilpin, *War and Change in World Politics* (Cambridge University Press, 1981) p. 17.
5 Antonio Cassese, *International Law* (2nd edition, Oxford University Press, 2005)p. 375.
6 Christine Gray, *International Law and the Use of Force* (3rd edition, Oxford University Press, 2008) p. 7; and Harold A. Young, 'Intrastate Conflicts: Refocus on the Intractable' (MPSA, 12 September 2017) <https://blog.mpsanet.org/2017/09/12/intrastate-conflicts-refocus-on-the-intractable/> accessed on 18 March 2021.
7 Marc Weller, *The Oxford Handbook of the Use of Force in International Law* (Oxford University Press, 2015) p. 19.
8 Report of the Secretary-General, 'Mobilizing Collective Action: The Next Decade for the Responsibility to Protect' (2016) A/70/999-S/2016/620, pp. 3–4.
9 Ibid.
10 The civil war was between the Hutu-led government and the Rwandan Patriotic Front (RPF). Officially, the war was supposed to end once both parties had signed the Arusha Accords in which they agreed to a power-sharing political structure. In reality, as soon as the Accords were signed, the Hutu extremists began their genocidal campaign to

scupper the implementation of the Accords. The death toll ranges were around 800,000 in addition to 250,000–500,000 rapes of the Tutsis; see Aidan Hehir, *Humanitarian Intervention: An Introduction* (Palgrave Macmillan, 2010) pp. 181–183; and 'Rwanda Genocide: 100 Days of Slaughter' (BBC, 4 April 2009) <https://www.bbc.co.uk/news/world-africa-26875506> accessed on 18 March 2021.

11 During the Bosnian War in 1993, Srebrenica was declared a 'safe area' through the SC Resolution 824, which was supposed to mean that the town was under the protection of the United Nations Protection Force; see, The United Nations Security Council Resolutions 824, S/RES/824; and Cedric Ryngaert and Nico Schrijver, 'Lessons Learned from the Srebrenica Massacre: From UN Peacekeeping Reform to Legal Responsibility' [2015] 62 *Netherlands International Law Review*, p. 219.

12 The Independent International Commission on Kosovo, *The Kosovo Report: Conflict, International Response, Lessons Learned* (Oxford University Press, 2000) pp. 70–72.

13 J.L. Holzgrefe and Robert Keohane (eds), *Humanitarian Intervention: Ethical, Legal and Political Dilemmas* (Cambridge University Press, 2005) p. 18.

14 The United Nations Charter, Article 2(4).

15 Ibid., Article 2(7).

16 Jennifer M. Welsh, *Humanitarian Intervention and International Relations* (Oxford University Press, 2003) p. 58.

17 Aidan Hehir, *Humanitarian Intervention: An Introduction* (Palgrave Macmillan, 2010) p. 135.

18 N.D. White, 'The Legality of Bombing in the Name of Humanity' [2000] 5(1) *Journal of Conflict and Security Law*, p. 32.

19 Antonio Cassese, 'Ex Iniuria Ius Oritur: Are We Moving Towards International Legitimation of Forcible Humanitarian Countermeasures in the World Community?' [1999] 10(1) *European Journal of International Law*, p. 25; and Bruno Simma, 'NATO, the UN and the Use of Force: Legal Aspects' [1999] 10(1) *European Journal of International Law*, p. 12; see also The Independent International Commission on Kosovo, *The Kosovo Report: Conflict, International Response, Lessons Learned* (Oxford University Press, 2000) p. 4.

20 'We the Peoples—The Role of the United Nations in the 21st Century' (2000), Millennium Report of the Secretary-General, p. 48 <https://www.un.org/en/events/pastevents/pdfs/We_The_Peoples.pdf> accessed on 14 April 2021.

21 The concept of 'Responsibility to Protect' is analysed in detail in Chapter 2.

22 'The Responsibility to Protect' [2001] The International Commission on Intervention and State Sovereignty.

23 Ramesh Thakur and William Maley, *Theorising the Responsibility to Protect* (Cambridge University Press, 2015) p. 21.

24 United Nations General Assembly (2009), 'Implementing the Responsibility to Protect' A/63/677.

25 Ibid., pp. 10–14.

26 Ibid., pp. 15–21.

27 Ibid., pp. 22–27.

28 Stephen Aris and Andreas Wenger, *Regional Organisations and Security: Conceptions and Practices* (Routledge, 2014) p. 81.

29 European Commission, 'Association of Southeast Asian Nations (ASEAN) (European Commission, updated 5 May 2020) <https://ec.europa.eu/trade/policy/countries-and-regions/regions/asean/index_en.htm> accessed on 10 January 2021; and Elaine Kurtenbach, 'ASEAN, China, Other Partners Sign World's Biggest Trade Pact' (The Diplomat, 16 November2020)<https://thediplomat.com/2020/11/asean-china-other-partners-sign-worlds-biggest-trade-pact/> accessed on 10 January 2021.

30 Office of the United States Trades Representatives, 'Association of the Southeast Asian Nations (ASEAN)' <https://ustr.gov/countries-regions/southeast-asia-pacific/association-southeast-asian-nations-asean> accessed on 10 January 2021.

31 In his statement, former president of the United States, Barack Obama recognised the significance of ASEAN in its role in pursuing regional peace and prosperity as well as being an international trade partner. Chinese President Xi Jinping acknowledged ASEAN as an essential trading partner and announced that China has made its relationship with ASEAN a priority; see, Remarks by President Obama at opening Session of US-ASEAN Summit (15 February 2016) <https://obamawhitehouse.archives.gov/the-press-office/2016/02/15/remarks-president-obama-opening-session-us-asean-summit> accessed on 7 December 2020; and Laura Zhou, '"Let's Build a Digital Silk Road": Xi Jinping Looks to Cement China's Ties with ASEAN' (South China Morning Post, 27 November 2020) <https://www.scmp.com/news/china/diplomacy/article/3111612/lets-build-digital-silk-road-president-xi-promises-ways-china> accessed on 7 December 2020.

32 The Economist, 'The Battle for China's Backyard' (The Economist, 27 February 2021) <https://www.economist.com/leaders/2021/02/27/the-rivalry-between-america-and-china-will-hinge-on-south-east-asia> accessed on 15 March 2021.

33 Ryan Zhang, 'Beating the Odds: How ASEAN Helped Southeast Asia Succeed' (Harvard Political Review, 15 March 2020) <https://harvardpolitics.com/asean-beats-the-odds/> accessed on 7 December 2020.

34 Shaun Narine, 'State Sovereignty, Political Legitimacy and Regional Institutionalism in the Asia-Pacific' [2004] 17(3) *The Pacific Review*, p. 426.

35 The Bangkok Declaration (1967), p. 1; The Declaration on a Zone of Peace, Freedom and Neutrality, Kuala Lumpur (1971); The Treaty of Amity and Cooperation (1976), Article 2 and The ASEAN Charter (2007).

36 Lina A. Alexandra, 'The Incipient Development of ASEAN: A Chance for Mutual Learning' [2013] *Instituto Affari Internazionali*, p. 65; see also International Committee of the Red Cross, 'Convention on the Prevention and Punishment of the Crime of Genocide' <https://ihl-databases.icrc.org/applic/ihl/ihl.nsf/States.xsp?xp_viewStates=XPages_NORMStatesParties&xp_treatySelected=357#panelReservation> accessed on 15 March 2021.

37 International Criminal Court, 'Signatories of the Rome Statute' <https://international-criminalcourtnashie.weebly.com/signatories-of-the-rome-statute.html> accessed on 15 March 2021.

38 Paul B. Stephan, 'Symmetry and Selectivity: What Happens in International Law When the World Changes' [2009] 10(1) *Chicago Journal of International Law*, p. 102.

39 William W. Burke-White, 'Power Shifts in International Law: Structural Realignment and Substantive Pluralism' [2015] 56(1) *Harvard International Law Journal*, p. 44.

40 Paul B. Stephan, 'Symmetry and Selectivity: What Happens in International Law When the World Changes' [2009] 10(1) *Chicago Journal of International Law*, p. 115.

41 Anthea Roberts, *Is International Law International?* (Oxford University Press, 2017) p. 14.

42 Ibid.; and Wim Muller, 'China: An Illiberal, Non-Western States in a West-centric, Liberal Order?' [2014] *Baltic Yearbook of International Law*, pp. 3–4.

43 Lauri Mälksoo, 'Russia and China Challenge the Western Hegemony in the Interpretation of International Law' (Blog of the European Journal of International Law, 15 July 2016) <https://www.ejiltalk.org/russia-and-china-challenge-the-western-hegemony-in-the-interpretation-of-international-law/> accessed on 11 May 2021.

44 Ibid.; and Wim Muller, 'China: An Illiberal, Non-Western States in a West-centric, Liberal Order?' [2014] *Baltic Yearbook of International Law*, pp. 6 and 9–10.

45 Anthea Roberts, et al., *Comparative International Law* (Oxford University Press, 2018) p. 162; and Anthea Roberts, *Is International Law International?* (Oxford University Press, 2017) p. 21.

46 Anthea Roberts, et al., *Comparative International Law* (Oxford University Press, 2018) and Anthea Roberts, *Is International Law International?* (Oxford University Press, 2017).

47 William W. Burke-White, 'Power Shifts in International Law: Structural Realignment and Substantive Pluralism' [2015] 56(1) *Harvard International Law Journal*.
48 Xue Hanqin, *Chinese Contemporary Perspectives on International Law* (Brill Nijhoff, 2012).
49 Lauri Malksoo, *Russian Approaches to International Law* (Oxford University Press, 2015); and Lauri Malksoo, 'Civilizational Diversity as Challenge to the (False) Universality of International Law' [2019] 9 *Asian Journal of International Law*.
50 Onuma Yasuaki, *International Law in a Transcivilizational World* (Cambridge University Press, 2017); and Onuma Yasuaki, *A Transcivilization Perspective on International Law* (Hague Academy of International Law, 2010).
51 B.S. Chimni, *International Law and World Order: A Critique of Contemporary Approaches* (Cambridge University Press, 2017) and B.S. Chimni, 'Third World Approaches to International Law: A Manifesto' [2006] 8(3) *International Community Review*.
52 Congyan Cai, *The Rise of China and International Law: Taking Chinese Exceptionalism Seriously* (Oxford University Press, 2019); and Congyan Cai, 'New Great Powers and International Law in the 21st Century' [2013] 24(3) *European Journal of International Law*.
53 'The Responsibility to Protect' [2001] The International Commission on Intervention and State Sovereignty, pp. 22 and 26; Report of the Secretary-General, 'The Role of Regional and Subregional Arrangements in Implementing the Responsibility to Protect' (2011), A/65/877-S/2011/393, pp. 2–3; and The United Nations, 'The 2005 World Summit: High-Level Panel Plenary Meeting of the 60th Session of the UN General Assembly' (UN Headquarter, New York, 14–16th September 2005) <http://www.un.org/en/events/pastevents/worldsummit_2005.shtml> accessed on 15 March 2021.
54 Bolarinwa Adediran, 'Implementing R2P: Towards a Regional Solution?' [2017] 9 *Global Responsibility to Protect*, p. 461.
55 Ibid., p. 468.
56 Ibid., pp. 469–470.
57 Ibid., p. 472.
58 Ibid., p. 474.

# 2 The Emergence of R2P in International Law

## 2.1 Introduction

This chapter focuses on the emergence of the principle of responsibility to protect. Its aim is to provide, at the beginning of the book, an overview of the current meaning and status of responsibility to protect in international law. The chapter first offers a discussion of the failures of the international community's responses to the humanitarian crises in Rwanda and Srebrenica in the mid-1990s and then, an analysis of the North Atlantic Treaty Organization's controversial Operation Allied Force in Kosovo in 1999. Following on this, this chapter discusses the origins of the responsibility to protect, which was first developed, in 2001, by the International Commission on Intervention and State Sovereignty in an effort to define a new guiding principle that could provide a valid answer to the problem of mass atrocities. After that, the chapter provides an overview of the gradual move of the responsibility to protect from the political to the legal space, a move that culminated in the adoption of the 2005 World Summit Outcome Document. The second part of the chapter looks at how the responsibility to protect has been thus far implemented on the ground. To date, the two conflict situations which have been most heatedly debated in connection with the responsibility to protect are those which started to occur in Libya and Syria in 2011. Finally, this chapter draws some conclusions as to the conceptual and practical problems that still hinder the full development and implementation of the responsibility to protect as an efficient principle in the battle against mass atrocities.

## 2.2 Rwanda, Srebrenica and Kosovo

As briefly mentioned in Chapter 1, in the mid-1990s, the international community failed to respond to two mass atrocity situations. The first one, which occurred in Rwanda in 1994, relates to the genocide of the Tutsi population.[1] This genocide took place in the context of an intra-state conflict, which had officially started in 1990 as a result of a deep-seated historical animosity between the two main ethnic groups in Rwanda, namely the Hutu and the Tutsi.[2] Prior to the colonisation of the country at the hands of Belgium, the distinction between the Hutus and Tutsis was not deeply embedded in the society.[3] The situation then worsened in 1959, when

DOI: 10.4324/9781003436799-2

the Hutus rebelled and overthrew the Belgian-backed Tutsi regime.[4] Following this change, thousands of Tutsis fled to Uganda and formed the Rwandan Patriotic Front (RPF).[5] Once the fighting started, the international community became involved and engaged in extensive mediation efforts to try to bring the violence to an end. These efforts resulted in the Arusha Accords/Peace Agreement, which aimed at establishing a new power-sharing political structure between the Hutu-led Rwandan Government and the Tutsis' RPF.[6] As part of the agreement and through the United Nations Security Council (SC) Resolution 872 of 1993, the United Nations (UN) established the UN Assistance Mission for Rwanda (UNAMIR) to monitor the ceasefire agreement and implement other conditions of the Accords.[7] The Hutu extremists were angered by the Accords and began a genocidal campaign against the Tutsi, because, as Réné Lemarchand put it, 'the wanton killing of Tutsi civilians . . . became the quickest and most "rational" way of eliminating all basis for compromise with the RPF'.[8] By the time the Accords were signed, the Hutu extremists had already established an effective organisational structure to implement their political plan of genocide.[9] Just before the Hutus initiated their genocidal campaign, the UN peacekeepers warned that extreme violence was very much likely to happen, but this warning was ignored.[10] Once the genocidal campaign started, the role of the UNAMIR had been reduced to being mere bystanders since it was not authorised to intervene militarily because it was not mandated under Chapter VII of the UN Charter.[11]

The second humanitarian crisis that revealed the incapacity of the international community to respond to mass atrocities was described by the former UN Secretary-General Kofi Annan as 'the worst [massacre] on European soil since the Second World War'.[12] This is the genocide that occurred in Srebrenica (Bosnia and Herzegovina) in July 1995. The violence in Bosnia-Herzegovina erupted when the latter sought independence from the former Federal Republic of Yugoslavia (FRY) in 1991 along with Croatia and Slovenia.[13] During the ensuing civil war, the Muslim population of Bosnia-Herzegovina was particularly targeted and subjected to torture, rape, murder, beatings, forced displacement, and destruction of property and cultural objects as part of the FRY and other Serbian paramilitary group's ethnic cleansing campaign.[14] Those who were able to, would flee to the closest designated UN 'safe areas/zones' that were supposedly protected by the United Nations Protection Force (UNPROFOR).[15] Ironically, these so-called 'safe zones' were not at all safe since the UN forces were ill-equipped and outnumbered compared with the Bosnian Serb army.[16] So, declaring Srebrenica a 'safe zone' did not deter the latter from increasing their attacks, which, in their view, were aimed at fighting terrorist activities from within the area.[17] Along with the increased attacks, there were numerous more indications that the Bosnian Serb's offensive campaign had started to escalate, including restrictions to food and medical supplies as well as restrictions of the peacekeepers' access to weapons in preparation for the main campaign of the full takeover of Srebrenica.[18] Despite indications that atrocities would be committed in Srebrenica, the SC did not take decisive action.[19] In the end, more than 8,000 Muslim men and boys were killed, an atrocity crime that the International Court of Justice (ICJ) has defined as genocide.[20]

What, then, did the UN do to prevent these two instances of genocide from occurring? Why had no one provided adequate protection to innocent civilians in the name of humanitarianism? From a legal perspective, these are not simple questions to answer. The concept of humanitarian intervention (HI) is one of the most controversial subjects in international law. As briefly mentioned in Chapter 1, there is no legal basis in international law for humanitarian intervention. Legally, this concept conflicts with two crucial provisions of the UN Charter, namely articles 2(4) and 2(7).[21] Politically, a notable concern of humanitarian intervention is around the issue of motives. Humanitarian interventions can easily be abused by powerful States by masking a self-serving agenda.[22] Another area of concern is who should have the right to intervene in humanitarian crises in another State: should it be individual States? Or regional organisations?

### *2.2.1 Humanitarian Intervention in Action*

Contrary to the cases of Rwanda and Srebrenica, a military intervention was launched to protect the Albanian population of Kosovo in 1999. In 1989, President Slobodan Milosević of the FRY, moved by his vision of 'One Serbia', repealed the autonomy of Kosovo. Following this change, President Milosević also started implementing discriminatory laws in Kosovo favouring the Serbs while oppressing the native Kosovar Albanians.[23] As a result of this form of oppression, the Albanians created the Kosovo Liberation Army (KLA) with the objective of liberating Kosovo from Serbian occupation.[24] Once military activities started to increase from both sides, the situation gained the attention of the international community.[25] The UN, through the SC, sought to mediate in order to put an end to the conflict, in which they failed.[26] As negotiations between the FRY and the Kosovar Albanians broke down, atrocities escalated to the level of ethnic cleansing, and the SC was gridlocked due to China and Russia threatening to veto any resolution that would authorise the use of force against the FRY.[27] At that point, a regional organisation, the North Atlantic Treaty Organization (NATO), launched a military operation, Operations Allied Force, to put an end to the conflict.[28] NATO's bombing campaign began on 24 March 1999, and it did not receive the authorisation of the SC. This intervention had a significant impact on international law debates concerning humanitarian intervention.[29] NATO was in direct violation of Article 2(4) of the UN Charter.[30] The UN Charter only provides two legal exceptions to Article 2(4): self-defence, which did not apply in the case of Operation Allied Force, and use of force authorised by the SC, which was not obtained.[31] A simple legal analysis would, therefore, point to the illegality of Operation Allied Force. That said, according to many, including Judge Bruno Simma and Antonio Cassese, while NATO intervention was, strictly speaking, illegal, it was also legitimate, a thesis which was also subscribed to the Independent International Commission on Kosovo.[32] After all, one could argue that one of the purposes of the UN is the promotion of human rights and, therefore, situations where systematic and grave human rights violations occur require intervention.[33] This is especially true if one considers that NATO's bombing campaign was a last-resort action taken after all diplomatic avenues and efforts had previously failed.[34] Thus, supporters of humanitarian intervention saw the NATO operation in Kosovo as a welcome indication that 'we are indeed entering the third age of human rights evolution: the era of enforcement'.[35]

The failure to act in relation to Rwanda and Srebrenica, on the one hand, and the legally controversial and problematic NATO operation in Kosovo, on the other, revealed the need for a different approach to mass atrocities in international law. The ensuing debate paved the way for the emergence of the principle of the responsibility to protect.

## 2.3 The International Commission on Intervention and State Sovereignty

As a result of the events in Rwanda, Bosnia, and Kosovo that were discussed previously, in 2000 the Canadian government decided to set up a commission to consider how the international community should respond to mass atrocity situations.[36] The following year, the International Commission on Intervention and State Sovereignty (ICISS) produced a report that encouraged States to reconceptualise the idea of sovereignty as a responsibility to protect and promote their own and other people's welfare and basic rights.[37] According to Gareth Evans, Ramesh Thakur, and William Maley, this idea of 'sovereignty as responsibility' represents one of the most important developments and breakthroughs in international politics in our time.[38]

Instead of the traditional concept of Westphalian sovereignty which gave States complete authority over their domestic affairs, the ICISS highlighted that the responsibility towards their citizens should be States' first priority.[39] In cases where a State is either unable or unwilling to protect its own citizens, then there should be 'a residual responsibility for other states to take up the slack'.[40] Crucially, this residual responsibility is not placed on States individually but, rather, as members of the international community. Therefore, if mass human rights violations occur and the State concerned fails to stop them, it becomes the responsibility of the international community to intervene for protection purposes.[41] The report of the ICISS also elaborated on the conditions that would justify an intervention. First, when there is a 'large-scale loss of life, actual or apprehended, with genocidal intent or not, which is the product either of deliberate state action, or state neglect or inability to act, or a failed state situation'.[42] Second, when there is 'large-scale "ethnic cleansing," actual or apprehended, whether carried out by killing, forced expulsion, acts of terror or rape'.[43]

While innovative in many respects, the ICISS left a number of questions unanswered, in particular the question of the 'right authority'. By noting that the Security Council has the 'primary'—rather than exclusive—responsibility under the UN Charter to authorise military action in the context of peace and security matters, the Commission left open the possibility for action without the authorisation of the SC. In the event that the SC is blocked or simply unable to come to an agreement in a crisis, the ICISS stated that Article 11 of the UN Charter gives the

United Nations General Assembly (GA) a fallback responsibility with regard to the maintenance of international peace and security.[44] However, the GA's power is limited to only making recommendations and not binding decisions. Nevertheless, the Report noted that even in the absence of an authorisation from the SC, if an intervention is to take place with the backing of a two-thirds vote in the GA, then it can be legitimately justified with powerful moral and political support.[45] More worryingly, this approach would also potentially validate the idea of humanitarian intervention carried out unilaterally by States, which was discussed earlier in this chapter.[46]

At the time of the publication of the ICISS report, R2P was merely an idea for the international community to consider. Many issues remained to be discussed, and more light needed to be shed on the meaning of this new concept. All these steps would be soon taken as part of a process of 'legalisation' of R2P, as will be discussed in the following section.

## 2.4 The Gradual Recognition of R2P in International Law

An important moment in the evolution of R2P happened in 2004, when the then Secretary-General of the UN, Kofi Annan, formally endorsed the concept in the report '*A More Secure World: Our Shared Responsibility*'. In particular, he expressly referred to:

> the emerging norm that there is a collective international responsibility to protect, exercisable by the Security Council authorising military intervention as a last resort, in the event of genocide and other large-scale killing, ethnic cleansing or serious violations of humanitarian law which sovereign governments have proved powerless of unwilling to prevent.[47]

This endorsement reflects upon the very fundamental concepts found in the ICISS report on R2P, which states that sovereignty entails duties and responsibility to defend people, whether they are domestic or abroad.[48] Furthermore, the 2004 report made a reference to the responsibility of all actors in the international community to protect every person in the face of mass human rights violations.[49]

While the UN Secretary-General's endorsement of R2P was certainly positive progress and a sign of its early development, it did not carry any significant legal value. Indeed, it could perhaps be better described as an indication of an important political commitment to support R2P. A year after the publication of this report, however, R2P was endorsed in a considerably more important document agreed by and supported by more than 170 States, that is, the 2005 World Summit Outcome. According to scholars such as Gareth Evans, the critical link between the ICISS report and the outcome of the World Summit was the real birth of R2P.[50] The 2005 World Summit was a once-in-a-generation opportunity where the vast majority of the world's heads of States and governments made decisions on areas of development, security, human rights and reform that would further the aims and objectives of the UN overall.[51] The Outcome document was adopted by the General Assembly in September 2005. Two paragraphs of the Summit Outcome Document deal specifically with the principle of the responsibility to protect, namely paragraphs 138 and 139. The former affirms that:

> Each individual State has the responsibility to protect its populations from genocide, war crimes, ethnic cleansing and crimes against humanity. This responsibility entails the prevention of such crimes, including their incitement, through appropriate and necessary means. We accept that responsibility and will act in accordance with it. The international community should, as appropriate, encourage and help States to exercise this responsibility and support the United Nations in establishing an early warning capability.[52]

The key part of Paragraph 139, instead, affirms that:

> The international community, through the United Nations, also has the responsibility to use appropriate diplomatic, humanitarian and other peaceful means, in accordance with Chapters VI and VIII of the Charter, to help protect populations from genocide, war crimes, ethnic cleansing and crimes against humanity. In this context, we are prepared to take collective action, in a timely and decisive manner, through the Security Council, in accordance with the Charter, including Chapter VII, on a case-by-case basis and in cooperation with relevant regional organisations as appropriate, should peaceful means be inadequate and national authorities manifestly fail to protect their populations from genocide, war crimes, ethnic cleansing and crimes against humanity.[53]

There are obvious connections between the Outcome Document and the ICISS report that were discussed in the previous section. For example, the wording in Paragraph 138 is similar to Section 4.20 of the ICISS report, which refers to the types of conscience-shocking situations that would trigger the implementation of R2P, typically including large-scale acts of ethnic cleansing, war crimes, crimes against humanity, and genocide.[54] Paragraph 139, instead, is related to Section 8.28 of the 2001 report, which refers to the responsibility of the international community to react if and when the four crimes are being committed.[55] However, despite embracing several aspects of the ICISS report, the World Summit Outcome introduced some fundamental changes.

First, the just cause threshold identified by ICISS, which, as noted before, was deemed too broad. By contrast, although there are similarities in the language, the Summit adopted a more restrictive version of the just cause, limiting R2P to only the case of four specific crimes: genocide, war crimes, crime against humanity, and ethnic cleansing. Another important change regards the question of 'right authority'. As noted before, the ICISS had affirmed, quite vaguely, that the SC should be the 'preferred' body to authorise any use of force for humanitarian purposes, which left open the possibility that individual States could act in the absence of a Security Council resolution.[56] Crucially, as it is made clear by paragraph 139, the Summit

Outcome recognised the Security Council as the only 'right authority'. First, the international community must act through the SC, and second, any form of intervention must be authorised by the latter. In doing so, the Outcome Document created a more limited version of R2P, perhaps also hoping that doing so would ensure its more effective application in the future. In fact, it has been argued that the variant of R2P endorsed by the Summit Outcome not only is a limited one but also one which does not add anything new to the existing UN Charter framework. This is so because the doctrine of R2P is not as revolutionary as it appears since it actually does not alter any of the legal instruments and powers of the international community, specifically the SC.[57] In accordance with Chapter VII of the UN Charter, the Council is empowered to implement both coercive and non-coercive measures in response to a threat to international peace and security. And since the definition of the concept of 'threat to peace' can be interpreted widely, the Council has always been able to authorise coercive measures in response to intrastate conflicts and/or humanitarian crises.[58]

Indeed, some critics of R2P, namely Stephen P. Marks and Nicholas Cooper, went even further to state that not only R2P is not as revolutionary as it appears to be, but its doctrine actually mirrors the doctrine of humanitarian intervention and that it was just merely 'old wine in a new bottle'.[59] James Pattison echoed this view by stating that although R2P is more politically acceptable since it involves more than just military intervention, it still includes a coercive element that reminds humanitarian intervention.[60]

A final point that needs to be made in relation to the central role of the SC is that the international community are prepared, through the Council, 'to take collective action, in a time and decisive manner' on a *case-by-case basis*. This clause gives the Council, specifically the permanent five members of the Council (P-5), a large room to manoeuvre when it comes to implementing R2P, which means that any decision taken, or lack thereof, would be completely under the Council's discretion.[61] This is problematic as political calculations inevitably inform the action of the P-5. According to Alex J. Bellamy, this will result in the SC acting inconsistently and unpredictably, as will be highlighted in the analysis of the Libyan and Syrian crises developed in Sections 2.5.1 and 2.5.2 later.[62]

### *2.4.1 Towards the Three-Pillar Structure of R2P*

The second turning point in the legal evolution of R2P was reached following the 2009 report of the then UN Secretary-General, Ban Ki-moon, 'Implementing the Responsibility to Protect'.

The significance of this report is that it outlined, for the first time, a clear three-pillar structure for the principle of the responsibility to protect. Pillar I refers to the responsibility of each State to protect its population against crimes against humanity, war crimes, ethnic cleansing, and genocide.[63] Pillar II refers to the responsibility of the international community to assist States in meeting their duty to protect.[64] Finally, Pillar III refers to the responsibility that member states of the UN have to respond collectively to crises in a timely and decisive manner through the Security Council.[65] This includes a range of tools, such as peaceful measures under Chapter VI of the UN Charter as well as more coercive measures available under Chapter VII of the Charter.[66] In the context of Pillar III, the 2009 report also suggested that the P-5 should refrain from using their vetoes carelessly, adding that they should decide in good faith before reacting to situations where there is a mass humanitarian catastrophe.[67] With regard to Pillar III, former Secretary-General Ban Ki-moon also suggested that the UN should make efforts to strengthen its relationship with regional and sub-regional organisations in order to facilitate rapid cooperation.[68]

In terms of implementation, the report did not suggest that the three Pillars have to be implemented in a sequential order. The report stated that 'there is no set sequence to be followed from one Pillar to another, nor it is assumed that one is more important than another'.[69] As explained by James Pattison, the possibility of going straight to implementing Pillar III measures without first exhausting Pillar II measures is particularly important in situations where atrocities have already reached a high level of severity.[70]

On the other hand, as argued by Jennifer M. Welsh, the three Pillars should, theoretically, be triggered in a sequential order.[71] However, Welsh acknowledges that, in practice, there is no rule against moving straight to the implementation of Pillar III without first exhausting Pillar II. This could create an opportunity for hasty attitudes towards the mobilisation of military force, which is problematic since the utilisation of military force should only be invoked as a last resort after all avenues have been exhausted. Since there are no set rules in regard to the implementation of the Pillars of R2P as of yet, it is problematic to fully advance R2P as an international norm to respond to mass atrocities.

## 2.5 The Implementation of R2P

After having outlined the meaning of R2P as currently formulated in international law, the second part of the chapter now turns to the phase of implementation of this principle. Before discussing the way in which R2P was implemented in the context of what has become, thus far, the two most notable conflict situations in which R2P was brought up, that is, Libya and Syria, it is important to highlight how UN bodies such as the Security Council, the General Assembly, and the UN Human Rights Council have all regularly called on this principle in their resolutions.

Since the 2005 World Outcome Summit, as of 2021, the SC has invoked R2P in more than 80 resolutions regarding crises in the Central African Republic, Côte d'Ivoire, Democratic Republic of the Congo, Liberia, Libya, Mali, Somalia, South Sudan, Syria, and Yemen.[72] Besides this, the Council has also invoked R2P in thematic resolutions concerning the prevention of genocide, armed conflict, and the restrictions of the trade of small arms and weapons.[73] At the same time, R2P has also been invoked by the UN Human Rights Council in more than 50 resolutions and by the GA in 13 resolutions.[74] On top of this, since 2009, the GA has been hosting Informal Interactive Dialogues on the Responsibility to Protect as a venue for States to discuss their positions and opinions on R2P, aimed at identifying the flaws and challenges that R2P faces in both practical and conceptual terms.[75] Since 2018, these annual informal dialogues have been formalised and officially included in the General Assembly's agendas.[76]

With this level of recognition and practice, it is safe to say that R2P's role as a guiding principle in the international community has been cemented. Gareth Evans shares this sentiment that R2P has become an important guiding principle in the international community and claims that the best evidence is the annual debates in the General Assembly even in the aftermath of the controversial Libyan intervention, which I will discuss later.[77] According to Evans, although there is no general consensus when it comes to the scope and implementation of Pillar III, no State disagrees with the fact that a sovereign State has the primary responsibility to protect its own people and that the international community has a responsibility to assist it to do so.[78] Evan further stated that there will always be disagreement as to what form of action should be taken in different cases, but the basic principles of R2P are agreed upon and not under threat.[79]

Alex J. Bellamy echoed Evans' view that R2P has reshaped international affairs.[80] Bellamy further stated that R2P is, albeit slowly and imperfectly, facilitating fundamental changes to the values, identities, and interests of States and societies. Bellamy also agreed that although there are disagreements over the implementation of R2P regarding Pillar III, the fundamentals of the concept are not under threat.

R2P supporters often stress that, after having been formally introduced in the realm of international law in 2005, R2P was successfully implemented for the first time in 2011 in Libya, where the Arab Spring had enflamed many people to take action.[81] Like its neighbouring countries, before the upheaval of the 'Arab Spring', Libya had a rather fragile civil society that was ruled under the authoritarian government of Colonel Muammar Gaddafi.[82] Under Colonel Gaddafi's regime, the people of Libya were subjected to oppressive policies, many of which violated basic human rights. This had created a rather dangerous disjunction between his regime and the people.[83] According to the International Crisis Group, Libya was 'a large pressure cooker ready to explode'.[84] The Arab Spring reached Libya when anti-government protests started in the eastern Libya city of Benghazi on 15 February 2011. This then escalated to a countrywide uprising.[85] The forces of Colonel Gaddafi responded to the uprising by deploying lethal force and attacking the demonstrators, causing the death of at least more than 100 civilians.[86] The disproportionate use of force by the government quickly turned a series of demonstrations into an insurrection. From this point on, the violence escalated, and fierce repression continued. Against this background, claims were made by various non-government organisations, such as Human Rights Watch, that the regime was violating international human rights law by deliberately targeting and killing demonstrators and innocent bystanders.[87]

Under these circumstances, the SC adopted Resolution 1970 condemning the violence and the use of force against civilians by government forces.[88] Importantly, the Resolution also called upon the Libyan authorities to uphold their responsibility to protect their population (Pillar I).[89] The Resolution also referred Libya to the International Criminal Court (ICC), recognising that the atrocities committed in the country could amount to crimes against humanity.[90] In an effort to try and pressure the regime to halt their violations, the SC further placed an arms embargo, travel ban, and asset freeze on Colonel Gaddafi's inner circle, who were responsible for the crimes committed against civilians.[91] In R2P terms, this resolution has implemented measures of Pillar III. However, Colonel Gaddafi's regime rejected the conditions and demands set out in Resolution 1970 and even refused to allow humanitarian aid convoys into various besieged towns.[92]

Weeks after the passage of Resolution 1970, while the violence between Colonel Gaddafi's forces and the protestors turned rebels continued, the options for the next decisive action were being weighed and according to Tim Dunne and Katharine Gelber, the debate in the international community centred on 'the responsibility to protect competing with other normative claims, such as the presumption against the use of force and the reluctance to interfere in the domestic jurisdiction of a member state'.[93] Ultimately, since all efforts had failed and all non-coercive measures had been exhausted, the principles of non-use of force and non-intervention gave way to R2P action through the passage of SC Resolution 1973.[94] This Resolution represents the first time that the SC has authorised the use of force for humanitarian purposes against a functioning State.[95] Resolution 1973 recalled the demands made in Resolution 1970 and further called upon the Libyan authorities to acknowledge their responsibility to protect their population and enter an overall immediate ceasefire.[96] Most importantly, in Paragraph 4, the Council authorised member states in cooperation with the Secretary-General to 'take all necessary measures' to protect the civilian population mandated under Chapter VII of the UN Charter.[97]

Resolution 1973 passed with ten votes in favour.[98] Even though there were no votes against, it is noteworthy that there were five abstentions, namely Brazil, China, Russia, Germany and India.[99] These five States were very careful not to condone the actions of the Libyan authorities.[100] However, they did not want to set a bold precedent for the use of military force for humanitarian purposes.[101] For example, China abstained from the vote despite acknowledging that it was 'deeply concerned by the continuing deteriorating of the situation in Libya'.[102] This should not come as a surprise, since China has always been an avid supporter of the strict interpretation of State sovereignty and has been sceptical of the implementation of Pillar III since the UN first adopted the concepts of R2P in 2005 (which will be discussed in detail in Chapter 8).[103] However, given that the gravity of the situation it considered these to be special circumstances calling for an abstention.[104]

At first glance, the intervention in Libya was a textbook case of how R2P should work. Non-coercive measures had failed to produce the expected results; Libyan authorities' level of violence against civilians had reached the threshold of crimes against humanity; hence, since Libya failed to protect its population from atrocity crimes, the responsibility to protect was passed on to the international community.[105]

### 2.5.1 Implementing Resolution 1973

The implementation of Resolution 1973 was not without controversies. The intervention authorised by the SC was led by NATO, whose airstrikes targeted Colonel Gaddafi's military capacity to attack civilians. Initially, it seemed that the NATO-led coalition was following the mandate of Resolution 1973. However, as the crisis went on, the coalition was accused of going beyond it. In particular, it was accused of overstretching the term 'all necessary measures' to support a hidden motive, notably regime change.[106] For example, it emerged that, despite the arms embargo placed under Resolution 1970, several states such as France were supplying weapons to the rebels.[107] Furthermore, NATO's operation also targeted Colonel Gaddafi's retreating forces and his hometown (Sirte), even though there were no threats to civilians present in that location.[108] Finally, rather than pursuing a ceasefire towards the end of the conflict, the NATO-backed rebels furthered their campaign to overthrow Colonel Gaddafi's regime, which ultimately led to his death. Seen from this perspective, the intervention in Libya appears more like an example of how R2P could be abused instead of, as noted before, a textbook example for R2P. In particular, the fact that the Western States involved in the operation ended up siding with rebels against Colonel Gaddafi signals an important potential problem with R2P. This is a problem that was mentioned earlier in this chapter in the context of a discussion of humanitarian intervention, namely the problem of the motives behind an intervention. If the NATO-led coalition failed to prioritise the protection of civilians, as mandated by Resolution 1973, and, instead, pursued regime change, questions arise as to the geopolitical dynamics affecting the implementation of this principle.[109] Hence, to what extent can R2P be really said to represent a better response to atrocity crimes than humanitarian intervention does?

### 2.5.2 Syria

The other conflict situation which, like Libya, attracted the attention of R2P commentators is the conflict that erupted in Syria in March 2011. The uprising in Syria started like the uprisings in Libya, Egypt, and Tunisia: non-violent anti-government demonstrators gathered as the wave of the Arab Spring swept through.[110] Just like Libya, the months that followed witnessed a rapid escalation of violence between the forces of President Bashar al-Assad and his oppositions. At the beginning, civilians were peacefully protesting against political oppression, poverty, unemployment, inequality, bureaucratic corruption, restrictions on freedom of speech, and the excessive use of martial law.[111] The turning point occurred when 15 teenagers were caught painting anti-government graffiti on the walls of their school. They were then arrested and when they were released there were signs of torture and mistreatment, which further enraged vast sectors of the Syrian population.[112] Following this event, increasing numbers of people took to the streets in what then turned into a countrywide call for the overthrow of President Assad's regime.[113] Assad responded by using force against the demonstrators prompting the latter to take up arms against the regime.[114] The violence escalated in the weeks and months that followed.[115] Several months after the start of the conflict, the Independent International Commission of Inquiry on the Syrian Arab Republic, appointed by the UN Human Rights Council in March 2011, concluded that crimes against humanity had been committed at the hands of government forces, including excessive use of force, extrajudicial executions, violations of children's rights, and sexual torture and violence.[116]

In theory, the situation in Syria should have been another 'textbook' example for the concept of R2P, following the precedent of Libya.[117] Instead, the international community's response to this crisis was very different. The SC was deadlocked due to the divisions between the P-5. Some members of the SC, including the United Kingdom, France, Germany, and Portugal, put forward a draft resolution which called on the Syrian government to acknowledge their responsibility to protect its population and strongly condemned the systematic gross violations of human rights and the use of force aimed at the Syrian civilian population.[118] However, despite not seeking to authorise any decisive action against the Syrian government, Russia and China opposed this resolution, threatening to veto it if it was put on the Council's agenda.[119] Russia explained that any draft resolution that would eventually authorise any sanction against Syria could 'be part of a hidden agenda aimed at once again instituting regime change', further referring to the intervention in Libya.[120] For similar reasons, two further draft resolutions were again vetoed by China and Russia, whose explanations of the vote hinted at their fear of regime change, which was not unfounded considering Libya.[121]

It is clear that Western members of the SC saw this conflict as a violent repression of civilians, human rights violations and excessive use of force by President Assad's regime.[122] By contrast, Russia saw President Assad's government as a victim of terrorism and violence. According to this narrative, violence was not used against civilians but rather to suppress a violent insurgency of criminals and terrorists.[123] It is also clear that Russia and China sought to prevent another instance of regime change following the events in Libya.[124] Their objections to impose any type of sanctions, including economic sanctions, on Syria fully revealed that politics will play a significant role in decision-making related to R2P action.[125]

## 2.6 Conclusions

This chapter suggests that R2P has come a long way since its creation in the 2001 report of the ICISS. It gained an official place as part of international law through the endorsement of the 2005 World Summit Outcome and, later, was further articulated in a 2009 report by the then UN Secretary-General, which formally introduced the three pillar-structure of R2P. This chapter highlights that the variant of R2P that has been legally validated at the international level is quite limited in scope. First, R2P can only be invoked in cases of 'genocide, ethnic cleansing, war crimes and crimes against humanity'. Second, action can only be taken when States are manifestly failing to protect their populations. Third, any actor who wishes to intervene in carrying out the international community's duty to protect must receive the SC's authorisation. This means that, in many respects, R2P has not added anything substantial to the existing UN Charter's legal framework.

Despite the above, according to the thesis, R2P promises, in theory, to remedy a number of legal and political problems that have traditionally affected the concept of humanitarian intervention. However, the analysis of the implementation of R2P conducted in the second part of the chapter highlights that important complications remain with regard to both the meaning and applicability of this principle. For example, although Libya was initially seen as a textbook case of R2P successfully working in practice, NATO overstretched the relevant UN mandate and ended up facilitating the overthrow of Colonel Gaddafi instead. In this sense, the Libyan intervention highlighted how R2P can be abused to mask the intervenor's ulterior motives such as the pursuit of regime change. The crisis in Syria similarly proved that R2P faces many challenges when it comes to implementation. Russia's and China's refusal to support any strong action against President Assad showed that politics plays a significant role in decision-making processes concerning R2P, even when severe humanitarian crises unfold and despite States' broad commitment towards action exemplified in the 2005 Summit Outcome Document.

While uncertainties continue to characterise R2P, the book takes the view that the latter has now come to represent a crucial principle in guiding the international community's efforts to tackle humanitarian crises. Given their prominent role in the SC, the position of the P-5 will be key for the further development of R2P. This calls for further investigations of great powers' approach to R2P. At the same time, given the global applicability of the principle, and its connection with regional conflict situations, it is also important to take a broader look at the way in which other States and regional organisations around the world approach R2P. With this in mind, the following chapter introduces the Association of Southeast Asian Nations before we move on to examine the way in which this regional organisation approaches R2P both conceptually and practically.

## Notes

1 Aidan Hehir, *Humanitarian Intervention: An Introduction* (Palgrave Macmillan, 2010) pp. 181–183.
2 Ibid., p. 180.
3 The Belgian administration introduced ethnic identity cards and privileged the Tutsis over the Hutus systematically, which then created more tension between the two ethnic groups; see, ibid.
4 Ibid., pp. 180–181.
5 The RPF aimed to protect the Tutsis refugees in Uganda and to take power again in Rwanda by invading northern Rwanda, which sparked the civil war; see, ibid.
6 Ibid.
7 United Nations Security Council Resolution 872 (1993), S/RES/872, p. 2.
8 Hate messages and encouragements to eliminate the Tutsis were broadcasted through radio stations, which led to a total of 800,000 of the Tutsi population and even moderate Hutus being killed; see, Nicolas J. Wheeler, *Saving Strangers: Humanitarian Intervention in International Society* (Oxford University Press, 2000) p. 212; and BBC, 'Rwandan Genocide: 100 Days of Slaughter' (BBC, 7 April 2014) <http://www.bbc.co.uk/news/world-africa-26875506> accessed on 14 December 2020.

9 Nicolas J. Wheeler, *Saving Strangers: Humanitarian Intervention in International Society* (Oxford University Press, 2000) p. 212.

10 Noticeably Major-General Roméo Dallaire of the UNAMIR requested permission to seize weapon caches and deploy more troops; see, Aidan Hehir, *Humanitarian Intervention: An Introduction* (Palgrave MacMillan, 2010) p. 190.

11 The only extent of the UN Chapter VII powers authorised for the UNAMIR was the imposition of an arms embargo on Rwanda even though the Security Council referred to 'the killings of members of an ethnic group with the intention of destroying such a group in whole or in part', which is punishable under international criminal law in SC Resolution 918 (1994); see, SC Resolution 918 (1994), S/RES/918; and Aidan Hehir, *Humanitarian Intervention: An Introduction* (Palgrave Macmillan, 2010) p. 188.

12 'Secretary-General's message to ceremony marking the 10th anniversary of the Srebrenica massacre (delivered by Mark Malloch Brown, Chef de Cabinet)' (The United Nations Secretary-General, 11 July 2005) <https://www.un.org/sg/en/content/sg/statement/2005-07-11/secretary-generals-message-ceremony-marking-10th-anniversary> accessed on 20 January 2021.

13 Leann Long, 'The Srebrenica Massacre' [2006] 15(2) *The Forensic Examiner*, p. 43; for this section of the Chapter, I chose to specifically focus on the atrocities in Srebrenica alone. However, I would like to point out that this does not mean that other human rights violations and international crimes/atrocities elsewhere are less significant.

14 Human Rights Watch, 'The Fall of Srebrenica and the Failure of UN Peacekeeping' [1995] 7(13) *Human Rights Watch*, p. 6.

15 The UNPROFOR was established through SC Resolution 743 (1992), and it was mandated to protect the 'safe areas' from armed attack or any other hostile actions. Srebrenica was designated as a 'safe zone' through SC Resolution 824 (1993); see The United Nations Security Council Resolution 743, S/RES/743 (1992), 819, S/RES/819 (1993) and 824, S/RES/824(1993); and Human Rights Watch, 'The Fall of Srebrenica and the Failure of UN Peacekeeping' [1995] 7(13) *Human Rights Watch*, p. 10.

16 Human Rights Watch, 'The Fall of Srebrenica and the Failure of UN Peacekeeping' [1995] 7(13) *Human Rights Watch*, pp. 10–11.

17 Ibid.

18 Ibid., pp. 11–18.

19 Once the campaign started, the UNPROFOR requested for air support from NATO, which was denied due to the Serb army's threat of attack on other UN compounds in the region, and once it was approved, it was too late, the atrocities had already happened; see, Human Rights Watch, 'The Fall of Srebrenica and the Failure of UN Peacekeeping' [1995] 7(13) *Human Rights Watch*, pp. 11–18.

20 *Application of the Convention on the Prevention and Punishment of the Crime of Genocide (Bosnia and Herzegovina v. Serbia and Montenegro)* Judgement, I.C.J. Reports 2007, para 297.

21 Article 2(4) states, 'All Members shall refrain in their international relations from the threat or use of force against the territorial integrity or political independence of any state'. Article 2(7), instead, states that 'Nothing contained in the present Charter shall authorize the United Nations to intervene in matters which are essentially in the domestic jurisdiction of any state; see The United Nations Charter, Article 2(4) and 2(7).

22 Jennifer M. Welsh, *Humanitarian Intervention and International Relations* (Oxford University Press, 2003) p. 58; and Aidan Hehir, *Humanitarian Intervention: An Introduction* (Palgrave Macmillan, 2010) p. 155.

23 The new strict segregation policies started to dismiss the Albanians from their posts and positions in the state school system and other organisations where it basically amounted to 'an apartheid in Kosovo', see The Independent International Commission on Kosovo, *The Kosovo Report: Conflict, International Response, Lessons Learned* (Oxford University Press, 2000) p. 49.

24 Klejda Mulaj, 'Resisting an Oppressive Regime: The Case of Kosovo Liberation Army' [2008] 31(12) *Studies in Conflict and Terrorism*, p. 1109.

25 Around the same time, the Bosnian war came to an end with the signing of the Dayton Peace Accords in 1995. The agreement might have put an end to the Bosnian war, but it had only enflamed the Albanians seeing as their reasonably peaceful civil resistance against the Serbs had been ignored. As a result of this, the KLA decided to change its tactics by escalating the violence aimed towards the Serbs in an effort to stop the systemic oppression opposed to them; see Aidan Hehir, *Humanitarian Intervention: An Introduction* (Palgrave Macmillan, 2010) p. 203.

26 At the same time, with the SC being 'gridlocked' without any actionable resolutions, they were still able to pass four resolutions officially to condemn this situation. SC Resolutions 1160 (1998), 1199 (1998), 1203 (1998), 1239 (1999), and 1244 (1999) all expressed grave concerns over the humanitarian catastrophe as a result of the conflict and condemned all acts of violence against the civilian populations. These resolutions also imposed an arms embargo and economic sanctions on the FRY and demanded the end of all hostilities; see SC Resolutions 1160 (1998), S/RES/1160, 1199 (1998), S/RES/1199, 1203 (1998), S/RES/1203, 1239 (1999), S/RES/1239, and 1244 (1999), S/RES/1244.

27 The Independent International Commission on Kosovo, *The Kosovo Report: Conflict, International Response, Lessons Learned* (Oxford University Press, 2000) p. 142.

28 Ibid., pp. 92–93; and Aidan Hehir, *Humanitarian Intervention: An Introduction* (Palgrave Macmillan, 2010) pp. 207–208.

29 MA. Arden Salihu, 'NATO Intervention in Kosovo in Light of Security Council Actions and International Law' [2013] 3(2) *ILIRIA International Review*, p. 292.

30 United Nations Charter, Article 2(4).

31 Christopher Greenwood, 'International Law and the NATO Intervention in Kosovo' [2000] 49(4) *International and Comparative Law Quarterly*, pp. 926–927.

32 The Independent International Commission on Kosovo, *The Kosovo Report: Conflict, International Response, Lessons Learned* (Oxford University Press, 2000) p. 4; Antonio Cassese, 'Ex Iniuria Ius Oritur: Are We Moving Towards International Legitimation of Forcible Humanitarian Countermeasures in the World Community?' [1999] 10(1) *European Journal of International Law*, p. 25; and Bruno Simma, 'NATO, the UN and the Use of Force: Legal Aspects' [1999] 10(1) *European Journal of International Law*, p. 12.

33 Christopher Greenwood, 'International Law and the NATO Intervention in Kosovo' [2000] 49(4) *International and Comparative Law Quarterly*, pp. 926–927.

34 The Independent International Commission on Kosovo, *The Kosovo Report: Conflict, International Response, Lessons Learned* (Oxford University Press, 2000) p. 4.

35 Aidan Hehir, *Humanitarian Intervention: An Introduction* (Palgrave MacMillan, 2010) p. 211.

36 Ramesh Thakur and William Maley, *Theorising the Responsibility to Protect* (Cambridge University Press, 2015) p. 19.

37 Ibid., pp. 13–14.

38 Ibid., p. 3.

39 Ibid., pp. 7–8.

40 Alex J. Bellamy and Tim Dunne, *The Oxford Handbook of the Responsibility to Protect* (1st edition 2006, Oxford University Press, 2016) p. 87.

41 Saulius Katuoka and Agne Cepinskyte, 'Response to Large-Scale Atrocities: Humanitarian Intervention and the Responsibility to Protect' [2010] 3 *Jurisprudencija*, p. 166.

42 'The Responsibility to Protect' [2001] The International Commission on Intervention and State Sovereignty, p. 32.

43 Ibid.

44 Ibid., p. 48.

45 Ibid.

46 Ibid.

47 High-Level Panel on Threats, Challenges and Change, *A More Secure World: Our Shared Responsibility* (New York: United Nations 2004), A/59/565, para 203.
48 Alex J. Bellamy and Tim Dunne, *The Oxford Handbook of the Responsibility to Protect* (1st edition 2006, Oxford University Press, 2016) p. 65.
49 Carsten Stahn, 'Responsibility to Protect: Political Rhetoric or Emerging Legal Norm?' [2007] 101(1) *The American Journal of International Law*, p. 105.
50 Ramesh Thakur and William Maley, *Theorising the Responsibility to Protect* (Cambridge University Press, 2015) p. 23.
51 The United Nations, 'The 2005 World Summit: High-Level Panel Plenary Meeting of the 60th Session of the UN General Assembly' (UN Headquarter, New York, 14–16 September 2005) <http://www.un.org/en/events/pastevents/worldsummit_2005.shtml> accessed on 20 January 2021.
52 United Nations General Assembly, *2005 World Summit Outcome,* resolution adopted by the General Assembly, 24 October 2005, A/RES/60/1, para 138.
53 Ibid., para 139.
54 'The Responsibility to Protect' [2001] The International Commission on Intervention and State Sovereignty, Section 4.20, p. 33.
55 Ibid, Section 8.28, p. 74.
56 Ibid., p. XII.
57 Mauro Barelli, 'Preventing and Responding to Atrocity Crimes: China, Sovereignty and the Responsibility to Protect' [2018] 23(2) *Journal of Conflict & Security Law*, p. 191.
58 Ibid.
59 Stephen P. Marks and Nicholas Cooper, 'The Responsibility to Protect: Watershed or Old Wine in a New Bottle?' [2010] 2(1) *Jindal Global Law Review*, p. 115.
60 James Pattison, *Humanitarian Intervention and the Responsibility to Protect: Who Should Intervene?* (Oxford University Press, 2010) pp. 250–251.
61 Mauro Barelli, 'Preventing and Responding to Atrocity Crimes: China, Sovereignty and the Responsibility to Protect' [2018] 23(2) *Journal of Conflict & Security Law*, p. 187.
62 Alex J. Bellamy and Tim Dunne, *The Oxford Handbook of the Responsibility to Protect* (1st edition 2006, Oxford University Press, 2016) pp. 262–264.
63 United Nations General Assembly, 'Implementing the Responsibility to Protect' (2009) A/63/677, pp. 10–14.
64 Ibid., pp. 15–21.
65 Ibid., pp. 22–27.
66 Ibid.
67 Alex J. Bellamy, 'The Three Pillars of the Responsibility to Protect' p. 49 <http://www.cries.org/wp-content/uploads/2015/09/006-bellamy.pdf> accessed on 20 January 2021.
68 Ibid.
69 United Nations General Assembly, 'Implementing the Responsibility to Protect' (2009) A/63/677, p. 2.
70 James Pattison, 'The Ethics of "Responsibility While Protecting": BRAZIL, The Responsibility to Protect, And Guidelines for Humanitarian Intervention' [2013] *Human Rights and Welfare Working Paper 71*, p. 7.
71 Alexander Betts and Phil Orchard, *Implementation and World Politics: How International Norms Change Practice* (Oxford University Press, 2014) p. 133.
72 'What Is R2P?' Global Centre for the Responsibility to Protect <https://www.globalr2p.org/what-is-r2p/> accessed on 20 January 2021.
73 Ibid.
74 Ibid.
75 United Nations Office on Genocide Prevention and the Responsibility to Protect <https://www.un.org/en/genocideprevention/general-assembly.shtml> accessed on 20 January 2021.
76 Ibid.

77 Alex J. Bellamy and Tim Dunne, *The Oxford Handbook of the Responsibility to Protect* (1st edition 2006, Oxford University Press, 2016) p. 914.
78 Ibid.
79 Ibid.
80 Alex J. Bellamy, *The Responsibility to Protect: A Defense* (Oxford University Press, 2015) p. 72.
81 Elvin Aghayev, 'Analysis and Background of the "Arab Spring" in Libya' (The Independent International Political Research Center, 20 August 2014) <http://www.iiprc.org/analysis-and-background-of-the-arab-spring-in-libya.html> accessed on 15 January 2017.
82 Eric Goldstein, 'Before the Arab Spring, the Unseen Thaw' (Human Rights Watch, 2012) <https://www.hrw.org/node/259729> accessed on 20 January 2021.
83 Aidan Hehir and Robert Murray, *Libya: The Responsibility to Protect and the Future of Humanitarian Intervention* (Palgrave Macmillan, 2013) p. 3.
84 Ibid., p. 4.
85 Alex J. Bellamy and Tim Dunne, *The Oxford Handbook of the Responsibility to Protect* (1st edition 2006, Oxford University Press, 2016) p. 769.
86 Jo Adetunji, Peter Beaumont and Martin Chulov, 'Libya Protests: More than 100 Killed as Army Fires on Unarmed Demonstrators' (The Guardian, 20 February 2011) <https://www.theguardian.com/world/2011/feb/20/libya-protests-benghazi-muammar-gaddafi> accessed on 20 January 2021.
87 Human Rights Watch, 'Libya: Governments Should Demand End to Unlawful Killings' (20 February 2011) <https://www.hrw.org/news/2011/02/20/libya-governments-should-demand-end-unlawful-killings> accessed on 18 January 2021.
88 United Nations Security Council Resolution 1970 (2011), S/RES/1970, pp. 1–3.
89 Ibid., p. 2.
90 Ibid.
91 Ibid., pp. 3–5 and 8–10.
92 Paul D. Williams and Alex J. Bellamy, 'Principles, Politics and Prudence: Libya, the Responsibility to Protect, and the Use of Military Force' [2012] 18(3) *Global Governance*, p. 278.
93 Tim Dunne and Katharine Gelber, 'Arguing Matters: The Responsibility to Protect and the Case of Libya' [2014] 6 *Global Responsibility to Protect*, p. 339.
94 Alex J. Bellamy, 'Libya and the Responsibility to Protect: The Exception and the Norm' [2011] 25(3) *Ethics and International Affairs*, p. 265.
95 Ibid., p. 263.
96 United Nations Security Council 1973 (2011), S/RES/1973, pp. 1–2.
97 Ibid., p. 3.
98 Those who voted in favour included Bosnia and Herzegovina, the United Kingdom, Colombia, France, Gabon, Lebanon, the United States, Portugal, Nigeria, and South Africa. China, Russia, Brazil, Germany, and India had abstained; see, SC Resolution 1973 (2011) voting summary <https://digitallibrary.un.org/record/699784?ln=en> accessed on 29 April 2021.
99 Ibid.
100 Paul D. Williams and Alex J. Bellamy, 'Principles, Politics and Prudence: Libya, the Responsibility to Protect, and the Use of Military Force' [2012] 18(3) *Global Governance*, p. 281.
101 Ibid.
102 Statement by the H.E. Ambassador Li BaoDong, Permanent Representative of China to the United Nations, at the Security Council Meeting on the Situation in Libya (Permanent Mission of the People's Republic of China to the UN (17 March 2011) <http://chnun.chinamission.org.cn/eng/chinaandun/securitycouncil/regionalhotspots/africa/t824183.htm> accessed on 20 January 2021.
103 Mauro Barelli, 'Preventing and Responding to Atrocity Crimes: China, Sovereignty and the Responsibility to Protect' [2018] 23(2) *Journal of Conflict & Security Law*, pp. 190–191.

104 Statement by the H.E. Ambassador Li BaoDong, Permanent Representative of China to the United Nations, at the Security Council Meeting on the Situation in Libya (Permanent Mission of the People's Republic of China to the UN (17 March 2011) <http://chnun.chinamission.org.cn/eng/chinaandun/securitycouncil/regionalhotspots/africa/t824183.htm> accessed on 20 January 2021.
105 Tim Dunne and Katharine Gelber, 'Arguing Matters: The Responsibility to Protect and the Case of Libya' [2014] 6 *Global Responsibility to Protect*, p. 327.
106 Alex J. Bellamy and Tim Dunne, *The Oxford Handbook of the Responsibility to Protect* (1st edition 2006, Oxford University Press, 2016) pp. 772–773.
107 Richard Spencer, 'France Supplying Weapons to Libyan Rebels' (The Telegraph, 29 June 2011) <http://www.telegraph.co.uk/news/worldnews/africaandindianocean/libya/8606541/France-supplying-weapons-to-Libyan-rebels.html> accessed on 20 January 2021.
108 Aidan Hehir and Robert Murray, *Libya: The Responsibility to Protect and the Future of Humanitarian Intervention* (Palgrave Macmillan, 2013) p. 197.
109 Alex J. Bellamy and Tim Dunne, *The Oxford Handbook of the Responsibility to Protect* (1st edition 2006, Oxford University Press, 2016) p. 772.
110 Ibid., p. 896.
111 Ibid.
112 Joe Sterling, 'Daraa: The Spark That Lit the Syrian Flame' (CNN, 1 March 2012) <http://edition.cnn.com/2012/03/01/world/meast/syria-crisis-beginnings/> accessed on 18 January 2021.
113 Alex J. Bellamy and Tim Dunne, *The Oxford Handbook of the Responsibility to Protect* (1st edition 2006, Oxford University Press, 2016) p. 897.
114 Lucy Rodgers, David Gritten, James Offers and Patrick Asare, 'Syria: The Story of Conflict' (BBC, 11 March 2016) <http://www.bbc.co.uk/news/world-middle-east-26116868> accessed on 18 January 2021.
115 Frank Gardner, 'Syria Blasts Signal Dangerous Escalation of Violence' (BBC, 10 May 2012) <http://www.bbc.co.uk/news/world-middle-east-18023668> accessed on 18 January 2021.
116 The United Nations Human Rights Council, 'Report of the Independent International Commission of Inquiry on the Syrian Arab Republic' (2011), A/HRC/S-17/2/Add.1, pp. 16–19.
117 Saira Mohamed, 'Syria, The United Nations, and the Responsibility to Protect' [2012] 106 *American Society for International Law Proceedings*, p. 225.
118 Draft United Nations Security Council Resolution, S/2011/612 <http://www.securitycouncilreport.org/atf/cf/%7B65BFCF9B-6D27-4E9C-8CD3-CF6E4FF96FF9%7D/Syria%20S2011%20612.pdf> accessed on 18 January 2021.
119 Jess Gifkins, 'The UN Security Council Divided: Syria in Crisis' [2012] 4 *Global Responsibility to Protect*, p. 382.
120 Ibid., p. 383.
121 United Nations Security Council, 'Security Council Fails to Adopt Two of the Draft Resolutions on Syria, Despite Appeals for Action Preventing Impending Humanitarian Catastrophe in Aleppo' (The United Nations, 8 October 2016) <https://www.un.org/press/en/2016/sc12545.doc.htm> accessed on 20 January 2021.
122 Jess Gifkins, 'The UN Security Council Divided: Syria in Crisis' [2012] 4 *Global Responsibility to Protect*, p. 389.
123 Ibid., p. 390.
124 Jaime A. FlorCruz, 'Russia, China and Partners Call for Non-Intervention in Syria and Iran' (CNN, 7 June 2012) <http://edition.cnn.com/2012/06/07/world/asia/china-russia-syria/> accessed on 20 January 2021.
125 Alex J. Bellamy and Tim Dunne, *The Oxford Handbook of the Responsibility to Protect* (1st edition 2006, Oxford University Press, 2016) p. 904.

# 3 The Association of the Southeast Asian Nations

## 3.1 Introduction

This chapter introduces the Association of the Southeast Asian Nations (ASEAN) as the chosen regional organisation at the centre of this book. As mentioned in Chapter 1, I have chosen to focus on ASEAN's position on the Responsibility to Protect for several reasons. Firstly, ASEAN is becoming an increasingly important actor in the international community. With important economic ties and partnerships with the United States (US), China, Japan, India, and the European Union (EU), ASEAN has significantly increased its geopolitical relevance.[1] Secondly, as discussed in this chapter, ASEAN and its members are known for taking a very conservative approach to the principles of sovereignty and non-intervention. Evidently, this stance is at odds with the fundamental concepts of Responsibility to Protect (R2P) that were discussed in the previous chapter. Therefore, it becomes particularly interesting to study this clash. In order to do so, it is necessary to first consider ASEAN's history, institutional structure, and decision-making processes.

The first part of this chapter focuses on the origins of ASEAN, its institutional structure as well as its decision-making mechanisms. Central to the organisation's *modus operandi* is the so-called 'ASEAN Way', which will be thoroughly discussed in the second part of the chapter. In essence, the ASEAN Way principles include State sovereignty, non-interference, the prohibition of the use of force in external relations, and consensus decision-making. Ultimately, the analysis in this chapter shows that ASEAN lacks the capacity to act independently from its individual members due to its strict adherence to the ASEAN WAY principles. In the context of this discussion, the last section of this chapter also analyses a more specific question, namely ASEAN's approach towards the issue of human rights.

## 3.2 ASEAN: Origins and Evolution

ASEAN was established on 8 August 1967, after the so-called confrontation, or 'Konfrontasi', that occurred in the period 1963–1966 between Malaysia and Indonesia. The Konfrontasi was a conflict that stemmed from Indonesia opposing the creation of the Federation of Malaysia (consisting of Malaya, Sabah, Sarawak, and Singapore) in 1963.[2] The then-President of Indonesia, Sukarno, led an aggressive

DOI: 10.4324/9781003436799-3

anti-colonial and nationalist government backed by the Indonesian Communist Party (PKI).[3] In 1963, he announced a *ganyang Malaysia* or ‘Crush Malaysia’ campaign, which amounted to a form of guerrilla warfare through the borders of Malaysia.[4] This conflict persisted up until Sukarno was ousted by a coup led by his former general, Muhammad Suharto in 1965.[5]

President Sukarno claimed that he did not object to the creation of the Federation as such, but rather, to the fact that the former colonial master, that is, Great Britain, would continue to meddle in the internal and external affairs of the newly created State.[6] In reality, things were different. As suggested by many authors, President Sukarno’s opposition to the formation of the Federation of Malaysia was motivated by his own geopolitical ambitions of uniting Malaya, Sabah, Sarawak, and Singapore under Indonesian rule.[7]

General Suharto, who had been secretly negotiating peace with Malaysia behind Sukarno’s back, officially abandoned the policy of Konfrontasi in 1966. Once General Suharto had formally installed himself as president, his new government declared a ‘New Order’ in Indonesia and abandoned President Sukarno’s agenda, refocused the country’s efforts towards restoring economic stability and growth while at the same time, contextually, adopting an anti-communist policy.[8] With this new policy, President Suharto vowed to destroy the remnants of the PKI.[9]

At the same time, the governments of Thailand, Singapore, Malaysia, and the Philippines also faced internal communist insurgencies. Malaysia was dealing with the Malayan Communist Party, Thailand with the Communist Party of Thailand, the Philippines with the Hukbalahap and, lastly, Singapore with the communist factions within the People’s Action Party.[10] Against this background, these five States met at the Bangkok Conference on 8 August 1967 with a view to creating a platform in which they could promote regional economic, social, political, and cultural growth. The platform would also aim at protecting regional peace and stability, on the one hand, and defeating the threat of communism, on the other.[11] This platform took the form of ASEAN. That the pursuit for stability and fear of communism were at the core of the project of establishing ASEAN is clear from the words of the then Prime Minister of Singapore, Lee Kuan Yew, who, while talking about the negotiations, noted that:

> The unspoken objective was to gain strength through solidarity ahead of the power vacuum that would come with an impending British and later a possible US withdrawal. . . . We had a common enemy—the communist threat in guerrilla insurgencies. . . . We needed stability and growth to counter and deny the communists the social and economic conditions for revolutions. . . . We were banding together . . . for political objectives, stability and security[12]

These sentiments were reflected in the formal outcome of the conference, that is, the Bangkok Declaration of 1967 which identified the following central aims for ASEAN: to accelerate economic growth, social progress, and cultural development in the region, on the one hand, and to promote regional peace and stability, on the other.[13]

The Bangkok Declaration also established ASEAN's four key structural components in order for the organisation to pursue the aforementioned goals. First, the ASEAN Ministerial Meeting, which consists of the Special Meetings of Foreign Ministers that may be convened as required.[14] Second, a Standing Committee which would carry out the work of the Organisation in between the Foreign Ministers Meeting.[15] Third, a combination of Ad-Hoc and Permanent Committees consisting of official specialists on specific subjects/issues.[16] And, fourth, a National Secretariat in each member state works as a reference point for the Organisation and is tasked with assisting the Special Meetings of the Foreign Ministers and the Standing Committee.[17]

At the time of its creation, ASEAN was a rather informal organisation. Rodolfo C. Severino, the then-Secretary General of the Organisation, once noted that ASEAN was created to foster cooperation among member states 'through informal understandings that impose[d] no legally binding obligations'.[18] Indeed, he continued, the Bangkok Declaration 'was a mere declaration of two pages setting forth the ends and means of the organisation'.[19] Furthermore, Severino explained that the cautious and slow beginning of ASEAN was understandable since the five founding members still harboured historical animosities and suspicions towards one another, including, for example, tension related to the Konfrontasi and a territorial dispute between the Philippines and Malaysia.[20]

Under those circumstances, it required not only time but faith in one another for the members to see past the deeply embedded historical legacies to commit themselves to the common objectives of ASEAN. Given the above, it is not surprising that it took almost a decade for ASEAN to convene its first-ever summit, in 1976. On that occasion, the member states concluded that it was essential to move to higher levels of cooperation in the political, economic, and social fields, and, with that in mind, agreed to sign two fundamental documents in the ASEAN architecture, namely the Declaration of ASEAN Concord and the Treaty of Amity and Cooperation in Southeast Asia (TAC).[21] The former aimed to promote peace, progress, prosperity, and the welfare of the peoples of the member states by consolidating earlier achievements and further expanding cooperation in the economic, social, cultural, and political fields.[22] In this regard, the Declaration of ASEAN Concord established five programmes of action, namely political, economic, social, cultural, and security.[23] In the political sphere, it established that the meeting of the heads of governments of member states should be held as and when necessary, and that member states would strengthen their political solidarity by promoting the harmonisation of views, coordinating actions and where possible and desired, taking common actions.[24] Lastly, this Declaration established the ASEAN Secretariat with the role of providing greater efficiency in the coordination of ASEAN organs and the implementation of ASEAN projects and activities.[25]

The second fundamental instrument adopted at the 1976 summit was the TAC. This Treaty, which, according to Lee Jones, represents the touchstone of the 'ASEAN Way', aimed to promote regional peace, stability, amity, and cooperation in the region with a view to contributing to fostering the organisation's strength, solidarity, and closer relationships.[26] In order to reach these goals, the TAC set out the fundamental principles that would guide inter-state relations among its signatories: mutual respect for each other's independence, sovereignty, equality, territorial integrity, and national identity; freedom from external interference, subversion, or coercion; renunciation of the threat or use of force; and peaceful settlement of disputes.[27] As stated by Hiro Katsumata, the importance of these principles cannot be overstated since they set out the fundamentals of the 'ASEAN Way', which will be discussed in detail in the following section.[28] Furthermore, what makes this treaty particularly significant is that, in addition to providing the code of conduct for its signatories, it enshrined it into legally binding norms rather than just political ones.[29] It is also worth noting that some authors have highlighted the broader implications of the TAC beyond ASEAN. Anja Jetschke, for example, affirmed that the TAC has become the centrepiece of the regional security framework in the wider East Asia region.[30] Since then, the principles of the TAC have been continually reaffirmed in every ASEAN summit and every ASEAN Foreign Minister's Meetings.[31] For example, on the 40th anniversary of the adoption of the TAC, the ASEAN Foreign Ministers released a joint statement emphasising how the TAC had served as a foundation for an integrated, peaceful, and stable ASEAN community.[32] The statement also underscored the continuing relevance and importance of the principles of the TAC in guiding inter-States relations.[33]

The next important step in the process of enhancing the cooperation and efficiency of the Association was taken during the 9th ASEAN Summit in 2003. On that occasion, the members of ASEAN adopted the Declaration of Concord II (Bali Concord II), which sought to further promote regional cooperation by creating three communities: the ASEAN Security Community, the ASEAN Economic Community, and the ASEAN Socio-Cultural Community.[34] The establishment of these communities made the organisational structure of ASEAN more precise and meant that any particular issue would now be delegated to the committee most relevant and suitable to tackle it. In particular, the ASEAN Political-Security Community (APSC) was envisaged to further promote cooperation in the crucial field of security with a view to ensuring that the people of ASEAN would live together in a harmonious and democratic environment.[35] For the purposes of this study, it is especially important to note that the APSC was given conflict prevention and conflict resolution tasks in order to achieve the aforementioned objectives. However, the APSC fully adheres to the set of shared norms and values included in the TAC that were discussed earlier, for example, renunciation of the threat and use of force, respect for state sovereignty and non-interference.[36] Therefore, not surprisingly, the APSC has always lacked the capacity to coordinate the foreign or defence policies of the member states which, instead, continue to enjoy their (sovereign) right to pursue individual foreign policies.[37] It is also worth mentioning that ASEAN Foreign Minister's Meetings (AMM) take place under the APSC umbrella. The AMM are responsible for the political-security cooperation and external relations in ASEAN.[38] These meetings produce ASEAN collective statements (once and if agreed by all members) in response to security and/or political issues, which will be highly relevant in the analyses of Chapters 5, 6, and 7 focusing on ASEAN's position on the East Timor, Rohingya, and West Papua crises.

### *3.2.1 The ASEAN Charter*

As noted by Severino, despite representing important steps in the institutional history of ASEAN, the Bangkok Declaration and the TAC combined had simply envisioned creating an association for regional cooperation.[39] It was the ASEAN Charter, adopted in 2007 through the 13th ASEAN Summit, that changed the nature of the organisation.[40] To begin with, by conferring upon ASEAN's 'legal personality' as an 'intergovernmental organization', the Charter signalled a crucial evolution from the initial voluntary nature of ASEAN.[41] On top of bestowing ASEAN with a legal personality, the ASEAN Charter aimed at evolving ASEAN into a more rules-based organisation. In fact, according to a document produced by the European Parliament Directorate-General for External Policies, one could say that the Charter elevated ASEAN's standing to the structural levels typical of the EU.[42] In addition, the Charter reiterated ASEAN's purposes of maintaining and enhancing regional peace, security, resilience, and prosperity, thus mirroring the Bangkok Declaration.[43] It also codified all of ASEAN's existing norms, rules, and values as previously enunciated under the TAC: renunciation of the threat and use of force, respect for sovereignty, non-interference into the internal affairs of member states, and reliance on peaceful settlement of disputes.[44]

Furthermore, the Charter formally codified ASEAN's existing organisational structure, placing the ASEAN Summit as the supreme policy-making body tasked with providing policy guidance and making decisions on key issues pertaining to the objectives of ASEAN.[45] As affirmed in Article 7 of the Charter, the Summit comprises ASEAN members' heads of States and is held twice a year. Headed by the Secretary-General, the ASEAN Summit provides guidance and takes into consideration key issues with the goals of pursuing the organisational goals which span over the areas of economic, social, political and security. Put simply, the Summit is on top of the chain of command of ASEAN. For example, in a situation of humanitarian crisis, this body would be pivotal. According to Article 7 of the ASEAN Charter, the Summit has the power to provide policy guidance and address emergency situations on issues affecting ASEAN and its members.[46] Thus, as will be discussed in Chapter 6, through the 32nd ASEAN Summit in 2018, ASEAN expressed concern and urged Myanmar to foster reconciliation with the Rohingya.[47] Furthermore, in the case of a serious breach of the Charter or non-compliance, the matter shall be referred to the Summit for decision.[48]

However, while the Summit might have 'soft' diplomatic powers, it lacks the power to enforce its recommendations.[49] As highlighted by Daniel Seah, this serves the purpose of safeguarding the members' sovereignty by allowing them to conduct their affairs and relations as they see fit.[50] Interestingly, proposals were initially made to strengthen the role of the Summit. For example, the Eminent Persons Group that was tasked with the drafting of the Charter had recommended that the Summit should have the authority to impose sanctions on its members in the event of serious violations of ASEAN's principles and obligations.[51] However, that proposal was met with strong opposition and was ultimately rejected. In a similar way, proposals were made by the Eminent Persons Group to introduce a provision in the ASEAN Charter allowing the organisation to expel its members in the event of a serious breach of ASEAN obligations.[52] As with the case of sanctions, however, this proposal was ultimately set aside.

In dealing with the organisation's *modus operandi*, Article 21 of the Charter reiterated the principle whereby decision-making shall be based on consultation and consensus.[53] Consensus is a form of decision-making which contrasts significantly with the majority rule and, more generally, with the use of any formalised procedure such as voting.[54] Consensus is defined as a decision made by all members of a group, thus representing the maximum area of common acceptance.[55] The consensus system ensures an agreement that is acceptable to all and helps achieve the 'universality or near universality' within a group.[56] Interestingly, while drafting the ASEAN Charter, the Eminent Persons Group had called for a more effective form of decision-making.[57] Although it agreed that decisions should be made through the process of consensus and consultation as a general rule, the Eminent Persons Group suggested that, in situations where consensus could not be achieved, decisions should be taken through voting on the basis of a simple majority, two-thirds, or three-quarter majority.[58] This proposal, however, was rejected.

This typology of decision-making seems most appropriate for ASEAN. Like in the case of the Summit discussed earlier, this broad commitment to consensus decision-making seeks to protect members' individual interests and sovereignty, while rejecting the voting mechanisms that typically lie at the core of Western-style institutions and governance.[59] The choice of consensus decision-making was inspired by the Malay practice of *mushawarah* (consultation) and *mufakat* (consensus).[60] This practice was used by Malay leaders to manage personal relations with other political chiefs in order to avoid resorting to the use of force.[61] *Mushawarah* only takes place among friends and neighbours, and it involves extensive discussions whereby participants are expected to adjust their views to a certain level in order to reach *mufakat* or a compromise and to ensure that the majority does not coercively impose their will on the minority.[62] According to Severino, this non-confrontational approach is particularly important in a region characterised by a high diversity of views and interests, so that decisions can only be made at 'a pace comfortable for all'.[63]

However, all this means that an ASEAN official decision can only be made in the absence of opposition by any member states.[64] It is not difficult to appreciate the negative consequences of this approach. As noted by Noel M. Morada, the system of consensus ends up even preventing sensitive issues from being brought forward for discussion.[65] Morada cited the examples of Thailand and Myanmar successfully preventing the discussion of, respectively, an escalation of violence in southern Thailand in 2015 and the crackdown against the Buddhist monks in 2007.[66] This, Morada noted, proves how the allegiance to consensus decision-making makes the ASEAN Charter's people-centred principles inferior to the principle of State sovereignty.[67] Ultimately, to Morada, the ASEAN Charter 'is one step forward and thirty-nine steps back' and it has further cemented ASEAN as a state-centric organisation.[68] Thus, as also aptly noted by Yi-Hung Chiou, despite the important changes introduced by the Charter, ASEAN remained as an organisation which is fundamentally meant to serve its members' national interests.[69]

Despite the limits inherent in consensus decision-making, the Charter marked a crucial departure from ASEAN's earlier and timid approaches to the questions of democracy and human rights. Article 1(7) of the Charter, in particular, affirms that one of the purposes of ASEAN is 'to strengthen democracy, enhance good governance and the rule of law, and to protect and promote human rights and fundamental freedoms, with due regards to the rights and responsibility of the member states'.[70] In conformity with this specific purpose, the Charter also states that ASEAN would establish an ASEAN human rights body, which will be analysed in detail in Section 3.4.1 later.[71]

## 3.3 The 'ASEAN Way'

As Helen Nesadurai argued, the Charter's most important achievement is its contribution to the institutionalisation and codification of the ASEAN Way principles into the organisation.[72] As it is clear from earlier discussions, ASEAN subscribes to a *modus operandi* which fully respects national sovereignty and the principle of non-interference in States' internal affairs. This key feature of the organisation is typically referred to as the ASEAN Way. According to Nesadurai, historical experiences help to explain the importance of the ASEAN Way for ASEAN States. In particular, colonialism, first, and interference by the USA, the Soviet Union, and China during and post the Cold War, later, created in the ASEAN States a clear preference for systems and mechanisms aimed at defending one's sovereignty and independence.[73] Without denying the importance of these historical events, Amitav Acharya has explained that the origins of the ASEAN Way are also to be found in the cultural sphere. Thus, the very idea of cooperation based on an interpersonal system of consultation rather than through inflexible institutionalised procedures is thought, in the region, to better promote progress while working towards mutual goals.[74] This point is well reflected in the words of Carlos Romulo, former Foreign Secretary of the Philippines, who once noted that, in the region, 'we often find that private talks over breakfast prove more important than formal meetings'.[75] For this reason, as was noted in the previous section, ASEAN's decision-making processes feature a high degree of informal and non-confrontational discussions aimed at reaching consensus.[76] As suggested by Yi-hung Chiou, this non-confrontational bargaining style—as opposed to the adversarial majority voting style of the West—has the merit of encouraging cooperation and solidarity while, at the same time, lessening disagreement.[77] As was noted earlier, however, this means that ASEAN would hardly take any decision that could undermine its members' sovereignty and/or interests.[78]

### *3.3.1 The Guiding Principles*

The key principles informing the 'ASEAN Way', as enshrined in the ASEAN Charter, are as follows: non-interference, consensus-based decision-making, national and regional resilience, respect for national sovereignty, the renunciation of the threat or use of force, and peaceful settlement of disputes.[79]

### *3.3.2 The Principles of Sovereignty and Non-Interference*

It is clear from what has been discussed so far in this chapter that the principle of sovereignty lies at the centre of the ASEAN Way. Indeed, sovereignty is linked with all the other principles defining the ASEAN Way, starting with the principle of consensus in decision-making. In the words of ASEAN's former Secretary-General, Phan Wannamethee, the latter represents 'a safety device to assure member states that their national interests will not be compromised, and nothing can be done against their will'.[80] ASEAN is, of course, not unique in giving prominence to the principle of sovereignty. As is well known, the UN Charter is based on the principle of the sovereign equality of States.[81] However, there are differences in how States interpret sovereignty today. In particular, Western States no longer adhere to what, in their view, is an outdated interpretation of the principle. As former UN Secretary-General Kofi Annan once put it, 'state sovereignty, in its most basic sense is being redefined . . . by the forces of globalisation and international cooperation' leading to a significant erosion of its meaning.[82] The ASEAN States, however, do not agree with this progressive take. According to Shaun Narine, ASEAN States' experience of colonialism and other forms of external interference has created a strong commitment to protecting their sovereignty.[83] Indeed, with the exception of Thailand, all nine members of ASEAN have been colonised at one point in their history: France colonised Cambodia, Vietnam, and Laos; Britain colonised Brunei, Malaysia, Myanmar, and Singapore; the United States colonised the Philippines; and the Netherlands colonised Indonesia. Furthermore, during the Cold War, the United States and the Soviet Union sought to gain important allies in the region, which became more unstable and volatile as a consequence.[84]

For the above reasons, the expression 'Westphalian sovereignty is' often used in the context of ASEAN. As explained by Robert Gilpin, Westphalian sovereignty posits that the State 'must answer to no higher authority in the international sphere . . . [and it] alone defines and protects the right of individuals and groups'.[85] References to this commitment to a strong version of sovereignty abound in ASEAN documents. For example, the Bangkok Declaration affirms that no actions or activities are 'to be used directly or indirectly to subvert national independence and freedom of states'.[86] The Declaration on a Zone of Peace, Freedom, and Neutrality (ZOPFAN), which was adopted by ASEAN in 1971, establishes that the organisation is 'inspired by the worthy aims and objectives of the UN, in particular by the principles of the respect for sovereignty and territorial integrity of all states'.[87] The 1976 TAC, which was discussed in Section 3.2 earlier, reaffirms the respect for sovereignty as a crucial pillar of the organisation. In particular, Article 2 of the TAC requires the contracting parties to be guided by 'mutual respect for the independence, sovereignty, equality, territorial integrity and national identity of all nations'.[88] The ASEAN Charter, as discussed in Section 3.2.1 earlier, is also fully aligned with this trend proclaiming the fundamental importance of 'the principles of sovereignty, equality, territorial integrity, non-interference, consensus and unity diversity'.[89]

In the ASEAN architecture, the corollary of sovereignty is the principle of non-interference. The centrality of this principle in the ASEAN structure was well captured by Amitav Acharya, who once described it as 'the single most important principle underpinning ASEAN regionalism'.[90] The reasons for the strong endorsement of this principle mirror those behind the commitment to sovereignty highlighted before, that is to say, a combination of colonial history and experiences of various other forms of interference.[91]

It is important, at this point, to clarify that the principle of non-interference endorsed by ASEAN should not be confused with the principle of 'non-intervention' recognised in international law.[92] Although these two terms are sometimes used interchangeably, ASEAN formally refers to the principle of 'non-interference', which, as will be discussed, has a much broader meaning than non-intervention. The latter is a firmly established principle of international law which has been affirmed, expressly or implicitly, in multiple international instruments and treaties.[93] For example, Eric Corthay has noted that, although the UN Charter does not explicitly stipulate an obligation for members to refrain from intervening in the internal affairs of other States, several provisions refer implicitly to the existence of a right of States to be free from external intervention. In particular, Corthay referred to Articles 2(1), 2(4), and 55 of the Charter.[94] More importantly, the principle of non-intervention has been expressly affirmed in several Resolutions of the UN General Assembly (GA), notably GA Resolution 2131 (1965), GA Resolution 2625 (1970), and GA Resolution 36/103 (1981).[95] Furthermore, the International Court of Justice (ICJ) in its judgement of *Nicaragua V. United States of America,* noted that 'the principle of non-intervention involves the right of every sovereign State to conduct its affairs without outside interference' and 'considers that [this] is part and parcel of customary international law'.[96]

While the principle of non-intervention represents a central principle of international law, to defining its actual meaning is not an easy task. As Corthay correctly pointed out, the principle of non-intervention does not prevent all forms of inter-state interactions.[97] Endorsing this position, Russell Buchan and Nicholas Tsagourias highlighted that the two key elements that define (illegal) intervention in international law are coercion and sovereignty.[98] In the words of the ICJ:

> A prohibited intervention must accordingly be one bearing on matters in which each State is permitted, by the principle of State Sovereignty to decide freely. One of these is the choice of a political, economic, social and cultural system, and the formulation of foreign policy. Intervention is wrongly when it uses methods of coercion in regard in such choices, which must remain free ones. The element of coercion, which defines, and indeed forms the very essence of, prohibited intervention is particularly obvious in the case of an intervention which uses force.[99]

To amount to an illegal intervention, then, the action of a State must display a coercive element (which does not necessarily need to be armed force) and be aimed at interfering with a matter falling within the sovereign domain of another State.[100]

The concept of non-interference endorsed by ASEAN, by contrast, has a much more expansive scope.[101] The key difference between non-intervention, as affirmed in international law, and non-interference, as articulated by ASEAN, lies in the fact that the principle of non-interference does not require the presence of coercion as a defining element. Criticising and making recommendations on matters in which States, using ICJ language, should be able to decide freely and without any attempt to coerce would, therefore, amount to a violation of the principle of non-interference while not qualifying as an unlawful intervention in international law.[102] Thus, as explained by Linjun WU, non-interference within ASEAN would include, for example, the prohibition of criticising the actions of other governments towards their own people.[103] This, as emphasised by Acharya, means that ASEAN will always hesitate to criticise members' governments in the event of human rights violations.[104]

Cultural considerations, like in the case of consensus decision-making, often feature as an additional explanation for ASEAN's commitment to a strict policy of non-interference. According to Nesadurai, for example, ASEAN leaders have recognised that their commitment to this principle is key given that so many diverse States have to work together on common problems.[105] In a similar way, Severino noted that 'with such a complex mixture of race, tribes, religions and cultures transcending national boundaries, and sensitivity of certain aspects of history, Southeast Asia countries are extraordinarily wary of the very possibility of interference by neighbours in one's internal affairs'.[106] Indeed, some have emphatically referred to the disastrous consequences that would follow from a regional failure to comply with the principle of non-interference: 'To abandon this time-honoured principle', noted by former Malaysia foreign minister Abdullah Ahmad Badawi, 'would set us on the path towards eventual disintegration'.[107]

Given the importance of non-interference in the region, it is not surprising that ASEAN instruments contain numerous references to this crucial principle. For example, the Bangkok Declaration affirms Member States' determination 'to ensure their stability and security from external interference in any form or manifestation'.[108] The operative paragraphs of ZOPFAN refer to the right of every state to lead its national existence free from outside interference in its internal affairs.[109] Likewise, Article 2 of the TAC explicitly refers to the right of every State to be free from external interference, subversion or coercion.[110] On its part, the ASEAN Charter affirms the importance of the right of each member state to lead its national existence free from external interference in its internal affairs.[111]

### *3.3.3 The Prohibition of the Threat and Use of Force*

As was explained before, aside from aiming at regional prosperity politically, socially, and economically, the establishment of ASEAN was also the product of the original members' desire to prevent conflict and tensions in the region, especially after the Konfrontasi.[112] Thus, along with its commitment to sovereignty and non-interference, ASEAN confers considerable relevance on the prohibition of the threat and use of force in international relations. ASEAN has made its commitment to this prohibition through its main declarations and treaties. The ZOPFAN affirmed, among other things, the Association's commitment to refrain from the threat or use of force in the internal affairs of States.[113] Article 2 of the TAC acknowledges the importance of settling disputes by peaceful means while renouncing coercive methods.[114] Likewise, Article 2(c) of the ASEAN Charter refers to ASEAN and its members' vow to reject any action involving the threat or use of force, while committing, through Article 2(d), to the peaceful settlement of disputes.[115]

The prohibition of the threat and use of force is of course one of the most important legal principles, enshrined in the UN Charter, that governs the relations between States. Article 2(4) of the UN Charter, in particular, affirms that 'All Members shall refrain in their international relations from the threat or use of force against the territorial integrity or political independence of any state, in any other manner inconsistent with the Purposes of the United Nations'.[116] In *Nicaragua v. United States of America*, the ICJ also confirmed that actions involving the use of force against another State are in breach of customary international law.[117]

The UN Charter, however, contains two exceptions to Article 2(4). The first one relates to the right of every State to self-defence (Article 51). The second, and more important one for the purposes of this book, refers to the ability of the United Nations Security Council (SC) to authorise the use of force in order to restore peace and security should non-coercive means prove to be ineffective.[118] This ability finds its legal basis in Chapter VII of the Charter, and, more generally, in the fact that the SC has the primary responsibility for the maintenance of international peace and security.[119] An example which was discussed in some detail in Section 2.5 of Chapter 2 is represented by the authorisation of the SC to use force in order to protect the civilian population in Libya through Resolution 1973 of 2011.

When it comes to regional organisations, a similar balance is sometimes struck. For example, the Constitutive Act of the African Union (AU) prohibits 'the use of force or threat to use force among Member States of the Union'.[120] Yet, in another passage, it recognises 'the right of the Union to intervene in a Member State pursuant to a decision of the Assembly [of Heads of State and Government] in respect of grave circumstances, namely: war crimes, genocide and crimes against humanity'.[121] In contrast to both the UN and the AU, ASEAN subscribes to an absolute prohibition of armed intervention, notably a circumstance which will inevitably inform its approach towards the type of conflict situations that lie at the centre of this book.

## 3.4 ASEAN and Human Rights

The final part of this chapter focuses on the specific question of human rights within the ASEAN architecture. As mentioned earlier, all States in the Southeast Asia region, with the exception of Thailand, suffered from colonial rule and exploitation. As noted by Ian Neary, this means that, following the process of decolonisation, they focused primarily, as newly created entities, on the need to stabilise their political and economic structures as noted through the adoption of the Declaration of ASEAN Concord (1976), TAC (1976), ZOPFAN (1971), and the Declaration of Concord II (2003), which was discussed in the earlier sections.[122] Under those circumstances, there was little appetite to invest time and efforts in the creation of a human rights apparatus; hence, there was no mention of human rights in any of the aforementioned foundational Declarations.[123] In a sense, then, Southeast Asia States chose to prioritise their political stability and economic development over the protection and promotion of human rights.[124] This lack of enthusiasm for human rights did not change over time. As was discussed in Chapter 1, Western States and especially the US' post-Cold War aggressive promotion of liberal values and practices through international human rights was resented by the governments of Southeast Asia.[125] The latter subscribe to a realist approach to human rights, which sees them as a form of 'unfortunate and sentimental intrusion into the real stuff of international relations- interstate power calculations'.[126] That said, ASEAN would later reverse, at least in part, its earlier negative attitudes towards human rights, making several important advancements over the span of 20 years. This evolution is well reflected in the adoption of the 1993 Bangkok Declaration, the 2004 Vientiane Action Programme, and the 2012 Human Rights Declaration.

### *3.4.1 The 1993 Bangkok Declaration on Human Rights*

Given that the idea of human rights was seen, at best, as purely a Western idea, and, at worst, as an instrument to advance Western imperialism, it is not surprising that, for years, no ASEAN's declaration or treaty included a reference to human rights.[127] This changed in 1993 when the Bangkok Declaration on Human Rights was established to provide an alternative narrative and understanding of human rights to the one offered by the West.[128] The adoption of the Bangkok Declaration marked the first time when ASEAN took an explicit stance on the issue of human rights.[129] In 1993, the world's leaders gathered for the Vienna World Conference to celebrate the 45th anniversary of the adoption of the 1948 Universal Declaration of Human Rights (UDHR). The Vienna Conference was designed to renew the international community's commitment to the protection and promotion of the UDHR.[130] At the end of this conference, the States involved adopted the Vienna Declaration and Programme of Action which reaffirmed their commitments and obligations to protect and promote fundamental human rights in accordance with the UN Charter.[131]

The ASEAN States were among the attendees of this conference. Rather than uncritically subscribing to the conference's conclusions, they expressed their concerns about Western States' emphasis on political and civil rights.[132] Two ASEAN leaders, in particular, Prime Ministers Lee Kuan Yew of Singapore and Mahathir Mohamad of Malaysia, called for a 'regional' approach to human rights. In their own words, 'human rights must be protected and promoted with due regard for specific cultural, social, economic and political circumstances'.[133] Prime Ministers Lee and Mahathir sought to promote an Asian approach to human rights based on the concept of 'Asian Values', an effort which is believed to have further distanced Asian social and political cultures from the West.[134] According to Prime Ministers Lee and Mahathir, Western values are incompatible with Asian values which, first, tend to prioritise community/family over individuals and, second, place more importance on stability and development over democracy. As stated by Prime Minister Mahathir, 'for Asians, the community, the majority comes first. The individual and minority must have their rights but not at the unreasonable expense of the majority'.[135] Prime Minister Lee furthered this position by saying that Asians must reject Western individualism and, instead, focus on promoting traditional intra-family relationship values.[136] Furthermore, Prime Ministers Lee and Mahathir argued that the need for development and stability in Asian societies were more important than the need for democracy. On top of this, they argued that democracy is often used by the West to disguise a plan to keep Asian countries subservient to the West, politically and economically.[137] Prime Ministers Lee and Mahathir also argued that democracy does not always lead to development and stability. As stated by Prime Minister Lee,

> A country must first have economic development, then democracy may follow. With a few exceptions, democracy has not brought good governance to new developing countries. Democracy has not led to development because the governments did not establish stability and discipline necessary for development.[138]

The ideas promoted by Prime Ministers Lee and Mahathir were formally articulated during a meeting in 1993 with other ASEAN's heads of States in Bangkok, leading to the adoption of the Bangkok Governmental Human Rights Declaration (Bangkok Declaration 1993).[139] The latter recognised that:

> while human rights are universal in nature, they must be considered in the context of a dynamic and evolving process of international norm-setting, bearing in mind the significance of national and regional particularities and various historical, cultural and religious backgrounds.[140]

This passage reflects ASEAN States' hostility towards the idea of 'universal' human rights, which, as was noted earlier, was perceived as a tool of Western neo-imperialist agendas.[141] It is clear from the above discussion that the adoption of this Declaration was not meant to signal any genuine intention by ASEAN to advance the cause of human rights in the region. Rather, as illustrated by Maznah Mohamad, the main objective of the Declaration was to give a more formal platform to ASEAN State's reservations and doubts towards the issue of the universality of human rights.[142] In line with this observation, no further notable development concerning human rights occurred within the organisation until 2004, that is, when the Vientiane Action Programme (VAP) was adopted. What is remarkable about the VAP is the fact that, in addition to including detailed plans for security, economic, and socio-cultural development, it made an explicit commitment to promoting human rights.[143] The VAP pledged to establish a network to promote education and public awareness on human rights and establish an ASEAN instrument on the protection and promotion of the rights of migrant workers, women and children.[144]

Authors like Mathew Davies have noted that, upon closer examination, the human rights clauses contained in the VAP are quite bland as they mainly tend to focus on raising awareness.[145] At the same time, once they are put in the context of ASEAN's history, the provisions of the VAP become considerably more important.[146] Indeed, Yongwook Ryu and Maria Ortuoste have noted that the VAP represents the first concrete step that ASEAN ever took towards the promotion of human rights, notably one step which would later inform the drafting of the ASEAN Intergovernmental Commission on Human Rights and the ASEAN Human Rights Declaration.[147]

### *3.4.2 The ASEAN Intergovernmental Commission on Human Rights*

As discussed in Section 3.2.1, the 2007 ASEAN Charter formalised ASEAN's commitment to establish a regional human rights body entrusted to promote and protect human rights and fundamental freedoms.[148] These references to human rights in the ASEAN Charter created some tension among member states. In the words of Ambassador Tommy Koh, the Singaporean member of the High-Level Task Force called to draft the ASEAN Charter, 'there was no issue that took up more of our time, no issue as controversial and which divided the ASEAN family so deeply as human rights'.[149] This division was particularly acute in relation to the nature and structure of the human rights body which would be created within the organisation.

According to James Munro, the negotiations on the creation of this new human rights body divided ASEAN members into two sharp camps, with only Singapore Thailand and Brunei choosing not to take any decisive position on the matter.[150] On the one hand, the liberal camp consisting of Indonesia, the Philippines, and Malaysia wanted not only to establish this human rights body but also to give it 'teeth' in order to increase the costs of non-compliance. They did not want this mechanism to simply have promotional powers but also strong powers such as that of imposing sanctions.[151] Indonesia, in particular, lobbied for the inclusion of provisions allowing not only sanctions but also the expulsion from the organisation in the event of serious breaches of a State's obligations.[152] On the other hand, the conservative camp consisting of Cambodia, Laos, Myanmar, and Vietnam raised concerns about the creation of such a human rights body, pointing to the perils of intrusive measures.[153] Myanmar, in particular, worked to prevent not only the proposed creation of a human rights mechanism but also the very inclusion of any reference to human rights and democracy in the Charter.[154] Eventually the two camps reached a compromise which consisted of the creation of the ASEAN Intergovernmental Commission on Human Rights (AICHR), which, as will be explained, is far from representing an autonomous regional watchdog with 'sharp teeth' and would act only as an advisory body.[155]

The AICHR as an intergovernmental human rights body has a number of important weaknesses. Firstly, being a consultative body, it only has the power to advise and promote human rights. Secondly, although it is expected to uphold international human rights standards as set out in the UDHR and the Vienna Declaration and Programme of Action, the AICHR Terms of Reference (TOR) mirrors the 1993 Bangkok Declaration in referring to the promotion of human rights within specific national and regional contexts, thus taking into account the relevant historical, cultural and religious backgrounds.[156] As noted by Hsien-Li Tan, this means that the AICHR must grant member States such a wide margin of appreciation to effectively end up protecting them from potential interferences concerning their human rights.[157] Thirdly, as established by the TOR, the members of the AICHR are appointed by the Heads of States and consist of mostly current or former government officials.[158] This circumstance confers on the body a highly political nature and contributes to impairing its independence. Fourthly, as noted by Narine, the decision-making process of the AICHR mirrors the consensual approach embedded in the ASEAN Way.[159] This means that the AICHR will not be able to advise or promote human rights in the absence of consensus among its members. It follows, as Amnesty International had warned, that each State could potentially be able to prevent any undesired action by the AICHR.[160] For all these reasons, authors like Yvonne Xin Wang have emphatically labelled the AICHR as 'the world's most toothless human rights body'.[161]

### *3.4.3 ASEAN Human Rights Declaration*

One of the mandates of the AICHR was to develop an ASEAN Human Rights Declaration. With this in mind, the AICHR created a Drafting Group in order to complete this task. In their drafting process, the Drafting Group had to uphold international human rights standards and at the same time take into account the different cultural, political, social, and religious backgrounds within the region.[162] As it happened during the negotiation for the creation of the AICHR, this drafting process once again divided ASEAN members into two distinct camps. The liberal camp (Thailand, Brunei, Singapore, Indonesia, Malaysia, and the Philippines) lobbied for a progressive declaration that would embrace universal human rights standards, while the conservative camp (Cambodia, Myanmar, Laos, and Vietnam) opposed such a course of action.[163] After extensive consultations a compromised agreement was reached in 2012, when the ASEAN Human Rights Declarations (ADHR) was adopted.[164]

The ADHR begins by reaffirming ASEAN and its members' commitment to the principles and purposes of the ASEAN Charter, the UN Charter, the UDHR and the Vienna Declaration and Programme of Action.[165] The ADHR has drawn most of its provisions from the aforementioned international instruments. The first set of articles affirm the rights to freedom of discrimination against race, sex, gender, language, religion, political opinion, culture, and economic status.[166] In terms of civil and political rights, the ADHR affirms that every person has the right to freedom of opinion and expression, to vote, to a fair and public trial, to seek asylum in another State, to personal liberty and security, and to be free from slavery and torture.[167] In terms of economic, social, and cultural rights, the ADHR affirms that every person has the right to join/form trade unions, to an adequate standard of living, to the highest standard of physical, mental, and reproductive health, to education, and to be free from economic and social exploitation.[168] The AHRD also affirms that 'the realisation of human rights must be considered in the regional and national context bearing in mind different political, economic, legal, social, cultural, historical and religious backgrounds'.[169]

Nicholas Doyle argued that the AHRD can be seen as a significant development in Southeast Asia considering the region's historical aversion to the issue of human rights.[170] For example, he claimed that the AHRD at least recognises certain human rights norms and formally endorsed them in writing.[171] Mathew Davies similarly noted that the creation of the AHRD is an important development considering, the exclusion of human rights provisions in all of ASEAN's previous instruments.[172] Despite these positive elements, the Declaration displays important weaknesses. To begin with, although the AHRD has drawn most of its provisions from the UN Charter, UDHR, and the European Convention on Human Rights, these rights must still be interpreted and applied in the light of the specific regional and national contexts. This, inevitably, opens the possibility that human rights violations could be tolerated under the pretext of national/regional peculiarities. Furthermore, the AHRD is more of a declaratory document given its non-legally binding nature.[173] It follows that the soft nature of the AHRD, combined with a toothless AICHR, cannot challenge the sanctity of the principles of sovereignty and non-interference embedded in the ASEAN architecture.[174]

The fact that the AHRD and the AICHR have little prospect of making a difference on the ground sheds light on ASEAN's lack of genuine commitment to the promotion and protection of human rights in the region. Indeed, it has been argued that the reasons for the creation of this human rights system in ASEAN are twofold. Firstly, there was a need to enhance the organisation's legitimacy. Authors like Hiro Katsumata have explained that the global community defines human rights as an element of legitimacy.[175] It follows that, by establishing the AICHR and the AHRD, ASEAN becomes a more credible and legitimate institution in the eyes of the international community.[176] Secondly, there was a need to deflect external criticism in relation to human rights. As explained by Munro, by relying on their own human rights bodies and instruments, ASEAN States would be able to avoid external criticisms of their human rights records by deferring the issue to their own, and more government-friendly, regional mechanisms.[177]

A final important point should be made in relation to the AICHR and atrocity crimes. As recognised by the 2005 World Summit Outcome, regional human rights institutions can play an important role in preventing atrocity crimes.[178] Early monitoring and reporting activities can be vital in this context. On the one hand, they can direct relevant actors towards engaging in prevention and mediation efforts; on the other, they can assist in and/or persuade the relevant governments to improve their human rights records, especially in light of the advantages deriving from the regional proximity.[179] It is evident that if the AICHR were to play any significant role in the battle against atrocity crimes, it would need to be granted full authority to investigate and report on serious human rights violations in ASEAN member states.

## 3.5 Conclusion

ASEAN has come a long way since its creation in 1967. It has evolved into a strong regional organisation whose member states cooperate in security, economic, and cultural issues and, to a limited extent, human rights. Although ASEAN initially started with a weak and informal organisational structure, it gradually evolved with the adoption of the Declaration of ASEAN Concord (1976) which expanded regional cooperation in the economic, social, cultural, and political fields.[180] The same year, ASEAN adopted a binding treaty regulating the way in which internal and external relations should be conducted, namely the TAC, which referred to principles such as the principle of mutual respect for each other's independence, sovereignty, equality, and territorial integrity. Another important step was taken to further enhance the efficiency and cooperation of the Association through the adoption of the Declaration of Concord II (Bali Concord II) in 2003. Among other things, this Declaration created the ASEAN Security Community, the ASEAN Economic Community, and the ASEAN Socio-Cultural Community, marking a significant improvement in the organisational structure of the organisation.[181] The most important step in the evolution of ASEAN is represented by the adoption of the ASEAN Charter in 2007. The latter transformed ASEAN into a more rules-based organisation with a legal personality and codified the fundamental principles of the ASEAN Way.[182]

The 'ASEAN Way' underpins the *modus operandi* of ASEAN. It consists of three main principles: first, respect for State sovereignty; second, non-interference in the internal affairs of States; and third, the prohibition of the use or threat of force. All ten members of ASEAN fully embrace these principles and consider the 'ASEAN Way' crucial for the functioning of the organisation. The principles of the 'ASEAN Way' have been deeply embedded into ASEAN's institutional structure through various treaties and declarations, both binding and non-binding such as, for example, the Zone of Peace, Freedom and Neutrality, the Treaty of Amity and Cooperation, and the ASEAN Charter. Another important component of the ASEAN Way consists of the consensus decision-making to which ASEAN has fully subscribed. The need to reach a consensus before any decision characterises the organisation while also limiting its scope of action. This *modus operandi* has been carefully chosen in order to protect the sovereignty and the national interests of each member state. Inevitably, then, ASEAN lacks the capacity to really act independently from its members.

This chapter also addresses the question of human rights within ASEAN. For historical and cultural reasons, human rights did not originally feature on the agenda of ASEAN. Things began to change in the early 1990s when ASEAN States adopted the 1993 Bangkok Declaration stressing the importance of Asian Values in interpreting and applying 'universal' human rights standards. This Declaration did not genuinely aim at enhancing the position of human rights in ASEAN. Yet, it marked the beginning of a gradual process that would culminate in the creation of the ASEAN Intergovernmental Commission on Human Rights and the adoption of the ASEAN Human Rights Declaration. This, however, does not mean that ASEAN has committed to effectively promoting and protecting human rights within the region. As discussed in this Chapter, the AICHR is only a consultative body which lacks the power to monitor, investigate, and criticise, let alone impose sanctions. On its part, the ADHR accepts that human rights must be interpreted and implemented in accordance with the different political, social and religious backgrounds within the region. On top of this, the ADHR is not legally binding. With a weak AICHR and a non-binding AHRD, the sanctity of the sovereignty of member states remains protected and embedded in the framework of ASEAN.

The features of ASEAN discussed in this chapter need to be taken into account in the analyses carried out in the subsequent chapters, especially in Chapters 5, 6, and 7, in order to provide a realistic assessment of the organisation's capacity/potential to accommodate and promote the application of the principles of R2P in the region. After this chapter's discussion of ASEAN's history, institutional structure, and *modus operandi*, the following chapter analyses ASEAN and ASEAN States' conceptual engagement with the three Pillars of R2P, before we turn to examine the case studies in Chapters 5, 6, and 7.

## Notes

1 European Commission, 'Association of Southeast Asian Nations (ASEAN) (European Commission, updated 5 May 2020) <https://ec.europa.eu/trade/policy/countries-and-regions/regions/asean/index_en.htm> accessed on 28 January 2021; Elaine Kurtenbach, 'ASEAN, China, Other Partners Sign World's Biggest Trade Pact' (The Diplomat, 16 November 2020) <https://thediplomat.com/2020/11/asean-china-other-partners-sign-worlds-biggest-trade-pact/> accessed on 28 January 2021.
2 Budiawan, 'How Do Indonesians Remember *Konfrontasi?* Indonesia-Malaysia Relations and the Popular Memory of "Confrontation" after the Fall of Suharto' [2017] 18(3) *Inter-Asia Cultural Studies*, p. 367.
3 Ibid.
4 John Subritzky, 'Britain, Konfrontasi, and the End of Empire in Southeast Asia, 1961–1965' [2000] 28(3) *The Journal of Imperial and Commonwealth History*, pp. 213–214.
5 Ibid., p. 224.
6 Budiawan, 'How Do Indonesians Remember *Konfrontasi?* Indonesia-Malaysia Relations and the Popular Memory of "Confrontation" after the Fall of Suharto' [2017] 18(3) *Inter-Asia Cultural Studies*, p. 367.
7 Greg Poulgrain, *The Genesis of Konfrontasi: Malaysia, Brunei, Indonesia 1945–1965* (C. Hurst & Co. Publishers, 1998) p. 142.
8 Lee Jones, *ASEAN, Sovereignty and Intervention in Southeast Asia* (Palgrave Macmillan, 2012) pp. 44–45.
9 Ibid., p. 46.
10 Ibid., p. 45.
11 Mohamad Faisol Keling, et al, 'The Development of ASEAN from Historical Approach' [2011] 7(7) *Asian Social Science*, p. 172.
12 Quoted in Lee Jones, *ASEAN, Sovereignty and Intervention in Southeast Asia* (Palgrave Macmillan, 2012) p. 46.
13 The ASEAN Declaration (Bangkok Declaration) (1967).
14 Ibid.
15 Ibid.
16 Ibid.

17 Ibid.

18 Address by Rodolfo C. Severino, Secretary-General of the Association of Southeast Asia Nations, at the International Law Conference on ASEAN Legal Systems and Regional Integration (2001), 'The ASEAN Way and the Rule of Law' <https://asean.org/?static_post=the-asean-way-and-the-rule-of-law>.

19 Ibid.

20 Ibid., and; Hiro Katsumata, 'Reconstruction of Diplomatic Norms in Southeast Asia: The Case for Strict Adherence to the "ASEAN Way"' [2003] 25(1) *Contemporary Southeast Asia*, p. 114.

21 Joint Communique the First ASEAN Heads of Government Meeting Bali, 23–24 February 1976 <https://asean.org/?static_post=joint-communique-the-first-asean-heads-of-government-meeting-bali-23-24-february-1976>

22 The Declaration of ASEAN Concord, Bali (1976).

23 Ibid.

24 Ibid.

25 'ASEAN Secretariat' <https://asean.org/asean/asean-secretariat/> accessed on 3 May 2021.

26 The Treaty of Amity and Cooperation in Southeast Asia (1976), Article 1; and Lee Jones, *ASEAN, Sovereignty and Intervention in Southeast Asia* (Palgrave Macmillan, 2012) p. 54.

27 The Treaty of Amity and Cooperation in Southeast Asia (1976), Article 2.

28 Hiro Katsumata, 'Reconstruction of Diplomatic Norms in Southeast Asia: The Case for Strict Adherence to the "ASEAN Way"' [2003] 25(1) *Contemporary Southeast Asia*, p. 106.

29 Kei Koga, 'Institutional Transformation of ASEAN: ZOPFAN, TAC, and the Bali Concord I in 1968–1976' [2014] 27(5) *The Pacific Review*, p. 732.

30 Stephen Aris and Andreas Wenger, *Regional Organisations and Security: Conceptions and Practices* (Routledge, 2014) pp. 84–85.

31 Chairman's Statement of the 37th ASEAN Summit (2020) para 43 <https://asean.org/storage/43-Chairmans-Statement-of-37th-ASEAN-Summit-FINAL.pdf> accessed on 30 April 2021; 30th ASEAN Summit (2017) para 18 <https://asean.org/wp-content/uploads/2017/04/Chairs-Statement-of-30th-ASEAN-Summit_FINAL.pdf> accessed on 30 April 2021; and Joint Communiqué of the 51st ASEAN Foreign Minister's Meeting (2018) para 16 <https://asean.org/wp-content/uploads/2018/08/51st-AMM-Joint-Communique-Final.pdf> accessed on 30 April 2021. For further statements and communiqué reaffirming the TAC, see <https://asean.org/asean/asean-structure/asean-summit/#99eddc04cd6d2f250>; and <https://asean.org/asean-political-security-community/asean-foreign-ministers-meeting-amm/>.

32 ASEAN Foreign Ministers' Statement on the Occasion of the 40th Anniversary of the Treaty of Amity and Cooperation in Southeast Asia (TAC) (2016) <https://asean.org/wp-content/uploads/2016/07/Statement-of-the-40th-Anniversary-of-the-TAC-ADOPTED.pdf> accessed on 30 April 2021.

33 Ibid.

34 Press Statement by the Chairperson of the 9th ASEAN Summit and the 7th + 3 Summit (2003) <https://asean.org/?static_post=press-statement-by-the-chairperson-of-the-9th-asean-summit-and-the-7th-asean-3-summit-bali-indonesia-7-october-2003> accessed on 30 April 2021.

35 ASEAN Political-Security Community Blueprint (2009), Section II.

36 Ibid., II (10).

37 Jean-Claude Piris and Walter Woon, *Towards a Rules-Based Community: An ASEAN Legal Service* (Cambridge University Press, 2015) p. 43.

38 ASEAN Foreign Ministers' Meeting <https://asean.org/asean-political-security-community/asean-foreign-ministers-meeting-amm/>.

39 Address by Rodolfo C. Severino, Secretary-General of the Association of Southeast Asia Nations, at the International Law Conference on ASEAN Legal Systems and Regional Integration (2001), 'The ASEAN Way and the Rule of Law' <https://asean.org/?static_post=the-asean-way-and-the-rule-of-law>.
40 Chairman's Statement of the 13th ASEAN Summit, 'One ASEAN at the Heart of Dynamic Asia'(Singapore, 2007)<https://asean.org/?static_post=chairman-s-statement-of-the-13th-asean-summit-one-asean-at-the-heart-of-dynamic-asia-singapore-20-november-2007> accessed on 30 April 2021.
41 The ASEAN Charter (2007), Article 3.
42 'ASEAN: Integration, Internal Dynamics and External Relations' [2013] European Parliament Directorate-General For External Policies, p. 4 <https://www.europarl.europa.eu/RegData/etudes/note/join/2013/433713/EXPO-AFET_NT(2013)433713_EN.pdf>.
43 The ASEAN Charter (2007), Article 1.
44 Ibid., Article 2.
45 Ibid., Article 7.
46 The ASEAN Charter (2007), Article 7.
47 The Chairman's Statement of the 32nd ASEAN Summit (2018) para 17 <https://asean.org/wp-content/uploads/2018/04/Chairmans-Statement-of-the-32nd-ASEAN-Summit.pdf> accessed on 30 April 2021.
48 The ASEAN Charter (2007), Article 20.
49 Amitav Acharya, 'A Regional Security Community in Southeast Asia?' [1995] 18(3) *The Journal of Strategic Studies*, p. 186.
50 Daniel Seah I, 'The ASEAN Charter' [2009] 58 *International and Comparative Law Quarterly*, p. 202.
51 Walter Woon, 'The ASEAN Charter Ten Years On' [2017] 39(2) *Contemporary Southeast Asia: A Journal of International and Strategic Affairs*, p. 248.
52 Ibid.
53 The ASEAN Charter (2007), Article 21.
54 Martha E. Gentry, 'Consensus as a Form of Decision-Making' [1982] 9(2) *Journal of Sociology and Social Welfare*, p. 233.
55 Ibid., p. 234.
56 Louis B. Sohn, 'Introduction: United Nations Decision-Making: Confrontation or Consensus?' [1974] 15(3) *Harvard International Law Journal*, p. 445.
57 Report of the Eminent Persons Group (EPG) on the ASEAN Charter (2006), p. 41.
58 Ibid.
59 Helen E.S. Nesadurai, 'The Association of Southeast Asian Nations (ASEAN)' [2008] 13(2) *New Political Economy*, p. 228.
60 Atena S. Feraru, 'ASEAN Decision-Making Process: Before and After the ASEAN Charter' [2015] 4(1) *Asian Development Policy Review*, p. 29.
61 Ibid.
62 Ibid.
63 Ibid.
64 Yi-hung Chiou, 'Unravelling the Logic of ASEAN's Decision-Making: Theoretical Analysis and Case Eminent Persons Group (EPG) that Was Tasked with the Drafting of the Charter Examination' [2010] 2(3) *Asian Politics & Policy*, p. 379.
65 Noel M. Morada, 'The ASEAN Charter and the Promotion of R2P in Southeast Asia: Challenges and Constraints' [2009] 1 *Global Responsibility to Protect*, p. 198.
66 Ibid.
67 Ibid.
68 Ibid., p. 206.
69 Yi-hung Chiou, 'Unravelling the Logic of ASEAN's Decision-Making: Theoretical Analysis and Case Examination' [2010] 2(3) *Asian Politics & Policy*, p. 375.
70 The ASEAN Charter (2007), Article 1 (7).

71 Ibid.
72 Helen E.S. Nesadurai, 'The Association of Southeast Asian Nations (ASEAN)' [2008] 13(2) *New Political Economy*, p. 226.
73 Ibid., p. 228.
74 Amitav Acharya, 'Culture, Security, Multilateralism: The "ASEAN Way" and Regional Order' [1998] 19(1) *Contemporary Security Studies*, pp. 58–59.
75 Ibid., p. 58.
76 Amitav Acharya, *Constructing a Security Community in Southeast Asia: ASEAN and the Problem of Regional Order* (3rd edition, Routledge, 2014) p. 63.
77 Yi-hung Chiou, 'Unravelling the Logic of ASEAN's Decision-Making: Theoretical Analysis and Case Examination' [2010] 2(3) *Asian Politics & Policy*, p. 375.
78 Ibid.
79 The ASEAN Charter (2007), Article 2.
80 Amitav Acharya, *Constructing a Security Community in Southeast Asia: ASEAN and the Problem of Regional Order* (3rd edition, Routledge, 2014) p. 67.
81 The United Nations Charter, Article 2(1).
82 Kofi Annan, 'Two Concepts of Sovereignty' (United Nations Secretary-General—via the Economist, 18 September 1999) <https://www.un.org/sg/en/content/sg/articles/1999-09-18/two-concepts-sovereignty> accessed on 3 May 2021.
83 Shaun Narine, 'State Sovereignty, Political Legitimacy and Regional Institutionalism in the Asia-Pacific' [2004] 17(3) *The Pacific Review*, p. 426.
84 Yukiko Nishikawa, 'The "ASEAN Way" and Asian Regional Security' [2007] 35(1) *Politics and Policy*, p. 45.
85 Robert Gilpin, *War and Change in World Politics* (Cambridge University Press, 1981) p. 17.
86 The Bangkok Declaration (1967), p. 1.
87 The Declaration on a Zone of Peace, Freedom and Neutrality, Kuala Lumpur (1971).
88 The Treaty of Amity and Cooperation (1976), Article 2.
89 The ASEAN Charter (2007), Preamble.
90 Amitav Acharya, *Constructing a Security Community in Southeast Asia: ASEAN and the Problem of Regional Order* (3rd edition, Routledge, 2014) p. 56.
91 Robin Ramcharan, 'ASEAN and Non-Interference: A Principle Maintained' [2000] 22(1) *Contemporary Southeast Asia*, p. 65. See also Lauren Dunn, et al., 'Western Interventionism Versus East Asian Non-Interference: Competing "Global" Norms in the Asian Century' [2010] 23(3) *The Pacific Review*, p. 297; and Amitav Acharya, *Constructing a Security Community in Southeast Asia: ASEAN and the Problem of Regional Order* (3rd edition, Routledge, 2014) p. 56.
92 Eric Corthay, 'The ASEAN Doctrine of Non-Interference in Light of the Fundamental Principle of Non-Intervention' [2015] 17(2) *Asian-Pacific Law & Policy Journal*, p. 3 (Footnote).
93 Ibid., p. 9.
94 United Nations Charter, Article 2(1), 2(4) and 55.
95 United Nations General Assembly Resolutions 2131(1965) A/RES/2131 (XX), 2625 (1970) A/RES/2625 (XXV) and 36/103 (1981) A/RES/36/103.
96 *Military and Paramilitary Activities in and Against Nicaragua (Nicaragua V. United States of America* (1986), Merits, Judgement, I.C.J. Report, para. 202.
97 Eric Corthay, 'The ASEAN Doctrine of Non-Interference in Light of the Fundamental Principle of Non-Intervention' [2015] 17(2) *Asian-Pacific Law & Policy Journal*, p. 14.
98 Russell Buchan and Nicholas Tsagourias, 'The Crisis in Crimea and the Principle of Non-Intervention' [2017] 19(2–3) *International Community Law Review*, p. 8.
99 *Military and Paramilitary Activities in and Against Nicaragua (Nicaragua V. United States of America* (1986), Merits, Judgement, I.C.J. Report, para. 205.

100 Eric Corthay, 'The ASEAN Doctrine of Non-Interference in Light of the Fundamental Principle of Non-Intervention' [2015] 17(2) *Asian-Pacific Law & Policy Journal*, p. 14.
101 Linjun Wu, 'East Asia and the Principle of Non-Intervention: Policies and Practices' [2000] 5(160) *Maryland Series in Contemporary Asian Studies*, p. 13.
102 Hitoshi Nasu, 'Revisiting the Principle of Non-Intervention: A Structural Principle of International Law or a Political Obstacle to Regional Security in Asia?' [2013] 3 *Asian Journal of International Law*, p. 29.
103 Although ASEAN as an organisation has never actually specified its strict interpretations of the practice of non-interference, this is how it has been perceived through analyses of the Association and its members' practices; see Linjun Wu, 'East Asia and the Principle of Non-Intervention: Policies and Practices' [2000] 5(160) *Maryland Series in Contemporary Asian Studies*, p. 13.
104 Eric Corthay, 'The ASEAN Doctrine of Non-Interference in Light of the Fundamental Principle of Non-Intervention' [2015] 17(2) *Asian-Pacific Law & Policy Journal*, p. 14.
105 Helen E.S. Nesadurai, 'The Association of Southeast Asian Nations (ASEAN)' [2008] 13(2) *New Political Economy*, p. 229.
106 Eric Corthay, 'The ASEAN Doctrine of Non-Interference in Light of the Fundamental Principle of Non-Intervention' [2015] 17(2) *Asian-Pacific Law & Policy Journal*, pp. 6–7.
107 Stephen Powell, 'ASEAN Debate on Democracy, Human Rights Hots Up' (Reuters, 26 July 1998) <https://www.burmalibrary.org/reg.burma/archives/199807/msg00594.html> accessed on 17 February 2021.
108 Linjun Wu, 'East Asia and the Principle of Non-Intervention: Policies and Practices' [2000] 5(160) *Maryland Series in Contemporary Asian Studies*, p. 4.
109 The Declaration on a Zone of Peace, Freedom and Neutrality, Kuala Lumpur (1971).
110 The Treaty of Amity and Cooperation (1976), Article 2.
111 The ASEAN Charter (2007), Article 2(a)(e) and (f).
112 Amitav Acharya, *Constructing a Security Community in Southeast Asia: ASEAN and the Problem of Regional Order* (3rd edition, Routledge, 2014) p. 46.
113 The Declaration on a Zone of Peace, Freedom and Neutrality, Kuala Lumpur (1971).
114 The Treaty of Amity and Cooperation (1976), Article 2 (d) (e).
115 The ASEAN Charter (2007), Article 2 (c) and (d).
116 The United Nations Charter, Article 2(4).
117 *Military and Paramilitary Activities in and Against Nicaragua (Nicaragua V. United States of America* (1986), Merits, Judgement, I.C.J. Report, para. 209 (4).
118 The United Nations Charter, Chapter VII, Article 42.
119 Ibid., Chapter VII.
120 Constitutive Act of the African Union (2000), Article 4 (f).
121 Ibid., Article 4 (h).
122 Saadia M. Pekkanen, et al., *The Oxford Handbook of the International Relations of Asia* (Oxford University Press, 2014) p. 594.
123 Ibid., p. 595.
124 Shaun Narine, 'Human Rights Norms and the Evolution of ASEAN: Moving without Moving in a Changing Regional Environment' [2012] 34(3) *Contemporary Southeast Asia: A Journal of International and Strategic Affairs*, p. 366.
125 Saadia M. Pekkanen, et al., *The Oxford Handbook of the International Relations of Asia* (Oxford University Press, 2014) p. 598.
126 David P. Forsythe, *Human Rights in International Relations* (Cambridge University Press, 2000) p. 48.
127 Shaun Narine, 'Human Rights Norms and the Evolution of ASEAN: Moving without Moving in a Changing Regional Environment' [2012] 34(3) *Contemporary Southeast Asia: A Journal of International and Strategic Affairs*, p. 368.
128 Ibid.

129 Ibid.
130 Ibid., pp. 367–368.
131 The Vienna Declaration and Action Programme (1993) I.
132 Shaun Narine, 'Human Rights Norms and the Evolution of ASEAN: Moving without Moving in a Changing Regional Environment' [2012] 34(3) *Contemporary Southeast Asia: A Journal of International and Strategic Affairs*, p. 368.
133 Ibid.
134 Maznah Mohamad, 'Towards a Human Rights Regime in Southeast Asia: Charting the Course of State Commitment' [2002] 24(2) *Contemporary Southeast Asia*, p. 233.
135 Mohd Azizuddin Mohd Sani, 'Mahathir Mohamad as a Cultural Relativist: Mahathirism on Human Rights' [2008] *Universiti Utara Malaysia*, p. 8.
136 Michael D. Barr, 'Lee Kuan Yew and the other "Asian Values" Debates' [2000] 24(3) *Asian Studies Review*, p. 319.
137 Ibid., p. 314.
138 Ibid., p. 324.
139 Shaun Narine, 'Human Rights Norms and the Evolution of ASEAN: Moving without Moving in a Changing Regional Environment' [2012] 34(3) *Contemporary Southeast Asia: A Journal of International and Strategic Affairs*, p. 368.
140 The Bangkok Governmental Human Rights Declaration (Bangkok Declaration 1993), para 8.
141 Maznah Mohamad, 'Towards a Human Rights Regime in Southeast Asia: Charting the Course of State Commitment' [2002] 24(2) *Contemporary Southeast Asia*, p. 236.
142 Ibid.
143 The Vientiane Action Programme (2004), Section 1.1 (ii).
144 Ibid., Section 1.1.14.
145 Mathew Davies, 'Explaining the Vientiane Action Programme: ASEAN and the Institutionalisation of Human Rights' [2013] 26(4) *The Pacific Review*, p. 387.
146 Ibid., p. 388.
147 Yongwook Ryu and Maria Ortuoste, 'Democratization, Regional Integration, and Human Rights: The Case of the ASEAN Intergovernmental Commission on Human Rights' [2014] 27(3) *The Pacific Review*, p. 360.
148 The ASEAN Charter (2007), Article 14.
149 James Munro, 'Why States Create International Human Rights Mechanisms: The ASEAN Intergovernmental Commission on Human Rights and Democratic Lock-in Theory' [2009] 10(1) *Asia-Pacific Journal on Human Rights and The Law*, p. 5.
150 Ibid., p. 13.
151 Ibid., pp. 13–14.
152 Ibid., p. 13.
153 Ibid., p. 15.
154 Ibid., p. 14.
155 James Munro, 'Why States Create International Human Rights Mechanisms: The ASEAN Intergovernmental Commission on Human Rights and Democratic Lock-in Theory' [2009] 10(1) *Asia-Pacific Journal on Human Rights and the Law*, p. 16; see also John Ciorciari, 'Institutionalizing Human Rights in Southeast Asia' [2012] 34(3) *Human Rights Quarterly*, p. 713.
156 The Bangkok Governmental Human Rights Declaration (Bangkok Declaration 1993), Para 8; and ASEAN Intergovernmental Commission on Human Rights (Terms of Reference) (2009), Section 1.
157 Hsien-Li Tan, *The ASEAN Intergovernmental Commission on Human Rights: Institutionalising Human Rights in Southeast Asia* (Cambridge University Press, 2011) p. 158.
158 ASEAN Intergovernmental Commission on Human Rights (Terms of Reference) (2009), Section 5.2.

159 Shaun Narine, 'Human Rights Norms and the Evolution of ASEAN: Moving without Moving in a Changing Regional Environment' [2012] 34(3) *Contemporary Southeast Asia: A Journal of International and Strategic Affairs*, p. 375.
160 Ibid.
161 Yvonne Xin Wang, 'Contextualizing Universal Human Rights: An Integrated Human Rights Framework for ASEAN' [2015] 25 *Duke Journal of Comparative & International Law*, p. 392.
162 Gerard Clarke, 'The Evolving ASEAN Human Rights System: The ASEAN Human Rights Declaration of 2012' [2012] 11(1) *Northwestern Journal of Human Rights*, p. 15.
163 Ibid., pp. 15 and 17–18.
164 Ibid., p. 19; see also Chairman's Statement of the 21st ASEAN Summit (2012) para 5 <https://www.asean.org/wp-content/uploads/images/documents/Chairman's%20Statement%20of%20the%2021st%20ASEAN%20Summit.pdf> accessed on 30 April 2021.
165 The ASEAN Human Rights Declaration (2012), Preamble.
166 Ibid., Article 1–9; Universal Declaration of Human Rights (1948) Article 2; and European Convention on Human Rights (1953) Article 14.
167 The ASEAN Human Rights Declaration (2012), Article 11–25.
168 Ibid., Article 26–34.
169 Ibid., Article 7.
170 Nicholas Doyle, 'The ASEAN Human Rights Declaration and the Implications of Recent Southeast Asian Initiatives in Human Rights Institution-Building and Standard-Setting' [2014] 63 *International and Comparative Law Quarterly*, p. 81.
171 Ibid.
172 Mathew Davies, 'The ASEAN Synthesis: Human Rights, Non-Intervention, and the ASEAN Human Rights Declaration' [2013] 14(2) *Georgetown Journal of International Affairs*, p. 54.
173 Nicholas Doyle, 'The ASEAN Human Rights Declaration and the Implications of Recent Southeast Asian Initiatives in Human Rights Institution-Building and Standard-Setting' [2014] 63 *International and Comparative Law Quarterly*, p. 98.
174 Shaun Narine, 'Human Rights Norms and the Evolution of ASEAN: Moving without Moving in a Changing Regional Environment' [2012] 34(3) *Contemporary Southeast Asia: A Journal of International and Strategic Affairs*, p. 375.
175 Hiro Katsumata, 'ASEAN and Human Rights: Resisting Western Pressure or Emulating the West' [2009] 22(5) *The Pacific Review*, p. 625.
176 Ibid.
177 James Munro, 'Why States Create International Human Rights Mechanisms: The ASEAN Intergovernmental Commission on Human Rights and Democratic Lock-in Theory' [2009] 10(1) *Asia-Pacific Journal on Human Rights and the Law*, p. 24.
178 Brooke Coe, 'Regional Human Rights Institutions and R2P: The Role of State Monitoring in Atrocity Prevention' [2017] 9(3) *Global Responsibility to Protect*, pp. 297–298.
179 Ibid.
180 The Declaration of ASEAN Concord, Bali (1976).
181 Press Statement by the Chairperson of the 9th ASEAN Summit and the 7th + 3 Summit (2003) <https://asean.org/?static_post=press-statement-by-the-chairperson-of-the-9th-asean-summit-and-the-7th-asean-3-summit-bali-indonesia-7-october-2003> accessed on 30 April 2021.
182 The ASEAN Charter (2007), Preamble and Article 3.

# 4 The Association of the Southeast Asian Nations and the 'Responsibility to Protect'

## 4.1 Introduction

The previous chapter analyses the background of the Association of the Southeast Asian Nations (ASEAN), the way in which it operates, its decision-making mechanisms, and the principles that it enshrines, known as the 'ASEAN Way'. Special attention was paid to ASEAN's interpretations of sovereignty, non-interference, non-use of force, and human rights. Chapter 2 develops a general analysis of the Responsibility to Protect (R2P), including its origins, meaning, and current status in international law. This chapter now brings the analyses from those two chapters together with the aim of examining ASEAN and ASEAN States' approaches to R2P.

In particular, this chapter focuses on the conceptual engagement with R2P within ASEAN. As mentioned in the previous chapter, unlike other regional organisations such as the European Union, ASEAN does not speak with one voice when it comes to issues regarding international law, especially on issues that may be in tension with the principles of sovereignty and non-intervention, as is the case with R2P. Given ASEAN's inability, as discussed in Chapter 3, to deliberate by the majority and speak with one voice, the core of this chapter's investigation will be on ASEAN States. In particular, I will be examining their individual statements that pertain to the three Pillars of R2P. While a variety of fora and statements will be considered, special attention will be paid to individual members' participation in the United Nations General Assembly (GA) informal meetings concerning R2P. Since 2009, the GA has conducted annual informal interactive dialogues on R2P in regard to the three Pillars, which have since been formalised to a formal debate in 2018. Generally, these are meetings where individual members of the United Nations (UN) discuss their positions and opinions on R2P and are aimed at identifying the flaws and challenges that R2P faces in both practical and conceptual terms. I will therefore focus my analysis on ASEAN States' governmental statements made during these dialogues. These dialogues are focused on different issues of R2P each year which have included: timely and decisive response (2012), State responsibility and prevention (2013), international assistance and the responsibility to protect (2014), a vital and enduring commitment: implementing the responsibility to protect (2015), mobilising collective action (2016), and implementing the responsibility to protect: accountability for prevention (2017).

DOI: 10.4324/9781003436799-4

Before proceeding, it is important to specify the way in which this examination will be carried out. A number of scholars have used different models in order to distinguish States on the basis of their level of support, or lack thereof, for R2P. For example, Professor Bellamy categorised States as R2P-engaged, Fence-sitters, and Opponents.[1] According to him, R2P-engaged States are those that vocally support and continue to contribute to the discussion on the R2P after the 2005 World Summit; Fence-sitters are States that acquiesced to the 2005 Outcome Document and have remained largely silent on issues regarding R2P since finally, Opponents States are those that have outright opposed and criticised all aspects of R2P.[2] Another model has been put forward by Jonas Claes, who has distinguished between States that are R2P Advocates, Critics and Rejectionists.[3] For Claes, the Advocates are those States that support all three Pillars of R2P.[4] The Critics are those who agree with Pillar I and II but stay wary in regard to Pillar III despite accepting that the United Nations Security Council (SC) should take action to protect populations from atrocity crimes.[5] Rejectionist States outright oppose the very idea and principles of R2P.[6]

For this chapter, I will be using three labels to categorise the ASEAN States as Wary Supporters, R2P-neutrals, or Opposers. These three labels fit better with the reality of ASEAN States' position on R2P. To rely specifically on Bellamy or Claes' categorisation would be inaccurate because, as will be shown, doing so would falsely suggest that some ASEAN States display high levels of support for R2P ('R2P-engaged' and 'advocates', respectively). As will be shown throughout this chapter, some ASEAN States, while not always enthusiastically supporting Pillar I and II of R2P, remain sceptical of Pillar III, and cannot therefore be qualified as being R2P-engaged or R2P advocates. Instead, I will refer to them as wary supporters (resembling Bellamy and Claes' categories of 'fence sitters' and 'critics'). R2P-neutral States, instead, are those that have neither denied nor publicly supported R2P, having had almost no public engagement with this issue at all. Lastly, I will label States that object to R2P altogether as Opposers (resembling Bellamy and Claes' category of 'rejectionists'). As will be analysed later in this chapter, an Opposer rejects the core ideas underpinning R2P due to its unwavering commitment to a narrow interpretation of State sovereignty and non-interference.

## 4.2 ASEAN

Chapter 3 clarifies that ASEAN operates on a consensus basis to ensure the highest respect for its members' sovereignty. Accordingly, in order for an ASEAN representative to present the collective view of ASEAN on a given issue while engaging with external parties, he/she would need to be mandated to do so by all member states and the latter would need to agree in advance on that view. It follows that, not surprisingly, no ASEAN collective statement can be found in any of the GA meetings mentioned in the introduction to this chapter. No statement issued by key bodies such as the ASEAN Summit or the ASEAN Foreign Ministerial Meetings directly referenced R2P either, including in 2005, the year when the very important 2005 World Summit Outcome was adopted.

On the other hand, since 2000 ASEAN has worked closely with the UN and officially obtained an observer status in the GA in 2006.[7] The partnership between these two organisations focuses on cooperation through the ASEAN communities: political-security, economic, and socio-cultural.[8] Through the political-security cooperation, the ASEAN-UN partnership aims to promote regional and international peace and security through various programmes of ASEAN-UN regional dialogues and training in peace-making and preventive diplomacy.[9] This partnership also aims to strengthen collaboration in peacekeeping and post-conflict peace-building. This is worth mentioning given that, as discussed in Chapter 2, peacekeeping operations represent one possible instrument for implementing the Pillar II of R2P. As of 2021, a total of 4,868 military and police personnel from 7 ASEAN States have been deployed to 10 UN peacekeeping operations.[10] While representing a potentially significant development, this should not be taken as an indirect form of support for R2P as such, given the lack of any express engagement with the issue.

In light of ASEAN's lack of engagement with R2P, in order to examine the way in which this principle has been welcomed, or resisted, within the organisation is necessary to focus on the individual positions of each member state.

## 4.3 Indonesia

Indonesia was one of the original founding members of ASEAN alongside Thailand, Singapore, Malaysia, and the Philippines. With the largest economy in the region and a commitment to cooperation, Indonesia has proven to have a significant influence on the direction that ASEAN has taken to the present day.[11] In terms of its position on R2P, Indonesia should be categorised as a wary supporter. It has endorsed the fundamentals of R2P, including Pillars I and II, but stays cautious when it comes to the actual implementation of the principle, especially in regard to Pillar III.

Indonesia endorsed the 2005 World Summit Outcome that brought R2P into the realm of international law but demonstrated to have reservations about this principle on several occasions. For example, GA 60th session called for the need to reach a large consensus on R2P, while also noting that the use of force should only be considered when all other means have failed.[12] At the 2006 GA Plenary Session on the Prevention of Armed Conflict, Ambassador Adiyatwidi Adiwoso voiced out Indonesian's concerns in unequivocal terms:

> the concept of the responsibility to protect should be approached very carefully, taking into account the sovereignty and the equality of all States. My delegation opposes the threatening of people, groups, or countries by others, and sees that as a counterproductive measure. While we realise that sanctions may be required in some exceptional circumstances, we believe that extreme care should be exercised in that regard.[13]

This statement shows that Indonesia did not oppose the concept of R2P altogether; rather, it raised doubts with regard to its actual implementation, especially in terms of its impact on State sovereignty. This concern was once again voiced out after the Secretary-General's 'Implementing the responsibility to protect' report was published in 2009 as a follow-up to the 2005 World Summit Outcome. A statement given at that time by Ambassador Dr. R.M Marty M. Natalegawa affirmed that Indonesia is not in disagreement with the three Pillars of R2P, while also specifying that Pillar III is just one of the options available in the most extreme cases and that, crucially, this Pillar includes also non-coercive and non-violent responses.[14] Again, on the occasion of the 2014 and 205 GA Informal Interactive Dialogue on R2P, Indonesia declared general support for R2P, specifically Pillars I and II, while also affirming that regional organisations should play a more important role in strengthening the responsibility. Instead, it never mentioned Pillar III.[15]

Finally, a statement made by Hasan Wirajuda, the then-Foreign Minister of Indonesia, on the occasion of the 2nd Roundtable Discussion on human rights in ASEAN, is worth reading here:

> When gross violations of human rights take place in a member country, invariably we shy away from discussing it in ASEAN meetings in deference to the principle of non-interference in the internal affairs of states. But in today's world, gross violations of human rights are no longer a purely domestic matter. They are also a matter of international concern. . . . Thus, if ASEAN members still feel that an incidence of gross violations of human rights is too sensitive an issue for open discussion in a meeting, then the logical alternative is to have it addressed within the neutral premises of a regional commission. To ignore it is no longer an option.[16]

This shows that Indonesia is willing to gradually step away from the narrow understanding of non-interference cherished by ASEAN, supporting the position that gross violations of human rights are a matter of international, and indeed, regional concern. Without mentioning R2P, this seems to provide strong support for the fundamentals of the principle included in Pillar I and II.

From these official statements, it can be said that Indonesia has endorsed the fundamental ideas behind R2P, namely that a sovereign State has the responsibility to protect its people from crimes against humanity, war crimes, ethnic cleansings and genocide (Pillar I), and that the international community should assist States in fulfilling that responsibility (Pillar II). With regard to Pillar III, however, Indonesia has shown signs of hesitation. While it has not openly disagreed with the possibility of coercive measures being taken under that Pillar, it has clearly indicated its preference for alternative non-coercive methods available under Chapter VI of the UN Charter.

### 4.4 Thailand

Thailand has always been among the most progressive ASEAN members. In fact, it sought to introduce (unsuccessfully) a more flexible notion of non-interference within the region.[17] The idea of 'flexible engagement' was promoted by Thailand's former Foreign Minister and later ASEAN's Secretary General, Surin Pitsuwan, who argued that the principle of non-interference should be modified to allow ASEAN members express their opinions in a constructive manner on issues that are transnational in nature.[18] Pitsuwan further emphasised that 'when a matter of domestic concern poses a threat to regional stability, a dose of peer pressure or friendly advice at the right time can be helpful'.[19] It is also worth noting that Pitsuwan was a member of the International Commission on Intervention and State Sovereignty (ICISS) Advisory Board, namely the Board which originally came up with the concept that state sovereignty implies a responsibility to protect the population from atrocity crimes and that this responsibility would be passed on to the international community if the State is unable or unwilling to do so.[20] Furthermore, as will be further discussed in Chapter 5, between 1999 and 2000, Thailand was the largest contributor of personnel for the International Force East Timor (INTERFET) among ASEAN States. INTERFET was led by the Australian military into East Timor during the violent crisis with Indonesia following a referendum for the secession of East Timor.[21]

In light of the above considerations, one would expect Thailand to be supportive of R2P. Indeed, on the occasion of the 2005 Summit Outcome, Thai Foreign Affairs Minister, Dr Kantathi Suphamongkhon, stated that his government saw 'merit in the idea of collective responsibility to protect people from genocide, war crimes, ethnic cleansing and crimes against humanity'.[22] However, since 2005, Thailand has stayed silent on the three Pillars of R2P. This can be due to Thailand's own internal political instabilities since the 2006 military coup which ousted the former Prime Minister Thaksin Shinawatra.[23] Due to Thailand's volatile political issues, it has shifted Thailand's position on R2P to one of 'neutrality'.[24]

However, at the 2013 GA Informal Interactive Dialogue on R2P, Thailand seemed to have reverted to its original position of wary supporter. Through this dialogue, Thailand's representative stated, firstly, that Thailand shares the view that States have the primary responsibility to protect their people from mass atrocities (Pillar I).[25] Furthermore, he also highlighted Thailand's support for Pillar II. However, there was no mention of Pillar III in this statement, which instead placed emphasis on prevention rather than reaction.

In 2015, 2016, and 2017, Thailand made very similar statements at the GA Informal Interactive Dialogues on R2P. In all the relevant statements, Thailand reaffirmed, in particular, its support for the basic tenets of R2P Pillar I and II.[26] Its view on Pillar III, however, was different. In its 2015 statement, Thailand pointed out that there are diverse views regarding the implementation of Pillar III, referring, in particular, to the suspicions surrounding the potential of unilateral military intervention without the SC authorisation.[27] It accordingly noted that, while there had already been several extensive discussions on Pillar I and II, the international community had barely touched the topic of Pillar III, which, crucially, is the centre of R2P controversies.[28] With this in mind, Thailand further encouraged the international community to have more open and in-depth discussions on Pillar III in order to develop clear and acceptable guidelines for its future implementation.[29] The 2016 statement hinted also at the importance of interpreting R2P as a preventive tool rather than a political one to be used to pursue regime change, while re-affirming Thailand's earlier concerns with the lack of clarity surrounding Pillar III, especially in relation to the criteria that would trigger it and the procedures that should be followed subsequently.[30] Thailand ended this statement by emphasising the need to guard against unilateral interventions.[31] Similar concerns were raised in 2017, when Thailand stated that the international community has failed to stop heinous crimes as a result of Pillar III being misused and misinterpreted (while the statement did not make a direct reference, it was mostly hinted at the 2011 NATO intervention in Libya that was discussed in Chapter 2), and emphasised, once again, the importance of preventive action.[32]

From the above discussion, it is clear that Thailand does not reject the ideas and principles underpinning R2P. However, despite having repeatedly voiced out its support for Pillar I and II, Thailand remains very cautious in regard to Pillar III, preferring preventive action over coercive responses. Accordingly, Thailand can be categorised as a wary supporter of R2P.

## 4.5 Malaysia

As was explained in Chapter 3, ASEAN was created after the insecurities and suspicions surrounding the Konfrontasi between Indonesia and the newly independent State of Malaysia. As a result of its unsteady independence in the first few years that resulted from external interferences infringing on its sovereignty, Malaysia has been suspicious of any concept that could be used as a 'trojan horse' by external actors to interfere in its domestic affairs. In light of this, one would expect Malaysia to be a strong opponent of R2P. Nevertheless, Malaysia has not objected to R2P as such. Instead, it has voiced support for Pillar I and II, while raising doubts and concerns about the scope and implementation of Pillar III.

Malaysia's position during the NATO intervention in Kosovo in 1999 is reflective of its overall stance. The Kosovo crisis and the resulting NATO intervention were influential in the creation of R2P. However, as discussed in Chapter 2, this intervention was criticised as it was without SC authorisation, hence constituting a direct violation of the UN Charter. During NATO's bombing campaign, in 1999, Russia submitted a draft resolution to the Security Council that demanded the cessation of the use of force and condemned NATO's actions as threats to international peace and security.[33] Between 1999 and 2000, Malaysia was one of the non-permanent members of the SC and voted against the adoption of this resolution. While affirming that the use of force should always be the last resort and sanctioned by the SC, Malaysia accepted that because of the excessive and wholly disproportionate use of force by the Serbian authorities resulting in humanitarian catastrophe 'such a tragic situation required an appropriate and prompt action by the world community'.[34]

In the same year as the NATO intervention in Kosovo, there was also the East Timor crisis that had resulted in the creation of INTERFET, authorised by the SC and led by the Australian army with the consent of the Indonesian government. This case study will be presented in detail in the following chapter, but here, it is crucial to note that with the SC's authorisation and Indonesia's consent, Malaysia had also contributed personnel to this peacekeeping mission.[35]

Turning to Malaysia's position on R2P at the 2005 World Summit, it is important to note Former Prime Minister Abdullah Ahmad Badawi's statement:

> I am aware of the growing consensus towards accepting that the existing provisions of the United Nations Charter regarding the use of force are sufficient to address the full range of security threats; that the only issue remaining is how to ensure that the use of force is applied only as instrument of last resort. Undoubtedly, this is a priority issue especially as it is connected to the question of responsibility to protect civilian populations from crimes against humanity. However, any intervention must give due recognition to Charter principles pertaining to sovereignty, territorial integrity and non-interference. While the Security Council would appropriately be the body to take decisions on these matters, it is Malaysia's view that provisions must also be made for the General Assembly to have an oversight role in this crucial matter of the use of force to deal with threats to international security.[36]

Prime Minister Badawi did not object to the fundamentals of R2P but expressed concerns and suspicions about the potential to resort to force and the implications for the principles of non-interference, sovereignty and territorial integrity. Furthermore, Prime Minister Badawi clearly demanded that the GA should also have a role in R2P situations.[37] Similar concerns were raised during the 2012 GA Informal Interactive Dialogue on R2P. In its statement, the Malaysian representative expressed the need for a chronological sequencing of the three Pillars of R2P to ensure that all measures must be tried first and that the decision to use force must be truly a last resort.[38] This is worth mentioning because this chronological model was rejected, as discussed in Chapter 2, by Secretary-General Ban Ki-moon's 2009 Report on 'Implementing the Responsibility to Protect'. In that report, the Secretary-General insisted that all Pillars are of the same significant value and there is no set sequence to be followed.[39] Furthermore, through this statement, Malaysia again raised the issue of selectivity and how *realpolitik* comes into play through the SC's decisions especially when it comes to the implementation of Pillar III.[40] Moreover, Malaysia also emphasised the role of regional organisations in assisting States in meeting their R2P commitment since they would have a more intimate understanding of the histories and cultures of the relevant States.[41] With these concerns, Malaysia suggested that the international community should be cautious in the implementation of R2P and that more discussions would be needed regarding its parameters, content, and framework.[42]

Malaysia reiterated its position at the 2014 GA Interactive Dialogue on R2P. Through this session, Malaysia emphasised the importance of Pillar II and how crucial international assistance would be when it comes to the responsibility to protect civilians from atrocity crimes.[43] It did not reject the concept of R2P, nor did it dispute the SC's power under the UN Charter to authorise military intervention in humanitarian crises but emphasised that Malaysia holds the principle of sovereignty above all else and that consent of a sovereign State should remain paramount when it comes to external international assistance.[44] This, of course, clashes with Pillar III of R2P whereby the SC could authorise the use of force without the consent of the target state if there has been a threat to international peace and security.[45] Malaysia ended this statement by affirming that R2P still requires more in-depth and comprehensive discussions in order to enable the international community to clearly define its understandings, implementations, and effects on the external and internal dimensions of States.[46]

Malaysia's statement during the 2015 GA Interactive Dialogue on R2P pointed out that the failure to act in a timely manner to prevent atrocities has undermined the concept of R2P.[47] Malaysia further emphasised the importance of non-military measures to respond and prevent escalations of atrocity crimes such as fact-finding missions, mediation, and public advocacy by international officials.[48]

Overall, Malaysia can be categorised as a wary supporter. It accepts the concept of 'sovereignty as responsibility' as well as the idea of the international community's responsibility in assisting States in meeting their R2P duties. However, Malaysia takes a very cautious approach to Pillar III. It notes that the use of force must be an absolute last-resort measure and warns against the risks of bias and selectivity in the implementation phase. On top of all that, it is telling that Malaysia has offered a very strong endorsement of the principle of sovereignty in the context of discussions on R2P.

## 4.6 Singapore

Singapore is another member of ASEAN who I would categorise as a wary supporter of R2P.

Like Malaysia, the Philippines, and Thailand, Singapore contributed personnel to the INTERFET during the East Timor crisis of 1999, showing its willingness to participate in peacekeeping operations under the authorisation of the SC and accepted by the host State.[49] Singapore has since publicly endorsed the concept of 'sovereignty as responsibility' and has even called on the permanent five members of the Security Council (P-5) to refrain from using their veto power in relation to humanitarian crises.[50]

Singapore is also the only ASEAN State that joined the 'Group of Friends of the Responsibility to Protect', established by Canada in order to facilitate and encourage dialogues on the workings of R2P at the UN.[51] An important aspect of this Group's lobbying efforts is that it promotes a full-scale implementation of R2P, including Pillar III. In 2016, the 'Group' expressed its support for Paragraphs 138 and 139 of the World Summit Outcome.[52] In 2019, during the 41st session of the Human Rights Council, the Group reiterated its support for Pillar I and II but also stressed the importance of acting in a timely manner in accordance with the UN Charter once the warning signs and risk factors have been identified.[53]

While it may be assumed that all members of the Group support all Pillars of R2P, this is not necessarily the case, as reflected in Singapore's statements. In fact, Singapore remains rather cautious when it comes to Pillar III. In 2009, during the GA

Informal Interactive Dialogue, Singapore issued a statement to make its position on R2P clear.[54] Differently from other ASEAN members, Singapore stated that the corollary to sovereignty is national responsibility and that States should view R2P as an ally of state Sovereignty and not as an adversary.[55] However, Singapore also showed its lack of trust in the SC as the key organ in implementing R2P, especially Pillar III. For example, it called on the SC to disregard political biases and agendas in order to act in a timely manner.[56] In order to lessen these controversies, it suggested that the GA should play a bigger role with respect to R2P since it offers more legitimacy due to its inclusive representation of the international community.[57] Thus, while Singapore is not against the actual implementation of Pillar III, it remains sceptical about the political dynamics affecting the SC decision-making process.

These concerns were again repeated through the GA's Informal Interactive Dialogue on R2P in 2012, 2015, and 2016.[58] First, Singapore referred to a general consensus among the international community on Pillars I and II, while noting a lack of agreement on Pillar III.[59] More specifically, Singapore noted that the real controversy is not about the non-coercive measures of Pillar III but rather the use of armed force to respond to atrocity crimes situations.[60] Second, Singapore once again raised its concerns with regard to the dynamics of the SC, noting that R2P could only work if the P-5 abandoned their vetoes, political biases, and double standards.[61]

Despite its concerns regarding Pillar III, generally, and the role of the SC in the implementation of this Pillar, specifically, Singapore is among the most supportive States within the region. It is also telling that Singapore never alluded to the importance of the principles of non-interference and sovereignty, while fully welcoming the concept of sovereignty as responsibility.

## 4.7 The Philippines

The Philippines is another member of ASEAN who I would categorise as a wary supporter of R2P, publicly supporting Pillar I and II of R2P but at the same time avoiding any direct reference to Pillar III and emphasising the importance of State sovereignty. Before analysing the Philippines' position on R2P, it is important to emphasise that during the East Timor crisis, the Philippines was the second largest personnel contributor within ASEAN after Thailand to the INTERFET.[62] This showed that the Philippines were willing to assume collective responsibility for the region's security problems.[63]

In 2004, a year before the adoption of the World Summit Outcome, the Philippines was one of the ten non-permanent members of the Security Council. At the time, the crisis that engrossed the SC was the Darfur conflict, which resulted in a mass humanitarian crisis. At the SC the Philippines affirmed that:

> Sovereignty also entails the responsibility of a State to protect its people. If it is unable or unwilling to do so, the international community has the responsibility to help that State achieve such capacity and such will and, in extreme necessity, to assume responsibility itself.[64]

Although it did not refer to it, the language in this statement reflected the one used in the ICISS Report which, as discussed in Chapter 2, brought for the first time the issue of R2P into the international law realm.[65] However, since the formal adoption of R2P in the 2005 World Summit Outcome, the Philippines has lessened its support for R2P. In 2016, Rodrigo Duterte was elected as president. The fact that Duterte is known to be a loyal supporter of the 'ASEAN Way' had an inevitable impact on the country's position on R2P.[66]

Through the 2014 Annual GA Interactive Dialogue on R2P, the Philippines reiterated its support for Pillar I but also emphasised the 'sacrosanct' nature of state sovereignty, referring to it as 'the building block of international law and the conduct of international relations'.[67]

The same position was taken during the 2015 and the 2017 GA Interactive Dialogue on R2P. The Philippines reiterated its support for Pillar I but at the same time confirmed its commitment to the principle of State sovereignty.[68] In 2015, it also made a reference to Pillar II, specifically in regard to regional institutions and their role in assisting States to fulfil their Pillar I duties.[69] It is also interesting to note that, in 2017, the Philippines mirrored Singapore's concerns with regard to the intentions of the P-5 at the SC. Thus, it called on the latter to be impartial in their decision-making and avoid using the veto for political/personal motives.[70]

As a wary supporter, the Philippines has, therefore, endorsed Pillar I and II of R2P but has remained cautious in regard to the scope and implementation of Pillar III.

## 4.8 Vietnam

Vietnam is another State that can be categorised as a wary supporter of R2P. Vietnam has typically shown a general endorsement of the fundamental concepts of Pillars I and II. For example, in 2008, during a Security Council meeting focused on the protection of civilians in armed conflicts, it stated that:

> it is States that bear primary responsibility to protect their own civilians and to deal with violence against civilians as well as violations of international humanitarian law. In order to help States fulfil their responsibilities, the United Nations can help improve their national capacity, provide technical assistance and work with them to conduct other awareness-raising activities, for instance through training courses.[71]

Echoing this position, Vietnam issued a statement at the 2009 GA's Plenary Meeting on the Responsibility to Protect affirming that 'the responsibility to protect, first and foremost, is a matter of State responsibility'.[72] Furthermore, Vietnam also emphasised the critical role that the international community plays when it comes to their responsibility to assist States in meeting their Pillar I commitments.[73] And rather than ignoring references to Pillar III, Vietnam stated that the latter 'requires clear and rational definition to avoid its possible confinement to coercive military force as the only alternative', thereby steering the emphasis towards the non-coercive measures.[74] This was reminiscent of earlier times when, at various UN fora, Vietnam made its commitment to the principles of state sovereignty and non-interference very clear. In 2004, for example, in response to former Secretary-General Kofi Annan endorsement of R2P in the report 'In larger freedom: towards development, security and human rights for all', Vietnam expressly stressed the importance of upholding the principles of territorial integrity, non-interference, national sovereignty, and peaceful settlements of disputes.[75] Also in the 2009 statement, Vietnam highlighted the same concerns that, as noted earlier, were raised by Singapore and the Philippines, that is, a general mistrust towards the ability of the P-5 to make decisions on Pillar III scenarios without selectivity and double standards.[76] Vietnam's overall support for the first two Pillars was also confirmed during the 2012 GA Interactive Dialogue on R2P.[77] Importantly, on that occasion it also made clear its determination to participate in any future discussions on R2P with a view to reaching a common ground and moved from 'words to deeds'.[78]

### 4.9 Cambodia

Cambodia had an unstable and violent history like Malaysia and Myanmar did. The genocidal Khmer Rouge regime, which followed years of civil wars and coups, was brought to an end by a Vietnamese military intervention in 1979. It is interesting to note that the current Prime Minister, Hun Sen, and his party, the Cambodian People's Party, which came to power after the Vietnamese intervention, welcomed the latter rather than regarding it as aggression or an act infringing on Cambodia's sovereignty given Cambodia's political history.[79] Despite this, Cambodia took a rather neutral approach to R2P when the principle first emerged internationally. At the time of the adoption of the 2005 World Summit Outcome, for example, it expressed support for that document but did not make any reference to R2P.[80] Subsequently, it remained largely silent on the matter. Indeed, Cambodia did not participate in any of the GA informal interactive dialogues on R2P that have been mentioned so far.

This neutral stance, however, changed in 2015 when Prime Minister Hun Sen publicly endorsed the fundamental concepts of R2P on the occasion of an international conference on the theme of R2P which took place in Phnom Penh. The conference marked the 10th anniversary of the adoption of the World Summit Outcome and focused on the interpretation and implementation of R2P. At this conference's opening address, Prime Minister Hun Sen solemnly affirmed, for the first time, Cambodia's commitment to R2P.[81] Furthermore, he added that while the UN Charter affirms the centrality of State sovereignty, 'it is also important to acknowledge that the exercise of sovereign rights carries with it certain obligations or responsibilities' and that 'R2P should be viewed as deepening the meaning of sovereignty in that it underscores the importance of states taking seriously their primary responsibility to protect their people against [atrocity crimes]'.[82] Endorsing also Pillar II of R2P, Prime Minister Hun Sen referred to the importance of both international and regional institutions in assisting States fulfil their Pillar I responsibility.[83]

All considered, despite the lack of participation in the UN fora concerning the conceptualisation of R2P, it can be said that the 2015 official endorsement of the principle makes Cambodia a wary supporter. The lack of any express reference to Pillar III is indicative of its reluctance to endorse the coercive dimension of R2P.

## 4.10 Laos

Being one of ASEAN's States with the lowest GDP per capita alongside Cambodia and Brunei, Laos has been traditionally preoccupied with the need to alleviate poverty, which is deemed to be the biggest threat to the State.[84] Accordingly, Laos has on past occasions used UN fora to call for international assistance to meet the challenges it faces as one of the least developed countries in the world such as poverty, reducing child and maternal mortality, malnutrition, and access to education and healthcare.[85] Laos also endorsed the 2005 World Summit Outcome but did not make any specific reference to R2P.[86] Crucially, Laos has not participated in any of the UN dialogues and meetings concerning R2P that have been considered in this chapter, notwithstanding, as seen so far, the large participation of other ASEAN States. For this reason, it seems appropriate to categorise Laos as a neutral State.

## 4.11 Brunei

Brunei's closest act that could be read as a form of support for R2P came in 2007, when its Foreign Affairs and Trade Minister endorsed the Commonwealth *Kampala Communique, a document which was produced following a meeting of the* Commonwealth Heads of Governments and which included a strong reference to R2P.[87] More specifically, the signatories of the Communiqué affirmed that the responsibility to protect populations from atrocity crimes is a fundamental Commonwealth value and reiterated their commitment to work together to ensure that R2P is carried out by the international community in accordance with the UN Charter.[88] This, however, is the only position taken by Brunei on the matter, as it chose, like Laos, not to participate in any of the UN activities concerning R2P that have been discussed in this chapter. For all these reasons, Brunei should be considered as an R2P-neutral State.

## 4.12 Myanmar

Myanmar, which will be the focus of a case study in Chapter 6, as an opposer of R2P, has been remarkably vocal in its unwavering support for the principles of sovereignty and non-interference. For example, on the occasion of the 2005 adoption of the World Summit Outcome at the GA, Myanmar made the following statement:

> While the United Nations must be reformed, its sacrosanct principles of national sovereignty, territorial integrity, equality, non-interference in internal affairs, settlement of disputes by peaceful means and non-use of force or threat of use of force should remain inviolate. These are the guiding principles that have withstood the test of time and are as relevant and valid today as on the day they were adopted.[89]

In 2014, Myanmar took part in the GA Informal Interactive Dialogue on R2P, where it talked about the international community's duty to provide international assistance to States.[90] Myanmar put emphasis on one specific aspect, namely the fact that this international assistance should only be provided at the request, and with the consent, of the State concerned.[91] More importantly, Myanmar expressed a firm rejection of Pillar III, further noting that intervening military in another sovereign State may well aggravate rather than solving a humanitarian crisis.[92] Furthermore, it raised the issue of great powers' motives and agendas behind R2P mandates.[93]

A similar objection to the coercive dimension of R2P came in 2015 during the GA Informal Dialogue on R2P when Myanmar affirmed that using force under the R2P umbrella would pose two problems: first, it would undermine the fundamental principles of the UN Charter; second, it would create the risk of misuses or abuses.[94] This statement further raised doubts as to how and who would decide when R2P should be applied, hinting at Myanmar's distrust in the Security Council.[95]

Not surprisingly, Myanmar's negative attitudes towards R2P have increased since its (mis)treatment of the Rohingya fell under the international spotlight. In 2017, Myanmar took part in the GA Informal Dialogue on R2P where its representative used that platform to emphasise that R2P can too easily be used to pursue political agendas, adding that Myanmar was not intent on, and does not have any intention to commit genocide or ethnic cleansing against any group.[96] In the latest development in Myanmar, on 1 February 2021, the Junta seized power from the National League for Democracy and detained President Win Myint, Aung San Suu Kyi, and other democratically elected officials in the context of a military coup.[97] In response to this, the people of Myanmar have gathered to protest nationwide to call for democracy to which the Junta has responded lethally leading to the deaths of more than 700 protestors as of 13 April.[98] As discussed earlier, in its 2014 Statement at the GA informal interactive dialogue, Myanmar is not against the assistance of the international community, per se, but, it must be with consent of the recipient State.[99] As such, on 24 April, Myanmar agreed to join the ASEAN emergency summit (Pillar II) to discuss the situation after calls from several ASEAN States (Indonesia, Singapore and Malaysia). The summit has reached a consensus on five points for the Junta to address the situation (which will be discussed in detail in Chapter 6).

## 4.13 Conclusion

This chapter examines ASEAN and ASEAN States' *conceptual* engagement with R2P with a view to identifying the degree of support that R2P as a principle is awarded within the organisation. While ASEAN, by virtue of its history, nature, and *modus operandi*, has not taken any collective stance on R2P, the analysis developed in the chapter has suggested that its member states are mostly characterised by a cautious support for R2P. As many as seven States, in fact, can be categorised as wary supporters of R2P, namely Indonesia, Singapore, the Philippines, Malaysia, Thailand, Vietnam, and Cambodia. In line with my definition of 'wary supporters', these States have generally, albeit not enthusiastically, endorsed the fundamental ideas underpinning R2P, and have shown various degrees of support for Pillars I and II, while remaining more reluctant to embrace the basics of Pillar III.

There are, of course, differences and nuances between these States. For example, Indonesia, Thailand, and Singapore have been more progressive than others. Indonesia has publicly stated that the principle of non-interference should not be used as a shield when it comes to humanitarian crises, as the latter represents an issue of international rather than domestic concern.[100] Similarly, Thailand brought forward the concept of 'Flexible Engagement' in order to promote interaction among ASEAN States with regard to conflict situations.[101] Singapore has also taken a rather bold position, suggesting that R2P should not be seen as an enemy but rather as an ally of State sovereignty.[102]

The chapter also shows that a common concern among wary supporters relates to the role that the SC plays in relation to the implementation of R2P, specifically in regard to Pillar III. Thus, Vietnam, the Philippines, Malaysia, and Singapore have all called for the P-5 to avoid selectivity and political bias in their decision-making in order to limit the potential abuse of R2P. As a potential solution to this problem, Singapore and Malaysia advocated the recognition of a bigger role for the GA, which, by virtue of its inclusivity and legitimacy, could guarantee a better chance of implementing R2P more objectively. A final important point should be made with respect to wary supporter States. In connection with their acceptance of Pillar II assistance, they have highlighted the importance of regional as opposed to international assistance. This was particularly evident in the case of Indonesia, Malaysia, and the Philippines.

While a clear majority of ASEAN States have shown positive, if cautious, attitudes towards R2P, this chapter highlights that two ASEAN States, namely Laos and Brunei, are better categorised as R2P-neutral. This is so because they have not directly engaged with, let alone shown evidence of support for, R2P during various UN meetings focused on the topic. At the same time, the lack of direct participation means that they did not get a chance to express a dissent about R2P either. Lastly, this chapter identifies one ASEAN State as an outright opposer of R2P, that is, Myanmar. Myanmar has rejected R2P publicly multiple times by claiming that R2P has no basis in international law and clashes with the fundamental principles of the UN Charter and international law.

One common feature seems to apply to all ASEAN States, namely their reluctance to accept the coercive dimension of Pillar III, which, as explained in Chapter 2, includes not only military force but also other non-consensual measures such as sanctions and referrals to the International Criminal Court. This reluctance to accept non-consensual measures is well-established in the ASEAN architecture. As discussed in Chapter 3, no ASEAN institution has the power to impose sanctions on member states. More generally, the history and status of ASEAN States as well as their traditional endorsement of the principles underpinning the ASEAN way, namely sovereignty, non-interference and non-use of force, explain the lack of support for Pillar III measures. It is important to point out that although none of the ASEAN States endorse Pillar III of R2P, they do not actually object to Chapter VII powers of the Security Council as such. Rather, they are wary of attempts to expand the interpretation of 'threat to international peace and security' under Chapter VII. As mentioned throughout this chapter, most ASEAN States already distrust the SC in implementing R2P and if humanitarian concerns are included within the scope of 'international threat to peace and security', this could potentially be abused to warrant unlawful and illegitimate interferences and interventions into the domestic affairs of sovereign States. ASEAN States' wariness is not completely unfounded as shown by the example of misuse of Chapter VII powers in the Libya Intervention in 2011 (as discussed in Chapter 2).

Having completed the analyses of ASEAN and ASEAN States' *conceptual* engagement with R2P, in the following chapters we look at how the latter have acted practically when faced with three humanitarian crises: the first in East Timor in 1999, which occurred before the formal introduction of R2P in the realm of international law; the second, more recently, in Myanmar; and the third, the current crisis in West Papua, at a time when R2P could have guided the ASEAN response.

## Notes

1 Alex J. Bellamy and Sara E. Davies, 'The Responsibility to Protect in the Asia-Pacific Region' [2009] 40(6) *Security Dialogue*, p. 551.
2 Ibid.
3 Jonas Claes, 'Protecting Civilians from Mass Atrocities: Meeting the Challenge of R2P Rejectionism' [2012] 4 *Global Responsibility to Protect*, pp. 70 and 72.
4 Ibid., p. 70. In relations, another model has also been put forward by Patrick Quinton-Brown, who differentiated between Cautious Supporters and Rejectionists where cautious supporters are States that have agreed to the principle of R2P but remain sceptical in regard to its implementation and scope, while Rejectionist States offers no support for R2P at all; See Patrick Quinton-Brown, 'Mapping Dissent: The Responsibility to Protect and Its State Critics' [2013] 5 *Global Responsibility to Protect*, p. 264.
5 Jonas Claes, 'Protecting Civilians from Mass Atrocities: Meeting the Challenge of R2P Rejectionism' [2012] 4 *Global Responsibility to Protect*, p. 72.
6 Ibid., p. 70.
7 Overview of ASEAN-United Nations Relations (2021) <https://asean.org/storage/Overview-of-ASEAN-UN-Cooperation-as-of-20-Jan-2021.pdf> accessed on 11 March 2021.
8 Ibid.
9 Ibid., p. 2.
10 Ibid.
11 Pattharapong Rattanasevee, 'Leadership in ASEAN: The Role of Indonesia Considered' [2014] 22(2) *Asian Journal of Political Science*, pp. 120–121.
12 United Nations General Assembly (2005), Sixtieth Session, 7th Plenary Meeting, A/60/PV.7, p. 5.
13 United Nations General Assembly, 'Prevention of Armed Conflict' (2006) A/60/PV.98, p. 19.
14 Statement by H.E. Dr. R. M Marty M. Natalegawa Ambassador, Permanent Representative of the Republic of Indonesia to the United Nations General Assembly (2009) "Integrated and coordinated implementation of and follow-up to the outcomes of the major United Nations conferences and summits in the economic, social and related field" (Agenda 44); and, "Follow-up to the outcome of the Millennium Summit" (Agenda 107) <http://indonesiamission-ny.org/menu_kiri/k2_special_political/k2Statement/ga072309.html> accessed on 8 March 2021.

15 Statement by the Deputy Permanent Representative of the Republic of Indonesia to the United Nations at the Informal Interactive Dialogue on the Report of the Secretary-General on 'Fulfilling Our Collective Responsibility: International Assistance and the Responsibility to Protect' (2014) <http://s156658.gridserver.com/media/files/indonesia-2.pdf> accessed on 8 March 2021; and Statement by H.E. Mr. Muhammad Anshor Chargé d'affaires ad interim Permanent Mission of the Republic of Indonesia to the United Nations at the United Nations General Assembly informal interactive dialogue on the Responsibility to Protect: 'A Vital and Enduring Commitment: Implementing the Responsibility to Protect' (2015) <https://www.globalr2p.org/resources/statement-by-indonesia-at-the-2015-un-general-assembly-informal-interactive-dialogue-on-the-responsibility-to-protect/> accessed on 8 March 2021.

16 Ibid.

17 Alex J. Bellamy and Catherine Drummond, 'The Responsibility to Protect in Southeast Asia: Between Non-Interference and Sovereignty as Responsibility' [2011] 24(2) *The Pacific Review*, p. 187.

18 Robin Ramcharan, 'ASEAN and Non-Interference: A Principle Maintained' [2000] 22(1) *Contemporary Southeast Asia*, pp. 75–76.

19 Eric Corthay, 'The ASEAN Doctrine of Non-Interference in Light of the Fundamental Principle of Non-Intervention' [2015] 17(2) *Asian-Pacific Law & Policy Journal*, p. 16.

20 Report of the International Commission on Intervention and State Sovereignty, 'The Responsibility to Protect' [2001] XI and p. 82.

21 Alan Dupont, 'ASEAN's Response to the East Timor Crisis' [2000] 54(2) *Australian Journal of International Affairs*, p. 167.

22 Statement by H.E. Dr Kantathi Suphamongkhon at the General Debate of the 60th Session of the UN General Assembly (2005) <https://www.un.org/webcast/ga/60/statements/thai050918eng.pdf> Accessed on 9 March 2021.

23 Peter Walker, 'Thai Military Claims Control After Coup' (The Guardian, 19 September 2006) <https://www.theguardian.com/world/2006/sep/19/thailand> accessed on 9 March 2021.

24 Hannah Ellis-Petersen, 'Thailand Military-Backed PM Voted after Junta Created Loose Coalition' (The Guardian, 5 June 2019) <https://www.theguardian.com/world/2019/jun/05/thailand-military-backed-pm-prayuth-chan-ocha-voted-in-after-junta-creates-loose-coalition> accessed on 9 March 2021.

25 Statement by His Excellency Mr. Chayapan Bamrungphon, Ambassador and Deputy Permanent Representative of Thailand to the United Nations, Thailand's Intervention at the Informal Interactive Dialogue on the subject of "Responsibility to Protect: State Responsibility and Prevention" (2013) p. 1 <http://s156658.gridserver.com/resources/500> accessed on 20 September 2019.

26 Thailand's Statement at the United Nations General Assembly Informal Interactive Dialogue on the Responsibility to Protect: 'A Vital and Enduring Commitment: Implementing the Responsibility to Protect' (2015) <https://www.globalr2p.org/resources/statement-by-thailand-at-the-2015-un-general-assembly-informal-interactive-dialogue-on-the-responsibility-to-protect/> accessed on 9 March 2021; "Mobilizing Collective Action: The Next Decade of Responsibility to Protect" (2016) <https://www.globalr2p.org/resources/statement-by-thailand-at-the-2016-un-general-assembly-informal-interactive-dialogue-on-the-responsibility-to-protect/> accessed on 9 March 2021; and 'Implementing the Responsibility to Protect: Accountability for Prevention' (2017) <https://www.globalr2p.org/resources/statement-by-thailand-at-the-2017-un-general-assembly-informal-interactive-dialogue-on-the-responsibility-to-protect/> accessed on 9 March 2021.

27 Ibid. (2015).

28 Ibid.

29 Ibid.

30 Thailand's Statement at the United Nations General Assembly Informal Interactive Dialogue on the Responsibility to Protect: 'Mobilizing Collective Action: The Next Decade of Responsibility to Protect' (2016) <https://www.globalr2p.org/resources/statement-by-thailand-at-the-2016-un-general-assembly-informal-interactive-dialogue-on-the-responsibility-to-protect/> accessed on 9 March 2021.

31 Ibid.

32 Thailand's Statement at the United Nations General Assembly Informal Interactive Dialogue on the Responsibility to Protect: 'Implementing the Responsibility to Protect: Accountability for Prevention' (2017) <https://www.globalr2p.org/resources/statement-by-thailand-at-the-2017-un-general-assembly-informal-interactive-dialogue-on-the-responsibility-to-protect/> accessed on 9 March 2021.

33 The United Nations Security Council Press Release, 'Security Council Rejects Demand for Cessation of Use of Force Against Federal Republic of Yugoslavia' (26 March 1999) SC/6659.

34 Ibid.

35 Alan Dupont, 'ASEAN's Response to the East Timor Crisis' [2000] 54(2) *Australian Journal of International Affairs*, p. 167.

36 Statement by the Honourable Abdullah Ahmad Badawi, Prime Minister of Malaysia and Head of the Malaysian Delegation to the High-Level Plenary Meeting of the 60th Session of the United Nations General Assembly (2005) p. 2 <https://www.un.org/webcast/summit2005/statements/malaysia050914eng.pdf> accessed on 9 March 2021.

37 Ibid.

38 Statement by H.E. Ambassador Hussein Haniff, Permanent Representative of Malaysia to the United Nations General Assembly Informal Interactive Dialogue on Responsibility to Protect: 'Responsibility to Protect: Timely and Decisive Response' (2012) <https://www.globalr2p.org/resources/statement-by-malaysia-at-the-2012-un-general-assembly-informal-interactive-dialogue-on-the-responsibility-to-protect/> accessed on 9 March 2021.

39 United Nations General Assembly (2009), 'Implementing the Responsibility to Protect' Report of the Secretary-General, A/63/677, p. 9.

40 Statement by H.E. Ambassador Hussein Haniff, Permanent Representative of Malaysia to the United Nations General Assembly Informal Interactive Dialogue on Responsibility to Protect: 'Responsibility to Protect: Timely and Decisive Response' (2012) <https://www.globalr2p.org/resources/statement-by-malaysia-at-the-2012-un-general-assembly-informal-interactive-dialogue-on-the-responsibility-to-protect/> accessed on 9 March 2021.

41 Ibid.

42 Ibid.

43 Statement by H.E. Ambassador Hussein Haniff, Permanent Representative of Malaysia to the United Nations General Assembly informal interactive dialogue on the Responsibility to Protect: 'Fulfilling Our Responsibility: International Assistance and the Responsibility to Protect' (2014) <https://www.globalr2p.org/resources/statement-by-malaysia-at-the-2014-un-general-assembly-informal-interactive-dialogue-on-the-responsibility-to-protect/> accessed on 4 March 2021.

44 Ibid.

45 United Nations General Assembly (2009), 'Implementing the Responsibility to Protect' Report of the Secretary-General, A/63/677, p. 22.

46 Ibid.

47 Malaysia's Statement at the United Nations General Assembly Informal Interactive Dialogue on the Responsibility to Protect: 'A Vital and Enduring Commitment: Implementing the Responsibility to Protect' (2015) <https://www.globalr2p.org/resources/statement-by-malaysia-at-the-2015-un-general-assembly-informal-interactive-dialogue-on-the-responsibility-to-protect/> accessed on 10 March 2021.

48 Ibid.
49 Alan Dupont, 'ASEAN's Response to the East Timor Crisis' [2000] 54(2) *Australian Journal of International Affairs*, p. 167.
50 Alex J. Bellamy and Sara E. Davies, 'The Responsibility to Protect in the Asia-Pacific Region' [2009] 40(6) *Security Dialogue*, p. 558.
51 'The Responsibility to Protect in Southeast Asia' [2009] The Asia-Pacific Centre for the Responsibility to Protect, p. 47.
52 Statement by the Group of Friends of the Responsibility to Protect in Geneva at the Informal Interactive Dialogue with the Under-Secretary-General Mr. Adama Dieng, Special Adviser to the Secretary-General on the Prevention of Genocide (2016) <https://www.globalr2p.org/resources/statement-delivered-on-behalf-of-the-group-of-friends-of-r2p-at-the-31st-session-of-the-human-rights-council-1/> accessed on 10 March 2021.
53 Statement delivered on behalf of the Group of Friends of R2P on Item 2 at the 41st session of the Human Rights Council (2019) <https://www.globalr2p.org/resources/statement-delivered-on-behalf-of-the-group-of-friends-of-r2p-in-geneva-on-item-2-at-the-41st-session-of-the-human-rights-council/> accessed on 10 March 2021.
54 Statement by Ambassador Vanu Gopala Menon, Permanent Representative of Singapore to the United Nations at the General Assembly Interactive Dialogue on the Responsibility to Protect (2009) <http://s156658.gridserver.com/media/files/singapore-2009-r2p-debate.pdf> accessed on 10 March 2021.
55 Ibid.
56 Ibid.
57 Ibid.
58 Singapore's Statement at the United Nations at the General Assembly Interactive Dialogue on the Responsibility to Protect: 'Responsibility to Protect: Timely and Decisive Response' (2012) <https://www.globalr2p.org/resources/statement-by-singapore-at-the-2012-un-general-assembly-informal-interactive-dialogue-on-the-responsibility-to-protect/> accessed on 10 March 2021; 'A Vital and Enduring Commitment: Implementing the Responsibility to Protect' (2015) <https://www.globalr2p.org/resources/statement-by-singapore-at-the-2015-un-general-assembly-informal-interactive-dialogue-on-the-responsibility-to-protect/> accessed on 24 April 2021; and 'Mobilizing Collective Action: The Next Decade of Responsibility to Protect' (2016) <https://www.globalr2p.org/resources/statement-by-singapore-at-the-2016-un-general-assembly-informal-interactive-dialogue-on-the-responsibility-to-protect/> accessed on 24 April 2021.
59 Ibid.
60 Ibid.
61 Ibid.
62 Alan Dupont, 'ASEAN's Response to the East Timor Crisis' [2000] 54(2) *Australian Journal of International Affairs*, pp. 167–168.
63 Ibid.
64 The United Nations Security Council Provisional 5040th meeting (2004) S/PV/.5040, p. 12.
65 Report of the International Commission on Intervention and State Sovereignty, 'The Responsibility to Protect' [2001] XI.
66 Regine Cabato, 'Duterte Highlights ASEAN Principle of Non-Interference' (CNN Philippines, 29 April 2017) <http://nine.cnnphilippines.com/news/2017/04/29/Duterte-ASEAN-speech-non-interference.html> accessed on 10 March 2021.
67 The Philippines' Statement at United Nations General Assembly interactive dialogue on the Responsibility to Protect: 'Fulfilling Our Collective Responsibility: International Assistance and the Responsibility to Protect' (2014) <https://www.globalr2p.org/resources/statement-by-the-philippines-at-the-2014-un-general-assembly-informal-interactive-dialogue-on-the-responsibility-to-protect/> accessed on 4 March 2021.

68 The Philippines' Statement at United Nations General Assembly interactive dialogue on the Responsibility to Protect: 'A Vital and Enduring Commitment: Implementing the Responsibility to Protect' (2015) <https://www.globalr2p.org/resources/statement-by-the-philippines-at-the-2015-un-general-assembly-informal-interactive-dialogue-on-the-responsibility-to-protect/> accessed on 4 March 2021.; and 'Implementing the Responsibility to Protect: Accountability for Prevention' (2017) <https://www.globalr2p.org/resources/statement-by-the-philippines-at-the-2017-un-general-assembly-informal-interactive-dialogue-on-the-responsibility-to-protect/> accessed on 4 March 2021.

69 Ibid. (2015).

70 Ibid. (2017).

71 The United Nations Security Council 5898th Meeting (2008) S/PV.5898, p. 14.

72 Statement by H.E. Ambassador Bui The Giang, Deputy Permanent Representative of Viet Nam, at the GA's Plenary Meeting on Responsibility to Protect (2009) <http://s156658.gridserver.com/media/files/vietnam-2009-r2p-debate.pdf> accessed on 10 March 2021.

73 Ibid.

74 Ibid.

75 The United Nations General Assembly 89th Plenary Meeting (2005) A/59/PV.89, pp. 21–22.

76 Statement by H.E. Ambassador Bui The Giang, Deputy Permanent Representative of Viet Nam, at the GA's Plenary Meeting on Responsibility to Protect (2009) <http://s156658.gridserver.com/media/files/vietnam-2009-r2p-debate.pdf> accessed on 10 March 2021.

77 Statement by Ambassador Pham Vinh Quang, Deputy Permanent Representative of the Socialist Republic of Vietnam at the United Nations General Assembly interactive dialogue on Responsibility to Protect: 'Responsibility to Protect: Timely and Decisive Response' (2012) <https://www.globalr2p.org/wp-content/uploads/2020/07/2012-IID-Viet-Nam.pdf> accessed on 10 March 2021.

78 Alex J. Bellamy and Sara E. Davies, 'The Responsibility to Protect in the Asia-Pacific Region' [2009] 40(6) *Security Dialogue*, p. 562.

79 Nicholas J. Wheeler, *Saving Strangers: Humanitarian Intervention in International Society* (Oxford University Press Reprinted 2010) p. 90.

80 The United Nations General Assembly Sixtieth Meeting, 22nd Plenary Meeting (2005) A/60/PV.22, p. 17.

81 Detailed conference report on 'The Responsibility to Protect at 10: Progress, Challenges and Opportunities in the Asia Pacific' (2015), p. 9 <https://r2pasiapacific.org/files/2823/r2p_at_10_conference_detailedreport.pdf> accessed on 23 April 2021.

82 Ibid.

83 Ibid., p. 10.

84 'The Responsibility to Protect in Southeast Asia' [2009] The Asia-Pacific Centre for the Responsibility to Protect, p. 30.

85 Statement by H.E. Dr. Khamlien Pholsena, Vice Minister of Planning and Investment of the Lao People's Democratic Republic at the Annual Ministerial Meeting on Least Developed Countries (LDCs) (2016) <https://www.un.int/lao/sites/www.un.int/files/Lao/final_statment_ldcs.pdf> accessed on 4 March 2021; and Statement by H.E. Dr Khiane Phansourivong, Permanent Representative of the Lao People's Democratic Republic to the United Nations at the Third Committee of the 73rd Session of the United Nations General Assembly, Agenda item 28 (2018) <https://www.un.int/lao/sites/www.un.int/files/Lao/statement_by_h.e._dr._khiane_phansourivong.pdf> accessed on 4 March 2021.

86 The United Nations General Assembly 12th Plenary Meeting (2007) A/62/PV.12, p. 9.

87 Commonwealth Heads of Government Meeting, The Kampala Communiqué (2007) para 5 <http://www.create-rpc.org/pdf_documents/Kampala_Communique.pdf> accessed on 3 May 2021.

88 Ibid.

89 Statement by His Excellency U Nyan Win, Minister for Foreign Affairs and Chairman of the Delegation of the Union of Myanmar at the High-Level Plenary Meeting of the 60th Session of the United Nations General Assembly (2005), p. 2 <https://www.un.org/webcast/summit2005/statements16/mya050916eng.pdf> accessed on 10 March 2021.

90 Statement by His Excellency Mr. Kyaw Tin, Permanent Representative of the Republic of the Union of Myanmar to the United Nations General Assembly Informal Interactive Dialogue on the Responsibility to Protect: 'Fulfilling Our Collective Responsibility: International Assistance and the Responsibility to Protect' (2014) <http://statements.unmeetings.org/media2/4493842/myanmar.pdf> accessed on 10 March 2021.

91 Ibid.

92 Ibid.

93 Ibid.

94 Ibid.

95 Ibid.

96 Statement by Myanmar at the United Nations General Assembly Informal Interactive Dialogue on the Responsibility to Protect 'Implementing the Responsibility to Protect: Accountability for Prevention' (2017) <http://s156658.gridserver.com/media/files/2017-iid-myanmar.pdf> accessed on 10 March 2021.

97 'Myanmar Coup: Aung San Suu Kyi Detailed as Military Seizes Control' (BBC, 1 February 2021) <https://www.bbc.co.uk/news/world-asia-55882489> accessed on 10 March 2021.

98 'Myanmar Coup: The People Shot Dead Since the Protests Began' (BBC, 13 April 2021) <https://www.bbc.co.uk/news/world-asia-56636345> accessed on 1 May 2021.

99 Statement by His Excellency Mr. Kyaw Tin, Permanent Representative of the Republic of the Union of Myanmar to the United Nations General Assembly Informal Interactive Dialogue on the Responsibility to Protect: 'Fulfilling Our Collective Responsibility: International Assistance and the Responsibility to Protect' (2014) <http://statements.unmeetings.org/media2/4493842/myanmar.pdf> accessed on 1 May 2021.

100 'The Responsibility to Protect in Southeast Asia' [2009] The Asia-Pacific Centre for the Responsibility to Protect, p. 21.

101 Robin Ramcharan, 'ASEAN and Non-Interference: A Principle Maintained' [2000] 22(1) *Contemporary Southeast Asia*, pp. 75–76.

102 Statement by Ambassador Vanu Gopala Menon, Permanent Representative of Singapore to the United Nations at the General Assembly Interactive Dialogue on the Responsibility to Protect (2009) <http://s156658.gridserver.com/media/files/singapore-2009-r2p-debate.pdf> accessed on 10 March 2021.

# 5 ASEAN and the East Timor Crisis

## 5.1 Introduction

Chapter 4 analyses the Association of Southeast Asian Nations (ASEAN) and its States' *conceptual* engagement with the responsibility to protect (R2P). Building on that discussion, this chapter and the following two chapters examine the ASEAN and ASEAN States' *practical* engagement with three humanitarian crises that have occurred in the region. This chapter, in particular, focuses on the 1999 East Timor crisis. Since the latter occurred before the adoption of the 2005 World Summit Outcome, this chapter enquires into how ASEAN and the ASEAN States responded to a humanitarian crisis before the formal emergence of R2P in the realm of international law. This response is then compared to the subsequent chapters, with their reactions, post-R2P emergence, to the current crises in the Rakhine State of Myanmar and West Papua of Indonesia. This will determine, among other things, whether those ASEAN States that conceptually endorsed at least some Pillars of R2P since 2015 have turned words into action.

This chapter is divided into five sections. The first section introduces the background of the East Timor crisis. The second section analyses the events that led to the crucial 5 May Agreement in 1999 whereby Portugal, Indonesia, and the United Nations (UN) agreed to hold a referendum to decide the fate of the East Timorese. Then, the third section discusses the creation of the United Nations Mission in East Timor. The fourth section analyses the events before and after the referendum, including the establishment of a UN peacekeeping mission, the International Force East Timor. The fifth and final section draws some conclusions as to the practical response of ASEAN and its members to the Timorese humanitarian crisis. The analysis developed in this chapter makes extensive use of primary sources such as official statements made at both international and regional fora, positions taken at the UN Security Council (SC) and voting patterns at the UN General Assembly (GA).

## 5.2 Background of the Crisis

Before East Timor came under Indonesian rule in 1976, it was colonised by Portugal in the sixteenth century. The country was known as Portuguese Timor until

DOI: 10.4324/9781003436799-5

Portugal abandoned the colony in 1974.[1] Portugal only initiated decolonising East Timor as a result of the Carnation Revolution, in which the left-wing Portuguese army staged a coup to overthrow the authoritarian Estado Novo regime.[2] Because Portugal rushed to rid itself of the burden of East Timor, there was no official handover of the administration to a local government. Lisbon's abandonment of its colony created a power vacuum, which resulted in the establishment of three political parties in this territory, each with different agendas as to what they hoped for the future of East Timor. The political parties consist of the Democratic Union of Timor (UDT), the Timorese Social Democratic Association (ASDT), which would later be renamed as the Revolutionary Front for Independent East Timor (FRETILIN), and the Timorese Democratic People's Union (APODETI).[3] FRETILIN worked towards full independence, UDT preferred a type of 'progressive autonomy' with continued Portuguese presence, and APODETI, which, as will be discussed later, had been created by Indonesia's State intelligence agency, sought to promote the integration of East Timor with Indonesia.[4]

Immediately after Portugal started to reduce its presence in East Timor, Indonesia appeared to be publicly supportive of the East Timorese's right to self-determination. Adam Malik, the then-Foreign Affairs Minister of Indonesia, stated that 'independence was the right of every nation with no exception for the people of Timor' and that Indonesia had no territorial ambitions and promised good relations with whomever would govern this territory after its independence.[5] However, the reality of Indonesia's position was rather different to what Malik had stated, especially once FRETILIN and UDT formed an alliance with the goal of negotiating with Portugal to create a transitional government that would ultimately lead to full independence.[6]

An independent East Timor posed a security problem to Indonesia because it could potentially become a hub for communism in the region. Over 90% of the population supported the alliance between the two pro-independence parties, FRETILIN and UDT.[7] FRETILIN, in particular, was feared by Indonesia because it had launched a new communist-like manifesto to 'revolutionise the social and economic structures of colonial inspiration in a general struggle against poverty, illiteracy and economic and political oppression'.[8] This did not sit well with President Suharto, the then-Indonesian President, who led an anti-communist regime and was very preoccupied about the region's stability, especially after the United States (US) started to withdraw from Vietnam.[9] A communist State in the region, especially if adjacent to the Indonesian province of West Timor, would have encouraged other local communist movements to rise up.[10] Consequently, while professing support for the East Timorese's right to self-determination, Indonesia actually worked against it. In particular, the Indonesian army engaged in Operasi Komodo, which was a covert operation within East Timorese political quarters aimed at building support for integration with Indonesia. This operation was conducted, initially, through propaganda and, later, through terror and military attacks.[11] One goal of this operation consisted, as mentioned earlier, in the creation of a pro-Indonesia political party, APODETI.[12] However, as APODETI failed to attract sufficient support among the population (about 5%), the agents of Operasi Komodo used other tactics, including a smear campaign across both West and East Timor warning that the latter had been infiltrated by Chinese, Vietnamese, and Soviet communist forces and that FRETILIN was riddled with Maoists.[13] At the same time, the Indonesian agents infiltrated in East Timor succeeded in persuading the leadership of the UDT to terminate their alliance with communist-controlled FRETILIN.[14] Instead of allying with APODETI, however, the UDT staged a pre-emptive coup in an attempt to preserve Timor's future independence.[15] They asked FRETILIN moderates to expel the leftists from their party and work together to pursue independence with the aid of the US.[16] FRETILIN, instead, not only rejected the offer but also recruited local forces to fight back against the UDT-led coup. As a result, civil war broke out in 1975.[17]

By that time, the majority of the Portuguese military had already left East Timor and the remaining sided with FRETILIN.[18] Consequently, by September of that year, FRETILIN had taken control of most parts of the country, restored order, and declared the independence of the 'Democratic Republic of East Timor'.[19] Indonesia, however, continued to falsely broadcast that East Timor was still locked in a violent civil war with an overflowing number of refugees fleeing to the Indonesian West Timor, a circumstance which was used as an indication that the crisis in East Timor was also threatening Indonesia's security and stability.[20] The fact that FRETILIN's declaration of independence was supported by then-communist States such as China, the Union of Soviet Socialist Republics, Vietnam, Cambodia, North Korea, and Laos further increased President Suharto's concerns about the spread of communism close to Indonesian borders.[21] In his own words:

> Indonesia has no territorial ambitions, we are concerned only about the security, tranquillity, and peace of Asia and the Southern Hemisphere. . . . FRETILIN has declared its independence unilaterally. . . . Portugal, however, is unable to control the situation. If this continues it will prolong the suffering of the refugees and increase the instability in the area . . . they [UDT and FRETILIN] are infected the same as is the Portuguese army with communism.[22]

As tension escalated, on 7 December 1975 Indonesia commenced a full-scale invasion of East Timor. By 17 July 1976, it successfully annexed East Timor as its 27th province.[23] Indonesia justified its invasion on multiple, if weak, grounds. For example, it invoked Article 51 of the UN Charter, stating that the armed intervention was in response to unprovoked attacks by FRETILIN forces into its borders.[24] It also claimed that it had intervened following an invitation from an East Timorese authority.[25] Further claims were made with regard to the non-viability of East Timor as an independent country, presenting the intervention as an attempt to benevolently absorb East Timor's burden.[26] Following Indonesia's intervention, the East Timorese were subjected to widespread violations of human rights, including extrajudicial execution, arbitrary detention, torture, and rape, on a level that, according to some accounts, constituted crimes against humanity.[27] At the same time, the Indonesian armed forces also committed war crimes, including widespread destruction and appropriation of properties, cruel treatments and tortures, taking hostages, and executions of civilians.[28] According to some estimates, in the two months following the commencement of the invasion, as many as 60,000 East Timorese were killed.[29]

## 5.3 The Initial Reaction of the International Community

Before looking at how ASEAN responded to Indonesia's forced annexation of East Timor and the mistreatment of East Timorese, it is useful to examine the reaction of the international community, as this will provide a sense of the gravity of the situation. To begin with, the Security Council convened a meeting on the 15th of December 1975 after it was notified by Portugal of Indonesia's invasion.[30] During this meeting, the Indonesian delegation justified the intervention on the grounds mentioned earlier, namely self-defence, intervention by invitation, and economic non-viability.[31] References were also made to the importance of preserving the stability of the whole region of Southeast Asia.[32] However, all these claims were rejected by the SC which, through Resolution 384, recognised the East Timorese's right to self-determination, and called on all States to respect the territorial integrity of East Timor.[33] Furthermore, Resolution 384 expressed concern over the loss of lives, condemned Indonesia's military intervention, demanded it to withdraw its troops, and invited Portugal to resume its role as the administering power.[34]

On 22 April 1976, before Indonesia's official annexation of East Timor, the SC passed another Resolution, that is Resolution 389, which reiterated most of the findings and demands of Resolution 384.[35] However, one notable difference is that Resolution 389 did not expressly condemn Indonesia's use of force. The language was watered down from 'deploring the intervention of the armed forces of Indonesia in East Timor' to 'call[ing] upon the Government of Indonesia to withdraw without further delay all its forces from the territory', which is noticeably more friendly.[36] These were the only two Resolutions passed by the SC in regard to this issue. After Resolution 389, the majority of the international community seemed to have accepted the fact that Indonesia's control of East Timor was necessary to maintain peace and stability.[37] Consequently, East Timor would not again be on the SC's agenda for another 23 years.

The GA too addressed the question of East Timor. First, on 12 December 1975, it passed Resolution 3485 which echoed SC Resolution 384 discussed earlier.[38] In December of the following year, the GA passed Resolution 31/53 reaffirming the inalienable right of the people of East Timor to self-determination and independence and deploring Indonesia's refusal to comply with the provisions of GA Resolution 3485 as well as SC Resolutions 384 and 389.[39] The voting on these two Resolutions by ASEAN States will be analysed in Section 5.3.2 later. After these two pronouncements, the GA continued to adopt similar resolutions until 1982.

### *5.3.1 The Initial Reaction of ASEAN*

In order to understand fully ASEAN's position in this crisis, it is important to take into account the history and nature of ASEAN. As discussed in Chapter 3, in the mid-1960s, Indonesia, Thailand, Malaysia, Singapore, and the Philippines were all facing internal communist insurgencies. Against this background, these five States met in 1967 and agreed to create a platform, which could be used to promote regional economic growth and stability, while at the same time defeating the threat of communism.[40] During the first decade of ASEAN's existence, its members were mainly intent on learning how to work with one another towards achieving the common objectives of ASEAN.[41] As discussed in Chapter 3, it was only ten years later, in February of 1976, that ASEAN States adopted the legally binding Treaty of Amity and Cooperation in Southeast Asia (TAC).[42] It is important to note that this happened shortly after Indonesia's invasion of East Timor.

The TAC essentially set out the fundamentals of the 'ASEAN Way', which, as discussed in Chapter 3, include mutual respect for each other's sovereignty, equality, territorial integrity, and national identity; freedom from external interference, subversion or coercion; renunciation of the threat or use of force; peaceful settlement of disputes, and consensus decision-making.[43] Having just signed a treaty which incorporated important State-centric principles within the ASEAN structure, it was unlikely that ASEAN States would take decisive action interfering in a member's internal affairs even though this member state had just violated the sovereignty of East Timor and essentially violated the principles of the ASEAN Way. In the name of unity and solidarity with its biggest founding member, ASEAN chose to ignore this fact.

As a result of this, ASEAN's collective response to the invasion of East Timor was very limited. In essence, the only relevant action was taken in 1976 when the ninth ASEAN Ministerial Meeting issued a Joint Communique concerning broadly the organisation's political-security cooperation and external relations.[44] The statement, carefully crafted to avoid offending Indonesia, is important because it showed ASEAN's general acceptance of the justifications provided by Indonesia for taking control of East Timor.[45] For example, for the sake of regional peace and security, the communique urged the UN to accept the assurances from Indonesia and the Provisional Government of East Timor that they would cooperate with the international community.[46] In particular, ASEAN accepted the validity of Indonesia's claim to have intervened following the invitation of the 'Popular Representative Assembly', without questioning whether the latter could lawfully represent the view of the people of East Timor. In doing so, the joint communique ignored the condemnation of Indonesia's military intervention included in SC Resolution 384 and the acts committed by the Indonesian armed forces that, according to various reports, amounted to crimes against humanity and war crimes. Finally, it is also telling that the ASEAN Summit, which, as discussed in Chapter 3, is the supreme body within the organisation, did not make any pronouncement on the crisis.

### *5.3.2 The Initial Reactions of ASEAN States*

At the time, ASEAN consisted of Indonesia, Malaysia, the Philippines, Thailand, and Singapore. In line with the ASEAN joint communique mentioned in the previous section, Malaysia, the Philippines, and Thailand showed solid support for

Indonesia. In doing so, these States were mainly motivated by the fear that a communist East Timor would endanger the security of the region. In an attempt to sway the international community's opinion on Indonesia and develop an alternative narrative, Malaysia, Thailand, and the Philippines co-sponsored two draft resolutions which were introduced at the 30th session of the GA in 1975.[47] These two draft resolutions neither condemned nor referred to the use of force by Indonesia. In fact, they omitted any reference to the role played by Indonesia in the crisis.[48] Furthermore, they downplayed the relevance of the declaration of independence issued by FRETILIN, suggesting that East Timorese were profoundly divided over their future. During the relevant discussions, the Philippines also referred to the need to prevent a 'power vacuum' in East Timor, which 'would threaten peace in the region' and asserted that Indonesia had been invited by the East Timorese to intervene to their help.[49] In place of these two drafts, the GA adopted Resolution 3485 by a vote of 69 to 11 with 38 abstentions. Thailand, Malaysia, and the Philippines were among the 11 States that voted against.[50] Contrary to the draft resolutions supported by the three ASEAN States, GA Resolution 3485 reaffirmed the right of the East Timorese to self-determination and strongly deplored the military intervention by the armed forces of Indonesia.[51] This resolution also called upon Indonesia to desist from further violation of the territorial integrity of Portuguese Timor and withdraw its forces. Finally, it urged the SC to take urgent action.[52]

It is important to note that Thailand, Malaysia, and the Philippines also subsequently voted against GA Resolution 31/53 which echoed Resolution 3485 in reaffirming the right of the East Timorese to self-determination and condemning Indonesia for its military intervention.[53] Furthermore, this resolution also rejected the claim that East Timor had been annexed to Indonesia since the East Timorese were not given a chance to exercise their right to self-determination.[54]

Thailand also tried, unsuccessfully, to amend the text of GA Resolution 3485 mentioned earlier. In particular, it sought to introduce a reference to the need to consult Indonesia in order to find a suitable solution to the crisis.[55] Further support to Indonesia was shown by Malaysia at an SC meeting convened on the 15th of December 1975 to discuss the situation of East Timor. In its statement, Malaysia asserted that Indonesia had intervened following the invitation of the East Timorese and blamed FRETILIN and Portugal for the 'lawlessness' and violence.[56]

The only other ASEAN member state at the time, Singapore, was initially hesitant to show support for Indonesia. For example, while, as noted before, Malaysia, the Philippines, and Thailand voted against GA Resolutions 3485 and 31/53, Singapore decided to abstain.[57] Singapore feared that Indonesia's forcible takeover of East Timor would set a bad precedent in the region, potentially encouraging future hostile regimes to take aggressive actions against a small State.[58] Tan Boon Seng, the then-Singapore's Deputy Secretary of the Ministry of Foreign Affairs, on 6 January 1976 affirmed that Indonesia should understand that Singapore was not prepared to automatically support its foreign policy at every sudden twists and turns.[59] Needless to say, Indonesia resented Singapore's hesitation, especially following its decision to abstain from GA Resolutions 3485 and 31/53.[60] In retaliation, Indonesia sought to boycott Singaporean initiatives within ASEAN by rejecting the country's promotion of the ASEAN Free Trade Area and excluding it from security and intelligence briefings.[61] As a result, Singapore gradually re-adjusted its position. From 1977 onwards, it started to vote against all GA Resolutions concerning East Timor that were critical of Indonesia.[62]

In sum, one could say that ASEAN and ASEAN States chose to ignore the widespread human rights violations suffered by the East Timorese and instead chose to support Indonesia in the name of the Association's unity and solidarity and with a view to preserving regional cooperation, peace and stability.[63]

## 5.4 The 5 May Agreement

Western powers were not too concerned about the situation of East Timor because they largely shared Indonesia's ambition to combat communism. Accordingly, following Indonesia's annexation of East Timor, the issue had promptly vanished from the SC's radar.

After absorbing East Timor as part of its territory, however, Indonesia governed the province violently, ultimately leading to civil unrest. One incident that stood out the most and caught the attention of Western audiences was the Santa Cruz massacre that occurred in 1991. On 12 November 1991, a group of pro-independence East Timorese marched in the Santa Cruz cemetery. It was reported that a scuffle took place between small numbers of demonstrators and security forces, which led to two soldiers being stabbed.[64] When the security forces reinforcements arrived, they opened fire and killed between 75 and 200 demonstrators.[65]

What was significant about this incident is the fact that it was caught on camera, thus widely exposing the brutality of the Indonesian troops.[66] Consequently, many Western States reversed their initial neutral position, a change of approach which was also facilitated by the fact that, by then, the fight against communism had been won.[67] For example, the Parliamentary Assembly for the Council of Europe condemned Indonesia's violent actions and demanded it to withdraw its troops from East Timor allowing the people of East Timor to exercise their right to self-determination. The Assembly also called for 'an arms embargo to Indonesia and suspension of all military support for Indonesia'.[68] The US Congress started to reduce its military aid to Indonesia and spearheaded action at the United Nations Commission of Human Rights to appoint a special rapporteur to 'assist in the resolution of the East Timorese conflict in pursuit of the right of self-determination by the East Timorese people'.[69]

Although these forms of external criticism placed some pressure on Indonesia, President Suharto was still confident in his ability to maintain the control of East Timor. In 1997, however, the stock markets crashed across Southeast Asia, resulting in the depreciation of the Indonesian currency by 50%.[70] This depreciation, along with mounting debts and rising unemployment resulted in widespread riots across Indonesia, ultimately leading to the resignation of Suharto and the appointment of B.J. Habibie as new president in 1998.[71] When President Habibie came into power, he inherited his predecessor's problem of a discredited regime that was in a fiscal crisis. Consequently, Indonesia's economy was entirely dependent on external Western donors. To secure foreign aid, President Habibie was forced to make significant changes with regard to, among others, democracy and human rights issues.

Inevitably, this new circumstance brought the issue of East Timor back into the spotlight. Amidst the precarious political and financial climate, President Habibie was unwilling to commit more resources to East Timor, which began to be regarded as a burden. Accordingly, he began to negotiate with the UN and Portugal to broker a deal.[72] At first, in 1998 President Habibie decided to offer East Timor only one option, namely a 'special status' within Indonesia which would give East Timor control over its own administration with the exception of defence and foreign policy.[73] This proposal was rejected by the leaders of the resistance, who instead called for a referendum supervised by the UN.[74] Then finally on 5 May 1999, Indonesia and Portugal signed an agreement, witnessed by the UN Secretary Kofi Annan, to hold a referendum on the status of East Timor.[75] The referendum question read as follows: 'Do you accept the proposed special autonomy for East Timor within the Unitary State of the Republic of Indonesia? Or, do you reject the proposed special autonomy for East Timor, leading to East Timor's separation from Indonesia?'[76] Article 5 of this agreement stated that if the East Timorese voted for special autonomy, then the Indonesian government would implement the appropriate constitutional framework for East Timor. By contrast, if the East Timorese voted against this proposed autonomy, then the Indonesian government would terminate its control over East Timor and restore its status to that in place before the annexation of 1976.[77]

On 7 May 1999, the SC endorsed the terms of this agreement through Resolution 1236 and expressed its intention to establish a UN mission to assist in arranging the referendum.[78] Following this, on 11 June, the SC adopted Resolution 1246 to officially establish the United Nations Mission in East Timor (UNAMET) to organise and conduct the popular consultation set for 8 August 1999.[79]

According to the UN-backed agreement, the Indonesian government, rather than UNAMET, carried the responsibility to maintain peace and security in preparation for the referendum.[80] Thus, UNAMET's police officers only acted in an advisory capacity to the Indonesian Police, while UNAMET's military liaison officers were only authorised to merely maintain contact with the Indonesian armed forces.[81] Although this was not ideal, the UN saw this as a time-limited offer from Habibie. In particular, given that Indonesia's political climate was rather unstable, and a general election was approaching, this opportunity could be rescinded by the next leader.[82]

Despite the intense activities occurring at the international level, it is telling that ASEAN remained passive and silent. For example, there was no official reaction from any of the key ASEAN bodies during the negotiation phase or even after the Agreement was reached and subsequently endorsed by the SC. Two months after the 5 May Agreement was signed, on 24–25 July 1999, ASEAN held its annual foreign minister meeting (AMM). In the joint communiqué, ASEAN foreign ministers applauded its members' efforts and progress in their regional economic and political cooperation.[83] The foreign ministers also emphasised the importance of the TAC (as discussed earlier and in detail in Chapter 3) and its continued relevance as the basic framework for governing inter-state relations and maintaining regional peace and stability.[84] It is also important that the foreign ministers expressed their concern about the humanitarian crisis occurring in Kosovo but did not refer at all to the situation in East Timor.[85]

Following this, ASEAN held its 3rd Informal Summit (the only one held in 1999) on 28 November. The Chairman's statement affirmed, generally, that the heads of ASEAN governments had a useful exchange of views on the current regional security and political developments.[86] However, the statement did not specify which issues the members had discussed.

By contrast, in their individual capacities, Thailand, the Philippines, Malaysia, and Singapore were actively involved in the negotiations. For example, Thailand provided its embassy in Lisbon for the Indonesian diplomats to negotiate with Portugal the modalities of the referendum.[87] Furthermore, all four States joined the UN's 'Friends of the Secretary-General' group to convince Indonesia to accept the negotiation for the future of East Timor.[88] Most importantly, all four States contributed to the personnel of UNAMET once it was established.[89] It is important to note, however, that the conduct of ASEAN States did not equate to acts of intervention in Indonesia's internal affairs. In fact, as discussed earlier, Habibie had agreed to the course of action proposed by the UN, including the sending of a UN mission.

By this time, another five States had joined ASEAN, namely Cambodia, Laos, Brunei, Myanmar, and Vietnam. None of these States, however, got directly involved in the negotiations for the 5 May Agreement or contributed to UNAMET. Taking a rather neutral position, they did not object to these developments either.

## 5.5 The Referendum

On the surface, it seemed that the situation in East Timor was gradually moving towards a positive and agreed solution. However, in the months leading up to the referendum there had been major obstacles for UNAMET to carry out its mandate. As mentioned earlier, the endorsement of the 5 May Agreement by the SC was rushed due to the fact that it was probably a time-limited opportunity because of Indonesia's internal political climate. Therefore, the SC unusually agreed to confer the responsibility to maintain peace and security in East Timor in preparation for the referendum solely on Indonesia, leaving an advisory role only to the officers of UNAMET.[90] This would not have been a problem had the Indonesian armed forces, Tentara Nasional Indonesia (TNI), acted in good faith. Instead, the decision by Habibie to offer the choice of independence in the Agreement was seen by the TNI General Wiranto as a weak move by a civilian president who did not possess a wholehearted commitment to the maintenance of Indonesia's unity.[91] General Wiranto had an entirely different view of East Timor: while President Habibie saw the referendum as an opportunity to save the country from the economic crisis, General Wiranto saw it as a potential loss to Indonesia's territorial integrity.[92] Consequently, the TNI started to train and arm a pro-Jakarta militia on the ground and subsequently launched a campaign of fear and intimidation in East Timor.[93] Ian Martin, who was then head of UNAMET, had raised concerns about the violence perpetrated by the TNI, claiming that this affected the ability of UNAMET officers to implement the mandate of the mission.[94] Therefore,

Martin advised the UN Secretary-General to postpone the referendum. Annan agreed that this delay was necessary. Accordingly, the mandate of UNAMET was extended by SC Resolution 1257.[95]

Despite an intensification of the violence in the weeks leading up to the referendum, 451,792 people out of approximately 823,386 registered to vote and there was 98.9% turnout on the day itself.[96] 21.5% voted for autonomy, while 78.5% voted for independence.[97] This, in theory, should have ended the unsettled status of East Timor, leading to its independence. Instead, the aftermath of the referendum was the worst-case scenario possible: once Annan announced the result, mass violence was unleashed across the territory, primarily targeting the pro-independence faction.[98]

## 5.6 The Post-Referendum Crisis: Reactions from the International Community

A few days after announcing the result of the referendum, Annan held a press conference in which he described the situation in East Timor as descending into anarchy. He further stated that Indonesia had failed in its responsibility to maintain peace and security in East Timor, in violation of the terms of the 5 May Agreement.[99] Annan also noted that TNI had failed to prevent the anti-independence militia from attacking UNAMET officers and its compound. In his view, Indonesia was either unable or unwilling to take effective steps to restore order.[100] For this reason, Annan urged President Habibie to accept the deployment of a UN peacekeeping mission and that if Habibie refused to do so then the TNI could not escape responsibility for crime against humanity.[101]

On an important side note, during this press conference, Annan was asked whether this situation could lead to another Kosovo. Annan answered that, in this case, the most concerned States were focused on putting collective pressure on Indonesia to consent to a peacekeeping force rather than contemplating military intervention.[102] This was reflected in the action taken by the SC, which sent a mission to Jakarta and Dili tasked with assessing the actual accounts of what was happening on the grounds through the UNAMET officers and to urge the Indonesian government to follow through with their 5 May Agreement by ensuring security in order to uphold the result of the referendum.[103] This mission confirmed that there was a large gap between how President Habibie presented the situation and what was actually happening. Habibie and General Wiranto had insisted that Indonesian armed forces could restore peace and security and outright rejected the possibility of international assistance.[104] Accordingly, President Habibie rejected any form of foreign military presence and said, 'that would send the wrong signal to Indonesians regarding the military and risk the Balkanization of Indonesia'.[105] Wiranto was even firmer stating that the pro-Indonesians were already angered by the presence of UNAMET and the introduction of external troops would only further increase the level of violence.[106] General Wiranto thought that a declaration of martial law would allow his forces to stabilise the situation.[107] UNAMET officers portrayed a very different situation.[108] They concluded that violence of that magnitude could not have happened without the backing of the TNI.[109] Most importantly, they concluded that there was strong prima facie evidence of abuses of international humanitarian law, as well as of widespread destruction, forced displacement, and executions that amounted to crimes against humanity.[110] Because it was clear that Indonesia would not be able to carry out its responsibility agreed upon in the 5 May Agreement, this mission emphasised the need for an international force mandated by the UN. That atrocity crimes had been committed was further confirmed by other sources. For example, a report commissioned by the UN Office of the High Commissioner for Human Rights estimated that after the referendum 900 people were unlawfully killed and at least 400,000 fled their homes under extreme duress.[111] Tragically, the East Timorese that did not flee quickly enough were subjected to 'extra-judicial killings, torture and ill-treatment, and sexual violence'.[112]

Given the gravity of the situation, a number of States in the region had already expressed their willingness to participate in an international peacekeeping force. These States included not only Australia (who offered to lead the mission) and New Zealand but also the Philippines and Malaysia.[113] This is important in R2P terms because it means that these two ASEAN countries were willing to help Indonesia (Pillar II) to meet its Pillar I responsibilities towards its population. At the same time, pressure was mounting on President Habibie from the US government and international financial institutions. At first, President Bill Clinton's administration approached this issue carefully by only insisting that the Habibie government should honour its commitments under the 5 May agreement.[114] The US position changed once Australia announced that it was willing to lead an international force in East Timor. President Clinton then started to demand more insistently that Indonesia must 'invite the international community to assist in restoring security'.[115] As the previous efforts proved to no avail, President Clinton then moved to cut ties with Indonesia in terms of military aid programmes, special forces training programmes, and financial assistance.[116] This prompted a response from both the International Monetary Fund and the World Bank, which coordinated a suspension of pending funds to Indonesia to increase pressure on the government. These moves were particularly effective because, as mentioned earlier, at that time Indonesia was affected by the Asian financial crisis, having experienced a significant devaluation of its currency. This meant that Indonesia's economy was heavily reliant on foreign assistance.

Indonesia's position started to change with the mounting pressures from President Clinton and the international financial community.[117] However, although President Habibie began to realise that agreeing to a peacekeeping force would be inevitable, he was still strongly opposed to Australia leading the mission since he was suspicious of the motives of the latter.[118] The then Thai Foreign Minister, Surin Pitsuwan, was instrumental in convincing President Habibie that none of the ASEAN States alone had the capability to lead the multinational force, and that, under the circumstances, Australia was the State best prepared and most willing to do so.[119] President Habibie then tasked Pitsuwan with rallying for contributions from individual ASEAN's States. Even though none of them could lead the peacekeeping mission, Indonesia wanted a strong ASEAN presence in the latter in an attempt to minimise the central role that Australia would play in the mission.[120]

In fact, General Wiranto was reported to have asked Surin to secure 'overwhelming ASEAN forces' as part of an international mission to East Timor.[121] Hoping that this plan would work, on 12 September, President Habibie informed Annan of Indonesia's readiness to accept an international peacekeeping force.[122] The following section examines how ASEAN States responded to the post-referendum violence and how they contributed to persuading Habibie to consent to a UN peacekeeping force.

### *5.6.1 Reactions from ASEAN and ASEAN States*

At that time, Thailand was arguably the most liberal among ASEAN States. Its government had a plan to lift the country 'to a higher ground of international morality, responsibility and credibility'.[123] For example, Pitsuwan wanted to soften the principles of the ASEAN Way, especially the principle of non-interference. In 1997, he stated that it was time 'that ASEAN's cherished principle of non-intervention be modified to allow it to play a constructive role in preventing or resolving domestic issues with regional implications'.[124] In line with this idea, in 1998 Pitsuwan proposed to other ASEAN members the concept of 'flexible engagement' which was also discussed in Chapter 4.[125] Despite some support from the Philippines, this proposal was ultimately rejected. Nevertheless, it can be said that the concept of 'flexible engagement' informed Thailand's approach to the East Timor crisis. Pitsuwan was concerned that ASEAN would risk becoming irrelevant should it do nothing when faced with a crisis of such magnitude. If the ASEAN States really wanted the region to be free from external interferences, he thought it was time to 'put . . . words into actions'.[126] With respect to providing international assistance to Indonesia, Pitsuwan further noted that ASEAN States' contribution to the UN peacekeeping mission would also benefit ASEAN.[127] That said, Thailand's engagement with the crisis was not really guided by humanitarian concerns nor was it aimed at stopping atrocity crimes in East Timor; rather, it was aimed at supporting a 'friend in need'.[128] In fact, it is important to stress that Thailand never criticised Habibie or the TNI.

Like Thailand, Malaysia was one of the first countries to offer to contribute to the UN peacekeeping force, even before President Habibie had consented to it.[129] At first, Mohamad Mahathir, the then-Prime Minister of Malaysia, criticised the West for having placed too much pressure on President Habibie to offer the referendum to the East Timorese when Indonesia was already coping with a change in leadership, was in the process of changing its system to democracy and was facing a serious financial crisis.[130] However, once the violence massively escalated after the referendum, Malaysia became worried of the spill-over effect that this could have on the whole region, including the large number of refugees who had already started to flee to its territory.[131] This is what motivated Malaysia's involvement in the crisis, and not a genuine concern about war crimes and crimes against humanity occurring in East Timor. In trying to persuade Habibie to accept UN peacekeeping, Malaysia made references to the shared values underpinning ASEAN by claiming that, as neighbours, ASEAN States understand each other better.[132] Although

Malaysia recognised that none of the ASEAN members had the capability to lead the UN force, it agreed that the latter should at least have 'a large ASEAN presence'.[133] As stated by the Malaysian Deputy Prime Minister at the time, Abdullah Ahmad Badawi, 'We don't wish to see any country appointing itself the protector or leader for this region. Asian countries are capable of looking after the region themselves and cherish peace for the region more than others'.[134]

The next country to consider is the Philippines. As mentioned earlier, when Pitsuwan introduced the concept of 'flexible engagement' to ASEAN, all other members rejected it with the exception of the Philippines.[135] The latter found the concept to be constructive in that it would allow neighbours to approach situations of local crisis without being accused of interfering with another country's internal affairs. That said, just like Thailand, the Philippines was not prepared to go further than that by, for example, calling for a more relaxed interpretation of the principle of State sovereignty. This can be seen, for example, in the position taken by the Philippines during a meeting of the SC focusing on East Timor at the time when it acted as an elected member of that body. On that occasion, the Philippines commended the effort of the Indonesian government to make the 5 May agreement happen, while it never criticised Indonesia for the violence in East Timor.[136] Thus, the Philippines stated, vaguely, that it was 'important that the violent groups and individuals who continue to sow terror and mayhem in the territory be stopped immediately'.[137] Manila did offer contributions to the UN peacekeeping mission even before Habibie had consented to it. However, it saw this as a friendly and peaceful offer aimed at assisting rather than punishing Indonesia.[138]

The internal political climate in the Philippines must also be taken into account in order to better understand its position. At the time, Manila was constrained by its own battle with separatist movements in Mindanao. In particular, the insurgency movement in Mindanao had resumed its fight for independence and demanded the UN organise a referendum as it did in East Timor.[139] Given that President Suharto had supported Manila's efforts in suppressing this separatist movement, Manila felt that it should equally support Indonesia with regard to the situation in East Timor.[140]

As it happened in the aftermath of the invasion, Singapore was the only ASEAN State which was hesitant to publicly declare its support for Indonesia in the post-referendum phase. Singapore's scepticism was mainly driven by the concerns that the crisis in East Timor would have 'spill-over' effects on the region and, most importantly, on Singapore's economy.[141] At that time, Singapore was still recovering from the Asian financial crisis of 1997, and this recovery depended on the maintenance of regional stability. Immediately after the violence, during a special meeting of the Security Council on East Timor, Singapore pointed out that Indonesia's decision to hold the referendum in East Timor had been premature since it was done without having obtained a national consensus on the matter.[142] Singapore might have been referring to the fact that the TNI was not on board with the decision to grant the East Timorese the referendum. Furthermore, Singapore indirectly called out the TNI's involvement by stating that 'the rogue elements in the army and police said to be among those responsible for the violence must be stopped'.[143] It also called for the result of the popular consultation to be respected. At the same time, Singapore reminded the international community that the East Timor crisis fell under Indonesia's sovereignty and that any international efforts to contribute to restoring order should obtain both Indonesia's consent and SC's authorisation.[144] In a sense, then, Singapore's position was quite ambiguous. While being critical of Jakarta, it called for the respect of Indonesia's sovereignty. To add to this complex position, Singapore refrained from demanding a large ASEAN contribution to the UN peacekeeping mission. According to its then UN Ambassador, ASEAN as an organisation lacked the practical capabilities required to restore order in East Timor.[145] As such, since Indonesia personally asked for individual contributions from ASEAN States, Singapore could not ignore it so blatantly, as shown in its contributions of personnel in the peacekeeping force below. When the UN peacekeeping mission was established, the ASEAN presence was significant. On September 1999, SC Resolution 1264 established the International Force East Timor (INTERFET) under Chapter VII of the UN Charter.[146] Out of the total 9,900 personnel in INTERFET, Thailand provided 1,580 personnel, both military and civilian, followed by the Philippines with 600 civilian personnel, Singapore with 254 military and civilian staff, and finally Malaysia with 30 civilian personnel.[147]

Finally, the response to the post-referendum crisis from Cambodia, Laos, Myanmar, Vietnam, and Brunei can be examined collectively given that each of these States showed strong solidarity with Indonesia, which derived from the concern about setting a dangerous precedent in the region by allowing foreign intervention to tame a local internal conflict.[148] For example, during the 4043rd Meeting of the SC, Vietnam called on all parties to respect the 5 May Agreement and applauded the Indonesian government for its efforts to restore peace and security in East Timor.[149] It also stressed that the deployment of a multinational force needed to have the consent of the Indonesian government and SC's approval.[150] Although Vietnam declined the request to contribute to the UN peacekeeping force, it did not do so due to a lack of will. Instead, Vietnam referred more generally to its lack of experience in sending military personnel to UN peacekeeping missions.[151]

The position of Cambodia can also be discerned by its statements at the SC 4043rd meeting mentioned earlier. After noting that it was already undergoing a complex process of transition and change, it commended Indonesia for its decision to give the East Timorese a referendum.[152] Furthermore, in a rather non-offensive way, Cambodia urged the Indonesian authorities to take steps to halt the violence and achieve the implementation of the 5 May Agreement in conjunction with the UN.[153] As to the peacekeeping force, Cambodia declined any involvement by referring to its internal poverty and weaknesses.[154]

Like Cambodia, Laos commended Indonesia for agreeing to hold the referendum and for its efforts to face up to its 5 May Agreement commitments through the SC 4043rd meeting.[155] Laos stated that in these difficult circumstances, Indonesia had done its best to resolve the situation.[156] Laos ended its statement by suggesting that the international community should let Indonesia shoulder its responsibilities and that any other initiatives going forward to resolve this problem would require the consent of Indonesia.[157]

On 13 September 1999, a spokesman for the Myanmar government noted that this crisis should not set a precedent for allowing external intervention into a State's internal affairs.[158] Myanmar also pointed out that ASEAN had not taken any coordinated decision as to whether ASEAN States should contribute to a UN peacekeeping force in East Timor.[159] As the decision to do so had been taken individually by some States, Myanmar did not feel under any obligation to contribute. This attitude can also be seen as Myanmar's Junta sympathising with Indonesia as it has faced many criticisms and condemnations from the international community in the past for it to hold a democratic national election.[160]

Brunei did not formally comment on the crisis, nor did it take any public action worthy of mention.

It is clear from this discussion that ASEAN States largely acted in solidarity with Indonesia. While individual responses were nuanced, all States refrained from taking an antagonist approach towards Indonesia. At the same time, their general support for and willingness to contribute to a consensual UN peacekeeping mission can be said to have contributed to Habibie's decision to give his consent to this external form of (non-coercive) intervention.[161] While this suggests that some States were willing to provide international assistance to Indonesia, there is very little to suggest that they were motivated by humanitarian concerns. Instead, they were mainly concerned about the spill-over effects of the crisis and its effects on regional stability.

## 5.7 Conclusion

The analysis developed in this chapter has shown that during the East Timor crisis ASEAN did not take any substantive action. The only exception was a Joint Communiqué issued by the ASEAN Foreign Ministerial Meeting in June 1976 that, rather than criticising it, effectively accepted Indonesia's weak justifications for the invasion of East Timor. In the name of solidarity with its biggest founding member, ASEAN conveniently chose to ignore the humanitarian dimension of the crisis. ASEAN's silence becomes even more problematic when one considers that both the SC and GA had condemned Indonesia and that a Security Council mission to East Timor had reported that war crimes and crimes against humanity had been committed by the TNI and/or TNI-sponsored militia against the East Timorese.

At the time of the invasion, ASEAN was composed of only five members: Indonesia, Thailand, the Philippines, Malaysia, and Singapore. With the exception of Singapore, which initially showed some discomfort in openly supporting Indonesian conduct, all of the ASEAN States stood in solidarity with Indonesia. When the crisis entered a different stage, namely the escalation of violence after the 30 August 1999 referendum leading to accusations of atrocity crimes, these States were again careful not to criticise Indonesia. However, when Annan called on President Habibie to consent to an international peacekeeping force, Thailand, Malaysia, Singapore, and the Philippines urged Indonesia to accept a UN mission. In addition, they all offered to contribute to this international peacekeeping force. These efforts, however, were hardly motivated by humanitarian considerations.

Firstly, these States were mainly concerned about the spill-over effects of this crisis on the region's stability. Second, their offers to take part in the UN mission followed a request by Indonesia to have a large ASEAN presence in the peacekeeping force. They were not, therefore, acting on the basis of a commitment to values such as human protection, nor were they willing to impose external views on Indonesia.

The responses of the other members who joined ASEAN at a later stage were quite different. Cambodia, Laos, Myanmar, Vietnam, and Brunei were less interested than the other ASEAN States in playing a more direct role in this crisis, mainly due to geographical reasons. Thus, these five States refrained not only from condemning Indonesia but also from urging it to consent to a peacekeeping mission.

The analysis developed in this chapter has shown how ASEAN and ASEAN States responded to a humanitarian crisis before the introduction of R2P in the realm of international law. The following chapter examines the current Rohingya crisis in Myanmar with a view to establishing whether ASEAN States' cautious endorsement of R2P since 2005 has had any effect on their approach to atrocity crime situations.

## Notes

1 Christine Chinkin, 'East Timor: A Failure of Decolonisation' [1999] 20 *Australia Year of Book of International Law*, p. 37.
2 G.V.C. Naidu, 'The East Timor Crisis' [1999] 23(9) *Strategic Analysis*, p. 1468.
3 Ibid., p. 1469.
4 Jill Joliffe, *East Timor: Nationalism and Colonialism* (University of Queensland Press, 1978) p. 79; and Roger S. Clark, 'Decolonization of East Timor and the United Nations Norms on Self-Determination and Aggression' [1980] 7(2) *The Yale Journal of World Public Order*, p. 5.
5 Jill Joliffe, *East Timor: Nationalism and Colonialism* (University of Queensland Press, 1978) p. 66.
6 Roger S. Clark, 'Decolonization of East Timor and the United Nations Norms on Self-Determination and Aggression' [1980] 7(2) *The Yale Journal of World Public Order*, p. 6.
7 Lee Jones, *ASEAN, Sovereignty and Intervention in Southeast Asia* (Palgrave Macmillan, 2012) p. 61.
8 Ibid., pp. 61–62.
9 Brad Simpson, '"Illegally and Beautifully", The United States, the Indonesian Invasion of East Timor and the International Community, 1974–1976' [2005] 5(3) *Cold War History*, p. 283.
10 Ibid., pp. 285–286.
11 Ibid.
12 Lee Jones, *ASEAN, Sovereignty and Intervention in Southeast Asia* (Palgrave Macmillan, 2012) p. 61.
13 Ibid., p. 62.
14 Ibid., pp. 62–63; see also Jill Jolliffe, *East Timor: Nationalism and Colonialism* (University of Queensland Press, 1978) pp. 84 and 96.
15 Ibid.
16 Ibid.
17 Ibid.
18 Roger S. Clark, 'Decolonization of East Timor and the United Nations Norms on Self-Determination and Aggression' [1980] 7(2) *The Yale Journal of World Public Order*, pp. 7–8.

19 Ibid.
20 Lee Jones, *ASEAN, Sovereignty and Intervention in Southeast Asia* (Palgrave Macmillan, 2012) p. 64.
21 Katsumi Ishizuka, *The History of Peace-building in East Timor: The Issues of International Intervention* (Foundation Books, 2010) p. 14.
22 Quoted in Deborah Mayersen and Annie Pohlman, *Genocide and Mass Atrocities in Asia: Legacies and prevention* (Routledge, 2013) p. 107.
23 Roger S. Clark, 'Decolonization of East Timor and the United Nations Norms on Self-Determination and Aggression' [1980] 7(2) *Yale Journal of World Public Order*, p. 10.
24 Roger S. Clark, 'East Timor and International Law' [1984] 2 *Mennesker og Rettigheter*, p. 33.
25 The invitation, however, came from the 'Popular Representative Assembly' set up by Indonesia; see Brad Simpson, '"Illegally and Beautifully", The United States, the Indonesian Invasion of East Timor and the International Community, 1974–1976' [2005] 5(3) *Cold War History*, p. 302.
26 A Publication of the United Nations Department of Political Affairs, Trusteeship and Decolonization: Issue on East Timor [1976] Vol.1, No.7, p. 14; and Jamsheed Marker, *East Timor: A Memoir of the Negotiations for Independence* (McFarland, 2003) p. 31.
27 Amnesty International, 'East Timor: Demand for Justice' (1999), ASA/21/191/1999, p. 4.
28 Ibid., pp. 15–16.
29 Ben Saul, 'Was the Conflict in East Timor "Genocide" and Why Does It Matter?' [2001] 2(2) *Melbourne Journal of International Law*, p. 510.
30 United Nations Security Council (1975), 1864th Meeting, S/PV.1864, para 1 <https://documents-dds-ny.un.org/doc/UNDOC/GEN/NL7/500/47/PDF/NL750047.pdf?OpenElement> accessed on 25 March 2021.
31 Ibid., para 69.
32 Ibid.
33 The United Nations Security Council Resolution 384, S/RES/384 (1975).
34 Ibid.
35 The United Nations Security Council Resolution 389, S/RES/389 (1976).
36 The United Nations Security Council Resolution 384, S/RES/384 (1975) and 389, S/RES/389 (1976).
37 Richard Burchill, 'The ICJ Decision in the Case Concerning East Timor: The Illegal Use of Force Validated' [1997] 2 *Journal of Conflict and Security Law*, p. 2.
38 The United Nations General Assembly Resolution 3485 (XXX) (1975), A/RES/3485 (XXX).
39 The United Nations General Assembly Resolution 31/53 (1976), A/RES/31/53.
40 Mohamad Faisol Keling, et al., 'The Development of ASEAN from Historical Approach' [2011] 7(7) *Asian Social Science*, p. 172.
41 Address by Rodolfo C. Severino, Secretary-General of the Association of Southeast Asia Nations, at the International Law Conference on ASEAN Legal Systems and Regional Integration, 'The ASEAN Way and the Rule of Law' (2001) <https://asean.org/?static_post=the-asean-way-and-the-rule-of-law> accessed on 28 March 2021.
42 Joint Communique The First ASEAN Heads of Government Meeting Bali, 23–24 February 1976 <https://asean.org/?static_post=joint-communique-the-first-asean-heads-of-government-meeting-bali-23-24-february-1976> accessed on 1 May 2021.
43 The Treaty of Amity and Cooperation in Southeast Asia (1976), Article 2.
44 Joint Communique of the Ninth ASEAN Ministerial Meeting (1976), para 23 <https://asean.org/?static_post=joint-communique-of-the-ninth-asean-ministerial-meeting-manila-24–26-june-1976> accessed on 1 May 2021.
45 Ibid.
46 Ibid.
47 United Nations General Assembly (1975), 30th Session, 4th Committee, Trusteeship (including Non-Self-Governing Territories), 2180th Meeting, A/C.4/SR.2180,

para 17–19 <https://digitallibrary.un.org/record/1286696?ln=en> accessed on 25 March 2021; and United Nations General Assembly (1975), 30th Session, Agenda item 88, 'Question of Territories under Portuguese Administration', Report of the Fourth Committee, A/10426, para 13 <https://digitallibrary.un.org/record/1325687> accessed on 26 March 2021.

48 Ibid.

49 The United Nations General Assembly (1975), 30th Session, 4th Committee, Trusteeship (including Non-Self-Governing Territories) 2188th Meeting, A/C.4/SR.2188, para 8–10 <https://digitallibrary.un.org/record/1314879?ln=en> accessed on 26 March 2021.

50 United Nations General Assembly (1975), 30th Session, 4th Committee, Trusteeship (including Non-Self-Governing Territories) 2188th Meeting, A/C.4/SR.2188, p. 412 <https://digitallibrary.un.org/record/1314879?ln=en> accessed on 26 March 2021.

51 The United Nations General Assembly Resolution 3485 (XXX) (1975), A/RES/3485 (XXX).

52 Ibid.

53 The United Nations General Assembly Resolution 31/53 (1976), A/RES/31/53; and United Nations General Assembly Voting Summary (1976) <https://digitallibrary.un.org/record/649327?ln=en> accessed on 25 March 2021.

54 The United Nations General Assembly Resolution 31/53 (1976), A/RES/31/53.

55 United Nations General Assembly (1975), 30th Session, 4th Committee, Trusteeship (including Non-Self-Governing Territories) 2187th Meeting, A/C.4/SR.2187, para 19 <https://digitallibrary.un.org/record/1315886?ln=en> accessed on 1 April 2021.

56 United Nations Security Council (1975), 1864th Meeting, S/PV.1864, para 152 <https://documents-dds-ny.un.org/doc/UNDOC/GEN/NL7/500/47/PDF/NL750047.pdf?OpenElement> accessed on 26 March 2021.

57 United Nations General Assembly Voting Summary, https://digitallibrary.un.org/record/650109?ln=en; (1975) and https://digitallibrary.un.org/record/649327?ln=en (1976) accessed on 25 March 2021.

58 Laura Southgate, *ASEAN Resistance to Sovereignty Violation: Interests, Balancing and the Role of the Vanguard State* (Bristol University Press, 2019) p. 55.

59 Ibid.

60 Ibid., pp. 55–56.

61 Ibid.

62 Ibid.

63 Hiro Katsumata, 'Reconstruction of Diplomatic Norms in Southeast Asia: The Case for Strict Adherence to the "ASEAN Way"' [2003] 25(1) *Contemporary Southeast Asia*, p. 114.

64 Human Rights Watch: Asia Watch, 'East Timor: The November 12 Massacre and Its Aftermath' [1991] 3(26) *Human Rights Watch*, p. 2 <https://www.hrw.org/legacy/reports/pdfs/i/indonesa/indonesi911.pdf> accessed on 2 May 2021.

65 Ibid., pp. 2–4.

66 Ali Alatas, *The Pebble in the Shoe: The Diplomatic Struggle for East Timor* (Aksara Karunia, 2006) p. 239; and Katsumi Ishizuka, *The History of Peace-building in East Timor: The Issues of International Intervention* (Foundation Books, 2010) p. 23.

67 Katsumi Ishizuka, *The History of Peace-building in East Timor: The Issues of International Intervention* (Foundation Books, 2010) p. 25.

68 Human Rights Watch: Asia Watch, 'East Timor: The November 12 Massacre and Its Aftermath' [1991] 3(26) *Human Rights Watch*, p. 16 <https://www.hrw.org/legacy/reports/pdfs/i/indonesa/indonesi911.pdf> accessed on 2 May 2021.

69 Ibid., p. 17.

70 Katsumi Ishizuka, *The History of Peace-building in East Timor: The Issues of International Intervention* (Foundation Books, 2010) p. 27.

71 Ibid.

72 Ibid., p. 28.
73 Ibid., p. 29.
74 'Resistance Leader Rejects East Timor Offer' (The BBC, 9 June 1998) <http://news.bbc.co.uk/1/hi/events/indonesia/latest_news/109595.stm> accessed on 22 March 2021.
75 The United Nations General Assembly, Report of the Secretary-General, 'Question of East Timor' (1999) S/1999/513.
76 Ibid., Annex II, B.
77 Ibid., Article 6.
78 The United Nations Security Council Resolution 1236 (1999), S/RES/1236.
79 The United Nations Security Council Resolution 1246 (1999), S/RES/1246.
80 The United Nations General Assembly, Report of the Secretary-General, 'Question of East Timor' (1999), S/1999/513, Article 3.
81 The United Nations Security Council Resolution 1246 (1999), S/RES/1246.
82 Jennifer M. Welsh, *Humanitarian Intervention and International Relations* (Oxford University Press, 2003) p. 149.
83 Joint Communiqué of the 32nd ASEAN Ministerial Meeting (1999) <https://asean.org/?static_post=joint-communique-the-32nd-asean-ministerial-meeting-amm-singapore-23-24-july-1999> accessed on 3 April 2021.
84 Ibid., para 20.
85 Ibid., para 41.
86 Chairman's Press Statement on ASEAN 3rd Informal Summit (1999), para 5 <https://asean.org/?static_post=chairman-s-press-statement-on-asean-3rd-informal-summit-manila-philippines-28-november-1999> accessed on 4 April 2021.
87 Lee Jones, *ASEAN, Sovereignty and Intervention in Southeast Asia* (Palgrave Macmillan, 2012) p. 158.
88 Ibid.
89 Ian Martin Vice President and Alexander Mayer-Rieckh, 'The United Nations and East Timor: From Self-Determination to State-Building' [2005] 12(1) *International Peacekeeping*, p. 130.
90 The United Nations Security Council Resolution 1246 (1999), S/RES/1246.
91 Kirsten E. Schulze, 'The East Timor Referendum Crisis and Its Impact on Indonesian Politics' [2001] 24(1) *Studies in Conflict and Terrorism*, p. 78.
92 Ibid., p. 79.
93 Geoffrey Robinson, 'People's War: Militias in East Timor and Indonesia' [2001] 9(3) *South East Asia Research*, p. 275.
94 Jennifer M. Welsh, *Humanitarian Intervention and International Relations* (Oxford University Press, 2003) pp. 148–149.
95 The United Nations Security Council Resolution 1257 (1999); and Letter from the Secretary-General Addressed to the President of the Security Council (1999) S/1999/830.
96 The United Nations Press Release, 'People of East Timor Reject Proposed Special Autonomy, Express Wish to Begin Transition to Independence, Secretary-General Informs Security Council' (1999) SG/SM/7119.
97 Ibid.
98 John Aglionby and John Gittings, 'Timor Vote Sparks Brutal Militia Attack' (The Guardian, 5 September 1999) <https://www.theguardian.com/world/1999/sep/05/indonesia.easttimor1> accessed on 22 March 2021.
99 The United Nations Press Release (1999), Transcript of Press Conference of Secretary-General Kofi Annan at Headquarters, SG/SM/7124.
100 Ibid.
101 Ibid.
102 Ibid.
103 Report of the Security Council Mission to Jakarta and Dili, 8–12 September 1999(S/1999/976) p. 1.

104 Ibid., p. 3.
105 Ibid.
106 Ibid.
107 Ibid.
108 Ibid., p. 5.
109 Ibid., p. 6.
110 Ibid., pp. 11–10.
111 Geoffrey Robinson, 'East Timor 1999: Crimes against Humanity': A Report Commissioned by the United Nations Office of the High Commissioner for Human Rights (2003), pp. 6 and 52.
112 Ibid., pp. 32–35.
113 The United Nations Press Release (1999), Transcript of Press Conference of Secretary-General Kofi Annan at Headquarters, SG/SM/7124.
114 Marianne Jago, 'InterFet: An Account of Intervention with Consent in East Timor' [2010] 17(3) *International Peacekeeping*, p. 384.
115 'The Fate of East Timor; In Clinton's Words: East Timor, Waco, Clemency Offer, and Other Issue' (The New York Times, September 10, 1999) <https://www.nytimes.com/1999/09/10/world/fate-east-timor-clinton-s-words-east-timor-waco-clemency-offer-other-issues.html> accessed on 22 March 2021.
116 Steven Mufson and Bradley Graham, 'U.S. and IMF Move to Isolate Indonesia' (Washington Post, 10 September 1999) <https://www.washingtonpost.com/wp-srv/inatl/daily/sept99/ustimor10.htm?> accessed on 22 March 2021.
117 Ibid., p. 383.
118 Ian Martin Vice President and Alexander Mayer-Rieckh, 'The United Nations and East Timor: From Self-Determination to State-Building' [2005] 12(1) *International Peacekeeping*, p. 132.
119 Alan Ryan, "Primary Responsibilities and Primary Risks' Australian Defence Force Participation International Force East Timor' [2000] 304 *Land Warfare Studies Centre*, p. 47.
120 Shaun Narine, 'Humanitarian Intervention and the Question of Sovereignty: The Case of ASEAN' [2005] 4(3–4) *Perspectives on Global Development and Technology*, p. 479.
121 Lee Jones, *ASEAN, Sovereignty and Intervention in Southeast Asia* (Palgrave Macmillan, 2012) p. 162.
122 Report of the Security Council Mission to Jakarta and Dili, 8–12 September, S/1999/976, p. 4.
123 Jürgen Haacke, 'ASEAN's Diplomatic and Security Culture: A Constructivist Assessment' [2003] 3 *International Relations of the Asia-Pacific Volume*, p. 68.
124 Amitav Acharya, *Whose Ideas Matter? Agency and Power in Asian Regionalism* (Cornell University Press, 2011) p. 127.
125 Eric Corthay, 'The ASEAN Doctrine of Non-Interference in Light of the Fundamental Principle of Non-Intervention' [2015] 17(2) *Asian-Pacific Law & Policy Journal*, p. 16.
126 Jürgen Haacke, 'ASEAN's Diplomatic and Security Culture: A Constructivist Assessment' [2003] 3 *International Relations of the Asia-Pacific Volume*, p. 67.
127 Lee Jones, *ASEAN, Sovereignty and Intervention in Southeast Asia* (Palgrave Macmillan, 2012) p. 170.
128 Ibid., p. 169.
129 The United Nations Press Release (1999), Transcript of Press Conference of Secretary-General Kofi Annan at Headquarters, SG/SM/7124.
130 'Press Conference by Prime Minister of Malaysia' (United Nations Press Release, 29 September 1999) <https://www.un.org/press/en/1999/19990929.malaysia.doc.html> accessed on 30 March 2021.
131 Lee Jones, 'ASEAN's Unchanged Melody? The Theory and Practice of "Non-Interference" in Southeast Asia' [2010] 23(4) *The Pacific Review*, p. 493.

132 Lee Jones, *ASEAN, Sovereignty and Intervention in Southeast Asia* (Palgrave Macmillan, 2012) p. 176.
133 Ibid.
134 Quoted in Jürgen Haacke, 'ASEAN's Diplomatic and Security Culture: A Constructivist Assessment' [2003] 3 *International Relations of the Asia-Pacific Volume*, p. 70.
135 Eric Corthay, 'The ASEAN Doctrine of Non-Interference in Light of the Fundamental Principle of Non-Intervention' [2015] 17(2) *Asian-Pacific Law & Policy Journal*, p. 16.
136 United Nations Security Council, 4043rd Meeting 'The situation in East Timor' (1999) S/PV.4043, p. 20.
137 Ibid.
138 The United Nations Press Release (1999), Transcript of Press Conference of Secretary-General Kofi Annan at Headquarters, SG/SM/7124.
139 Lee Jones, *ASEAN, Sovereignty and Intervention in Southeast Asia* (Palgrave Macmillan, 2012) p. 172.
140 Ibid.
141 Ibid., p. 174.
142 United Nations Security Council, 4043rd Meeting 'The situation in East Timor' (1999) S/PV.4043 (Resumption), p. 20.
143 Ibid.
144 Ibid.
145 Lee Jones, *ASEAN, Sovereignty and Intervention in Southeast Asia* (Palgrave Macmillan, 2012) p. 174.
146 The United Nations Security Council Resolution 1264 (1999), S/RES/1264, p. 2.
147 Laura Southgate, *ASEAN Resistance to Sovereignty Violation: Interests, Balancing and the Role of the Vanguard State* (Bristol University Press, 2019) p. 145.
148 Lee Jones, *ASEAN, Sovereignty and Intervention in Southeast Asia* (Palgrave Macmillan, 2012) p. 166.
149 United Nations Security Council, 4043rd Meeting 'The situation in East Timor' (1999) S/PV.4043 (Resumption), p. 17.
150 Ibid.
151 Lee Jones, *ASEAN, Sovereignty and Intervention in Southeast Asia* (Palgrave Macmillan, 2012) p. 167.
152 United Nations Security Council, 4043rd Meeting 'The situation in East Timor' (1999) S/PV.4043 (Resumption), p. 5.
153 Ibid.
154 Lee Jones, *ASEAN, Sovereignty and Intervention in Southeast Asia* (Palgrave Macmillan, 2012) p. 168.
155 United Nations Security Council, 4043rd Meeting 'The situation in East Timor' (1999) S/PV.4043 (Resumption), p. 9.
156 Ibid.
157 Ibid.
158 'Myanmar Solidarity with Indonesia "Brothers"' (AFP, 13 September 1999) <https://www.burmalibrary.org/reg.burma/archives/199909/msg00559.html> accessed on 30 March 2021.
159 Ibid.
160 Moe Gyo, 'East Timor and Burmese Democracy' [1999] 7(8) *The Irrawaddy* <https://www2.irrawaddy.com/article.php?art_id=1653&page=1> accessed on 30 March 2021.
161 Report of the Security Council Mission to Jakarta and Dili, 8–12 September, S/1999/976, p. 4.

# 6 ASEAN and the Rohingya Crisis

## 6.1 Introduction

This chapter analyses the Association of Southeast Asian Nations (ASEAN) and its States' response to Myanmar's violent crackdown on the Rohingya minority living in Rakhine State from 2016 onwards. What has often been referred to as the 'Rohingya crisis' has a deep-rooted historical background with various violent episodes occurring for over half a century.[1] This crisis resembles the concept of 'intractable conflict', that is, a conflict perceived as being about essential goals, for example, territory, self-determination, or religious freedom, which are fundamental for a group's survival and existence.[2] Because these goals are typically in direct contradiction with another group's ambitions, intractable conflicts tend to result in a large loss of lives and destruction. The numbers of the Rohingya crisis are in line with this description. According to the 2018 report of the independent fact-finding mission on Myanmar established by the United Nations Human Rights Council, the estimated number of deaths until then was over 10,000.[3] In addition, it has been estimated that, as of the summer of 2019, 740,000 Rohingya refugees had reached Bangladesh, 95,644 Thailand, 170,460 Malaysia, and 800 Indonesia.[4] As will be discussed in this Chapter, the United Nations (UN) fact-finding mission in Myanmar concluded that genocide, crimes against humanity and war crimes have been committed in Rakhine State.[5]

Contrary to the case of East Timor, this humanitarian crisis unfolded after the emergence of R2P in the realm of international law. As discussed in Chapter 2, the commission of any of the three crimes mentioned earlier could in principle trigger a responsibility to protect (R2P) response by the international community. This is particularly important considering that, as shown in Chapter 4, the majority of ASEAN States have conceptually endorsed, if cautiously, Pillar I and II of R2P. Pillar II, in particular, requires the intervention of the international community to assist a State which is failing in its responsibility to protect its population. In this context, an organisation like ASEAN could play a relevant role in providing external assistance.

With all this in mind, this chapter examines whether, and if so how, ASEAN, collectively, and the ASEAN States, individually, took any concrete action aimed at protecting the Rohingya inspired by the principles underpinning R2P. The chapter

DOI: 10.4324/9781003436799-6

is divided into five sections. The first section introduces the historical background of the Rohingya humanitarian crisis. The second section discusses, more specifically, the events of the current crisis starting from the 2016 wave of violence. The third section examines the international community's reaction to this crisis, while the fourth section focuses on the response of ASEAN and ASEAN States. The fourth section also analyses the 2021 coup. The last section of the chapter draws some final conclusions.

## 6.2 Background of the Crisis

The Rohingya is a Muslim ethnic group who predominantly resides in Rakhine State, which is located on the Western coast of Myanmar. The Rohingya consider themselves as indigenous to Rakhine State, and date their presence there to ancient times. According to Anthony Ware and Costas Laoutides, the arrival of the Rohingya in Rakhine preceded the arrival of the ethnic Rakhine and the British between the sixth and fourteenth centuries in various waves.[6] However, the Burmese majority and the ethnic Rakhine (both Buddhists) argue that the arrival of the Muslim population only came during the colonial era, starting from 1862 when Myanmar became part of British India, thus highlighting a first (temporal) level of complexity surrounding this crisis.[7] Under colonial rule, there was an increase in migration into Myanmar consisting of traders, labours, and entrepreneurs, who were mostly Chinese and Indians (Hindus and Muslims).[8] This was encouraged by the British.[9] Furthermore, to their convenience, the British employed the policy of Divide and Rule that divided the governance of Myanmar into two: the Ministerial Burma (inhabited by the Burmese Buddhist majority and ruled by the British) and the Peripheral Regions (inhabited mostly by the Muslim minorities and ruled by their own chosen leaders).[10] This preferential treatment for the Muslim minorities over the Buddhist majorities (Burmese and ethnic Rakhine) fuelled the mistrust and hatred of the latter.[11] The Buddhists felt threatened by the Muslim minorities by the fact that they had to compete for economic resources and territory. This environment persisted until the arrival of the Japanese troops in 1942 during World War II, which only exacerbated the existing tensions. The Burmese Buddhist majority took this opportunity to join forces with the Japanese to push the British out of Myanmar, while the Rohingya Muslims remained loyal to the British.[12] The British mobilised the Rohingya volunteers, mostly for intelligence and guerrilla operations, with the promise that they would be given a form of partial independence or a 'Muslim national area' free from Burmese rule.[13] The fact that the Rohingya cooperated with the British, however, was seen by the Buddhists as a form of betrayal.[14] Three years later, the Burmese switched side to join forces with the British in exchange for early independence.[15] Once the British made this separate alliance with the Burmese, they swiftly abandoned their original promise to the Rohingya. This led to a short revolt by the Rohingya, who petitioned to include the northern Rakhine State in what was then East Pakistan (today's Bangladesh).[16] Since the Buddhists had already seen the Rohingya's initial cooperation with the British as a betrayal, this further attempt to secede from Myanmar and join

Bangladesh made things worse. According to the Buddhist majority, this attempt to join another country proved that the Rohingya was not a *taing-yin-tha* (which translates as being Indigenous to the territory) because a *taing-yin-tha* would never attempt to secede from the motherland.[17] This perspective carries a considerable significance to our understanding of the crisis because it would be later used as reasoning behind the institutional discrimination against the Rohingya.

### *6.2.1 Myanmar Independence*

In 1948, Myanmar was officially declared an independent sovereign State free from colonial rule (then known as the Union of Burma). Under U Nu, the first Prime Minister of Myanmar, the Rohingya enjoyed political inclusion and were recognised as a *taing-yin-tha*. For example, in the first Constituent Assembly Elections in 1947, the Rohingya were allowed to vote.[18] Furthermore, while the first Constitution of Myanmar, which was written under British rule in 1947, did not explicitly mention the Rohingya by name, it set out a framework that allowed the Rohingya to qualify as citizens. In particular, Section 11(iii) of the constitution stated that every person born or of parents who had been alive during the commencement of this constitution would be recognised as a citizen of the Union.[19] Furthermore, Section 11(iv) stated that:

> Every person who was born in any of the territories which at the time of his birth was included within His Majesty's dominions and who has resided in any of the territories included within the Union for a period of not less than eight years in the ten years immediately preceding the date of the commencement of this constitution or immediately preceding the 1st January 1942 and who intends to reside permanently.[20]

More importantly, Myanmar did not institutionally differentiate between an indigenous race or a citizen given that Section 10 of the Constitution established only one type of citizenship throughout the Union.[21] Against this institutional background, it is telling that, in 1954, U Nu referred to the Rohingya by name in a public speech stating, 'The people living in Buthidaung and Maungdaw Townships are Rohingya, ethnic of Burma'.[22]

### *6.2.2 The 1962 Coup*

Unfortunately, hopes for further political inclusion of the Rohingya proved to be short-lived. The Burmese Socialist Programme led by General Ne Win, which took power following a coup on 2 March 1962, had a very different vision for Myanmar, namely one inspired by the idea of 'Burman Unity'.[23] According to the latter, all the diverse ethnic groups of Myanmar may be different in culture, language or traditions but are in essence members of a single family of races with a common historical origin.[24] Under Prime Minister Ne Win, the definition of *taing-yin-tha* had also changed to include only those who had permanently settled in Myanmar before the British arrived.[25] Prime Minister Ne Win further securitised and politicised the concept of *taing-yin-tha,* demonising all those groups which were not regarded as Indigenous, especially the Muslims.[26] Prime Minister Ne Win capitalised on the fact that, as discussed earlier, Muslims joined forces with the British against the Burmese during World War II and had attempted to secede from Myanmar. At the same time, he conveniently ignored the fact that there are differences in the Muslims minorities and that the Rohingya, specifically, had been in Rakhine State for centuries before the British had arrived. He argued that, because all Muslims migration only began during the colonial era, they could not be considered as *taing-yin-tha.*[27] *Instead, they were categorised as Bengali (considered as illegal immigrants from Bangladesh), posing a threat to Myanmar's security and sovereignty.*[28]

As a result of this mindset, Prime Minister Ne Win started to pursue a ruthless policy of exclusion and discrimination against the Rohingya. He began with the nationalisation of businesses across the whole economy, which aimed at marginalising the non-*taing-yin-tha,* including all Chinese, Indians, and Muslims.[29] Then, in 1978, the Tatmadaw, that is, the Burmese army, launched a violent widescale census operation known as Operation Nagamin, which was intended to clear out all illegal immigrants.[30] Those involved in this operation were initially meant to simply check for individuals' documents but eventually engaged in violent acts such as rape, torture, and murder, as well as in the destruction of mosques, homes, and properties.[31] This operation failed to recognise the fact that the Rohingya, as a Muslim minority, had been in Rakhine State before the British arrival. Instead, the Tatmadaw treated them as illegal immigrants.

Gradually, restrictive policies were introduced to make it harder for the Rohingya to join any civil service, and to prevent them from joining the armed forces.[32] The final step of this campaign consisted of the passing of the 1982 Citizenship Law, which is still in force today. According to this Law, there are three categories of citizenship in Myanmar: full citizenship, associate citizenship, and naturalised citizenship. Under this law, the power to grant any type of citizenship is given to the 'Central Body', which is composed of the Ministers of Home Affairs, Defence, and Foreign Affairs, all enjoying complete discretion over the process.[33] First, to qualify as a full citizen, a person needs to be of an ethnicity recognised as *taing-yin-tha*, that is to say, belonging to an ethnic group who has settled in Myanmar from a period anterior to '1185 B.E., 1823 A.D.' as their permanent home.[34] This singles out the Rohingya from constitutional recognition because after 1962 the State has refused to acknowledge the Rohingya's presence in Rakhine State before the arrival of the British. Secondly, associate citizenship is recognised to those who had applied for citizenship under the 1948 Union Citizenship Act or have an ongoing application.[35] According to Amnesty International, when the 1948 Union Citizenship Act was passed, most of the Rohingya were either unaware of this Act or did not understand the significance of it. Their failure to apply for citizenship under this Act made them ineligible to later apply for associate citizenship under the 1982 Law.[36] The few who sought to apply for associate citizenship faced other challenges, such as the inability to provide original ID documents due to the latter having been destroyed during the census Operation Nagamin that was mentioned earlier.[37]

Finally, the criteria that one must meet in order to obtain naturalised citizenship include (1) being able to speak well one of the national languages; (2) being of good character; and (3) being of sound mind.[38] These provisions are quite vague. For example, the law does not provide any information as to what would constitute a good character or a sound mind. As a result of this, the Central Body mentioned earlier has been entrusted to confer citizenship certificates and enjoys full discretion in determining who meets or does not meet those criteria.[39] Another problem related to this route for obtaining citizenship is that it would imply that the Rohingya are foreigners, whereas prior to 1962 they were recognised as *taing-yin-tha*.[40] Put simply, the legal framework set up by the Citizenship law prevents the Rohingya from being recognised as citizens as well as *taing-yin-tha*, thereby rendering them stateless.

Since the days of Prime Minister Ne Win's rule, the Rohingya's predicament has only continued to worsen. As a result of years of pent-up animosity and distrust between the Rohingya and the Buddhists, a large wave of violence broke out in Rakhine State in 2012. Although this 2012 wave is not the focus of this chapter, it would later lead to the main events of 2016, and, for this reason, it will be briefly discussed later.

### *6.2.3 The 2012 Violence*

According to Human Rights Watch, this wave of violence began on 28 May 2012 with the rape and murder of Thida Htwe, an ethnic Rakhine woman, in Ramri in southern Rakhine State, allegedly committed by three Muslim men.[41] The State media and the ethnic Rakhines were quick to demonise the 'Bengali' (Rohingya) for this heinous crime, which sparked the long-simmering communal tension between the two ethnic groups.[42] In the following days, the level of violence steadily intensified. A Rakhine mob attacked and killed 10 Rohingya men (who had no connection to the murder and rape of Thida Htwe) travelling by bus in a nearby town of Toungup.[43] In retaliation, thousands of Rohingya rioted, destroyed properties, and killed an unknown number of ethnic Rakhine.[44] The violence then quickly spread across Rakhine State, forcing President Thein Sein to declare a state of emergency. Crucially, the Tatmadaw was instructed to deploy troops to towns under curfew, but not before 98 people had been killed, 123 injured and 5,338 homes had been destroyed.[45] In these statistics, the number of Rohingya killed and injured as well as Rohingya's homes destroyed were a lot higher than in the ethnic Rakhine community.[46] The deployment of the Tatmadaw was supposed to keep order but, according to Human Rights Watch, it ended up favouring the ethnic Rakhine, for example standing by or joining in when the latter burned down Rohingya's homes.[47]

## 6.3 The 2016 Wave of Violence

According to some estimates, in September 2015 the number of internally displaced persons, across 68 camps, was 143.514, most of whom were Rohingya.[48] The latter had to live under dire conditions without proper shelters and adequate healthcare and with limited access to food and clean water.[49] At the same time, those in Rakhine State faced an even worse reality, as, in addition to poor living conditions, they also experienced arbitrary arrests, extrajudicial killings, as well as physical and sexual assaults.[50]

Against this background, on 9 October 2016, several hundred local armed Muslim men launched simultaneous attacks on three Border Guard Police (BGP) posts in Maungdaw and Rathedaung townships, located near the north-western border with Bangladesh.[51] These attacks were claimed by the Arakan Rohingya Salvation Army (ARSA), which had been created to fight for Rohingya freedom against the government's discrimination and persecution.[52] According to an International Crisis Group report, these attacks resulted in the deaths of nine police officers and eight attackers. At the same time, the rest made off with 62 firearms and more than 10000 rounds of ammunition.[53] The clashes between the ARSA and the BGP lasted until 12 October, when ARSA launched a violent campaign to take over the north-western State.[54] ARSA claimed responsibility for many violent attacks through a series of videos that called for other Rohingya to join the Jihad to liberate northern Rakhine State, while also appealing for foreign support, weapons and fighters.[55] The videos explicitly stated that ARSA's objectives were to stop the persecution of the Rohingya and secure their rights and greater freedom as citizens of Myanmar and not to impose Sharia law onto others.[56]

In response to these violent attacks and challenges to the unity of Myanmar, the Tatmadaw along with the BGP launched a major counter-operation aimed at recovering the looted weapons and arresting those involved in the attacks.[57] To achieve its goal, the Tatmadaw engaged in clearance operations that quickly descended into chaos with the burning of properties, shooting suspects on sight, seizures, destruction of food stocks, and rape of women and girls.[58] It is estimated that between 9 October and 2 December, over 20000 Rohingya fled to Bangladesh to escape these atrocities.[59] At the same time, the Tatmadaw started to arm and encourage the establishment of a non-Muslim local militia.[60] The conflict further escalated following a series of attacks using improvised explosive devices on government forces in the area. In response, the Tatmadaw deployed more ground troops and started using attack helicopters.[61] The Tatmadaw claimed that it was conducting lawful military operations against Islamic terrorist groups.[62] The same position would be taken later by State Counsellor Aung San Suu Kyi when she represented Myanmar before the International Court of Justice (ICJ). In that context, she affirmed that the accusations of 'inter-communal violence' had been exaggerated and mis-constructed and that the Tatmadaw had only acted to neutralise a terrorist threat against Myanmar.[63]

However, news stories of mass killings, rape, destruction of food and water sources, and villages continued to emerge.[64] The 2018 report of the Independent International Fact-Finding Mission on Myanmar set up by the UN Human Rights Council was unambiguous in this regard. Based on the information gathered, this mission found that 'crimes including murder, imprisonment, enforced disappearance, torture, rape, sexual slavery and other forms of sexual violence, persecution and enslavement' had been committed by the Tatmadaw as part of widespread and systematic attacks on the Rohingya civilian population.[65] Crucially, the fact-finding mission concluded that war crimes and crimes against humanity had been committed in Rakhine State and that there were sufficient evidence and information to warrant the prosecution of Tatmadaw senior officials for the crime of genocide too.[66] All this clearly suggests that a mass atrocity situation had materialised and that an R2P response should have been conceived.

## 6.4 The Reactions of the International Community

This section examines the reaction of the international community to this crisis. While special attention will be paid to the actions taken by a number of UN bodies, the response of the Organisation of Islamic Cooperation will also be considered. This will provide a useful context within which to discuss, later, the positions taken by ASEAN and the ASEAN States.

The first UN body that will be discussed is the Human Rights Council. As mentioned earlier, the Council set up, through resolution 34/22 of 24 March 2017, a Fact-Finding Mission with the task of establishing the facts and circumstances of the alleged human rights violations by the military and security forces in Rakhine State.[67] In a subsequent resolution, passed in December 2017, the Council expressed concern over the reports of systematic mass human rights violations carried out by the Myanmar security forces, further noting that these atrocities were likely to constitute crimes against humanity.[68] It is important to highlight that, although these two resolutions did not directly invoke R2P, they did use R2P language by stressing that States have the primary responsibility for the respect and protection of human rights and by calling upon both international and regional actors to assist Myanmar.[69]

Further evidence of the international concern surrounding this crisis comes from the action taken by the United Nations General Assembly (GA). In response to the 2016 violence, the GA adopted three Resolutions: 72/248 (24 December 2017), 73/264 (22 December 2018), and 74/246 (27 December 2019). These resolutions condemned the ARSA attacks on the BGP posts and expressed concern about the scale of abuses and discrimination in Rakhine State, calling for the end of the military operations.[70] Furthermore, the GA echoed the Human Rights Council's concern for the Rohingya's statelessness due to the enactment of the 1982 Citizenship Law (discussed earlier) and also urged the Myanmar government to implement the recommendations of the Advisory Commission on Rakhine State.[71] The GA also condemned the human rights violations set out in the report of the UN Fact-Finding Mission that was mentioned before.[72] Finally, the GA encouraged the international community, including ASEAN, to provide assistance to Myanmar in the fulfilment of its international human rights commitments.[73]

Compared to those of the Human Rights Council and the General Assembly, the response of the UN Security Council (SC) was quite timid. Three months after the second phase of violence, on 6 November 2017, the SC released a presidential statement, instead of a resolution, condemning the ARSA's attacks on the BGP posts and expressing grave concern over the reports of human rights violations and abuses taking place in the Rakhine State.[74] While condemning the violence, the SC reaffirmed its commitment to the sovereignty, political independence, and territorial integrity of Myanmar. Furthermore, using typical R2P Pillar I language, the SC stressed 'the primary responsibility of the Government of Myanmar to protect its population including through respect for the rule of law and respect, promotion and protection of human rights'.[75] In addition, the SC also called upon the government to take all necessary measures to counter incitement to violence or hatred and restore peace and inter-communal harmony through peaceful dialogue.[76] Another response from the SC was through the adoption of Resolution 2669 in 2022, where it expressed its concerns on the instability in Myanmar, which poses a risk to the sustainable return of the Rohingya refugees that fled to Bangladesh after the 2016–2017 waves of violence in Rakhine State.[77] The Resolution further called upon the Myanmar government to address the root causes of the crisis in Rakhine State. Several things stood out through this Resolution.[78] First, there was no mention of the crimes perpetrated by the Tatmadaw against the Rohingya, which were listed out in the 2018 UN-commissioned fact-finding mission. Second, there was no urging of the government to assume its primary responsibility to protect its citizens, Third, this Resolution was brought on by the 2021 coup (which will be discussed later) and was not motivated by the humanitarian concerns for the Rohingya. Fourth, and lastly, this Resolution still reaffirmed its support for the sovereignty and territorial integrity of Myanmar,

Initially, the fact that the Security Council released a presidential statement rather than passing a resolution is *per se* very important. This means that the five permanent members of the Council (P-5) could not agree on the text of a resolution. In fact, it was reported that China and Russia consistently blocked any attempt to pass a resolution that would condemn Myanmar.[79] This was not the first time that Beijing, which promotes a rigid interpretation of the principles of sovereignty and non-intervention, protected Myanmar at the Security Council.[80] The position of China matters because although the latter is not a member of ASEAN, it does have a special relationship with this regional organisation and has strong links with several individual member states.[81] China's detailed positions on R2P and this crisis will be discussed in Chapter 8. Regarding the latest resolution it adopted on the matter, for the reasons listed earlier, the SC still made sure that the language used was respectful towards Myanmar.

### *6.4.1. The Organisation of Islamic Cooperation*

The Organisation of Islamic Cooperation (OIC) is the second-largest international organisation after the UN. It is made up of 57 Muslim States and aims to protect the interests of Muslims all over the world.[82] Because of its large membership that spans over four continents, the OIC can be a powerful player in the international arena. For this book, the position of the OIC towards the Rohingya crisis is particularly relevant because three ASEAN States are also members of the OIC, namely Indonesia, Malaysia and Brunei.

The OIC has been very critical of the Myanmar government. For example, in September 2017, it released a declaration expressing deep concern over the systematic brutal acts perpetrated by the security forces in Rakhine State, claiming that the situation had reached the level of ethnic cleansing.[83] The Declaration called upon the Myanmar government to stop all violence against the Rohingya and to stop the 'continuous attempts to obliterate their Islamic culture and identity'.[84] The Declaration also requested that its members consider restricting economic relations and suspending trade agreements with Myanmar until the government ensures the safe return of the IDPs and refugees, and ceased violence and persecution against the Rohingya.[85]

Subsequent resolutions adopted in 2018 welcomed the UN Human Rights Council's decision to constitute a fact-finding mission and criticised Myanmar's lack of cooperation with this mission.[86] Furthermore, the OIC backed one of its members, The Gambia, in lodging an application with the ICJ against Myanmar for violations of the Genocide Convention (which is a form of measure of Pillar III of R2P).[87]

In the latest response by the OIC to this crisis, in 2023, along with the EU, it sponsored a draft resolution introduced to the GA that explicitly condemned all the abuses perpetrated against the Rohingya by the Tatmadaw and expressed its concerns over the Rohingya's statelessness propagated by the 1982 Citizenship Law.[88] Furthermore, the draft resolution also expressed the group's and other co-sponsor's concern following the 'unjustified declaration of the state of emergency on 1 February 2021' (which will be discussed later).

## 6.5 The Reaction of ASEAN

The first part of this chapter has highlighted several important points. First, a humanitarian crisis unfolded in Rakhine State. Second, Myanmar was accused by various parties, including UN organs, of having committed atrocity crimes. Third, various international bodies highlighted the gravity of the situation and called for international action, including action by ASEAN.[89] That said, as discussed before, the United Nations was not in a position to take effective R2P action. Due to internal dynamics, the Security Council could not take steps under Pillar III, while Myanmar's refusal to receive international support made Pillar II measures unviable. As discussed in Chapter 1, under these circumstances regional organisations could play an important role in addressing atrocity crimes situations. Accordingly, this section examines ASEAN's response to the crisis.

To begin with, ASEAN's response to the 2012 violence was quite timid. For example, both a foreign ministers' statement issued on 17 August and a chairman's statement following the 21st ASEAN Summit on 18 November affirmed ASEAN's support for the democratisation process taking place in Myanmar, and expressed ASEAN's readiness, upon the request of the latter, to provide humanitarian assistance in Rakhine State.[90] Crucially, these pronouncements did not make any reference to the persecution of the Rohingya, nor did they call upon the Myanmar government to stop the ongoing violence. More importantly, pleasing the Myanmar government, they did not use the term 'Rohingya'.

As discussed earlier, the 2012 wave of violence was less severe compared to the 2016 wave. However, ASEAN's overall approach to the crisis did not change following the escalation of violence and human rights violations. The 30th ASEAN Summit, which took place in April 2017, was the first to be held after the eruption of violence in late 2016. Remarkably, the chairman's statement did not refer to the situation in Rakhine State at all. The only indirect reference that was made to the crisis was expressed in the following terms:

> We reaffirmed our commitment to addressing the irregular movement of persons in the region. We reiterated the need to explore the establishment of a Task Force to respond to crisis and emergency situations rising from irregular movement of persons in Southeast Asia.[91]

However, the cause of these 'irregular movements of persons' was not mentioned. It is telling, instead, that the statement reaffirmed the principles of the Treaty of Amity and Cooperation in Southeast Asia (TAC), namely mutual respect for State sovereignty, non-interference, and non-use or threat of force that govern inter-state relations in the region.[92] This early failure to address the humanitarian crisis was not an isolated one. On future occasions, ASEAN continued to avoid referring to the situation in Rakhine State as a humanitarian crisis and calling upon Myanmar to duly protect its population.[93]

Things, however, changed following the launch of the Tatmadaw's clearing operations in response to the ARSA's attack in August 2017. After meeting with the members' foreign ministers on 24 September 2017, ASEAN's chairman released a statement on the situation in Rakhine State. This was the first time in ASEAN history that a chairman's statement explicitly addressed a member's internal affairs. Although this was in some respect a significant development, a closer look at the language used in the statement tells a different story. The statement, for example, did not refer to the Rohingya by name. It raised concerns about the recent developments in Rakhine State, condemning the attacks against the Myanmar security forces and all other acts of violence that resulted in the loss of lives, destruction of properties, and displacement of people.[94] Furthermore, it referred to the situation in Rakhine State as a complex inter-communal issue with deep historical roots, urging all parties to avoid actions that would worsen the situation on the ground.[95] Finally, the statement affirmed ASEAN's support for the government's efforts to bring peace and stability in Rakhine State.[96] The same position was expressed in the official statements which followed in 2018,[97] 2019,[98] 2020,[99] 2021,[100] 2022,[101] and 2023.[102] The Joint Communique released on the occasion of ASEAN Foreign Ministerial Meetings (AMM) in 2018,[103] 2019,[104] 2020,[105] 2021,[106] 2022,[107] and 2023[108] reaffirmed the same points.

In essence, ASEAN did not show any humanitarian concern about the situation of the Rohingya. It did not use any R2P-based language and did not take any concrete action aimed at addressing the crisis. These official pronouncements could have at least acknowledged Myanmar's primary responsibility to protect its population given that, as discussed in Chapter 4, all ASEAN States had endorsed the Pillar I of R2P back in 2005. Furthermore, although the references to ASEAN's commitment to support the government's effort to bring peace and stability in

Rakhine State resembled the language typical of Pillar II, these promises seemed more like a friendly encouragement rather than a concrete commitment to assist or a call for Myanmar to assume its primary responsibility.

## 6.6 The Reactions of ASEAN States

The following section provides an analysis of individual States' responses to this humanitarian crisis. As will be shown, there are important differences in the way in which ASEAN States approached this crisis.

### *6.6.1 Malaysia*

Out of all ASEAN members, Malaysia has been the most critical of Myanmar. Malaysia was among the first countries to react to the plight of the Rohingya. Soon after the Tatmadaw's clearance operations had commenced, Prime Minister Najib Razak publicly accused Aung Sung Suu Kyi of inaction and called for the UN to stop the ongoing *genocide*.[109] It is important to note that Najib described the situation as genocide well before the publication of the 2018 Report of the Independent International Fact-finding Mission on Myanmar. He also sought to promote a sort of ASEAN intervention by stressing that when grave humanitarian crises occur ASEAN must set aside its principle of non-interference and uphold its commitment, enshrined in the ASEAN Charter, to ensure the protection of human rights.[110] This was the first time that an ASEAN State called for this type of intervention in the internal affairs of another member states without the consent of the latter. Not surprisingly, Myanmar accused Najib of violating ASEAN's rule of non-interference and considered lodging an official complaint with ASEAN for this infringement.[111]

Malaysia's involvement in the crisis did not wane over time. On 19 January 2017, it hosted an extraordinary session of the Council of Foreign Ministers of the Organization of Islamic Cooperation on the situation of the Rohingya. The resolution passed on that occasion urged Myanmar's government to prevent the worsening of the crisis and expressed concern about the human rights violations faced by the Rohingya.[112] During another meeting of the OIC, Malaysia's Minister of Foreign Affairs condemned the 'disproportionate response' by Myanmar and called for the immediate stop of all military operations.[113] It also called for the perpetrators of crimes against humanity to be held accountable and for the international community to save the Rohingya.[114] Malaysia also supported the OIC's decision to back The Gambia's application against Myanmar before the ICJ for violations of the Genocide Convention. It is, therefore, clear that Malaysia used the Organization of Islamic Cooperation as an international platform to advocate for collective action to stop the relevant atrocities and hold the perpetrators to justice.

Malaysia took another unprecedented step when, in September 2017, it distanced itself from an ASEAN chairman's statement on the situation in Rakhine.[115] According to Malaysia, the statement misrepresented the reality of the situation and failed to incorporate its concerns about the clearance operations. Hence, for Malaysia the statement was not based on consensus and should have not been issued.[116] Malaysia also maintained a very critical position of Myanmar at the UN. In particular, it voted for GA Resolutions 72/248, 73/264, and 74/246, which condemned Myanmar for its clearance operations and referred to widespread atrocities being committed against the Rohingya.[117] A very strong statement was made at the 74th Session of the GA on 25 September 2019. On that occasion, Prime Minister Mahathir Mohamad accused Myanmar of genocide and called upon the international community to urgently take action given Myanmar's unwillingness to protect the Rohingya.[118]

Overall, while no express reference to R2P was made, it can be said that Malaysia has called for R2P action. The references to atrocity crimes, genocide, and the failure of Myanmar to protect the Rohingya as well as the call for international action clearly resemble R2P language. Malaysia was described in Chapter 4 as a wary supporter of R2P, having endorsed Pillar I and II without hesitation while remaining more cautious with regard to the implementation and scope of Pillar III.[119] In this case, however, it would seem that Malaysia was also prepared to back coercive action against Myanmar.

### 6.6.2 Indonesia

Indonesia is another predominantly Muslim ASEAN State. Given the influx of Rohingya refugees into its territory, it was in Indonesia's best interest to help resolve this issue. On 4 August 2012, in response to that year's eruption of violence against the Rohingya, Indonesian President Susilo Bambang Yudhoyono asked Myanmar's President Thein Sein in a letter to solve the deadly conflict quickly and to stop the attacks on the Rohingya.[120] On top of this, Yudhoyono also called upon Myanmar to accept international observers to review the situation in Rakhine State and ended the letter by offering Indonesia's assistance in solving this conflict.[121]

On 3 September 2017, immediately after the escalation of violence, President Joko Widodo stressed the need to act instead of merely making statements of condemnation. He further affirmed Indonesia's commitment to help resolve this humanitarian crisis in conjunction with the international community.[122] Right after this statement, Widodo sent his Minister of Foreign Affairs to meet with Aung San Suu Kyi to present a proposal from the Indonesian government called the 4+1 Formula to address the crisis.[123] There are four elements in the Formula: 'stability and security, maximum self-restraint and refrain from violence, protection for everyone in Rakhine State regardless of ethnicities and religions, and the importance of open access for humanitarian aids'.[124] In an effort to assist Myanmar, Indonesia also launched the Indonesian Humanitarian Alliance for Myanmar to provide aid in terms of education, healthcare and relief in Rakhine State.[125]

As a member of the Organization of Islamic Cooperation, Indonesia has not been as vocally critical of Myanmar as Malaysia. At the same time, although it did not distance itself from the strong official positions taken by the OIC, Indonesia did use its position as a member of this organisation to urge the members of the Muslim community and the international community to constructively engage with Myanmar in order to address the root causes of the violence against the Rohingya community.[126]

Within the UN, Indonesia voted in favour of UN Human Rights Council Resolution S-27/1 and GA Resolutions 72/248, 73/264, and 74/246, which, among other things, condemned Myanmar's military operations and called for the Myanmar government to remedy the Rohingya's statelessness.[127] Furthermore, in January 2019 Indonesia joined the Security Council as a non-permanent member.[128] Interestingly, Indonesia had announced that its main priorities in the Council would include creating a 'global ecosystem of peace and stability by advancing peacekeeping and peacebuilding, promoting greater engagement and synergy between the council and regional organisations in conflict prevention, and ensuring synergy between sustaining peace and global development'.[129] In spite of these aspirations, there was not much that Indonesia could do as a member of the Council, given that, as noted earlier, this body was effectively prevented from taking any concrete action against Myanmar due to the opposition of China and Russia.

All considered, Indonesia was critical of Myanmar without being as vocal as Malaysia was. According to Mohamad Rosyidin, it can be said that Jakarta employed 'quiet diplomacy' as opposed to the West and Malaysia's preference for 'megaphone diplomacy'.[130] This approach can have some merits. According to Rosyidin, by focusing on humanitarian assistance instead of condemning and calling for punishment, Indonesia sought to provide an effective solution to protect civilians during a humanitarian crisis, facilitated by the fact that Myanmar would treat Jakarta as a friend and not an enemy.[131]

### *6.6.3 Brunei*

Brunei is another predominantly Muslim ASEAN country. It was certainly less vocal than Malaysia and did not get as involved as Indonesia. However, contrary to many ASEAN States, it still voted in favour of GA Resolutions 72/248, 73/264, and 74/246, which, as noted before, condemned the human rights violations committed by the Tatmadaw as part of its clearance operations and urged Myanmar to remedy the Rohingya's statelessness.[132] In addition, Brunei is a member of the Organisation of Islamic Cooperation. Despite not taking any direct action, it did not distance itself from the pronouncements discussed earlier that were critical of Myanmar.

### *6.6.4 Singapore*

Due to geographic reasons, Singapore did not receive any refugees in its territory and was not directly affected by the humanitarian crisis. Its position, accordingly, was quite neutral. On 8 September 2017, for example, it issued the following statement:

> The situation in Rakhine State is a complex inter-communal issue with deep historical roots. All the parties involved must avoid actions that will further worsen the situation on the ground and work together to foster viable and long-term solutions, so that the affected communities can rebuild their lives.[133]

This statement clearly echoed the content of the ASEAN Chairman's statement adopted on 24 September 2017 which was discussed earlier.[134] It did not refer to the Rohingya specifically, nor did it refer to the situation as a humanitarian crisis but rather as an inter-communal issue. Singapore also stated that it was prepared to work with Myanmar in its efforts to restore peace and stability and to provide humanitarian assistance in accordance with the principles of the ASEAN Charter.[135] Following on this statement, on 19 October 2017, Singapore pledged $100,000 through the ASEAN Humanitarian Assistance Centre to help the humanitarian efforts in Rakhine State.[136] It is also important to note that Singapore abstained on GA Resolutions 72/248, 73/264, and 74/246 that condemned the clearance operations by the Tatmadaw.[137]

### 6.6.5 *Thailand*

Between 2014 and 2023, Thailand was run by a military dictatorship under General Prayut Chan-ocha and has been embroiled in political unrest erasing the democratic legacy of its famed foreign minister, Surin Pitsuwan. Consequently, Thailand has been largely preoccupied with repressing its own people's call for democracy.[138] This seems to have had an effect on its position in the Rohingya crisis.

After the 2017 escalation of violence in Rakhine State, on 1 October, Thailand's foreign ministry stated that it was closely following the situation in Rakhine and would provide aid to the governments of Myanmar and Bangladesh (where Rohingya refugees mostly fled to).[139] Thailand placed great emphasis on the importance of providing humanitarian support to a fellow member, as it did during the East Timor crisis in 1999.[140] Other than that, it had minimal direct involvement in the crisis, preferring to side with the ASEAN collective (and weak) response.[141] In accordance with this position, it is telling that Thailand abstained on GA Resolutions 72/248, 73/264 and 74/246, choosing not to join in with Malaysia, Indonesia and Brunei in condemning the clearance operations.[142]

### 6.6.6 *Cambodia*

Cambodia has been a supporter of Myanmar amidst international pressure and criticism. Cambodia's Prime Minister, Hun Sen, once stated that he opposed any attempt to internationalise the Rohingya crisis, which, instead, should be regarded as being part of Myanmar's domestic affairs.[143] Hun Sen also referred to the ASEAN Charter, which forbids members from interfering in each other's internal affairs.[144] In line with this pro-Myanmar stance, Cambodia voted against GA Resolutions 72/248, 73/264, and 74/246, choosing not to condemn the clearance operations against the Rohingya.[145] Cambodia's defence of Myanmar could also be explained by additional factors other than a simple compliance with ASEAN traditional principles. In particular, its position could be motivated by an interest in increasing economic cooperation with the country. In a meeting with the Myanmar ambassador, Hun Sen stated that Cambodia supports Myanmar's efforts to repatriate the Rohingya refugees from Bangladesh.[146] Additionally, in the meeting, Hun

Sen also discussed the strengthening of relationships between the two nations in terms of trade and tourism, which was welcomed by the Myanmar ambassador.[147] In Chapter 4, Cambodia was described as a wary supporter of R2P. In fact, Hun Sen once even stated that

> R2P should be viewed as deepening the meaning of sovereignty in that it underscores the importance of states taking seriously their primary responsibility to protect their people against genocide, war crimes, crimes against humanity and ethnic cleansing.[148]

However, from its position on this crisis, Cambodia showed a lack of a serious commitment to the implementation of R2P.

#### *6.6.7 Laos, Vietnam, and the Philippines*

Laos expressed its solidarity with Myanmar by voting against GA Resolutions 72/248, 73/264, and 74/246.[149] Other than that, it has remained largely silent about the situation. This seems in line with its description in Chapter 4 as an R2P neutral State. Vietnam was labelled in Chapter 4 as a wary supporter of R2P because it supports the fundamental concepts of Pillar I and II but rejects Pillar III. However, its stance on this crisis suggests that it lacks a genuine commitment to the implementation of R2P altogether. For example, it voted against GA Resolutions 72/248, 73/264 and 74/246.[150] Between 2020–2021, Vietnam acted as a non-permanent member of the Security Council. On 4 February 2020, the SC held a meeting to discuss the provisional measures issued by the ICJ on Myanmar.[151] Vietnam sided with China to prevent the Council from reaching a consensus on a potential statement.[152]

Finally, the President of the Philippines, Rodrigo Duterte, had initially referred to the Rohingya situation as genocide and announced that the Philippines was ready to provide sanctuary for the victims.[153] However, Duterte quickly retracted this statement and issued an apology to Aung Sung Suu Kyi, 'I will apologise to you, but if you have noticed my statement was almost a satire. . . . I am not ready to intervene in your [internal affairs]'.[154] Duterte clarified that he was speaking against the European Countries that had accused Myanmar of rampant human rights violations but did little to actually help the Rohingya.[155] To show solidarity with Myanmar, The Philippines voted against GA Resolutions 72/248, 73/264, and 74/246 and the UN Human Rights Council Resolution S-27/1, choosing not to support the international condemnation of the clearance operations by the Tatmadaw.[156]

### 6.7 The February 2021 Coup

In the most recent development in Myanmar, on 1 February 2021, the Junta headed by General Min Aung Hlaing arrested President Win Myint, the *de facto* head of State Aung San Suu Kyi and their associates in a military coup.[157] General Hlaing defended the military actions by stating that there were irregularities in the national election in November 2020 and promised to hold new elections to achieve a 'true and disciplined democracy'.[158] Since then, there has been a series of nationwide protests against the Junta calling for democracy. The Junta responded with forceful measures including the use of live ammunition, which has resulted in the deaths of more than 700 protestors as of 13 April 2021.[159] The fact that General Hlaing is acting as the head of government is important for this study because he is among those named in the 2018 report of the UN Fact-Finding Mission as responsible for crimes against humanity, war crimes and genocide committed against the Rohingya.[160] This means that any hopes for the current government to cooperate with the international community to solve the Rohingya crisis is minimal.

According to Gareth Evans, the current situation in Myanmar must be treated as an R2P case since it resembles the early days of the one-sided violent repression of peaceful dissents that occurred in Libya and Syria.[161] In particular, Evans noted that the Tatmadaw is guilty of crimes against humanity. According to him, coercive measures of Pillar III other than military force should be employed, including, for example, arms embargos, sanctions, and criminal prosecutions.[162]

The SC in its two presidential statements highlighted that this development has the potential to exacerbate the existing challenges in Rakhine State, while also condemning the violence against peaceful protestors and calling upon the military to exercise its utmost restraint.[163] Furthermore, the statements still affirmed Myanmar's sovereignty and territorial integrity. Since then, Myanmar has also been subjected to a new wave of international condemnation from individual States such as the US, the UK, Japan, and Australia.[164] In 2022, in a expressing a firmer stance on the matter, the SC adopted Resolution 2669. In this Resolution, the SC demands all forms of violence to cease, urges the Junta to release all arbitrarily detained prisoners, calls upon the Junta to cooperate with ASEAN, and lastly, it also urges the Junta to address the root causes of the crisis in Rakhine State.[165]

ASEAN expressed its initial concerns about the situation on 2 March through its informal Foreign Minister's Meeting (IAMM), calling on all parties to refrain from instigating further violence and working towards a peaceful solution.[166] However, the IAMM statement did not condemn the Junta for the coup and the arrest of President Myint, Aung San Suu Kyi, and their associates. More importantly, the IAMM did not refer to the use of lethal force by the Junta against pro-democracy protestors.

On 24th of April, however, in its first unprecedented mediation effort, ASEAN held an emergency summit to discuss the situation in Myanmar. For the first time in its history, ASEAN has employed the power of Article 7 of the ASEAN Charter that states that ASEAN summits can be convened in order to address emergency situations affecting ASEAN and its members.[167] In the following Chairman's statement, ASEAN expressed its deep concern for the escalation of violence in Myanmar and presented its 'Five-Point Consensus'.[168] According to these five points, (1) all parties should immediately halt any violence; (2) all parties concerned shall commence constructive dialogue to seek a peaceful solution; (3) a special ASEAN envoy shall facilitate mediation of the dialogue process; and (4) ASEAN shall provide humanitarian assistance; (5) the special ASEAN envoy shall visit Myanmar to meet with all parties concerned.[169] In addition, the statement underscored the importance of Myanmar's effort in addressing the situation in Rakhine State.

A closer examination of the language used suggests that the 'Five-Point Consensus' has been carefully crafted not to criticise or infringe upon the sovereignty of Myanmar. First, the statement and the consensus reached did not condemn the violent power grab by the Junta.[170] Second, the imperative words used were *shall* and not *must*, which act more as a suggestion rather than a demand for the Junta to follow the consensus points. Third, the consensus did not explicitly call upon the Junta to stop violating the human rights of the people but rather called upon 'all parties' to exercise restraint when in reality the events have shown a one-sided violence against the civilian population. Lastly, since the 'Five-Point Consensus' did not demand a strict timeline from the Junta to implement the suggestions, it is entirely dependent on General Hlaing when and if he sees fit to do so. As for the references made to the situation in Rakhine State, the chairman's statement still did not refer to the Rohingya by name in an attempt not to antagonise the Junta.

In its second consecutive unprecedented effort to address this crisis, in the ASEAN Summits in 2021, 2022 and 2023, ASEAN collectively barred Min Aung Hlaing from attending since his regime has so far failed to implement any points of the 'Five-Point Consensus'.[171] Furthermore, ASEAN also announced that Myanmar will not be assuming its ASEAN chairmanship in 2026 and the responsibility has passed over to the Philippines instead.[172] As was discussed earlier in the chapter, ASEAN does not have any mechanism or precedents to refer to in an event of non-compliance by any of its members such as this. ASEAN is, to put it simply, 'stuck between a rock and a hard place' as it cannot be seen as not putting any efforts into solving this crisis, which would deem it irrelevant in the regional and international community. At the same time, the degree of responses varies among ASEAN members so even if some wants there to be a stronger response, it would have to be from an individual capacity and not a collective one since ASEAN operates under a consensus method.

As for individual State efforts, Indonesia has been spearheading the regional effort to address the situation diplomatically. Immediately after the coup, President Joko Widodo along with Malaysian Prime Minister Muhyiddin Yassin led the call for a special IAMM to discuss the matter.[173] However, there was no response until the 2nd of March when ASEAN held an IAMM (as discussed earlier). During the IAMM, Indonesia did not directly condemn the Junta but stated that 'the wish and goodwill of ASEAN to help will be unable to be carried out if Myanmar doesn't open its door to ASEAN'.[174] Indonesia added that there should be no foreign intervention, but that ASEAN should be ready to help Myanmar in any way.[175] Indonesia was also decisive in calling for an emergency ASEAN summit on the situation.[176] During the latter, it affirmed that the situation in Myanmar is unacceptable and that violence must stop immediately.[177] Since then, Indonesia has continued to implement methods of 'quiet diplomacy' such as dialogues in an effort to resolve the matter.[178]

During the IAMM, Malaysia called for the release of President Myint, Aung San Suu Kyi and their associates and encouraged dialogue between the parties concerned.[179] On 20 March, Prime Minister Muhyiddin also said that the use of lethal force against unarmed civilians was unacceptable and this 'deplorable situation must stop immediately'.[180] Prime Minister Muhyiddin further stated that Malaysia along with the ASEAN community cannot afford to see a fellow member and neighbour be so destabilised at the hands of a selected few for their own interests.[181] This statement is the strongest view adopted by an ASEAN member against General Hlaing so far. At the emergency summit, Prime Minister Muhyiddin affirmed that ASEAN's policy of non-interference should not lead to inaction if a domestic situation such as this 'jeopardizes security, and stability of ASEAN and the wider region'.[182] In its latest response, since Myanmar has so far failed to implement the 'Five-Point Consensus', Malaysia has called on stronger measures; however, it did not specify which measures.[183]

Singapore's Prime Minister, Lee Hsien Loong, on 3 March stated that the use of lethal force against civilians and unarmed demonstrators is unacceptable and is disastrous internationally and domestically.[184] Singapore had joined Brunei, Indonesia, and Malaysia in calling for ASEAN to hold an emergency summit to discuss this situation.[185] Singapore's Foreign Minister Vivian Balakrishnan stated, like Indonesia did, that there should be no foreign intervention, but that ASEAN should stand ready to help in any way.[186] During the emergency summit, Lee agreed with the 'Five-point Consensus' but added that the Junta should also release President Win Myint and Aung San Suu Kyi.[187] Lee further stated that during the summit, General Hlaing did not oppose ASEAN playing a constructive role and would consider the points that were raised.[188]

As the current ASEAN chair, Brunei said that it welcomed and was working with Malaysia and Indonesia to prepare for the emergency summit to discuss the situation.[189] Brunei has not released any other statement on the matter. Thailand, in contrast to Malaysia and Singapore, has merely expressed its grave concern over the situation but has not condemned the coup nor the use of lethal force against pro-democracy protestors.[190] This is understandable since Prime Minister Prayut Chan-o-cha himself came into power by a coup in 2014. Not surprisingly, within days of the coup in Myanmar, Prayut had voiced his support for General Hlaing's quest for 'democracy'.[191] Since then, Thailand had a new Prime Minister, Srettha Thavisin who stated the 'Five-point Consensus' and at the same time vows to also engage with the Junta bilaterally to help resolve the crisis since Thailand and Myanmar share borders.

Immediately after the coup, Prime Minister Hun Sen said that this situation falls within the internal affairs of Myanmar and that Cambodia does not interfere with the latter.[192] In the subsequent years, Prime Minister Hun Sen met with General Min Aung Hlaing to discuss the implementation of the 'Five-point Consensus' and vowed Cambodia's assistance in brokering peace and stability in Myanmar.[193]

Vietnam, currently a member of the SC, joined China and Russia in working towards preventing the imposition of measures against Myanmar.[194] Furthermore, on 9 April, while addressing the Arria Formula meeting on Myanmar at the SC, Ambassador Dang Dinh Quy stated that the international community should make constructive contributions to help Myanmar stop all violence and promote an environment where conductive dialogue and reconciliation between the parties can take place.[195] Since then, Vietnam continues to call on all parties to exercise restraint and urges for the implementation of the 'Five-point Consensus' to resolve the conflict.[196]

The Philippines has supported Myanmar even after the recent coup. In a statement to the UN Human Rights Council, it not only affirmed its support for Myanmar's progress towards democracy but also praised the role of the military in preserving the country's territorial integrity and national security.[197] Furthermore, the Philippines strongly emphasised the primacy of national efforts towards democratic reforms as opposed to external efforts aimed at imposing a solution on a country. The Philippines ended its statement by reaffirming its support for the sovereignty and territorial integrity of Myanmar.[198] Since 2022, the Philippines has sworn in a new President, Ferdinand Marcos Jr, which subtly changed the Philippines' stance on the matter. President Marcos Jr is less vocal in his support for the Junta and has instead expressed that this issue is difficult for ASEAN to solve since Myanmar has not been cooperative in implementing the 'Five-point Consensus'.[199] However, he did not emphasise any other methods to employ to solve this crisis in the near future.

In sum, the ASEAN States that have been more critical of Myanmar's actions against the Rohingya, namely Indonesia, Malaysia, Brunei, and Singapore, are also the ones that have been more active in criticising the coup and the violence against civilians. By contrast, those who had defended Myanmar from the accusation of atrocity crimes against the Rohingya, namely Cambodia, Thailand, Vietnam, and the Philippines, are now supporting General Hlaing. ASEAN, on its part, has reached an important agreement on the 'Five-point Consensus', which lists the steps for the Junta to take in order to resolve the crisis. However, although this represents an important development, a closer examination of the language used has revealed that it has been carefully crafted to avoid forceful language against the Junta.

## 6.8 Conclusion

During the Rohingya crisis, ASEAN stood in solidarity with Myanmar. It avoided interfering in Myanmar's internal affairs and in no way did it attempt to violate Myanmar's sovereignty. Even after the UN Fact-Finding Mission concluded that crimes against humanity, war crimes, and genocide had been committed against the Rohingya, ASEAN remained largely supportive of Myanmar's handling of the crisis. Furthermore, it is telling that ASEAN accepted Myanmar's government practice of referring to the Rohingya as Bengali or as the Muslim minority in Rakhine State. Through its Summits, Meetings of Foreign Ministers and chairman's statements, ASEAN offered its assistance to Myanmar; however, these appeared to be weak promises lacking a genuine commitment to human protection. Strong, concrete forms of assistance were not considered, and no pressure was placed on Myanmar to accept or request external help.

This chapter also suggests that those ASEAN countries that were not directly affected by the spill-over effect of the Rohingya crisis and/or were mainly preoccupied with their own internal problems, for example, Thailand, Singapore,

Cambodia, the Philippines, and Laos, essentially supported the very weak approach chosen by ASEAN. However, as discussed in Chapter 4, these States (with the exception of Laos) have conceptually endorsed Pillar I and II of R2P, when faced with an atrocity crimes situation they ignored it and, instead, chose to act in solidarity with a fellow ASEAN member. This shows that their endorsements of R2P were merely political and that they were not willing to act on it.

By contrast, two ASEAN countries, namely Indonesia and Malaysia, took a much stronger stance on the crisis than ASEAN and other ASEAN States did. Although Indonesia chose a softer diplomatic route in its efforts to resolve this crisis, it referred, albeit indirectly to all three Pillars of R2P. It acknowledged that Myanmar had failed its Pillar I responsibilities; it has employed measures of Pillar II to assist Myanmar, but, at the same time, it warned that Pillar II tactics might not be sufficient; and called for action from the international community to help resolve this crisis. However, it did not specify what type of measure was needed.

The ASEAN State that acted the most unconventionally is Malaysia. Never before in ASEAN's history had a member spoken and acted so strongly against another. Not only has Malaysia spoken out harshly against Myanmar's government, but also actively called for decisive action against the perpetrators of the crimes against the Rohingya. Although it did not specifically refer to R2P, Malaysia has condemned Myanmar for failing its Pillar I responsibilities and acknowledged that while ASEAN and the UN offered their assistance (Pillar II), Myanmar has been unwilling to accept it. As a result, Malaysia has called for the international community to take action without actually using the words of R2P, although it did not specify what type of action it had in mind. This is extraordinary compared to its attitude during the East Timor crisis, where it repeatedly gave diplomatic support to Indonesia and only joined INTERFET after Indonesia had given its consent to the deployment of the force. Overall, the analysis in this chapter has suggested that R2P has not guided the way in which ASEAN and ASEAN States approached this humanitarian crisis.

## Notes

1 Multiple articles by both academics and non-academics have referred to this situation as the Rohingya crisis, including by Jobair Alam, 'The Current Rohingya Crisis in Myanmar in Historical Perspective' [2019] 39(1) *Journal of Muslim Minority Affairs*; Eleanor Albert and Lindsay Maizland, 'The Rohingya Crisis' (Council on Foreign Relations, 23 January 2020) <https://www.cfr.org/backgrounder/rohingya-crisis> accessed on 3 May 2021; and Reuters <https://www.reuters.com/article/us-myanmar-rohingya-timeline-idUSKBN25H03Y> accessed on 7 April 2021. Anthony Ware and Costas Laoutides, 'Myanmar's "Rohingya" Conflict: Misconceptions and Complexity' [2019] 50(1) *Asian Affairs*, p. 72.

2 Daniel Bar-Tal, *Intractable Conflicts: Socio-Psychological Foundations and Dynamics* (Cambridge University Press, 2013) p. 37.

3 Report of the International Independent Fact-Finding Mission on Myanmar (2018) A/HRC/39/64, (IV) 4(a).

4 Adam Bemma, 'Rohingya Refugee Voices Amplify Across Southeast Asia' (The Jakarta Post, 8 July 2019) <https://www.thejakartapost.com/life/2019/07/08/rohingya-refugee-voices-amplify-across-southeast-asia.html> accessed on 5 June 2020.

5 United Nations Human Rights Council, 'Report of the International Independent Fact-Finding Mission on Myanmar' (2018) A/HRC/39/64, Section VI.
6 Anthony Ware and Costas Laoutides, *Myanmar's 'Rohingya Conflict'* (Hurst & Company, 2018) pp. 78–79.
7 Jobair Alam, 'The Current Rohingya Crisis in Myanmar in Historical Perspective' [2019] 39(1) *Journal of Muslim Minority Affairs*, p. 3.
8 Martin Smith, 'The Muslim Rohingya of Burma' [1995] Conference Paper at the Burma Centrum Netherlands, p. 5 <http://www.netipr.org/policy/downloads/19951211-Rohingyas-of-Burma-by-Martin-Smith.pdf> accessed on 2 April 2021.
9 Jobair Alam, 'The Current Rohingya Crisis in Myanmar in Historical Perspective' [2019] 39(1) *Journal of Muslim Minority Affairs*, p. 3.
10 These Muslim minorities included the Rohingya and Indian Muslims.
11 Jobair Alam, 'The Current Rohingya Crisis in Myanmar in Historical Perspective' [2019] 39(1) *Journal of Muslim Minority Affairs*, p. 6.
12 Anthony Ware and Costas Laoutides, *Myanmar's 'Rohingya Conflict'* (Hurst & Company, 2018), p. 14.
13 A.F.K Jilani, *A Cultural History of Rohingya* (Dhaka: Ahmed Jilani, 2001) p. 89.
14 Ibid.
15 Jobair Alam, 'The Current Rohingya Crisis in Myanmar in Historical Perspective' [2019] 39(1) *Journal of Muslim Minority Affairs*, p. 5.
16 Anthony Ware and Costas Laoutides, *Myanmar's 'Rohingya Conflict'* (Hurst & Company, 2018), p. 101.
17 Ibid., pp. 94 and 101.
18 Jobair Alam, 'The Current Rohingya Crisis in Myanmar in Historical Perspective' [2019] 39(1) *Journal of Muslim Minority Affairs*, p. 8.
19 The Constitution of the Union of Burma, 1947, Chapter II, Section 11 (iii) <https://www.ilo.org/dyn/natlex/docs/ELECTRONIC/79573/85699/F1436085708/MMR79573.pdf> accessed on 3 May 2021.
20 Ibid., Section 11 (iv).
21 Ibid., Section 10.
22 Jobair Alam, 'The Current Rohingya Crisis in Myanmar in Historical Perspective' [2019] 39(1) *Journal of Muslim Minority Affairs*, p. 8; and refer to the footnote in the article.
23 Anthony Ware and Costas Laoutides, *Myanmar's 'Rohingya Conflict'* (Hurst & Company, 2018) p. 103; and Nick Cheesman, 'How in Myanmar "National Races" Came to Surpass Citizenship and Exclude Rohingya' [2017] 47(3) *Journal of Contemporary Asia*, p. 466.
24 Ibid., p. 118; and Ibid., p. 465.
25 Anthony Ware and Costas Laoutides, *Myanmar's 'Rohingya Conflict'* (Hurst & Company, 2018) p. 22.
26 Nick Cheesman, 'How in Myanmar "National Races" Came to Surpass Citizenship and Exclude Rohingya' [2017] 47(3) *Journal of Contemporary Asia*, p. 467.
27 Anthony Ware and Costas Laoutides, *Myanmar's 'Rohingya Conflict'* (Hurst & Company, 2018) p. 124.
28 Ibid., p. 125; and Eleanor Albert and Lindsay Maizland, 'The Rohingya Crisis' (Council on Foreign Relations, 23 January 2020) <https://www.cfr.org/backgrounder/rohingya-crisis> accessed on 3 May 2021.
29 Anthony Ware and Costas Laoutides, *Myanmar's 'Rohingya Conflict'* (Hurst & Company, 2018) p. 16.
30 Martin Smith, 'The Muslim Rohingya of Burma' [1995] Conference Paper at the Burma Centrum Netherlands, pp. 9–10 <http://www.netipr.org/policy/downloads/19951211-Rohingyas-of-Burma-by-Martin-Smith.pdf> accessed on 2 April 2021.
31 Ibid.
32 Jobair Alam, 'The Current Rohingya Crisis in Myanmar in Historical Perspective' [2019] 39(1) *Journal of Muslim Minority Affairs*, pp. 8–9.

33 Burma Citizenship Law (1982), Chapter VI <https://www.refworld.org/docid/3ae6b4f71b.html> accessed on 5 May 2021.
34 Ibid., Chapter II, Section3.
35 Ibid., Chapter III.
36 Amnesty International, 'Myanmar: The Rohingya Minority: Fundamental Rights Denied' (2004) ASA 16/005/2004, p. 9 <https://www.amnesty.org/download/Documents/92000/asa160052004en.pdf> accessed on 8 April 2021.
37 Md. Mahbubul Haque, 'Rohingya Ethnic Muslim Minority and the 1982 Citizenship Law in Burma' [2017] 37(4) *Journal of Muslim Minority Affairs*, p. 458.
38 Burma Citizenship Law (1982), Chapter IV, Section 44 <http://un-act.org/publication/view/myanmars-citizenship-law-1982/> accessed on 15 May 2020.
39 Md. Mahbubul Haque, 'Rohingya Ethnic Muslim Minority and the 1982 Citizenship Law in Burma' [2017] 37(4) *Journal of Muslim Minority Affairs*, p. 458.
40 Ibid.
41 Human Rights Watch, '"The Government Could Have Stopped This": Sectarian Violence and Ensuing Abuses in Burma's Arakan State' [2012] p. 18.
42 'Bengali' is used by the Burmese majority as a derogatory term to refer to the Rohingya as illegal immigrants; see Flavia Krause-Jackson and Daniel Ten Kate, 'Myanmar Rape-Murder Sparks Outrage Over Abuse of Muslims' (Bloomberg, 31 August 2012) <https://www.bloomberg.com/news/articles/2012-08-31/myanmar-rape-murder-sparks-outrage-over-abuse-of-muslims> accessed on 2 April 2021; and Shafiur Rahman, 'Myanmar's "Rohingya" vs "Bengali" Hate Speech Debate (The Diplomat, 21 December 2019) <https://thediplomat.com/2019/12/myanmars-rohingya-vs-bengali-hate-speech-debate/> accessed on 2 April 2021.
43 Human Rights Watch, '"The Government Could Have Stopped This": Sectarian Violence and Ensuing Abuses in Burma's Arakan State' [2012] p. 18.
44 'Final Report of Inquiry Commission on Sectarian Violence in Rakhine State' (Republic of the Union of Myanmar, 8 July 2013), p. 9 <https://www.burmalibrary.org/docs15/Rakhine_Commission_Report-en-red.pdf> accessed on 3 May 2021.
45 Ibid., p. 19.
46 Ibid., p. 20; With 66 deaths, 72 injured and 4,188 homes destroyed in the Rohingya community compared to 32 deaths, 51 injured and 1,150 homes destroyed in the ethnic Rakhine community.
47 Also, through this wave of atrocities, Thein Sein's government refused to acknowledge the Rohingya as *taing-yin-tha*; see Human Rights Watch, 'Burma: Government Forces Targeting Rohingya Muslims' (Human Rights Watch, 31 July 2012) <https://www.hrw.org/news/2012/07/31/burma-government-forces-targeting-rohingya-muslim s> accessed on 17 April 2021.
48 'Disenfranchisement and Desperation in Myanmar's Rakhine State: Drivers of a Regional Crisis' (ASEAN Parliamentarians for Human Rights, October 2015) pp. 3 and 7 <https://reliefweb.int/sites/reliefweb.int/files/resources/APHR_Rakhine-State-Report.pdf> accessed on 2 April 2021.
49 Ibid., pp. 14–15.
50 Ibid., p. 7.
51 'Myanmar: A New Muslim Insurgency in Rakhine State' [2016] 283 *International Crisis Group, Asia Group Report*, p. 6.
52 Ibid., p. 14.
53 Ibid., p. 6.
54 Anthony Ware & Costas Laoutides, *Myanmar's 'Rohingya Conflict'* (Hurst & Company, 2018) p. 50.
55 Ibid.
56 'Myanmar: A New Muslim Insurgency in Rakhine State' [2016] 283 *International Crisis Group, Asia Group Report*, p. 14.

57 Ibid., p. 6.
58 Ibid.
59 Adam Withnall, 'Burma: 21,000 Rohingya Muslims Flee to Bangladesh amid "Attempted Genocide"' (The Independent, 6 December 2016) <https://www.independent.co.uk/news/world/asia/burma-21000-rohingya-muslims-flee-bangladesh-attempted-genocide-a7458091.html> accessed on 2 April 2021.
60 'Myanmar: A New Muslim Insurgency in Rakhine State' [2016] 283 *International Crisis Group, Asia Group Report*, p. 8.
61 Ibid., p. 10.
62 Statement by Statement by Ambassador U Hau Do Suan, Permanent Representative of Myanmar to the United Nations at the United Nations High-level Conference of Heads of Counter-Terrorism Agencies of Member States (28–29 June 2018) <https://www.un.org/counterterrorism/ctitf/sites/www.un.org.counterterrorism.ctitf/files/S2-Myanmar.pdf> accessed on 18 March 2021.
63 Marlise Simons and Hannah Beech, 'Aung San Suu Kyi Defends Myanmar Against Rohingya Genocide Accusations' (The New York Times, 23 January 2020) <https://www.nytimes.com/2019/12/11/world/asia/aung-san-suu-kyi-rohingya-myanmar-genocide-hague.html> accessed on 18 March 2021.
64 '"Hundreds of Rohingyas" Killed in Myanmar Crackdown' (Al Jazeera, 3 February 2017) <https://www.aljazeera.com/news/2017/02/rohingyas-killed-myanmar-crackdown-170203101817841.html> accessed on 18 March 2021.
65 United Nations Human Rights Council, 'Report of the International Independent Fact-Finding Mission on Myanmar' (2018) A/HRC/39/64, Section VI.
66 Ibid.
67 The United Nations Human Rights Council Resolution 34/22 (2017), A/HRC/RES/34/22, p. 11.
68 The United Nations Human Rights Council Resolution S-27/1 (2017), A/HRC/RES/S-27/1, p. 2.
69 The United Nations Human Rights Council Resolution 34/22 (2017), A/HRC/RES/34/22, p. 2; and The United Nations Human Rights Council Resolution S-27/1 (2017), A/HRC/RES/S-27/1, p. 1.
70 The United Nations General Assembly Resolution 72/248 (2017), A/RES/72/248, pp. 2–3.
71 Ibid., pp. 1(n) and 3.
72 The United Nations General Assembly Resolution 73/264 (2018), A/RES/73/264, pp. 2 and 4.
73 The United Nations General Assembly Resolution 74/246 (2019), A/RES/74/246, p. 8.
74 Statement by the President of the Security Council (2017) S/PRST/2017/22 <https://www.securitycouncilreport.org/atf/cf/%7B65BFCF9B-6D27-4E9C-8CD3-CF6E4FF96FF9%7D/s_prst_2017_22.pdf> accessed on 18 March 2021.
75 Ibid.
76 Ibid.
77 The United Nations Security Council Resolution 2669 (2022), S/RES/2669.
78 Ibid.
79 'China, Russia Block U.N Council Concern about Myanmar Violence' (Reuters, 17 March2017)<https://www.reuters.com/article/us-myanmar-rohingya-un-idUSKBN16O2J6> accessed on 2 April 2021.
80 Mauro Barelli, 'Preventing and Responding to Atrocity Crimes: China, Sovereignty and the Responsibility to Protect' [2018] 23(2) *Journal of Conflict & Security Law*, pp. 177 and 197.
81 Among other things, China became a signatory of the Treaty of Amity and Cooperation in Southeast Asia (TAC) in 2003; 'Accession to the Treaty of Amity and Cooperation in Southeast Asia by China' (ASEAN, 1 October 2003) <https://asean.org/

accession-to-the-treaty-of-amity-and-cooperation-in-southeast-asia-by-china/> accessed on 8 April 2021.

82 Organisation of Islamic Cooperation <https://www.oic-oci.org/page/?p_id=52&p_ref=26&lan=en> accessed on 2 April 2021.

83 Organisation of Islamic Cooperation, Declaration of the Contact Group on Rohingya Muslims of Myanmar (2017) Section 2 <https://www.oic-oci.org/upload/documents/acm_2017_rohingya_rep_en.pdf> accessed on 2 April 2021; and Organisation of Islamic Cooperation Resolutions on Muslim Communities and Muslim Minorities in the Non-OIC Member States Adopted to the 45th Session of the Council of Foreign Ministers (2018) Resolution No.4/45-MM, p. 14.

84 Organisation of Islamic Cooperation, Declaration of the Contact Group on Rohingya Muslims of Myanmar (2017) Section 5 <https://www.oic-oci.org/upload/documents/acm_2017_rohingya_rep_en.pdf> accessed on 2 April 2021.

85 Ibid., Section 21.

86 The Organisation of Islamic Cooperation Resolutions on Muslim Communities and Muslim Minorities in the Non-OIC Member States Adopted to the 45th Session of the Council of Foreign Ministers (2018) Resolution No.4/45-MM, p. 15.

87 'Questions and Answers on Gambia's Genocide Case Against Myanmar before the International Court of Justice' (Human Rights Watch, 5 December 2019) <https://www.hrw.org/news/2019/12/05/questions-and-answers-gambias-genocide-case-against-myanmar-international-court> accessed on 18 March 2021.

88 The United Nations General Assembly (2023), Seventy-eighth session Third Committee, 'Situation of Rohingya Muslims and other minorities in Myanmar' A/C.3/78/L.40/Rev.1.

89 For example, the 2018 Report of the Independent International Fact-Finding Mission on Myanmar urged ASEAN to develop strategies to ensure the accountabilities for perpetrators of the crimes committed amongst other suggestions; see United Nations Human Rights Council, Report of the international independent fact-finding mission on Myanmar (2018) A/HRC/39/64, Section IX (115).

90 'Statement of ASEAN Foreign Ministers on the Recent Developments in the Rakhine State, Myanmar' (2012) <https://www.asean.org/wp-content/uploads/images/archive/documents/Statement%20of%20ASEAN%20FM%20on%20Recent%20Developments%20in%20the%20Rakhine%20State.pdf> accessed on 2 April 2021; and Chairman's Statement of the 21st ASEAN Summit (2012) para 55 <https://www.asean.org/wp-content/uploads/images/documents/Chairman's%20Statement%20of%20the%2021st%20ASEAN%20Summit.pdf> accessed on 2 April 2021.

91 Chairman's Statement of the 30th ASEAN Summit (2017) para 30 <https://asean.org/wp-content/uploads/2017/04/Chairs-Statement-of-30th-ASEAN-Summit_FINAL.pdf> accessed on 2 April 2021.

92 Ibid., paras 18 and 19.

93 For example, on 5 August 2017, the Joint Communique of the 50th ASEAN Foreign Ministers' Meeting (AMM), simply referred to a commitment to address the 'influx of irregular movement of persons in Southeast Asia' without actually discussing the atrocities in Rakhine State; see Joint Communique of the 50th ASEAN Foreign Ministers' Meeting, 'Partnering for Change, Engaging the World' Para 34 <https://asean.org/storage/2017/08/Joint-Communique-of-the-50th-AMM_FINAL.pdf> accessed on 17 April 2021.

94 ASEAN Chairman's Statement on the Humanitarian Situation in Rakhine State (2017) <https://asean.org/wp-content/uploads/2017/09/1.ASEAN-Chairmans-Statement-on-the-Rakhine.pdf> accessed on 2 April 2021.

95 Ibid.

96 Ibid.

97 Chairman's Statement of the 32nd ASEAN Summit (2018), para 17 <https://asean.org/wp-content/uploads/2018/04/Chairmans-Statement-of-the-32nd-ASEAN-Summit.pdf> accessed on 2 April 2021; and Chairman's Statement of the 33rd ASEAN Summit (2018) para 37 <https://asean.org/storage/2018/11/33rd_ASEAN_Summit_Chairman_s_Statement_Final.pdf> accessed on 2 April 2021.

98 Chairman's Statement of the 34th ASEAN Summit (2019), para 43 <https://asean.org/storage/2019/06/Final_Chairs-Statement-of-the-34th-ASEAN-Summit-rev.pdf> accessed on 2 April 2021; and Chairman's Statement of the 35th ASEAN Summit (2019), para 37–38 <https://asean.org/storage/2019/11/Chairs-Statement-of-the-35th-ASEAN-Summit-FINAL.pdf> accessed on 2 April 2021.

99 Chairman's Statement on the 36th ASEAN Summit (2020), para 54 <https://asean.org/storage/2020/06/Chairman-Statement-of-the-36th-ASEAN-Summit-FINAL.pdf> accessed on 4 April 2021; and Chairman's Statement on the 37th ASEAN Summit (2020), para 75 <https://asean.org/storage/43-Chairmans-Statement-of-37th-ASEAN-Summit-FINAL.pdf> accessed on 4 April 2021.

100 Chairman's Statement on the 38th and 39th ASEAN Summit (2021), para 85 <https://asean.org/chairmans-statement-of-the-38th-and-39th-asean-summits/> accessed on 27 February 2024.

101 Chairman's Statement on the 40th and 41st ASEAN Summit (2022), paras 87–88 <https://asean.org/wp-content/uploads/2022/11/01-Chairmans-Statement-of-the-40th-and-41st-ASEAN-Summits-rev.pdf> accessed on 27 February 2024.

102 Chairman's Statement on the 42nd and 43rd ASEAN Summit (2023), paras 111 and 134–135 <https://asean.org/chairmans-statement-of-the-42nd-asean-summit/> and <https://asean.org/wp-content/uploads/2023/09/CHAIRMAN-STATEMENT-OF-THE-43RD-ASEAN-SUMMIT-FIN-2.pdf> accessed on 27 February 2024.

103 Joint Communique of the 51st ASEAN Foreign Ministers' Meeting (2018) para 56 <https://asean.org/wp-content/uploads/2018/08/51st-AMM-Joint-Communique-Final.pdf> accessed on 2 April 2021.

104 Joint Communiqué of the 52nd ASEAN Foreign Ministers' Meeting (2019), para 63–64 <https://asean.org/storage/2019/07/CIRCULATE-Joint-Communique-of-the-52nd-AMM-FINAL.pdf> accessed on 4 April 2021.

105 Joint Communiqué of the 53rd ASEAN Foreign Ministers Meeting (2020), para 78–79 <https://asean.org/storage/2020/09/FINAL-Joint-Communique-of-the-53rd-AMM.pdf> accessed on 4 April 2021.

106 Joint Communiqué of the 54th ASEAN Foreign Ministers Meeting (2021), para 74 <https://asean.org/wp-content/uploads/2021/08/Joint-Communique-of-the-54th-ASEAN-Foreign-Ministers-Meeting-FINAL.pdf> accessed on 27 February 2024.

107 Joint Communiqué of the 55th ASEAN Foreign Ministers Meeting (2022), para 96 <https://asean.org/wp-content/uploads/2022/08/Joint_Communique-of-the-55th-AMM-FINAL.pdf> accessed on 27 February 2024.

108 Joint Communiqué of the 56th ASEAN Foreign Ministers Meeting (2022), para 116 <https://asean.org/wp-content/uploads/2023/07/The-56th-AMM-Joint-Communique.pdf> accessed on 27 February 2024.

109 'Malaysian PM Urges World to Act Against "Genocide" of Myanmar's Rohingya' (The Guardian, 4 December 2016) <https://www.theguardian.com/world/2016/dec/04/malaysia-pm-urges-world-to-act-against-genocide-of-myanmars-rohingya> accessed on 4 April 2021.

110 Ibid.

111 Praveen Menon, 'Malaysia PM Opens Thorny Debate in Accusing Myanmar of Genocide' (Reuters, 9 December 2016) <https://www.reuters.com/article/us-myanmar-rohingya-malaysia/malaysia-pm-opens-thorny-debate-in-accusing-myanmar-of-genocide-idUSKBN13Y0IY> accessed on 4 April 2021.

112 Organization of Islamic Cooperation, Resolution on the Situation of the Rohingya Muslim Minority in Myanmar Present to the Extraordinary Session of the OIC Council of Foreign Ministers on the Situation of the Rohingya Muslim in Myanmar (2017) <https://www.oic-oci.org/docdown/?docID=574&refID=64> accessed on 18 March 2021.

113 Statement by the Malaysian Minister of Foreign Affairs at the OIC Contact Group on the Rohingya Muslim Minority in Myanmar (19 September 2017) <https://www.kln.gov.my/web/nam_windhoek/news-from-mission/-/blogs/statement-by-

the-minister-of-foreign-affairs-at-the-oic-contact-group-on-the-rohingya-muslim-minority-in-myanmar-new-york-19-september-2017> accessed on 18 March 2021.

114 Ibid.

115 'Malaysia's Dissent on Myanmar Statement Reveals Cracks in ASEAN Façade' (Reuters, 25 September 2017) <https://www.reuters.com/article/us-myanmar-rohingya-malaysia-idUSKCN1C0124> accessed on 4 April 2021.

116 Ibid.

117 The United Nations General Assembly Voting Record on Resolution 72/248 (2017) <https://digitallibrary.un.org/record/1470211?ln=en> accessed on 4 April 2021; Resolution 73/264 (2018) <https://digitallibrary.un.org/record/1657120?ln=en> accessed on 4 April 2021; and Resolution 74/246 (2019) <https://digitallibrary.un.org/record/3841021?ln=en> accessed on 4 April 2021.

118 '"Genocide": Malaysian PM Mahathir Urges International Community to Act on Rohingya Issue' (Channel News Asia, 25 September 2019) <https://www.channelnewsasia.com/news/asia/malaysia-mahathir-rohingya-urges-world-to-act-united-nations-11940210> accessed on 18 March 2021.

119 Refer to Chapter 4 for a detailed analysis on Malaysia's position on R2P.

120 'Indonesia Calls for Independent Probe' (The Irrawaddy, 7 August 2012) <https://www.irrawaddy.com/news/burma/indonesia-calls-for-independent-rohingya-probe.html> accessed on 24 April 2021.

121 Ibid.

122 'Indonesian Minister to Raise Rohingya Plight with Suu Kyi' (AP News, 3 September 2017) <https://apnews.com/article/e9c79d7ae7ce4e7ab102dedf8e26e4ae> accessed on 4 April 2021.

123 'Foreign Affairs Minister Meets with Aung San Suu Kyi to Discuss Rakhine Humanitarian Crisis' (Cabinet Secretariat of the Republic of Indonesia, 4 September 2017) <https://setkab.go.id/en/foreign-affairs-minister-meets-with-aung-san-suu-kyi-to-discuss-rakhine-humanitarian-crisis/> accessed on 23 April 2021.

124 Ibid.

125 Ibid.

126 Sheany, 'Indonesia Urges OIC, International Community, to Address Myanmar Conflict' (Jakarta Globe, 11 September 2017) <https://jakartaglobe.id/news/indonesia-urges-oic-international-community-address-myanmar-conflict/> accessed on 24 April 2021.

127 The United Nations General Assembly Voting Record on UNHRC Resolution S-27/1 (2017), p. 6; GA Resolution 72/248 (2017) <https://digitallibrary.un.org/record/1470211?ln=en> accessed on 4 April 2021; Resolution 73/264 (2018) <https://digitallibrary.un.org/record/1657120?ln=en> accessed on 4 April 2021; and Resolution 74/246 (2019) <https://digitallibrary.un.org/record/3841021?ln=en> accessed on 4 April 2021.

128 Anbar Jayadi, 'With a Seat on the UN Security Council, What Can Key ASEAN Member Indonesia Do to Solve the Rohingya Crisis?' (The Conversation, 24 September 2018) <https://theconversation.com/with-a-seat-on-the-un-security-council-what-can-key-asean-member-indonesia-do-to-solve-the-rohingya-crisis-102915> accessed on 18 March 2021.

129 Dio Herdiawan Tobing, 'Will Indonesia Bring the Rohingya Issue to UN Security Council? Jakarta Post Contributor' (The Strait Times, 25 June 2018) <https://www.straitstimes.com/asia/se-asia/will-indonesia-bring-the-rohingya-issue-to-un-security-council-jakarta-post-contributor> accessed on 18 March 2021.

130 Mohamad Rosyidin, 'Reconciling State's Sovereignty with Global Norms: Indonesia's Quite Diplomacy in Myanmar and the Feasibility of the Implementation of Responsibility to Protect (R2P) in Southeast Asia' [2020] 12(1) (Special Issue) *Global Responsibility to Protect*, p. 31.

131 Ibid., p. 34.
132 The United Nations General Assembly Voting Record on Resolution 72/248 (2017) <https://digitallibrary.un.org/record/1470211?ln=en> accessed on 4 April 2021; Resolution 73/264 (2018) <https://digitallibrary.un.org/record/1657120?ln=en> accessed on 4 April 2021; and Resolution 74/246 (2019) <https://digitallibrary.un.org/record/3841021?ln=en> accessed on 4 April 2021.
133 'Singapore Urges Calm from All Sides in Myanmar Conflict, Offers to Work with ASEAN to Provide Humanitarian Aid' (The Straits Times, 8 September 2017) <https://www.straitstimes.com/singapore/singapore-says-ready-to-work-with-myanmar-to-restore-peace-and-stability-in-rakhine-state> accessed on 18 March 2021.
134 ASEAN Chairman's Statement on the Humanitarian Situation in Rakhine State (2017) <https://asean.org/wp-content/uploads/2017/09/1.ASEAN-Chairmans-Statement-on-the-Rakhine.pdf> accessed on 2 April 2021.
135 'Singapore Urges Calm from All Sides in Myanmar Conflict, Offers to Work with ASEAN to Provide Humanitarian Aid' (The Straits Times, 8 September 2017) <https://www.straitstimes.com/singapore/singapore-says-ready-to-work-with-myanmar-to-restore-peace-and-stability-in-rakhine-state> accessed on 18 March 2021.
136 Lydia Lam, 'Singapore Pledges $100,000 in Humanitarian Aid to Help in Myanmar's Rakhine Crisis' (The Straits Times, 19 October 2017) <https://www.straitstimes.com/singapore/singapore-pledges-100000-in-humanitarian-aid-to-help-in-myanmars-rakhine-crisis> accessed on 18 March 2021.
137 The United Nations General Assembly Voting Record on Resolution 72/248 (2017) <https://digitallibrary.un.org/record/1470211?ln=en> accessed on 4 April 2021; Resolution 73/264 (2018) <https://digitallibrary.un.org/record/1657120?ln=en> accessed on 4 April 2021; and Resolution 74/246 (2019) <https://digitallibrary.un.org/record/3841021?ln=en> accessed on 4 April 2021.
138 'Thailand "Run Against Dictatorship" Draws Thousands' (The BBC, 12 January 2020) <https://www.bbc.co.uk/news/world-asia-51082419> accessed on 18 March 2021.
139 'Thailand Says Closely Watching Myanmar Crisis, Ready to Provide Aid' (Reuters, 1 October 2017) <https://www.reuters.com/article/us-thailand-myanmar-rohingya/thailand-says-closely-watching-myanmar-crisis-ready-to-provide-aid-idUSKCN1C60XN> accessed on 18 March 2021.
140 Refer to Chapter 5 for a detailed analysis of the East Timor Crisis.
141 'Thailand Says Closely Watching Myanmar Crisis, Ready to Provide Aid' (Reuters, 1 October 2017) <https://www.reuters.com/article/us-thailand-myanmar-rohingya/thailand-says-closely-watching-myanmar-crisis-ready-to-provide-aid-idUSKCN1C60XN> accessed on 18 March 2021.
142 The United Nations General Assembly Voting Record on Resolution 72/248 (2017) <https://digitallibrary.un.org/record/1470211?ln=en> accessed on 4 April 2021; Resolution 73/264 (2018) <https://digitallibrary.un.org/record/1657120?ln=en> accessed on 4 April 2021; and Resolution 74/246 (2019) <https://digitallibrary.un.org/record/3841021?ln=en> accessed on 4 April 2021.
143 Sao Phal Niseiy, 'Cambodia's Prime Minister Is Wrong about Myanmar's Rohingya Issue' (The Diplomat, 9 February 2017) <https://thediplomat.com/2017/02/cambodias-prime-minister-is-wrong-about-myanmars-rohingya-issue/> accessed on 18 March 2021.
144 Ibid.
145 The United Nations General Assembly Voting Record on Resolution 72/248 (2017) <https://digitallibrary.un.org/record/1470211?ln=en> accessed on 4 April 2021; Resolution 73/264 (2018) <https://digitallibrary.un.org/record/1657120?ln=en> accessed on 4 April 2021; and Resolution 74/246 (2019) <https://digitallibrary.un.org/record/3841021?ln=en> accessed on 4 April 2021.
146 Khuon Narim, 'Cambodia, Myanmar discuss Rohingya refugees' (Khmer Times, 11 September 2019) <https://www.khmertimeskh.com/642106/cambodia-myanmar-discuss-rohingya-refugees/> accessed on 18 March 2021.

147 Ibid.
148 Detailed Conference Report on 'The Responsibility to Protect at 10: Progress, Challenges and Opportunities in the Asia Pacific' (2015), p. 9 <https://r2pasiapacific.org/files/2823/r2p_at_10_conference_detailedreport.pdf> accessed on 3 May 2021.
149 The United Nations General Assembly Voting Record on Resolution 72/248 (2017) <https://digitallibrary.un.org/record/1470211?ln=en> accessed on 4 April 2021; Resolution 73/264 (2018) <https://digitallibrary.un.org/record/1657120?ln=en> accessed on 4 April 2021; and Resolution 74/246 (2019) <https://digitallibrary.un.org/record/3841021?ln=en> accessed on 4 April 2021.
150 Ibid.
151 'UN Fails to Take Action on Order Against Myanmar on Rohingya' (Aljazeera, 5 February 2020) <https://www.aljazeera.com/news/2020/2/5/un-fails-to-take-action-on-order-against-myanmar-on-rohingya> accessed on 5 April 2021.
152 Ibid.
153 '"Philippines" Duterte Cites "Genocide" in Myanmar, Says Will Take Refugee' (The Straits Time, 5 April 2018) <https://www.straitstimes.com/asia/se-asia/philippines-duterte-cites-genocide-in-myanmar-says-will-take-refugees> accessed on 18 March 2021.
154 '"Philippines" Duterte Apologizes to Suu Kyi for Myanmar "Genocide" Remark' (Reuters, 13 April 2018) <https://www.reuters.com/article/us-philippines-duterte-myanmar-idUSKBN1HK0HJ> accessed on 17 April 2021.
155 Ibid.
156 The United Nations General Assembly Voting Record on UNHRC Resolution S-27/1 (2017), p. 6; GA Resolution 72/248 (2017) <https://digitallibrary.un.org/record/1470211?ln=en> accessed on 4 April 2021; Resolution 73/264 (2018) <https://digitallibrary.un.org/record/1657120?ln=en> accessed on 4 April 2021; and Resolution 74/246 (2019) <https://digitallibrary.un.org/record/3841021?ln=en> accessed on 4 April 2021.
157 'Myanmar Coup: Aung San Suu Kyi Detailed as Military Seizes Control' (BBC, 1 February 2021) <https://www.bbc.co.uk/news/world-asia-55882489> accessed on 4 April 2021.
158 'Myanmar Coup Leader Defends Action Amid Mass Protests' (BBC, 8 February 2021) <https://www.bbc.co.uk/news/world-asia-55975746> accessed on 5 April 2021.
159 'Myanmar Coup: The People Shot Dead Since the Protests Began' (BBC, 13 April 2021) <https://www.bbc.co.uk/news/world-asia-56636345> accessed on 17 April 2021.
160 United Nations Human Rights Council, 'Report of the International Independent Fact-Finding Mission on Myanmar' (2018) A/HRC/39/64, Section VII (92).
161 Gareth Evans, 'The Responsibility to Protect the People of Myanmar' (Australian Institute of International Affairs, 8 April 2021) <https://www.internationalaffairs.org.au/australianoutlook/the-responsibility-to-protect-the-people-of-myanmar/> accessed on 10 April 2021.
162 Ibid. For a similar view, see Simon Adams, 'Myanmar's Deadly Coup and the Responsibility to Protect' (Global Centre for the Responsibility to Protect, 25 March 2021) <https://www.globalr2p.org/publications/myanmars-deadly-coup-and-the-responsibility-to-protect/> accessed on 10 April 2021.
163 Statement by the President of Security Council (2021), S/PRST/2021/5 <https://www.securitycouncilreport.org/atf/cf/%7B65BFCF9B-6D27-4E9C-8CD3-CF6E4FF96FF9%7D/s_prst_2021_5.pdf> accessed on 5 April 2021; SC/14697 <https://press.un.org/en/2021/sc14697.doc.htm> accessed on 27 February 2024.
164 'Global Condemnation Follows Bloodiest Day Since Myanmar Coup' (Bangkok Post, 28 March 2021) <https://www.bangkokpost.com/world/2090927/global-condemnation-follows-bloodiest-day-since-myanmar-coup> accessed on 5 April 2021.
165 The United Nations Security Council Resolution 2669 (2022), S/RES/2669.
166 Chair's Statement on the Informal Ministerial Meeting (IAMM) (2021) <http://www.asean2021.bn/Theme/news/iamm-02.03.21.aspx> accessed on 4 April 2021.

167 The ASEAN Charter (2007), Article 7.
168 Chairman's Statement on the ASEAN Leaders' Meeting (2021) pp. 3–4 <https://asean.org/storage/Chairmans-Statement-on-ALM-Five-Point-Consensus-24-April-2021-FINAL-a-1.pdf> accessed on 26 April 2021.
169 Ibid., p. 4.
170 'ASEAN Demands "Immediate Cessation of Violence" in Myanmar' (Aljazeera, 24 April 2021) <https://www.aljazeera.com/news/2021/4/24/myanmar-coup-leader-in-jakarta-for-southeast-asian-summit> accessed on 26 April 2021.
171 'ASEAN Summit Begins Without Myanmar After Top General Barred' (Aljazeera, 26 October 2021) <https://www.aljazeera.com/news/2021/10/26/asean-summit-begins-without-myanmar-after-top-generals-exclusion#:~:text=Myanmar%20not%20at%20ASEAN%20summit,end%20violence%20in%20the%20country.&text=Southeast%20Asian%20leaders%20have%20begun,exclusion%20of%20its%20top%20general.> accessed on 27 February 2024; 'Southeast Asian Leaders Struggle with Myanmar Crisis at Summit' (Aljazeera, 11 November 2022) <https://www.aljazeera.com/news/2022/11/11/southeast-asia-leaders-struggle-with-myanmar-crisis-at-summit> accessed on 27 February 2024; and Goh Chiew Tong, 'ASEAN Is "At a Loss for Ideas" on How to Address Myanmar Crisis, Says Indonesia's Ex Foreign Minister (CNBC, 5 September 2023) <https://www.cnbc.com/2023/09/05/asean-at-a-loss-for-ideas-on-myanmar-crisis-ex-indonesian-minister.html> accessed on 27 February 2024.
172 'Myanmar Will Not Be Allowed ASEAN Leadership in 2026' (Aljazeera, 5 September 2023) <https://www.aljazeera.com/news/2023/9/5/myanmar-will-not-be-allowed-asean-leadership-in-2026> accessed on 27 February 2024.
173 'Indonesia, Malaysia Seeking ASEAN Meeting on Myanmar after Coup' (Bangkok Post, 5 February 2021) <https://www.bangkokpost.com/world/2063259/indonesia-malaysia-seeking-asean-meeting-on-myanmar-after-coup> accessed on 4 April 2021.
174 Sebastian Strangio, 'ASEAN Foreign Ministers Meet to Discuss Myanmar Crisis' (The Diplomate, 3 March 2021) <https://thediplomat.com/2021/03/asean-foreign-ministers-meet-to-discuss-myanmar-crisis/> accessed on 4 April 2021.
175 Sebastian Strangio, 'Singapore Joins Calls for Emergency ASEAN Summit on Myanmar' (The Diplomat, 26 March 2021) <https://thediplomat.com/2021/03/singapore-joins-calls-for-emergency-asean-summit-on-myanmar/> accessed on 5 April 2021.
176 'Malaysia PM Backs Indonesia's Call for ASEAN Summit on Myanmar' (Bangkok Post, 20 March 2021) <https://www.bangkokpost.com/world/2086847/malaysia-pm-backs-indonesias-call-for-asean-summit-on-myanmar> accessed on 4 April 2021.
177 Niniek Karmini, 'ASEAN Leaders Tell Myanmar Coup General to End Killings' (AP News, 25 April 2021) <https://apnews.com/article/aung-san-suu-kyi-global-trade-indonesia-myanmar-singapore-2959338f61cbe0b0b7c6dd7599ee6e2c> accessed on 26 April 2021.
178 'Indonesia Says "Positive" Signs from Myanmar's Warring Camp on Dialogue Effort (Reuters, 24 November 2023) <https://www.reuters.com/world/asia-pacific/indonesia-says-positive-signs-myanmars-warring-camps-dialogue-effort-2023-11-24/> accessed on 27 February 2024.
179 Sebastian Strangio, 'ASEAN Foreign Ministers Meet to Discuss Myanmar Crisis' (The Diplomate, 3 March 2021) <https://thediplomat.com/2021/03/asean-foreign-ministers-meet-to-discuss-myanmar-crisis/> accessed on 4 April 2021.
180 'Malaysia PM Backs Indonesia's Call for ASEAN Summit on Myanmar' (Bangkok Post, 20 March 2021) <https://www.bangkokpost.com/world/2086847/malaysia-pm-backs-indonesias-call-for-asean-summit-on-myanmar> accessed on 4 April 2021.
181 Ibid.
182 Ibid.
183 'Malaysia Calls for "Strong" Measures on Myanmar as ASEAN Meets' (Aljazeera, 5 September 2023) <https://www.aljazeera.com/news/2023/9/5/malaysia-calls-for-strong-measures-on-myanmar-as-asean-meets#:~:text=Senior%20General%20Min%20

Aung%20Hlaing,ASEAN%20summit%20two%20months%20later.> accessed on 27 February 2024.
184 Sebastian Strangio, 'ASEAN Foreign Ministers Meet to Discuss Myanmar Crisis' (The Diplomate, 3 March 2021) <https://thediplomat.com/2021/03/asean-foreign-ministers-meet-to-discuss-myanmar-crisis/> accessed on 4 April 2021.
185 Sebastian Strangio, 'Singapore Joins Calls for Emergency ASEAN Summit on Myanmar' (The Diplomat, 26 March 2021) <https://thediplomat.com/2021/03/singapore-joins-calls-for-emergency-asean-summit-on-myanmar/> accessed on 5 April 2021.
186 Ibid.
187 'ASEAN Demands 'Immediate Cessation of Violence' in Myanmar' (Aljazeera, 24 April 2021) <https://www.aljazeera.com/news/2021/4/24/myanmar-coup-leader-in-jakarta-for-southeast-asian-summit> accessed on 26 April 2021.
188 'Myanmar: Army General Behind Coup "Agrees Violence Must Stop" After Regional Leaders Summit' (Sky News, 24 April 2021) <https://news.sky.com/story/general-behind-myanmar-coup-agrees-violence-must-stop-after-regional-leaders-summit-12285766> accessed on 26 April 2021.
189 'Brunei Calls for ASEAN Meeting to Discuss Myanmar Situation' (VOA News, 5 April 2021) <https://www.voanews.com/east-asia-pacific/brunei-calls-asean-meeting-discuss-myanmar-situation> accessed on 5 April 2021.
190 Kay Johnson and Panarat Thepgumpanat, 'Analysis: Myanmar's Neighbour Thailand Unlikely to Toughen Stance on Coup' (Reuters, 2 April 2021) <https://www.reuters.com/article/us-myanmar-politics-thailand-analysis-idUSKBN2BP0LN> accessed on 5 April 2021.
191 Ibid.
192 'Cambodia Leader Hun Sen Terms Myanmar Coup "Internal Affairs"' (VOA Cambodia, 1 February 2021) <https://www.voacambodia.com/a/cambodian-leader-hun-sen-terms-myanmar-coup-internal-affairs-/5759503.html> accessed on 5 April 2021.
193 'Cambodia PM Hun Sen's Visit with Myanmar Military Chief Sparks Protest' (The Guardian, 8 January 2022) <https://www.theguardian.com/world/2022/jan/08/cambodian-pm-hun-sens-visit-with-myanmar-military-chief-sparks-protests> accessed on 27 February 2024; and Ben Sokhean, 'ANOTHER SHOT: Mr Hun Sen Will to Hold Talks with Myanmar Junta Again' (Khmer Times, 12 October 2023) <https://www.khmertimeskh.com/501375066/another-shot-mr-hun-sen-willing-to-hold-talks-with-myanmar-junta-again/> accessed on 27 February 2024.
194 Michelle Nichols, 'U.N. Security Council Wrestles with Threat of Action Over Myanmar Coup' (Reuters, 10 March 2021) <https://www.reuters.com/article/us-myanmar-politics-un-idUSKBN2B209S> accessed on 5 April 2021.
195 'Vietnam Calls on World Community to Help Myanmar Prevent Violence' (VN Explorer, 10 April 2021) <https://vnexplorer.net/vietnam-calls-on-world-community-to-help-myanmar-prevent-violence-a2021146179.html> accessed on 10 April 2021.
196 Nguyen Tien, 'Vietnam Calls for End of Violence to End in Myanmar' (Vietnam Express International, 17 November 2023) <https://e.vnexpress.net/news/news/vietnam-calls-for-end-of-violence-in-myanmar-4582791.html> accessed on 27 February 2024.
197 The Philippine's Statement for the Special Session of the Human Rights Council on the Human Rights Implications of the Crisis in Myanmar (2021) <https://dfa.gov.ph/dfa-news/statements-and-advisoriesupdate/28619-philippine-statement-for-the-special-session-of-the-human-rights-council-on-the-human-rights-implications-of-the-crisis-in-myanmar-12-february-2021> accessed on 5 April 2021.
198 Ibid.
199 'Philippines' Marcos Says Myanmar a Difficult Problem for ASEAN' (The Straits Times, 20 November 2023) <https://www.straitstimes.com/asia/se-asia/philippines-marcos-says-myanmar-a-difficult-problem-for-asean> accessed on 27 February 2024.

# 7 ASEAN and West Papua

## 7.1 Introduction

This chapter analyses the Association of Southeast Asian Nations (ASEAN) and its States' response to the protracted conflict in West Papua, Indonesia, since the 1960s. What shall now be referred to as the West Papua crisis, is a lesser-known and understudied conflict since Indonesia prohibits foreign media, non-governmental organisations (NGOs), and humanitarian groups from reporting in West Papua. Nonetheless, it is a crisis that is still occurring within Southeast Asia that involves an ASEAN State. Crucially, what makes West Papua an appropriate case study for this book is the fact that there are multiple reports and academic studies that argue that R2P crimes have been committed in the region.[1] As a result of this, it is imperative that we analyse how ASEAN and its States respond to this ongoing conflict and whether R2P is applied in any capacity.

With this in mind, this chapter is divided into five sections. The first section introduces the historical background of West Papua. The second section discusses West Papua under Indonesia's rules from 1963 to the present. The third section analyses how the international community has reacted to this conflict, while the fourth section focuses on ASEAN and its member states' reactions. The last and fifth section draws some final conclusions.

## 7.2 Background

West Papua is a region that geographically covers most of the western peninsulas of the island of New Guinea, which is the world's second-largest island located in Melanesia in the southwestern Pacific Ocean. The island was named by Spanish explorers in 1546, who thought that the inhabitants resembled the Guineans of West Africa.[2] West Papua has been inhabited by Papuan peoples who are Melanesians, a cultural and ethnic grouping which includes most of the people living in the Southwest Pacific (in countries such as Papua New Guinea, Fiji, Vanuatu, the Solomon Islands, and New Caledonia), which comprised of a tremendous ethnolinguistic diversity with 1,319 languages being spoken in the region.[3]

Although many explorers from the United Kingdom, France, Germany, Portugal, and Spain made incursions into West Papua, it was the Dutch that had successfully

DOI: 10.4324/9781003436799-7

annexed West Papua, which they called *New Guinea.*[4] *Whilst the Dutch established both military and administrative posts in West Papua, their intervention into local activities were minimal. It was due to the facts that the Dutch thought that the island possessed too great a challenge with too meagre material rewards for them to colonise it directly and fully.*[5] Whilst being under Dutch colonial rule had affected the culture, religion, and institution building in the West Papua society, it was predominantly felt in the coastal areas and the large parts of the mountainous inlands remained largely undisturbed until the early twentieth century.[6]

When World War II broke out in 1939, the Japanese military succeeded in occupying countries in Southeast Asia and the South Pacific within the span of six months.[7] The Japanese troops effectively occupied West Papua from 1942 to 1944 as well as Indonesia from 1942 to 1945.[8] When the United States (US) detonated atomic bombs over the Japanese cities of Hiroshima and Nagasaki, respectively, Japan surrendered unconditionally six days later, on 15 August 1945, which brought the end of World War II. That same month, Indonesia took the opportunity to proclaim independence from the Netherlands, which was ensued with diplomatic and armed resistance. That is until 1949 when the Netherlands finally officially recognised Indonesia's independence after having succumbed under international pressure to do so.[9]

When Indonesia successfully proclaimed its independence, it also included West Papua (it was then known as Irian Jaya) as part of its territory. From Jakarta's perspective, West Papua's importance stemmed from several imperatives. Firstly, Jakarta was viewed inside as a successor State to the Dutch sovereignty over the whole of the Netherlands East Indies, which included West Papua, meaning that any denial of Indonesia's sovereignty over West Papua would imply that the decolonisation and 'national revolution' were incomplete.[10] Secondly, the continued Dutch presence in West Papua was perceived as a threat and national affront since it would mean that the former had not fully given up its 'colonial ways'.[11] Thirdly, whilst West Papua was not on Jakarta's radar in the early colonial years, between 1936 and 1939 a Dutch geologist working for Shell Oil, Jean-Jacques Dozy made a significant discovery of natural resources deposits such as gold, petroleum, natural gas, and forests in the region, which substantially increased its attractiveness to the Indonesia government and other foreign parties to gain control over it.[12] Fourthly, on top of being a region being rich in vital and scarce resources, West Papua is geo-strategically located at the intersection of the interests of major powers in the international community—the US, China, Japan, and Australia.[13]

To galvanise a sense of unity and nationalism among Indonesians, following the initial failure of Indonesia to persuade the Dutch to relinquish sovereignty over West Papua, in the National Day Address of President Sukarno in August 1950, he stated that:

> This is not a trifling question: this is a major issue. I fear that the Netherlands does not yet understand that the Irian question is a major issue to us. . . . The Irian question is a question of colonialism or non-colonialism, a question of colonialism or independence. Part of our country is still colonised by the

> Dutch. This is a reality and we do not accept this. . . . If a settlement by negotiation cannot be arrived at within this year a major conflict will arise over the issue of who will be in power in that island from then onward. Fr once again I declare: we will not stop fighting, we will continue fighting, and we will keep on fighting whatever may come until Irian has been returned to our fold.[14]

On the other hand, whilst Indonesia was adamant on gaining West Papua as part of its territory, the Netherlands was preparing the latter for its independence. The Dutch at the time had begun preparations of nation building for West Papua to assume independence by 1970, with the support of the United Nations.[15] Political parties, labour unions, a general election law, and Papuan People's Congress were established to foster a sense of Papuan's national identity. On 1 December 1961, the Morning Star Flag, which represented West Papua independence was formally raised for the first time.[16]

Officially, the reasons that were given by the Dutch to deny Indonesia's sovereignty over West Papua were as follows: (1) Papuans were essentially ethnologically different from the rest of Indonesia as they were Melanesians of origin. (2) Papuans were poor and uneducated; therefore, they needed different political arrangements that would be more suitable, politically, socially, and economically. (3) Since the Papuans were uneducated and backwards, they needed to be 'tutored' towards self-determination and independence.[17] Whilst these were the official justifications the Dutch had given, according to Dr. Bilveer Singh, between 1950 and 1962, the strategic importance of Papua to the Dutch was increasingly referred to as the key *raison d'être* for the latter to continue its presence in the former's territory.[18] Three arguments were given for this line of analysis. First, military bases in West Papua would be advantageous for the Dutch to utilise in order to protect its economic interests in Indonesia in the event of it being threatened. Second, the Dutch continued presence in the territory contributed to the West's defence strategy to contain communism that was emerging in the region. Third, the Dutch's presence would safeguard Australian strategic and security interests in West Papua and New Guinea.[19] Even with all their efforts, the Dutch ultimately failed to assist the Papuans in gaining their independence, and their sovereignty was instead handed over to Indonesia.

Why? The end of World War II led the international community to face a new security environment and strategic challenges, forcing States to re-evaluate and adjust their interests accordingly. With the onset of the Cold War, the rivalry between the Western Bloc and Eastern Bloc highlighted the importance of geopolitics and security terms that came to be defined in strict ideologies and political terms, essentially between capitalist liberal democracy and autocratic communism.[20] The issue of West Papua's independence was initially unimportant to the international community, and it was assumed that its decolonisation process would eventually be settled. That is until Indonesia realised it could be strategically exploiting the Cold War realities and successfully re-framed the issue as a fight against the spread of communism. With this reconceptualisation, and the realisation that Indonesia as the largest country in Southeast Asia that also straddled important sea lanes of communication, and with large reserves for raw materials, it could be a powerful ally against communism expansion in the region, this diplomatic dispute over the sovereignty of West Papua between Indonesia and the Netherlands then became one of the forefront issues in the international political community.

As stated earlier, Indonesia had decided to exploit the Cold War rivalries to have its victory over the Dutch and annexe West Papua as part of its territory, and ultimately, it was successful in doing so. Historically, Indonesia had maintained a policy of non-alignment, meaning it was inclined towards neither the Soviet nor the American bloc.[21] However, Indonesia started to take an anti-Western attitude when the Western Bloc was somewhat indifferent towards this issue of West Papua. It was emphasised by then Indonesia Vice-President Mohammad Hatta:

> The United States stand on neutrality in the feud between Indonesia and the Netherlands over the West Irian does, in fact, give support to the Dutch. . . . Indonesia cannot understand why the United States should assume such half-hearted posture in this matter. The United States has been the moving force in setting up NATO and SEATO to halt the spread of Communism influence and power in Europe and Asia. Yet to permit West Irian to continue indefinitely as a bone of contention between Indonesia and the Netherlands is to afford Communism an opportunity to spread in Indonesia. . . . It (The United States) wants to eradicate Communism, but its policy merely helps the spread. In addition it leaves Indonesia with a sense of grievance.[22]

Indonesian's sentiment towards the Americans was then cleverly exploited by the Soviets. Starting in 1956, the relationship between Indonesia and Russia blossomed, with Moscow supporting Indonesia over the West Papua issue. Furthermore, the Soviet's aid for Indonesia even amounted to a third of available aid for non-aligned nations, which Jakarta used for a military build-up.[23] Indonesia's preferential treatment by the Soviets was further emphasised by the former being the only country to receive MG021 fighters outside the Soviet Union bloc.[24] This close relationship between the two was reiterated by Communist Party leader Nikita Khrushchev, who visited Indonesia in 1960 and was emphasised by President Sukarno, 'the friendship between the Soviet Union and Indonesia is not a formal friendship between States, but the friendship that reaches from heart to heart'.[25]

Seeing this as an imminent threat of a Communist-oriented regime in Indonesia, the US pivoted their policy on the matter to attempt to win over the Indonesians. Amidst the circumstances, the Netherlands attempted to have the United Nations (UN) take over West Papua in 1961 via a UN Trusteeship, which was invoked under Article XII of the UN Charter. The proposal, however, failed to gain the required two-thirds majority in the General Assembly (GA) due to the fact that the Americans had changed their position on the matter.[26] On 2 April 1962, US President John F. Kennedy sent a secret letter to the Dutch Prime Minister Dr. J.E. de Quay to convey that it was imperative that the Dutch renege on their position of giving West Papua its independence and warned that a war would signal a victory for communism.[27] This warning was against the background of Indonesia's threatening to use force to expel Dutch forces from the island, which was emphasised through President Sukarno's establishment of the *TRIKORA* (which is an Indonesian acronym for *Tri Komando Rakyat* or 'Three People's Demands'). As stated, the *TRIKORA* was essentially tasked to forcefully expel Dutch forces from the island and essentially to plant the Indonesian flag on Papuan soil. The *TRIKORA* also detailed that it would invade the island with 75,000 Indonesian soldiers supported by warships brought from Eastern Europe.[28] After having realised that they would not be militarily assisted by the US, the United Kingdom (UK), and Australia (its allies), the Netherlands complied with an agreement believing that it would serve as an eventual route for a plebiscite among the Papuans within a period of one year.[29] It is crucial to note that the Dutch did not consult the Papuans before complying with this agreement. However, the Indonesians were initially unsatisfied with the plan and demanded that West Papua be transferred to its jurisdiction directly and immediately. Indonesia even threatened that it would resort to using force unless its demands were met. Although the US was on Indonesia's side on the matter, it did not want an armed conflict to break out in the region; because of this position, the US warned Indonesia that if an armed conflict was to break out, Indonesia alone would shoulder the responsibility. As a result of this, Indonesia withdrew its threat of armed invasion and on 15 August 1962, the New York Agreement was signed by Indonesia and the Netherlands under the auspices of the UN.[30]

### *7.2.1 The New York Agreement*

Article II of the Agreement states that the Netherlands would transfer the administration of West Papua over to a United Nations Temporary Executive Authority (UNTEA) established by the UN Secretary-General.[31] The UNTEA will transfer the administration of West Papua to Indonesia in accordance with Article XII, once the first phase of the UNTEA administration is completed. The first phase of the UNTEA entailed that UNTEA would replace all Dutch officials by 1 May 1963 and to fill in any remaining administrative posts with Indonesian personnel.[32] Under the first phase, the UNTEA also had the responsibility to publicise and inform the Papuans of their sovereignty being transferred under Indonesia's jurisdiction and the terms of their self-determination.[33]

The second phase of the UNTEA entailed that UN security forces would be replaced by Indonesian security forces after the first phase was completed. Crucially, as part of the second phase, Indonesia is to invite the Secretary-General to appoint a representative who will implement the Secretary-General's responsibilities to assist, advise, and participate in arrangements which are the responsibilities of Indonesia for the 'Act of Free Choice'.[34] Indonesia then had the responsibility to make the appropriate arrangements in preparation for this opportunity for the Papuans to exercise their freedom of choice, which included: consultations with representative councils on procedures and appropriate methods to be followed after the population had expressed their will; to determine the actual date of the exercise of free choice; to formulate questions that would permit the population with the choice between remain with Indonesia or sever ties with Indonesia; and to determine the eligibility of all adults to participate in the act of self-determination in accordance with international practice.[35]

Furthermore, the New York Agreement also emphasised that the UNTEA and Indonesia would guarantee the full rights, which included the rights of free speech, freedom of movement, and assembly of the Papuans.[36]

With the inclusion of the finer details included in the Agreement, UNTEA and Indonesia commenced the preparations for the 'Act of Free Choice'.

### *7.2.2 The Act of Free Choice*

In preparations for the 'Act of Free Choice' and in accordance with the New York Agreement, by 1 May 1963, the Indonesians officially took over the administration of West Papua and there were no more UNTEA officials in the territory despite repeated requests by the Papuans for them to stay. Immediately, the Indonesians made their authority known in the territory by bringing in 30 warships and 20 aeroplanes for the occasion.[37] With no UN presence, the Indonesian military was essentially unrestrained. There were reports that the military cleaned out the shops and storehouses from the locals and within months there was an acute shortage of food and consumer goods.[38] Furthermore, the military even engaged in harsh tactics to curb the rise of Papuan nationalism, which included mass arrests and even torture. At the same time, the local economy was being exploited along with the compulsory use of the Indonesian language in schools even though the transfer of West Papua's sovereignty to Indonesia was not fully completed.[39] With the rise in human rights violations and abuses perpetrated by the Indonesian military, the pro-independence Papuan resistance movement known as the *Organisasi Papua Merdeka* (OPM) emerged in 1962, which was joined by Papuans all over the region.[40] In 1965, the OPM started launching armed attacks against the Indonesian military, to which the latter responded with unproportionate violence that resulted in killings, disappearances, and rape.[41] These operations included: *Operasi Sadar* (1965–1967), *Operasi Brathayudha* (1967–1969), and *Opersi Wibawa* (1969).[42] These abuses were targeting civilian Papuans as well as OPM and resistance fighters. Around the same period of time, the Indonesian government also established the *Merah Putih* (Red and white) in 1964 with the sole aim of gathering and sustaining massive pro-Indonesian support for the 'Act of Free Choice' later on.[43] In order to build up support, this movement also employed the method of education for the Papuans so that they would choose to stay integrated with Indonesia.

Then in August 1968, the Bolivian ambassador to the UN, Fernando Ortiz-Sanz arrived in West Papua as the Secretary-General's representative to 'advise, assist and participate' under Article 18 of the New York Agreement, in the Indonesian organised act of self-determination, the 'Act of Free Choice'.[44] The first part of the struggle for Ortiz-Sanz's responsibility was the tedious debate on the manner in which the 'Act of Free Choice' would be conducted. The Indonesians insisted on *Musyawarah*-type (consensus decision-making) voting, which would involve votes from community leaders from various districts of West Papua as opposed to the one-man one-vote mechanism.[45] The Indonesians opposed this system on the grounds of logistics and impracticality.[46] This issue was eventually resolved in the Indonesian's favour. Furthermore, Ortiz Sanz also found his mission to be underfunded, understaffed, and constantly struggling to ensure that the Indonesian government would adhere to the New York Agreement and international law/practices.[47] Essentially, the Indonesian government was able to employ their preferred method of conducting the act of self-determination by successfully pressuring the West Papuan provincial assembly to sanction the creation of eight assemblies to determine who is eligible to participate in the 'Act of Free Choice'.[48] Eventually, the eight assemblies selected 1,026, 1,024 of whom eventually voted on the 'Act of Free Choice' later in the year.[49]

As mentioned earlier, with the increase of violent interventions by the Indonesian military in West Papua, OPM and various insurgencies activities were also increasing in the name of Papuan nationalism. However, these incidents were always met with an unproportionate response from the Indonesian government, which included strafing on various villages such as Paniai that resulted in killing dozens and thousands of displaced Papuans.[50] With the surge of anti-Indonesia sentiment, the Indonesian military began making public violent threats against Papuan leaders who advocated voting for independence.[51] Consequently, on 2 August 1969, expectantly, the 1,024 Papuans selected to vote in the 'Act of Free Choice' unanimously voted in favour of Indonesia's control of West Papua.[52] The UN took note of the result through Resolution 2504 with no objections even after allegations that the preparations and mechanisms that were undertaken were fraudulent, full of coercion, and against international practice.[53] After the vote, it was reported that there were at least 30,000 deaths of Papuans through the campaigns of intimidation, torture, rape, and killing by the Indonesian military.[54] At the same time, Ortiz-Sanz even expressed his disappointment and dissatisfaction with the Indonesian government regarding the whole process and explicitly stated that the 'Act of Free Choice' was conducted in accordance with Indonesian practice, implying that it was against international law and practice.[55]

We might ask ourselves that in a case such as this, with clear violations of international law and the self-determinations of the Papuans, how could Indonesia legally gain control over West Papua? As with anything occurring in either the regional or international community, *realpolitik* considerations are always present and prioritised. Just as the initial dispute between the Netherlands and Indonesia, the driving force behind the Dutch's decision to cede its control of West Papua was because of the US' position. The UN recognising Indonesia's sovereignty over West Papua is by the US' design as it needed Indonesia as an ally in order to have access to its natural resources and to gain another ally during the Cold War. As mentioned earlier, with an area of 420,000 square km, West Papua has a huge economic potential due to its large untapped reserves of natural resources such as gold, petroleum, natural gas, and forests which after the 'Act of Free Choice' has become part of Indonesia's territory.[56] Although this was discovered in the 1930s by the Dutch, they were unable to exploit it due to World War II. An additional factor that played a crucial role in the US' support for Indonesia annexing West Papua as part of its territory and why Indonesia was so confident in its ability to do so because the Indonesian government and the US-based Freeport-McMoran signed a contract to exploit the Grasberg Mine, which is the world's largest gold and copper mine located in Timika, West Papua, in April 1967, two years before the 'Act of Free Choice' and eventual integration into Indonesia.[57] Freeport's role in West Papua has functioned as one of the main continuous sources of environmental, labour, and human rights abuses, which will be discussed in detail in the following section.

## 7.3 West Papua Under Indonesia's Rule

Before I start the analysis of West Papua's treatment under Indonesia's rule, it is crucial to note that in the few years leading up to the 'Act of Free Choice' in 1969, the highly violent and repressive practice perpetrated by the Indonesian military was due to a change in leadership. In 1967, General Suharto ousted President Sukarno in a coup and enacted his vision of the New Order in order to strengthen and unify Indonesia.[58] Under President Suharto, a vicious cycle of violent political, social, cultural, and economic oppression of the Papuans constitutes crimes against humanity and genocide that are still occurring today. As was discussed in Chapter 2, the concept of Responsibility to Protect (R2P) exclusively covers four crimes: war crimes, ethnic cleansing, crimes against humanity, and genocide.[59] This section analyses Indonesia's treatment of West Papua from 1969 to present and it will come to the conclusion that Indonesia had indeed committed crimes against humanity and arguably also genocide against the Papuans. As a result of R2P crimes having been committed, in my opinion, it is appropriate that I analyse it in detail.

Immediately after the official annexation of West Papua into Indonesia, the Suharto administration began enacting policies and programmes as efforts to 'Indonesianise' the Papuans. The 'Indonesianisation' efforts included the banning of raising the Morning Star flag (which is a symbol of Papuan nationalism) and traditional Papuan apparel, as well as restricting cultural practices and symbols.[60] Furthermore, the Papuans are traditionally predominantly Christian, as part of the New Order policy, mosques and the spread of Islam and Javanese started to emerge in Christian-dominated Papuan villages in efforts to impede the Papuans' right to religion.[61] Furthermore, part of the effort to steer the Papuans away from their traditional fundamental culture was to replace one of their staple food sources, which was *syko*. One *syko* plant can feed one family for between six months to one year; however, the Indonesian government deemed it as being unhealthy and instead replaced it with rice.[62] The Papuans were then forced to destroy their indigenous food and used the lands to plant rice instead. As a result of this policy, the Papuans were then started to be dependent on Jakarta for food source. Additionally, even the local ethnic Papuan languages were violently oppressed, and Papuan history was not taught in school (especially the part where they were freed from the Netherlands) since they were seen as treacherous and anti-Indonesian.[63] All these policies enacted onto the Papuans were part of the New Order regime exert control, preserved centralism, and essentially crushed Papuan's identity and nationalism.

Furthermore, on top of the cultural oppression that the Papuans were facing, the Indonesian military also increased its operations, in both quantity and violent intensities. Whilst there were probably countless incidents and operations, I will list the ones that stood out in terms of a number of deaths in this sub-section.[64] In 1970, there was a reported incident in the Lereh district that a unit of the Indonesian armed forces (ABRI) *Udayana* division massacred 500 Papuans.[65] Between 1977 and 1978, it was a particularly violent period of years in West Papua. Whilst there is no official record of the number of deaths, in 1981, Eliezener Bonay, a former governor of West Papua testified before the Tribunal on Human Rights in West Papua that the death toll, was around 3,000.[66] Furthermore, according to Reverent Obet Komba, a well-known priest in the Baliem Valley, reported that there was an estimate of 11,000 deaths in Jayawijaya alone due to gunshots, torture, disease, and hunger.[67] It is also estimated that within that time period, there were an additional 9,000 deaths in Wamena, Pyramid, Kurulu, Kelila, Bokondini, and Kobakma, and a further 2,000 deaths in the Eastern Highlands.[68]

As a result of the military brutality, the anti-Indonesian government grew rapidly and, in turn, caused the Papuans to support and join the OPM. Consequently, the military employed the pretext of fighting against the OPM freedom fighters that were allegedly destabilising the region in order to kill innocent civilian Papuans. For example, in 1977–1978, the military executed major operations in the Jayawijaya highlands that involved the military strafing a group of villages including Akimuga, which is about 40 kilometres from Timika; the villages combined had an estimate of more than a thousand population.[69] According to Benny Giay, a theologian, social anthropologist, and human rights activist, he concluded that in the Indonesian military operations between the years leading up to the 'Act of Free Choice' and the mid-1980s, the Papuan death toll was somewhere between 100,000 and 500,000, depending which account you attain.[70] These brutal operations were justified by the Indonesian military as a fight against Papuan's separatism, specifically forces of the OPM, which could in turn destabilise Indonesia as a whole. However, these death tolls were of civilian populations too as the military were indiscriminate about who they targeted or who posed collateral damage. Unfortunately, we will never know the exact number of Papuan deaths since its inclusion into Indonesia's territory as journalists are not permitted in West Papua. Even non-government organisations and humanitarian agencies, especially foreign ones, are banned in West Papua. The Indonesian government justified this policy as a way to protect its sovereignty as it claimed that any reporting would intrude on its internal affairs and fuel Papuan nationalistic separatism sentiments.

### *7.3.1 Transmigration*

When it comes to analysing the cultural oppression and physical violations of the Papuans, it is imperative to analyse it along with the transmigration (*transformasi*) policy that the Indonesian government enacted in West Papua from 1970 to the present. The transmigration policy has been one of the main mechanisms employed by the Indonesian government to essentially undermine the Papuan's self-determination and their distinct ethnic identity. The transmigration programme was initially enacted by the Dutch colonial regime and was continued by the Indonesian government. This programme was essentially part of a cultural assimilation project, which as stated earlier included the use of the Indonesian language, the replacement of Christianity with Islam, and an overall ban of any Papuan cultural practices, which were seen as primitive and backwards.[71] The transmigration programme was implemented by migrating people from densely populated areas such as Java, Bali, and Sulawesi to sparsely populated areas in West Papua.[72] The arrival of transmigrants into West Papua presented fundamental challenges to the identity of the Papuans. The Papuans were essentially chased out of their ancestral land, and on top of this, the transmigrant also took over the businesses and much of the administration, leaving the Papuan marginalised in their own motherland.[73] By 1984, approximately 700,000 hectares of land had been confiscated from the indigenous Papuans without them being given proper compensation.[74] Unfortunately, it is difficult to locate the accurate official statistics on the demographic in West Papua since information is limited from the government and the continuous restrictions on NGOs or media. However, according to the International Work Group for Indigenous Affairs, as of 2022, the total population of West Papua was 4.378 million, more than 50% of whom were from the transmigration programme.[75] Concerning this percentage in West Papua demographics, indigenous Papuans are now a minority in their own motherland. This can be considered as an internal colonisation since the local indigenous population is slowly reducing whilst its land and resources continue to be exploited. Furthermore, as part of the transmigration programmes, the allocation of resources and funds has also been unfair with more priorities given to the transmigrant, which includes education, access to healthcare, and employment opportunities. For example, in 2013, 32% of Papuans lived below the poverty line compared to the national average of 12.5%.[76] Furthermore, according to a study conducted by Dr. Jim Elmslie, a political scientist, he found that in the 15–44 years age group, Papuans had an illiteracy rate of 34.83% in 2011, compared to the national average of just 2.30%.[77] Due to the vast inequalities that exist between the Papuan and the rest of Indonesian society, which has been exacerbated by the transmigration programme, this has also been one of the fundamental sources of Papuans' grievances towards the Indonesian government and Indonesia as a whole.

### *7.3.2 Freeport McMoran*

When it comes to analysing the human rights violations in West Papua, it is imperative that the role of the mining giant corporation Freeport-McMoran is also included as it has been one of the main sources of the predicament that the Papuans were and continues to be in. As stated in Section 7.2.2, two years before the 'Act of Free Choice' referendum was held, there was already a contract signed between the Indonesian government and Freeport. This contract gave Freeport the exclusive license to exploit the Grasberg mine, which is the world's largest gold and third-largest copper mine located in Timika, West Papua.[78] Under this contract,

Indonesia would receive a compensation fee, a 9.3% minority shareholder stake, and tax revenue.[79] The contract entailed that Freeport had a concession to explore the 10,908-hectre mining area until 2041, with a possibility for an extension.[80] As a result of this preferential treatment for Freeport and its operations, it gave this corporation the right to seize land from the indigenous Papuan without having had to pay compensation.[81] The Indonesian military and police having collaborated with Freeport, then began to relocate the ethnic Amungme, Sempan, and Kamoro peoples who lived in the areas aside from the mine for hundreds of years down to Timika, where they suffered from starvation and diseases they had never been exposed to on the mountain.[82] Once the indigenous populations had been evicted from the areas surrounding the Grasberg mine, the region effectively became a militarised zone and was only open to Freeport officials and the Indonesian security forces.[83] What was once a communal area and hunting grounds for the indigenous Papuans had become a money-making pit for Freeport and the Indonesian government/military/police. In the first quarter of 2023 alone, Freeport earned a revenue of $5.39 billion.[84]

With its records of high revenues from the mine, Freeport became the highest taxpayer to the Indonesian government.[85] And since the Indonesian military and police helped with the establishment and protection of the mine operation, they receive bonuses and annual payments in excess of tens of millions of dollars given by Freeport annually.[86] These payments were not made to government or military institutions but direct payments to the military/government/police personnel. In 2006, the New York Times investigative report obtained documents that showed from 1998 to 2004, Freeport paid nearly $20 million to the Indonesian military/police personnel.[87] With this arrangement, any obstacles or objections to Freeport operations from the indigenous Papuans have been and most likely will continue to be violently oppressed by the Indonesian security apparatus.

In addition to the wealth and resource extractions of West Papua by Freeport through its exploitation of the Grasberg mine, this corporation has also done irreversible destruction to the surrounding natural environment. According to a report prepared by *Lembaga Peduli Masyarakat Wilaya Mimika Timur Jau* (LEPEMAWIL), a coalition of grassroots civil society organisations predominantly consists of women and youth groups to address the environment and human rights issues that are affecting the Indigenous Papuans in the Mimika (where the Grasberg mine is located) and Timika (the region next to Mimika). Freeport operation did not have the proper mechanisms to dump their disposals, therefore, they have been dumping the toxic waste directly into the river, particularly the Ajikwa River, that as a result has destroyed the nearby forests and wildlife in the rivers that the indigenous Papuans' livelihoods had depended on for centuries.[88] Freeport had initially vowed that they would use the waste for road construction but this has not been materialised. Furthermore, because of the contaminations from the mine, the Ajikwa River's fish stocks and biodiversity have been greatly affected, which resulted in the trees drying up and the deaths of millions of fish.[89] Furthermore, as a result of Freeport's activity, the whole area surrounding the Grasberg mine has had its biodiversity and ecosystem destroyed, which in turn also destroyed the livelihoods and cultural practices of the indigenous Papuans from the areas.[90] On top of the environmental degradation, the indigenous Papuans who still live near the Ajikwa River have gotten sick from the polluted water.[91] In response to this, Freeport has vowed that it will undertake measures such as proper housing, access to healthcare, and education for the local communities in order to rectify the issues; unfortunately, these conditions still ensue.[92]

Due to Freeport's activities in West Papua and its treatment of the indigenous populations, resentments from the latter further emerged that led to them fighting back through collaborations with the OPM. As such in 1977, the OPM under Kelly separatist leader Kelly Kwalik attacked and managed to halt Freeport's operations of the mine's slurry line that carried the ore down to the coast.[93] In response to this, the Indonesian military executed an operation that killed at least 800 Papuans and displaced thousands into the mountains.[94] With increasing opposition to Freeport's operations, the New Order government even banned the Papuans from protesting. According to a report in the Indonesian Church Council Conference, there were several human rights violation patterns between 1994 and 1995. These included: the inhuman arrest of people who were accused of being separatist fighters or members of the OPM; the disappearance of family members of people who were accused of being supporters of OPM or the separatism sentiments; indiscriminate violence against civilians; houses and properties being destroyed by the Indonesian military apparatus; and the constant monitoring of the local Papuans to inflict fear into their mentalities.[95]

Presently, Freeport is still operating in West Papua with an exclusive right to explore the Grasberg mine until 2041 in accordance with the original contract signed with the Indonesian government in 1967. As of late 2023 and 2024, Freeport and the Indonesian government are in negotiations over the possibility of extending the contract to another 20 years after 2041. Indonesian Foreign Minister Bahlil Lahadalia stated that the negotiations between the two parties are almost complete, emphasising that the main condition to be agreed upon is the possible increase of the Indonesian government's stake in Freeport from 51.2% to 61.2%. Crucially, it should be noted that the negotiations for the extension of the contract between the Indonesian government and Freeport did not include any stipulation regarding the Papuans just as it had not during the original contract. As a result of this, in the last decade or so until the present day, there have been multiple strikes from the Papuan workers against Freeport, mostly regarding inhumane treatment of the workers, welfare, proper protection, and unfair wages that sometimes involved the use of violence by the Indonesian security apparatus to suppress the protests.[96]

### *7.3.3 Present Days*

As emphasised previously, human rights violations stemming from Freeport violations are still occurring since Freeport is still in operation. However, no efforts have been made to rectify the grievance towards the Papuans, which is the same case for the transmigration policy and the cultural and physical oppression/violations that are instrumental to the plight of the Papuans. Before I proceed to the following section of analysing whether the Indonesian government's treatment of the Papuans since its annexation amounts to the crime of genocide and/or crimes against humanity in accordance with international law, I will briefly discuss the recent developments in West Papua that are pertinent for this case study.

Throughout the years, with different Indonesian administrations, the circumstance in West Papua also fluctuates. As was discussed in the previous sections, under Presidents Sukarno and Suharto's regimes, the Papuans faced highly violent oppressive treatment. Unfortunately, since then, with the last few administrations, whilst it can be argued that it has been as violent, the Papuans are still facing intense oppression, socially, politically, culturally, and economically. In 1998, Indonesia and the world saw an end to 32 years of Suharto's authoritarian regime, which was subsequently replaced by President BJ Habibie that commenced the era known as *Reformasi*.[97] The *reformasi* was known as the transition of Indonesia's governance from an authoritarian to a more democratic era. With this political transition, the Papuan elites saw this as an opportunity to capitalise on the weak position of the Indonesian central government and renewed demands for independence and trials to human rights violations perpetrated by the Indonesian security apparatus during Presidents Sukarno and Suharto's regime.[98] Unfortunately, the Papuan's request for a referendum regarding its secession was rejected as President Habibie's cabinet was still dominated by the New Order and military elites, who were extremely against any talks of independence.[99] After rejecting the Papuan's aspiration for independence, President Habibie's administration subsequently proposed a Special Autonomy in West Papua to somewhat appease the locals. After a year of being in office, President Habibie withdrew his presidency nomination since he was without adequate support from parliament; he was then succeeded by President Abdurrahman Wahid. It was under President Wahid's administration that the negotiations for the Special Autonomy took place. Similarly to President Habibie, President Wahid took a more accommodative approach that emphasised dialogues and negotiations. Although for a short period of time, the Papuans were hopeful, their optimisms were quickly squashed with President Wahid was impeached and was subsequently succeeded by President Megawati Sukarnoputri.[100] Unlike her predecessors' approaches to the issue of West Papua's self-determination and autonomy, President Megawati had a hardline approach to it and preferred to implement repressive means in response.[101] When President Megawati finally signed the Special Autonomy Law in November 2001, it was celebrated among the Papuans. Included in the Law were the authorisation of the Indigenous peoples to become leaders in their territory; the right to fly the Morning Star flag; the rights over fund allocations; affirmative action; human rights protections; and mechanisms to address past human rights abuses.[102] Although, at first glance, it seemed that the plight of the Papuans was starting to get better, not only that the implementation of the Special Autonomy Law was stalled but also President Megawati instated Presidential Instruction No. 1/2003 to divide West Papua into three provinces: West Irian Jaya, Central Irian Jaya, and Irian Jaya.[103] On top of not having consulted with the Papuan elites, this policy has been considered as an attempt to divide the independence movement, which would make the Papuans more vulnerable.[104] This legal division of West Papua still persists in the present days and has been a source of resentment for the Papuan against the Indonesian central government. Furthermore, several stipulations that were included in the Special Autonomy Law still have not been implemented such as the establishment of a mechanism to address past human rights violations and the fact that raising the Morning Star flag is still currently banned and would only be allowed if it is raised alongside the Indonesian flag, with the latter having to be raised higher than the former.[105]

Then in 2021, under President Joko Widodo (Jokowi) administration, the Indonesian government added a second amendment comprising 20 revisions to the Papua's Special Autonomy Law, which was enacted without consultation with the representatives of the Papuans as stipulated in the original law.[106] The central government argued that these revisions were added to ensure better accountability and improved delivery of public goods and services. However, to the Papuans, this was seen as a deduction of power of representative institutions for Indigenous Papuans as well as the recentralisation of fiscal power and control over administrative regions back to the central government.[107]

With this background laid out, because the multi-layered oppression of the Papuan still persists, the Papuans on occasion held protests to express their grievances against the central government. However, these protests have always been met with excessive force and further oppression of the Papuans.[108] As a result of this, the OPM's armed faction is still active and has repeatedly renewed calls for independence.[109]

### *7.3.4 Arguments for the Crime of Genocide*

After having analysed the background and continued predicament of the Papuans under Indonesian's rule, in this section and the following section, I will analyse whether the violations and abuses perpetrated by the Indonesian policies and security apparatus amount to the crimes of genocide and crimes against humanity. Why specifically these two crimes? It is because genocide and crimes against humanity are R2P crimes, which in theory, the State has a responsibility to both protect and prevent it from occurring to its population. And in the event where the State is unable or unwilling to do so, the residual responsibility is then passed on to the international community.[110]

The legal definition of genocide in accordance with the Convention on the Prevention and Punishment of the Crime of Genocide (1948) (Convention), Article II:

> In the present Convention, genocide means any of the following acts committed with intent to destroy, in whole or in part, a national, ethnical, racial or religious group, as such: (a) Killing members of the group; (b) Causing serious bodily or mental harm to members of the group; (c) Deliberately inflicting on the group conditions of life calculated to bring about its physical destruction in whole or in part; (d) Imposing measures intended to prevent births within the group; (e) Forcibly transferring children of the group to another group.[111]

Article I of this Convention stated that the crime of genocide may take place in the context of an armed conflict, international or non-international but also in the context of a peaceful situation.[112] Crucially, it must be noted that there are two main elements of the crime of genocide, mental and physical elements. The physical element of genocide entails the acts that are listed earlier, and the mental element is the '*intent* to destroy, in whole or in part, a national, ethnical, racial or religious group, as such.[113] While the physical element is easier to prove, the mental element of the crimes is challenging to determine since perpetrators would not necessarily make this clear.

If we are to proceed with this understanding of genocide alone, then it is challenging to make the case that the continued Indonesian oppression of the Papuans amounts to genocide resembling the Holocaust, the Rwandan genocide, or the Rohingya genocide.[114] Unlike these genocides, there have not been any systemic patterns of mass killings or any period of large-scale intense campaign of killings against the Papuans. Therefore, rather than being treated as a case of genocide, the plight of the Papuans is perceived as a case of extreme political and cultural oppression. In response to this, Kjell Anderson, a social scientist argued that just because the case of the Papuans does not fit in with the narrow perception of genocide perceived under the context of the holocaust, does not mean that genocide is not happening to the Papuans, in which I concur with.[115] According to Anderson, there needs to be a new legal framework for genocide to account for cases like West Papua where the perpetrators knowingly commit acts that contribute to the eventual destruction of a group over a period of time, to which he has labelled as a '*cold genocide*' as opposed to the widely recognised/accepted understanding of genocide in accordance to the Convention, '*hot genocide*'.[116] On one hand, *hot genocides* are characterised by an intense hatred that the perpetrator has towards the victim group and this hatred is perceived as a sense of existential threat against their survival.[117] Furthermore, usually in cases of *hot genocide,* the campaigns of mass killings would occur in an intensely short period of time (usually several years) through direct killings, concentration camps, and outright assaults.[118] With this line of analysis, the Holocaust, Rwandan genocide, Srebrenica genocide, Kosovo genocide, and Rohingya genocide, are *hot genocides*. On the other hand, *cold genocides* are characterised as being motivated by the assumed supremacy of the perpetrators over the victims, which may be manifested as pity, indifference, or annoyance/inconvenience.[119] As opposed to the intense period of mass killings in *hot genocides, cold genocides* occur over long periods of time, decades even, with low-intensity mechanisms employed against the victims.[120] One crucial factor between the concepts of *hot genocides* and *cold genocides* is that the perpetrators in the former intend to destroy the victim group completely (as perceived in the Convention), whereas the latter may be accomplished through extreme marginalisation or subjugation of the victim group.[121] Furthermore, according to the understanding of the Convention and *hot genocides,* cultural destruction/oppression is not considered as an element of genocide, whereas in certain cases of *cold genocides,* cultural destruction/oppression can be seen as an element of genocide. It is because for certain groups such as the Papuans, cultural practices are essential to the group's physical survival.

With this in mind, I argue that the Indonesian government and its security apparatus have been committing genocide against the Papuans both in terms of understandings from the Convention and *cold genocide*. Even if the Indonesian government argues that it did not in the past and does not presently have specific genocidal intent towards the Papuans, their policies, and treatments of the Papuans since the annexation of West Papua proves otherwise. Referring to Article II (a) and (b) or the Convention, as was discussed in Section 7.3, over the 60 years of being under Indonesia's rule, there have been over 500,000 Papuan deaths by Indonesian security apparatus, according to Benny Wenda, the world-renowned West Papuan independence leader and activist.[122] Furthermore, on top of killings, the Papuans have also been exposed to torture, disappearances, unlawful detentions, and rape, which has undoubtedly inflicted serious generational mental harm against the group. Since there is neither a specific amount of time nor the number of deaths mentioned in the Convention to signify that a case has reached the legal threshold of the crime of genocide, then I argue that in this case it has for the Papuans. Furthermore, referring to Article II section (c) of the Convention, with the continuous resources and environmental exploitation as well as relocation of the Papuans (especially regarding Freeport's operations, unfair allocation of wealth and resources from the central government, and transmigration programme), the Indonesian has been inflicting on the Papuans' way of life and has resulted in continuous decline of the Papuan populations throughout these few decades.[123] With special attention paid to the transmigration programme, it has been argued by scholars from Yale Law School, with which I concur, that is highly unlikely that it was implemented without the knowledge that it would bring about the eventual destruction of the West Papuan population.[124] In order to make space for the transmigrants, the Indonesian government removed the Papuans from their traditional to other areas with which they were not accustomed to. Because of this, the Papuans were exposed to terminal diseases such as HIV/AIDS, to which they do not have access to proper healthcare for treatments. Among all Indonesian provinces, West Papua has the highest proportion of people living with HIV/AIDS.[125] Without access to proper healthcare or education about diseases, the Indonesian government must know that this will eventually affect the Papuans' mortality and fertility rate.

Furthermore, on top of the continuous physical eradication of the Papuans, their distinct ethnic, cultural, historical, and linguistic legacy is also being eradicated by the multifaceted Indonesian policies enacted upon them. This includes the transmigration programmes, Freeport operations, and the discriminatory policies against the Papuan (such as the ban of the Morning Star flag and cultural practices). These policies can effectively be labelled as the 'Indonesianisation' of the Papuans. As briefly mentioned earlier, some ethnic groups attach their physical survival to cultural survival as well, it is what essentially makes the group distinct. If the Papuans lose their distinct cultural identity that comes with thousands of years of history and cultural practices, they will soon be forgotten. So not only that the Papuans are being slowly eradicated physically, but they are also being eradicated culturally/

ethnically as well. Again, as emphasised earlier, in response to this, even if the Indonesian government's policies over the years lack intentionality and urgency, but yet, they still do have genocidal implications in the sense that it has been attacking the sustainability of the Papuans, they still have a responsibility to reassess their approach or be accountable for the genocidal policies that they continue to enact onto the Papuans. This is one such case that can be argued that the genocidal policies enacted upon the Papuans since the 1960s are a by-product or collateral of economic development (Freeport) and modernisation of a region, and not an intentional will by the Indonesian government to eradicate the Papuans as a group. Nevertheless, it has been and continues to happen, and how can the Papuans continue to survive within a highly marginalised, militarised, and hegemonic state that would eventually end with its eradication?

### *7.3.5 Arguments for Crimes Against Humanity*

In the case where my arguments for the crime of genocide are not permissible, in this section, I will argue that the Indonesian government has at least committed repeated acts of crimes against humanity. The perpetuation of this crime is appropriate for this book as it is also one of R2P crimes; hence, it should in theory invoke responsive actions from the State or international community. Crimes against humanity is defined in Article 7 of the Rome Statute of the International Criminal Court as:

> For the purpose of this Statute, "crime against humanity" means any of the following acts when committed as part of a widespread or systemic attack directed against any civilian population with knowledge of the attack: (a) murder; (b) extermination; (c) enslavement; (d) deportation or forcible transfer of population; (e) imprisonment; (f) torture; (g) rape or any other form of sexual violence; (h) persecution against any identifiable group or collectivity on political, racial, national, ethnic, cultural, religious, gender; (i) enforced disappearance of persons; (j) the crime of apartheid; (k) other inhumane acts of a similar character intentionally causing great suffering, or serious injury to body or to mental or physical health.[126]

Firstly, as discussed in detail in the previous sections, there are various reports that prove that the Indonesian government and its security apparatus have been killing Papuans over the years, which means that they are chargeable under the Rome Statute Article 7 (a). Secondly, the Indonesian security apparatus has been engaged in the torture, disappearances, and arbitrary arrests of Papuans, which constitute unequivocal acts of the sections (d)(e)(f)(g), and (k) of this article. Grave concerns have been raised even by UN Special Rapporteurs on the rights of indigenous people, on extrajudicial, summary, or arbitrary executions, and on the human rights of internally displaced persons, Morris Tidball-Binz, Francisco Cali Tzay, and Cecilia Jimenez-Damary. In their joint statement, the UN Special Rapporteurs stated that they received allegations that extrajudicial killings, rapes, enforced disappearances, tortures, inhumane treatment, and forced displacements by the Indonesian security forces.[127] According to their statement, they estimated that as of 2022, the numbers of Papuans internally displaced are between 60,000 and 100,000.[128] The Special Rapporteurs also emphasised that these allegations may just be the tip of the iceberg and that there must be ample of incidents that went unreported since independent monitors, NGOs and media are still not allowed into the region.

As such, with this report and the collection of analyses in the previous sections, it arrives at the conclusion that, even if, my arguments that the Indonesia government and its apparatus have committed genocide and continue to against the Papuans are not legally permissible, we cannot argue against the proofs that the former has committed substantial acts of crimes against humanity over the years against the latter. As a result of this, it shows that the Indonesian government has committed not one but two crimes against the principle of R2P, which should, in theory, invoke responses from the international and regional community, which will be discussed if they have done so in the following chapter.

## 7.4 The Reactions of the International Community

This section examines the reactions of the international community to the continuous crisis of the Papuans in West Papua, Indonesia. Following the patterns from the previous chapters, I will start with the examination of reactions from the UN bodies, which will be followed by reactions from the European Parliament and relevant individual States. It is important that I analyse the reactions from these actors in order to assess whether they have explicitly invoked the Pillars of R2P or merely used R2P language without referencing the concept or not at all.

Unlike the previous case studies of East Timor and the Rohingya crises where I analyse the reactions of international and regional actors to a specific period of time where the crisis erupted along with humanitarian crises as a result, instead for the case of the Papuans, I will analyse the reactions in 1969 (after the Act of Free Choice), the last few years and if there are any reactions that stand out.

The first UN bodies that will be discussed are the human rights apparatus, the Human Rights Council (UNHRC) and the Office of the High Commissioner for Human Rights (OHCHR). There were no reactions from either the OHCHR or the UNHRC after the result of the Act of Free Choice was announced as these bodies were only created in 1993 and 2006, consecutively. Unlike in responses to the East Timor and Rohingya crises, there have been no resolutions nor fact-finding missions since the Indonesian government is still adamant on refusing foreign interventions in any form. Nevertheless, these two bodies still release statements to make their positions clear on the matter. In 2013, the UN High Commissioner for Human Rights, Navi Pillay released a statement to express concerns over the crackdown on pro-independence protestors that involved the violations of freedom of speech and expression, unlawful imprisonments, killings, and arrests. The Commissioner also urged Indonesia to allow international journalists and UN Special Rapporteurs into West Papua to investigate the reports of human rights violations, which have been denied.[129]

In 2020, Ravina Shamdasani, a spokesperson for the OHCHR released a statement expressing the body's disturbance at reports of a series of extrajudicial killings, unlawful arrests, unlawful imprisonments, and harassment of activists and protestors that were happening in West Papua.[130] Although Shamdasani did not clearly state it, these acts committed by the Indonesian security apparatus approximate to acts of crimes against humanity. However, this specific R2P crime was not mentioned nor R2P language was used in this statement. In 2022, as was discussed in the previous section, three UN Special Rapporteurs reported the humanitarian crisis in West Papua has been deteriorating with reports of extrajudicial killings, rapes, enforced disappearances, tortures, inhumane treatment, and forced displacements by the Indonesia security forces, which I have argued that these are acts of crimes against humanity.[131] Although this was not explicitly mentioned in the Rapporteurs' report, the Rapporteurs once again called upon the Indonesian government to allow an independent investigation to be carried out to which the latter replied by saying that the former's report is biased, and it has denied allegations that it is responsible for the displacements of the Papuans.[132] Furthermore, the Indonesian government emphasised that the region needs to be militarised because of the 'armed criminal group' activities (pro-independence group). In 2023, Alice Wairimu Nderitu, Under Secretary-General, Special Advisor to the Secretary-General on the Prevention of Genocide, released a report as an update to the UNHRC in which she included West Papua as an area of rising concern. In the report, Nderitu stated that the human rights situation in Papua remains deeply concerning, which includes alleged 'harassment, arbitrary arrests, and detention of Papuans and non-recognition of indigenous Papuans that has enabled the alleged appropriation of indigenous lands'.[133] Following the other statements made, this report also ended with urging the Indonesian government to allow independent humanitarian assessment. Lastly in 2024, a dialogue session was carried out between Indonesia and experts of the Human Rights Committee under the auspices of the OHCHR. In this session, the experts expressed their concerns over the extrajudicial killings and excessive use of force against the Papuans and inquired as to why Indonesia had not conducted public investigations or released the findings of an internal investigation, if there were any.[134] Indonesia responded by stating that it has implemented affirmative actions aimed at improving the lives of the Papuans and that through the Special Autonomy Law, the Indonesian government has ensured a larger presentation of the Papuans in local government and has also increased the allocation of funds to the regional development.[135] The Indonesian government has subsequently blamed the armed separatist groups for the violence, killings, and human rights violations that occurred in West Papua, thereby avoiding any responsibility. It is important to note that whilst there have not been any references made to R2P, the repeated requests by various UN human rights apparatus are a form of indirectly instrumentalising Pillar II of R2P. Unfortunately, as discussed earlier, this action requires the consent of Indonesia, which is still adamant about refusing it until the present day.

Another UN body that is of significance to this case study is the UN Special Committee on Decolonisation (C24), which is mandated to

> (i) examine the application of the Declaration on the Granting of Independence to Colonial Countries and Peoples and (ii) to make suggestions and recommendations on the progress and extent of the implementation of the Declaration (on the granting of independence to colonial countries and peoples).[136]

In 2017, the exiled Papuan leader, Benny Wenda presented a petition signed by 1.8 million Papuans (70% of the Papuans' population) to the C24. The petition, which Wenda said had to be smuggled across Papua since it was banned by the Indonesian government, asked the UN to appoint a special Rapporteur to investigate the human rights abuses in the region, and 'to put West Papua back on the decolonisation committee agenda and ensure that their right to self-determination . . . is respected by holding an internationally supervised vote'.[137] Wenda further stated, 'After decades of suffering, decades of genocide, decades of occupation, we open up the voice of the West Papuan people which lives inside this petition. My people want to be free'.[138] Unfortunately, the chair of the C24 rejected this petition saying that it was outside the mandate of the Committee and that the Committee will not do anything against Indonesia (who is a member of the C24). In response to this, Indonesia also emphasised that West Papua region is a sovereign part of Indonesia is an indisputable fact and internationally recognised after the 1969 Act of Free Choice. Wenda and the Papuans' right to self-determination had once against been withheld.

In terms of reactions from the UN General Assembly (GA), it has also been limited. No resolution has been adopted. The only time the issue of the West Papua crisis was brought up was by the Pacific Island countries who share the root of Melanesian ethnicity with the Papuans. In 2016 (Nauru, Marshall Islands, Tuvalu, Vanuatu, Solomon Islands, Tonga, and Palau) and 2017 (Solomon Islands, Tuvalu and Vanuatu), the Pacific Island countries raised the plight of the Papuans during the 71st and 72nd Sessions of the GA, where they collectively called upon the principle of self-determination to be respected and for the human rights violations to be investigated.[139] In response to these statements, Indonesia emphasised that the issue of West Papua is an internal matter and that no States should interfere with it. As of the latest session of the GA in 2023, the 78th session, unfortunately, the issue of West Papua was not brought up.[140] It is also important to note that although the Pacific Island States raised the issue of the West Papua crisis, R2P was not referred in any capacity nor its language such as 'it is the responsibility of Indonesia to protect its people'.

Lastly for the UN bodies, the UN Security (SC) is the supreme decision-making body when it comes to responding to humanitarian crises as it has the authority to invoke both non-coercive and, most importantly, coercive measures. Furthermore, as was discussed in detail in Chapter 2, Section 2.4, the SC is the only 'right authority' that has the power to mandate any form of intervention by any State or group of States when it comes to invoking the R2P Pillars. Unfortunately, in the case of the West Papua crisis, there has been no reaction from the SC, which could be explained by the fact that the US is a member of the permanent members of the SC (p-5). And with the US and Indonesia's close relationship, it comes as no surprise that the West Papua issue would not be on the agenda of the SC.

As of 2024, both the Dutch and European parliaments have issued statements demanding that the OHCHR representatives be allowed into West Papua for a fact-finding mission in order to investigate the human rights violations perpetrated by the Indonesian security apparatus.[141] Whilst these are appropriate steps that these actors urged the Indonesian government to take, again, no references to R2P were made.

As for individual State responses to the West Papua crisis, one that stands out is the US since it is a superpower and is a member of the P-5 that wields significant diplomatic power in the international community.[142] As was discussed in detail in Section 7.2.2, the US was the fuel to Indonesia's ambition to annex West Papua into their territory in the first place and it was essentially because of the US that the Dutch gave up on its dispute with Indonesia over West Papua. It was due to the US realising the strategic importance that Indonesia holds since the late 1950s and 1960s. As a result of this, the US continues to have a close relationship with Indonesia until the present day. Even with continuous various reports that emerged over the years regarding allegations of genocide, crimes against humanity, and multitudes of human rights abuses perpetrated against the Papuans, the US continues to specifically have a close relationship with the Indonesia military, the *Tentara Nasional Indonesia* (TNI). It is precisely the TNI that is the main source of the reported violations perpetrated against the Papuans. Pushing this fact aside, the US continues to hold both bilateral and multilateral military training and assistance programmes with the TNI.[143] Whilst attention on the West Papua crisis fluctuates throughout the years depending on different administrations and lawmakers in Congress usually through congressional reporting on the situation, there has only been one development in the relationship between the US and Indonesia that stood out. In 2002, there was a shootout between Freeport, which resulted in the death of two American citizens that was perpetrated by the TNI.[144] As a result of this, the US Congress voted to ban International Military Education and Training and Foreign Military Financing for Indonesia until certain conditions were met. The conditions listed were transparency in the military budget and accountability for rights violations in East Timor, West Papua, and Aceh.[145] However, these bans did not last long and were lifted in 2005. An important factor here that called the US Congress into action was that there were American citizens involved and not the fact that the Papuans face violations from the TNI every day. Whilst this can be understood to an extent as the US implying methods of Pillar III of R2P, it is hard to believe that it was done so for the good of the Papuans. It is more likely that the US was responsive because it did not want to be seen as not pursuing justice for the deaths of its citizens, hence, why it was lifted only after three years. Since then, there have been no concrete actions from the US regarding the West Papua crisis.

## 7.5 The Reaction of ASEAN and ASEAN States

A crucial factor that played into my decision-making when it came to choosing a third appropriate case study for this book is the face that West Papua is Indonesia's territory and Indonesia is a member of ASEAN. Because of this, it is even more imperative that I analyse ASEAN and its member states' responses or lack thereof to this crisis in order to see whether they still abide by the ASEAN Way when it comes to applying the concepts of sovereignty, non-interference and human rights in their foreign relations with their fellow ASEAN member, or abide by their *conceptual* endorsements of R2P.[146] In this section, I will examine to see whether ASEAN as an organisation had any responses to the West Papua crisis.

Since ASEAN was formed in 1967 and did not convene its first summit until 1976 when the cooperation between members was more structurally organised, there were no official reactions to the result of the Act of Free Choice. As was discussed in Chapter 3, Section 3.3, ASEAN as an organisation operates under a set of rules known as the ASEAN Way, which consists of non-interference, consensus-based decision-making, national and regional resilience, respect for the national sovereignty, the renunciation of the threat or use of force, and peaceful settlement of disputes.[147] ASEAN was not created to challenge its members, especially with issues that are considered as an internal affair of that member. Since R2P can be an intrusive concept, especially when it comes to Pillar III, ASEAN did not have a collective response or standing when it comes to it.[148] As a result of this, through the ASEAN Summits (the Summit is ASEAN's supreme policy-making body) and the ASEAN Foreign Ministerial Meetings, there had been no mention of West Papua at all. This can easily be explained by stating the fact that Indonesia is the biggest member in terms of economy and population; therefore, no other members wanted to be seen as interfering with Indonesia. Since there was never any mention of West Papua through any of the ASEAN apparatus, it comes as no surprise that no references were made to R2P regarding this crisis.

Expectantly, the same can be said about the rest of ASEAN members. Throughout the years, there have been no reactions or even comments from Thailand, Singapore, Malaysia, the Philippines, Vietnam, Cambodia, Myanmar, Brunei, and Laos regarding West Papua. For the same justification stated earlier, it does not hold any weight the fact that all ASEAN members endorsed R2P as a concept, whilst it varies on the degree when it comes to the three Pillars, the members all endorsed the basic concept of R2P, which is the responsibility to protect your population from the four crimes. On top of abiding by the ASEAN Way, the ASEAN members placed higher importance on their strategic relationships and *real politik* considerations with Indonesia rather than calling upon the protection of the Papuans.

## 7.6 Conclusion

For the last 55 years, the world has been seeing the Papuans robbed of the right to self-determination, and as a population, they have been subjected to continuous abuses that as I argued earlier, amount to the crime of genocide and crimes against humanity perpetrated by the Indonesian government along with its security apparatus. In 2005, when the UN adopted the concept and Pillars of R2P, it was thought to be a game changer when it comes to responding to humanitarian crises around the world. Every single member of the UN endorsed the reconceptualised perception of sovereignty, which along with it, carries the responsibilities of States to protect their people from genocide, crimes against humanity, ethnic cleansing, and war crimes, and in the event that the State is either unable or unwilling to, then the residual responsibility would fall onto other actors in the international community since we are all interconnected. There were high hopes when R2P was endorsed by the international community, and most importantly ASEAN member states. As mentioned earlier, whilst ASEAN member states' *conceptual* endorsements of R2P vary in degrees, regarding the three Pillars of R2P, they all endorse Pillar I. Pillar I refers to the responsibility of each State to protect its population against the aforementioned four crimes. In theory, the ASEAN members should have called upon Indonesia to uphold its Pillar I responsibility since throughout the years the latter's security apparatus had been and continues to commit acts of crimes against humanity and crucially, genocide against the Papuans. Whilst we have said in theory this is what should have happened, this non-responsive stance taken by the ASEAN members also comes as no surprise. The ASEAN members are notoriously known to strictly abide by their ASEAN Way, especially the rule on non-interference. An additional factor that strengthens their commitment to the rule on non-interference is the fact that ASEAN member states' domestic climates are mostly highly volatile, which occasionally involve incidents of human rights violations. As a result of this, when a crisis occurs within any of the member states, the rest do not want to necessarily speak out when it easily be seen as hypocritical. Lastly, after having examined ASEAN and its member states' reactions to the West Papua crisis along with the East Timor, and Rohingya crises, we can be confident in saying that their *conceptual* endorsements of R2P have not been translated into action, since they all stand in solidarity with Indonesia.

The following chapter focuses on examining China's approaches to the three Pillars of R2P and its reactions to the three case studies of East Timor, Rohingya, and West Papua in order to analyse the correlations between China and ASEAN member states.

## Notes

1 Independent legal and academic experts from Yale University, Sydney University, the Asia Human Rights Commission, and many more have argued that genocide has been committed in West Papua since having been annexed as part of Indonesia in 1969. Their works are Elizabeth Brundige, et al., 'Indonesian Human Rights Abuses in West Papua: Application of the Law of Genocide to the History of Indonesian Control' [2004] *The Allard K. Lowenstein International Human Rights Clinic Yale Law School*; Jim Elmslie and Camellia B. Webb-Gannon, 'A Slow-Motion Genocide: Indonesia Rule in West Papua' [2013] *Griffith Journal of Law and Human Dignity*; and 'The Neglected Genocide: Human Rights Abuses Against Papuans in the Central Highlands, 1977–1978' [2013] *Asian Human Rights Commission.*

2 Bilveer Singh, *Papua: Geopolitics and the Quest for Nationhood* (Routledge, 2017) p. 18; and Kjell Anderson, 'Colonialism and Cold Genocide: The Case of West Papua' [2015] 9(2) *Genocide Studies and Prevention: An International Journal*, p. 12.

3 Kjell Anderson, 'Colonialism and Cold Genocide: The Case of West Papua' [2015] 9(2) *Genocide Studies and Prevention: An International Journal*, p. 12; and M. Lynn Landweer and Peter Unseth, 'An Introduction to language use in Melanesia' [2012] 214 *International Journal of the Sociology of Language*, pp. 1–3.
4 Bilveer Singh, *Papua: Geopolitics and the Quest for Nationhood* (Routledge, 2017) p. 19.
5 Ibid.
6 'The Neglected Genocide: Human Rights Abuses Against Papuans in the Central Highlands, 1977–1978' [2013] Asian Human Rights Commission, p. 3.
7 Bilveer Singh, *Papua: Geopolitics and the Quest for Nationhood* (Routledge, 2017) pp. 23–24.
8 'The Neglected Genocide: Human Rights Abuses Against Papuans in the Central Highlands, 1977–1978' [2013] Asian Human Rights Commission, p. 3.
9 Ibid.
10 Bilveer Singh, *Papua: Geopolitics and the Quest for Nationhood* (Routledge, 2017) pp. 61–62.
11 Ibid.
12 'The Neglected Genocide: Human Rights Abuses Against Papuans in the Central Highlands, 1977–1978' [2013] Asian Human Rights Commission, p. 4.
13 Bilveer Singh, *Papua: Geopolitics and the Quest for Nationhood* (Routledge, 2017) p. 58.
14 Robert C. Bone, Jr., *The Dynamics of the Western New Guinea (Irian Barat) Problem* (Cornell University, 1958) pp. 85–86.
15 'The Neglected Genocide: Human Rights Abuses Against Papuans in the Central Highlands, 1977–1978' [2013] Asian Human Rights Commission, p. 1.
16 Ibid., p. 4; this date and the flag would later become a controversial form of expression but still remain an important symbolic gesture for the Papuans.
17 Bilveer Singh, *Papua: Geopolitics and the Quest for Nationhood* (Routledge, 2017) p. 63.
18 Ibid.
19 Ibid., pp. 63–64.
20 Ibid., p. 56.
21 Ibid., p. 86.
22 Mohammad Hatta, 'Indonesia between the Power Blocs' [1958] 36 *Foreign Affairs*, pp. 486–489.
23 Bilveer Singh, *Papua: Geopolitics and the Quest for Nationhood* (Routledge, 2017) pp. 88–89; and Guy J. Pauker, 'The Soviet Challenge In Indonesia' [1962] 40(40) *Foreign Affairs*, pp. 612–627.
24 Wynfred Joshua and Stephen Gilberd, *Arms for the Third World: Soviet Military Aid and Diplomacy* (Johns Hopkins University Press, 1969) p. 73.
25 Bilveer Singh, *Papua: Geopolitics and the Quest for Nationhood* (Routledge, 2017) p. 88.
26 John Martinkus, *The Road: Uprising in West Papua* (Black Inc, 2020) pp. 14–15.
27 Bilveer Singh, *Papua: Geopolitics and the Quest for Nationhood* (Routledge, 2017) p. 91.
28 Brian May, *Indonesian Tragedy* (Singapore: Routledge & Kegan Paul Ltd, 2001) p. 165.
29 Bilveer Singh, *Papua: Geopolitics and the Quest for Nationhood* (Routledge, 2017) p. 91; it looks as though Indonesia was once again successful in exploiting the Cold War rivalry of using the context of containing the spread of communism to its advantage just like it did in the case of East Timor in the early days, which was discussed in Chapter 5.
30 Ibid.
31 The New York Agreement (1962) Article II.
32 Ibid., Article IX.
33 Ibid., Article X.
34 Ibid., Articles XIII and XVII.
35 Ibid., Article XVIII.

36 Ibid., Article XXII.
37 John Martinkus, *The Road: Uprising in West Papua* (Black Inc, 2020) p. 16.
38 Ibid.
39 Elizabeth Brundige, et al., 'Indonesian Human Rights Abuses in West Papua: Application of the Law of Genocide to the History of Indonesian Control' [2004] *The Allard K. Lowenstein International Human Rights Clinic Yale Law School*, pp. 14–15.
40 'History of West Papua' <https://www.freepapuamovement.org/about-us/> accessed on 4 February 2024.
41 Elizabeth Brundige, et al., 'Indonesian Human Rights Abuses in West Papua: Application of the Law of Genocide to the History of Indonesian Control' [2004] *The Allard K. Lowenstein International Human Rights Clinic Yale Law School*, p. 15.
42 'Human Rights in Papua: An Overview' (Watch Indonesia, 4–5 June 2003) <https://www.watchindonesia.de/6878/human-rights-overview-papua?lang=en> accessed on 4 February 2024.
43 Bilveer Singh, *Papua: Geopolitics and the Quest for Nationhood* (Routledge, 2017) p. 97.
44 United Nations General Assembly, Report of the Secretary-General Regarding the Act of Self-Determination in West Irian, (1969) A/7723, para 1.
45 Bilveer Singh, *Papua: Geopolitics and the Quest for Nationhood* (Routledge, 2017) p. 93.
46 Ibid.
47 Elizabeth Brundige, et al., 'Indonesian Human Rights Abuses in West Papua: Application of the Law of Genocide to the History of Indonesian Control' [2004] *The Allard K. Lowenstein International Human Rights Clinic Yale Law School*, p. 16.
48 Ibid.
49 United Nations General Assembly, Report of the Secretary-General Regarding the Act of Self-Determination in West Irian, (1969) A/7723, para 6; criticisms emitted from various actors including the OPM as this number was a mere 0.1% of the population of Papuans at the time, in which the result would not be fairly and fully representative of the actual will of the people.
50 Elizabeth Brundige, et al., 'Indonesian Human Rights Abuses in West Papua: Application of the Law of Genocide to the History of Indonesian Control' [2004] *The Allard K. Lowenstein International Human Rights Clinic Yale Law School*, p. 17.
51 Ibid., p. 18.
52 Ibid.
53 The United Nations General Assembly Resolution 2504 (1969) A/RES/2504(XXIV).
54 'Fifty Years of Corporate Exploitation: The Story of US Mining Giant Freeport & Papua's Stolen Sovereignty (Part One)' (Corporate Accountability Law, 28 February 2022) <https://corpaccountabilitylab.org/calblog/2022/2/28/fifty-years-of-corporate-exploitation-the-story-of-us-mining-giant-freeport-amp-papuas-stolen-sovereignty-part-i> accessed on 4 February 2024.
55 Elizabeth Brundige, et al., 'Indonesian Human Rights Abuses in West Papua: Application of the Law of Genocide to the History of Indonesian Control' [2004] *The Allard K. Lowenstein International Human Rights Clinic Yale Law School*, p. 18.
56 Emir Chairullah, *Indonesia's Failure in Papua: The Role of Elites in Designing, Implementing and Undermining Special Autonomy* (Routledge, 2022) p. 88.
57 Ibid.
58 It is also crucial to point out that it was so the Indonesian military under General Suharto that committed war crimes and crimes against humanity against the East Timorese, which was discussed in detail in Chapter 5, Section 5.2. Emir Chairullah, *Indonesia's Failure in Papua: The Role of Elites in Designing, Implementing and Undermining Special Autonomy* (Routledge, 2022) p. 88.
59 United Nations General Assembly, *2005 World Summit Outcome*, resolution adopted by the General Assembly, 24 October 2005, A/RES/60/1, para 138.

60 Julius Cesar I. Trajano, 'Ethnic Nationalism and Separatism in West Papua, Indonesia' [2010] 16 *Journal of Peace, Conflict and Development*, p. 18.
61 Ibid.
62 Bilveer Singh, *Papua: Geopolitics and the Quest for Nationhood* (Routledge, 2017) p. 102.
63 Ibid., p. 99.
64 Even if I intend to list out all the operations and incidents between the Indonesian military that resulted in the deaths of civilians, it would be beyond the bounds of possibilities because there were/are cases where it was not reported. This is because Indonesia had treated West Papua essentially as a military zone with limited access to outsiders, hence, it is highly unlikely that all cases were reported.
65 Elizabeth Brundige, et al., 'Indonesian Human Rights Abuses in West Papua: Application of the Law of Genocide to the History of Indonesian Control' [2004] *The Allard K. Lowenstein International Human Rights Clinic Yale Law School*, p. 19.
66 'The Neglected Genocide: Human Rights Abuses Against Papuans in the Central Highlands, 1977–1978' [2013] Asian Human Rights Commission, p. 7.
67 Ibid.
68 Ibid.
69 Elizabeth Brundige, et al., 'Indonesian Human Rights Abuses in West Papua: Application of the Law of Genocide to the History of Indonesian Control' [2004] *The Allard K. Lowenstein International Human Rights Clinic Yale Law School*, p. 19.
70 John Martinkus, *The Road: Uprising in West Papua* (Black Inc, 2020) p. 20.
71 Kjell Anderson, 'Colonialism and Cold Genocide: The Case of West Papua' [2015] 9(2) *Genocide Studies and Prevention: An International Journal*, p. 13.
72 Bilveer Singh, *Papua: Geopolitics and the Quest for Nationhood* (Routledge, 2017) p. 103.
73 Ibid; and R.J. May, 'Fifty Years after the "Act of Free Choice": The West Papua Issue in a Regional Context' [2021] *The Department of Pacific Affairs*, p. 3.
74 Jeffrey S. Bachman, *Cultural Genocide: Law, Politics, and Global Manifestations* (Routledge, 2021) pp. 184–185.
75 'The Indigenous World 2022: West Papua' (International Work Group for Indigenous Affairs, 2022) <https://iwgia.org/en/indonesia/4660-iw-2022-west-papua.html?highlight=WyJ3ZXN0Iiwid2VzdCdzdXdldCdlbiIsInBhcHVhIiwicGFwdWEncyIsInBhcHVhJyIsIndlc3QgcGFwdWEiXQ==> accessed on 6 February 2024.
76 Jim Elmslie, 'Economic and Social Indicators in West Papua' (Pacific Institute of Public Policy, 2013).
77 Ibid.
78 Emir Chairullah, *Indonesia's Failure in Papua: The Role of Elites in Designing, Implementing and Undermining Special Autonomy* (Routledge, 2022) p. 88.
79 Ibid.
80 Ibid.
81 John Martinkus, *The Road: Uprising in West Papua* (Black Inc, 2020) pp. 31–32.
82 Ibid., p. 32.
83 Julius Cesar I. Trajano, 'Ethnic Nationalism and Separatism in West Papua, Indonesia' [2010] 16 *Journal of Peace, Conflict and Development*, p. 23.
84 'Freeport-McMoran Profit Plunges on Reduced Production' (Mining Technology, 24 April2023)<https://www.mining-technology.com/news/freeport-mcmoran-profit-plunges/?cf-view> accessed on 7 February 2024.
85 John Martinkus, *The Road: Uprising in West Papua* (Black Inc, 2020) p. 32.
86 Ibid.
87 Raymond Bonner and Jane Perlez, 'Inquiry Sought on Mining Company' (The New York Times, 29 January 2006) <https://www.nytimes.com/2006/01/29/world/asia/inquiry-sought-on-mining-company.html> accessed on 7 February 2024.

88 'Freeport Mining and Its Environment Impacts on the Riverine Ecosystem' (Lembaga Peduli Masyarakat Wilaya Mimika Timur Jau, 24 June 2022) p. 3 <https://www.ohchr.org/sites/default/files/2022-06/Solidarity%20for%20Indigenous%20Papuans1.pdf> accessed on 7 February 2024.

89 Ibid., pp. 6–7.

90 Ibid., pp. 8–12.

91 Ibid., pp. 12–13.

92 Ibid., pp. 13–14.

93 John Martinkus, *The Road: Uprising in West Papua* (Black Inc, 2020) pp. 32–33.

94 Ibid.

95 Emir Chairullah, *Indonesia's Failure in Papua: The Role of Elites in Designing, Implementing and Undermining Special Autonomy* (Routledge, 2022) pp. 92–93.

96 'Strike Prolonged in Controversial Papuan Mine' (Aljazeera, 9 November 2011) <https://www.aljazeera.com/economy/2011/11/9/strike-prolonged-in-controversial-papuan-mine> accessed on 10 February 2024; 'Protestor Killed in Indonesia Mine Strike' (The Guardian, 10 October 2011) <https://www.theguardian.com/world/2011/oct/10/indonesian-forces-striking-mine-workers> accessed on 10 February 2024; Cecilia Jamasmie, 'Strike Hits Freeport's Grasberg Mine in Indonesia' (Mining, 3 October 2016) <https://www.mining.com/strike-hits-freeports-grasberg-mine-in-indonesia/> accessed on 10 February 2024; 'Jokowi Urged to Resolve Freeport Worker Strike Amid Share Talks with CEOs' (West Papua Daily, 17 November 2023) <https://en.jubi.id/jokowi-urged-to-resolve-freeport-worker-strike-amid-share-talks-with-ceos/> accessed on 10 February 2024.

97 Emir Chairullah, *Indonesia's Failure in Papua: The Role of Elites in Designing, Implementing and Undermining Special Autonomy* (Routledge, 2022) p. 58.

98 Ibid., pp. 58–59.

99 Ibid., pp. 62–63; it should also be noted that a crucial factor that was most likely considered in the Indonesian elites' consideration when it came to this referendum negotiation was that they were extremely against it as Indonesia was facing secession sentiments in East Timor around the same time, which was discussed in detail in Chapter 5.

100 Emir Chairullah, *Indonesia's Failure in Papua: The Role of Elites in Designing, Implementing and Undermining Special Autonomy* (Routledge, 2022) p. 81.

101 Ibid., pp. 81–82.

102 Ibid., p. 103.

103 Ibid.

104 Ibid., pp. 64–65.

105 Johnny Blades, 'West Papua: The Issue That Won't Go Away For Melanesia' (Lowy Institute Analysis, 2020) p. 26; and 'West Papuans Jailed for Raising Banned Morning Star Flag' (RNZ, 2 September 2022) <https://www.rnz.co.nz/international/pacific-news/473973/west-papuans-jailed-for-raising-banned-morning-star-flag> accessed on 10 February 2024.

106 Made Supriatma, 'The Second Amendment to Papua's Special Autonomy Law and the Recentralization of Power to Jakarta' (ISEAS Perspective, 2021) <https://www.iseas.edu.sg/articles-commentaries/iseas-perspective/2021–123-the-second-amendment-to-papuas-special-autonomy-law-and-the-recentralization-of-power-to-jakarta-by-made-supriatma/> accessed on 10 February 2024.

107 Ibid.

108 Kate Lamb, 'West Papua Protests: Indonesia Deploys 1,000 Soldiers to Quell Unrest, Cuts Internet' (The Guardian, 22 August 2019) <https://www.theguardian.com/world/2019/aug/22/west-papua-protests-indonesia-deploys-1000-soldiers-to-quell-unrest> accessed on 10 February 2024; Rory James, '"We Are Living in a War Zone": Violence Flares in West Papua as Villagers Forced to Flee' (The Guardian, 11 May 2021) <https://www.theguardian.com/world/2021/may/11/

we-are-living-in-a-war-zone-violence-flares-in-west-papua-as-villagers-forced-to-flee> accessed on 10 February 2024.

109 'New Zealand Calls for Pilot to Be Freed a Year after Papua Kidnapping' (The Jakarta Post, 5 February 2024) <https://www.thejakartapost.com/world/2024/02/05/new-zealand-calls-for-pilot-to-be-freed-a-year-after-papua-kidnapping.html> accessed on 10 February 2024.

110 United Nations General Assembly, *2005 World Summit Outcome*, resolution adopted by the General Assembly, 24 October 2005, A/RES/60/1, paras 138–139.

111 Convention on the Prevention and Punishment of the Crime of Genocide (1948), Article II.

112 Ibid., Article I.

113 Ibid., Article II.

114 The Rwandan genocide is discussed in Chapter 2, Section 2.2 and the Rohingya genocide is discussed in detail in Chapter 6, Section 6.3.

115 Jeffrey S. Bachman, *Cultural Genocide: Law, Politics, and Global Manifestations* (Routledge, 2021) p. 93.

116 Anderson has done a remarkable job at conceptually distinguishing between *cold* and *hot genocides* in Chapter 7 of Jeffrey S. Bachman, *Cultural Genocide: Law, Politics, and Global Manifestations* (Routledge, 2021).

117 Ibid., pp. 193–194.

118 Ibid., p. 194.

119 Ibid.

120 Ibid.

121 Ibid.

122 'Benny Wenda: Genocide Is Happening in West Papua' (united Liberation Movement for West Papua, 17 November 2023) <https://www.ulmwp.org/benny-wenda-genocide-is-happening-in-west-papua#:~:text=Over%2060%20years%20of%20genocidal,been%20killed%20by%20Indonesian%20forces.> accessed on 11 February 2024.

123 Elizabeth Brundige, et al., 'Indonesian Human Rights Abuses in West Papua: Application of the Law of Genocide to the History of Indonesian Control' [2004] *The Allard K. Lowenstein International Human Rights Clinic Yale Law School*, pp. 63–67.

124 Ibid., pp. 69–70.

125 John Wing and Peter King, 'Genocide in West Papua? The Role of Indonesian State Apparatus and a Current Needs Assessment of the Papuan People' (The Centre for Peace and Conflict Studies, 2005) pp. 8–10.

126 The Rome Statute of the International Criminal Court (1998), Article 7.

127 'Indonesia: UN Experts Sound Alarm on Serious Papua Abuses, Call for Urgent Aid' (United Nations Human Rights Office of the High Commission Press Release, 1 March 2022) <https://www.ohchr.org/en/press-releases/2022/03/indonesia-un-experts-sound-alarm-serious-papua-abuses-call-urgent-aid> accessed on 12 February 2024.

128 Ibid.

129 'Pillay Concerned About Persistent Violence and Abuses in Papua (Indonesia)' (Office of the High Commissioner for Human Rights Press Release, 2 May 2013) <https://www.ohchr.org/en/press-releases/2013/05/pillay-concerned-about-persistent-violence-and-abuses-papua-indonesia?LangID=E&NewsID=13287> accessed on 13 February 2024.

130 'Comment by UN Human Rights Office Spokesperson Ravina Shamdasani on Papua and West Papua, Indonesia' (Office of the High Commissioner for Human Rights Press Release, 30 November 2020) <https://www.ohchr.org/en/statements/2020/11/comment-un-human-rights-office-spokesperson-ravina-shamdasani-papua-and-west?LangID=E&NewsID=26551> accessed on 13 February 2024.

131 'Indonesia: UN Experts Sound Alarm on Serious Papua Abuses, Call for Urgent Aid' (United Nations Human Rights Office of the High Commission Press Release, 1 March 2022) <https://www.ohchr.org/en/press-releases/2022/03/indonesia-un-experts-sound-alarm-serious-papua-abuses-call-urgent-aid> accessed on 12 February 2024.

132 'Indonesia Dismisses U.N Experts' Call to Probe Alleged Abuses in Papua' (Reuters, 2 March 2022) <https://www.reuters.com/world/asia-pacific/indonesia-dismisses-un-experts-call-probe-alleged-abuses-papua-2022-03-02/> accessed on 13 February 2024.

133 'Remarks by Ms. Alice Wairimu Nderitu, Under Secretary-General, Special Advisor to the Secretary-General on the Prevention of Genocide' (United Nations Press Release, 4 July 2023) <https://www.un.org/en/genocideprevention/documents/Remarks_Alice%20Wairimu%20Nderitu_Special%20Adviser_53rd_Session_HRC_Interactive_dialogue%20.pdf> accessed on 13 February 2024.

134 'In Dialogue with Indonesia, Experts of the Human Rights Committee Commend Measures Promoting Women's Political Participation, Raise Questions on Air Pollution and Water Pollution, and on Excessive Use of Force against Indigenous Papuans' (Office of the High Commissioner for Human Rights Press Release, 12 March 2024) <https://www.ohchr.org/en/news/2024/03/dialogue-indonesia-experts-human-rights-committee-commend-measures-promoting-womens> accessed on 12 March 2024.

135 Ibid.

136 'Special Committee on Decolonization' (United Nations) <https://www.un.org/dppa/decolonization/en/c24/about> accessed on 13 February 2024.

137 Ben Doherty and Kate Lamb, 'West Papua Independence Petition Is Rebuffed at the UN' (The Guardian, 30 September 2017) <https://www.theguardian.com/world/2017/sep/30/west-papua-independence-petition-is-rebuffed-at-un> accessed on 13 February 2024.

138 Ibid.

139 'Seven Countries Support West Papua at the UN General Assembly!' (Free West Papua Campaign, 27 September 2016) <https://www.freewestpapua.org/2016/09/27/seven-countries-support-west-papua-at-the-un-general-assembly/> accessed on 13 February 2024; and 'Fiery Debate Over West Papua at UN General Assembly' (RNZ, 27 September 2017) <https://www.rnz.co.nz/international/programmes/datelinepacific/audio/201860156/fiery-debate-over-west-papua-at-un-general-assembly> accessed on 13 February 2024.

140 Jayanty Nada Shofa, 'Indonesia Says No One Brings Up Papua Issue at Recent UNGA Forum' (Jakarta Globe, 29 September 2023) <https://jakartaglobe.id/news/indonesia-says-no-one-brings-up-papua-issue-at-recent-unga-forum> accessed on 13 February 2024.

141 'Meeting in European Parliament Demands UN Visit to West Papua' (United Liberation Movement for West Papua, 22 January 2024) <https://www.ulmwp.org/meeting-in-european-parliament-demands-un-visit-to-west-papua> accessed on 13 February 2024; and 'Hearing in Dutch Parliament Calls for UN Visit to West Papua' (United Liberation Movement for West Papua, 29 February 2024) <https://www.ulmwp.org/hearing-in-dutch-parliament-calls-for-un-visit-to-west-papua> accessed on 5 March 2024.

142 Another State that is appropriate to examine its responses or lack thereof is China as it is also a superpower and a member of the P-5.

143 'CARAT Indonesia 2022 Kicks Off with Indonesia and U.S Navy and Marine Corps' (The United States Navy, 7 December 2022) <https://www.navy.mil/Press-Office/News-Stories/Article/3238091/carat-indonesia-2022-kicks-off-with-indonesian-and-us-navy-and-marine-corps/> accessed on 13 February 2024; and 'Indonesian, US Troops Begin "Super Garuda Shield" Joint Drills' (The Jakarta Post, 31 August 2023) <https://www.thejakartapost.com/indonesia/2023/08/31/indonesian-us-troops-begin-super-garuda-shield-joint-drills.html> accessed on 13 February 2024.

144 'The West Papua Report: March 2004' (East Timor & Indonesia Action Network, 2004) <https://www.etan.org/issues/wpapua/rfk2/0403wpap.htm> accessed on 13 February 2024.

145 'U.S Congress Maintains Restrictions on Military Assistance for Indonesia' (East Timor & Indonesia Action Network, 21 November 2004) <https://www.etan.org/news/2004/11appr.htm> accessed on 13 February 2024.

146 ASEAN and Its Individual States' *conceptual* engagement with R2P Pillars are analysed in detailed in Chapter 4.
147 The ASEAN Charter (2007), Article 2.
148 Pillar III refers to the responsibility that member states of the UN have to respond collectively to crises in a timely and decisive manner through the Security Council. This includes both non-coercive and coercive measures.

# 8 The Association of the Southeast Asian Nations and China

## 8.1 Introduction

In the previous chapters, I have discussed both the *conceptual* and *practical* engagements of the concept of Responsibility to Protect (R2P) by the Association of the Southeast Asian Nations (ASEAN) and its ten member states. These previous analyses have shown that the commitments to implement the Pillars of R2P by ASEAN and its members are mostly weak and by some, completely non-existent.[1] As a result of this, it acts as an obstacle for R2P to fully become a guiding principle in international law when it comes to responding to humanitarian crises. Most importantly, looking at these analyses from a broader level, ASEAN and its member states' engagements with R2P largely mirror that of China. Since China is a superpower, the similarities between ASEAN and its states' engagements with R2P and China cannot be understated. Whilst China is only one State, the United States (US) has described it as 'the most consequential geopolitical challenge' and 'the only competitor with both the intent to reshape the international order and, increasingly, the economic, diplomatic, military, and technological power to advance the objective'.[2] As a result of this, a new dominant non-western interpretation of R2P and its principles that are embedded in international law could emerge that could change the current status quo in the international community. Therefore, it is important to examine the correlation between China and ASEAN states' approaches to R2P in detail.

With this in mind, this chapter is divided into six sections. The first analyses China's positions on principles of international law that are vital to the concept and implementation of R2P, which are sovereignty, non-interference, use of force, and human rights. The second analyses China's *conceptual* engagements with the Pillars of R2P in order to see the correlations between ASEAN and its member states. In the third, fourth, and fifth sections, we analyse China's reactions to the East Timor, Rohingya, and West Papua crises, respectively. And in the sixth section, we draw final conclusions on China's engagement with R2P and its correlations with ASEAN and its member states.

## 8.2 China and (R2P) Principles of International Law

As mentioned in Chapters 1 and 2, and in the previous section, the concepts of R2P interact with established principles of international law/norm, namely, sovereignty, non-interference, use of force, and human rights. As such, it is important for us to

DOI: 10.4324/9781003436799-8

establish where China stands on these issues before analysing its application to the implementation of R2P and its Pillars.

To fully grasp China's perceptions of the concept of sovereignty, non-interference, and non-use of force today, Judge Xue Hanqin of the International Court of Justice explained, regarding the Westphalian sovereignty concept, 'for Europeans, the system by now is 360 years old, but for non-European countries, particularly the Asian and African countries, it is applicable to them for only 60 years'.[3] Judge Xue then explained how international law is based on a foreign (Western) legacy that non-European States had to adopt as the normative framework to conduct their international relations. According to Judge Xue, these States did not merely accept the principles of international law enshrined in the United Nations (UN) Charter because they had to, but because these principles reflected values that they had been fighting for, one of them being sovereignty.[4] As such, the significance of sovereignty, non-interference, and non-use of force to China cannot be over-emphasised. China's intense dedication to its sovereignty can be explained by its own historical experiences with foreign powers during the 'century of humiliation' until the end of World War II.[5] Since then, the government of China, the Chinese Communist Party, has made the protection of its sovereignty from external interferences the top priority and always urges for peaceful conduct in foreign relations. China's perception of the concept of non-interference is one that is rather narrow, which includes three terms: denounces comments, suggestions, or criticisms being made against itself or other States' internal affairs; considers the political regime of a State as an exclusive internal affair; and strongly denounces coercive interferences of any kind into a State's internal affairs.[6] Regarding the use of force, according to China's narrow perception, There are only two exceptions, which are responding to circumstances that are deemed to be a threat to international peace and security by the United Nations Security Council (SC) under Article 39 of the UN Charter and the right to individual or collective self-defence under Article 51 of the UN Charter.[7] As such, China conducts its foreign relations based on the Five Principles of Peaceful Coexistence adopted in 1954: (1) mutual respect for each other's territorial integrity and sovereignty; (2) non-aggression; (3) non-interference; (4) equality and cooperation for mutual benefit; and (5) peaceful co-existence.[8] These principles were then also subsequently adopted in the preamble of the Constitution of the People's Republic of China in 1982.[9] Since its rise to a superpower status, China is still a staunch and principled defender of the concept of sovereignty, non-interference and non-use of force in the international community, which will be shown in the later sections.

When it comes to human rights, I cannot say that it shares the same significance to China as the concepts of sovereignty, non-interference and the use of force. Nevertheless, that is not to say that China completely disregards it. However, although China somewhat upholds the principle of human rights, it has made very clear that its application should reflect on the diversities of States, China stated that

> it respects the principle of the universality of human rights and considers that all countries have an obligation to adopt measures to promote and protect human rights in accordance with the purposes and principles of the Charter

of the United Nations and the relevant provisions of international human rights instruments, in the light of their national realities.[10]

This means that China urged the international community to take into account the diversities in developments, cultures, histories, and even political regimes when it comes to promoting and implementing the protection of human rights. China still holds this position in the present day.[11]

Before I start the examination on how China approaches these principles of international law under the R2P umbrella, essentially how China approaches the Pillars of R2P, *conceptually,* it is crucial to emphasise that China's perceptions of sovereignty, non-interference, use of force, and human rights, mirror that of the ASEAN Way. As was discussed in Chapter 3, Section 3.3, the ASEAN Way is a set of principles that are legally enshrined in the ASEAN Charter, which guides the relations of ASEAN and its members and members-to-members. The ASEAN Way principles are as follows: non-interference, consensus-based decision-making, national and regional resilience, respect for the national sovereignty, the renunciation of the threat or use.[12] Furthermore, on top of adhering to the same principles in their foreign relations, China, ASEAN, and its member states hold similar narrow perceptions of these concepts such as the three terms of non-interference mentioned earlier, as well as, applying national perceptions on the implementation of the protection of human rights. Later, I will examine whether their similarities will continue when it comes to the *conceptual* engagements with the Pillars of R2P.

## 8.3 China and R2P

When the concept of R2P was first introduced to the international community through the International Commission on Intervention and State Sovereignty (ICISS) report in 2001, China initially rejected the notion that the concepts of sovereignty and non-interference had been reconceptualised.[13] In 2005 when the World Summit Outcome document was adopted by the United Nations General Assembly (GA), China released a statement that it acknowledged that the scope of R2P had been limited to the four crimes but warned that all parties should refrain from expanding the norm.[14] In the same statement, China endorsed the idea that national governments have the primary to protect their citizens (Pillar I) and assistance from the international community is only welcomed when it abides by the principles of the UN Charter, namely respect for sovereignty, and non-interference (Pillar II).[15] Regarding coercive measures, China stated that it should be a last resort but did not fully reject it (Pillar III).

In 2009 during the GA session on R2P, China once again emphasised that R2P's application was limited towards the four crimes, Pillar I responsibilities, and Pillar II with the consent of the host State.[16] China ended its statement by highlighting that R2P does not constitute a rule of international law; therefore, no States should employ it as a diplomatic pressure on others. Since then, China has engaged with the GA's Informal Interactive Dialogues on R2P with other members of the communities, in a non-consecutive manner, in the years 2011,[17] 2013,[18] 2014,[19] 2015,[20]

2016,[21] and 2017.[22] In the years mentioned, China have had the same response to the Dialogues on R2P; which emphasised national governments bearing the primary responsibility to protect their citizens from the four crimes; the international community in providing assistance should be in a consensual capacity and abide by the principles of the UN Charter; emphasised on dialogues and negotiations; lastly, regarding the use of coercive measures, it should always be a last resort and be authorised by the SC. From these statements, it is accurate to deduce that China endorses Pillar I and Pillar II of R2P but still remains wary of Pillar III, which would categorise China as a wary supporter of R2P. With this categorisation in mind, referring back to Chapter 4, as many as seven out of ten ASEAN member states are also categorised as wary supporters of R2P. China and these seven ASEAN States share the same concerns when it comes to the implementation of coercive measures under Pillar III of R2P.

Although China remains wary of R2P, especially when it comes to Pillar III, it should be highlighted that China has been very active in contributing to UN peacekeeping missions all over the world, both monetarily and physically. Over the past three decades, China has sent over 50,000 peacekeepers to participate in UN missions in more than 20 countries, which makes it the largest troop contributor among the five permanent members of the SC (P-5).[23] China is also the second biggest contributor to the UN peacekeeping funds, accounting for 15.21%.[24] Whilst these contributions were made without any references to R2P, it can be indirectly viewed as China's support for Pillar II measures, since peacekeeping missions are in consensual manners.

Now that I have examined China's *conceptual* engagement with R2P and have categorised it as a wary supporter, in the following section, I will analyse whether China's position will translate into action and whether it still largely mirrors that of ASEAN and its member states.

## 8.4 China and East Timor Crisis

As discussed in Chapter 5, the East Timor crisis erupted in 1999 into a humanitarian crisis due to the violent campaigns responding to the referendum result of the East Timorese expressing their right to self-determination to secede from Indonesia's rule. Although this crisis occurred before the birth of R2P, as stated in Chapter 1 and Chapter 5, it is still important to my overall analyses to understand China's reaction to a mass humanitarian crisis, how it applies principles of international law that later turned into reconceptualised principles of R2P and most importantly, to examine whether China's position mirror ASEAN and its member states.

In an initial response to Indonesia's invasion of East Timor in 1975, China's opposition was expressed through the SC adopting Resolution 384, which recognised the East Timorese right to self-determination and deplored the armed intervention by Indonesia.[25] Instead, China recognised the Revolutionary Front for Independent East Timor's (East Timor's resistance movement with communist ties) declaration of independence.[26] In the following year, China again expressed its position on the matter through SC Resolution 389 which reiterated the same findings as Resolution 384, except the SC did not deplore Indonesia's use of force in East Timor.[27] Other than expressing its position through the SC, China made no other comments on the matter and the issue of East Timor subsided until 1999.

In 1999 after multiple factors that were discussed in Chapter 5, it led Indonesia to hold a referendum for the East Timorese to exercise their right to self-determination under the auspices of the UN. Whilst China did not individually express its position on the matter, it was done through the SC passing Resolutions 1236 and 1246 establishing the United Nations Mission in East Timor to organise and conduct the referendum.[28] Whilst the situation looked to be improving on paper, it was the onset of mass violence that had started prior to the referendum and increased in intensity and scale by the time the referendum was completed and the East Timorese chose to secede from Indonesia. The magnitude of the violence had amounted to crimes against humanity reported by a UN mission sent by the SC (which had to have been approved by China).[29] As a result of this, talks of establishing a peacekeeping force occupied the international community; however, China was somewhat passive. Due to internal factors, Indonesia consented to a UN-mandated peacekeeping force, which was passed through the SC Resolution 1264 that established the International Force East Timor (INTERFET) under Chapter VII of the UN Charter.[30] Allowing this peacekeeping force to materialise does not mean that China supported coercive responses to a mass humanitarian crisis since it was in a consensual capacity. Therefore, INTERFET did not interfere or infringe upon Indonesia's sovereignty. In R2P terms, this response was the implementation of Pillar II.

China's responses to the East Timor crisis mirrored the ASEAN States in the sense that respect for Indonesia's sovereignty was always prioritised throughout this crisis. Whilst individual ASEAN States' responses were nuanced, all States refrained from taking an antagonist approach towards Indonesia, just as China did. China along with ASEAN member states' generally supported INTERFET because of its non-coercive consensual nature, hence it was a peacekeeping and not peace-*enforcement* mission. If that had been the case, it is hard to imagine China voting for the creation of this peacekeeping mission and it would have exploited its power to veto.

## 8.5 China and the Rohingya Crisis

In this section, we will turn to analyse China's reactions/responses to the Rohingya crisis that erupted in 2016, which still has not been solved today. The Rohingya crisis is one of an intractable nature that has different waves of violence throughout the years. 2016–2017 was the worst-ever recorded humanitarian crisis that had stemmed from decades of struggles that the Rohingyas had endured under the Myanmar government. What kickstarted this particular wave of violence was an attack by an insurgent, group Arakan Rohingya Salvation Army (ARSA), to which the Myanmar army, the Tatmadaw launched clearance operations in what it claimed as lawful military operations against an Islamist terrorist group.[31] According to the 2018 report of the Independent International Fact-Finding Mission on Myanmar set up by the UN Human Rights Council, it was reported that war crimes,

crimes against humanity, and genocide had been committed in Rakhine State by the Tatmadaw.[32] Since these are R2P crimes and they occurred after the adoption of R2P by the GA along with China, theoretically, we should expect a level of response/assistance on the matter.

In response to the eruption of this humanitarian crisis, China released a statement condemning the violent attacks in Rakhine State and emphasised on the Myanmar's government to maintain peace and stability but did not blame the Tatmadaw.[33] Through the SC, the only initial response was a presidential statement, instead of a resolution, condemning the ARSA's attacks expressing grave concern over the reports of human rights violations and abuses taking place in the Rakhine State without explicitly referencing the R2P crimes that had been committed against the Rohingya, while also affirming the sovereignty of Myanmar.[34] Furthermore, the statement used R2P language regarding Pillar I by stressing that it was the primary responsibility of Myanmar to protect its population. The reason why only a presidential statement that did not carry any diplomatic or legal weight was issued was due to China and Russia blocking any statements or resolutions that would explicitly condemn the Myanmar government.[35] Myanmar's protection at the SC comes to a large extent from its special relationship with China. Following the imposition of international sanctions against Myanmar in the 1980s, China became the Tatmadaw's primary supplier of military hardware, and, in return, Myanmar started to supply China with raw materials for the Chinese market.[36] In recent years China also perceived Myanmar as a strategic interest that can cement China's presence in the Southeast Asia region and give it access to the Indian Ocean, which can be utilised for oil/gas pipelines since these two States share a border, trading route, and access for the People's Liberation Army Navy Vessels.[37] Hence, China has prioritised diplomatic and economic protection on Myanmar throughout the years.

Contrasting with the West's wave of coercive actions such as sanctions, embargoes and calls for interventions in Rakhine State, China employed a different method in an effort to solve this crisis, which is Pillar II in R2P terms. After its statement through the SC, China independently proposed a three-phase plan for the crisis: (1) ceasefire; (2) bilateral dialogue between Myanmar and Bangladesh since the Rohingyas had fled to the latter after the clearance operations; and (3) strive for a long-term solution.[38] Whilst China did not invoke the R2P concept when it proposed this plan, this can indirectly be seen as an attempt to implement Pillar II of R2P. At the same time, China also donated 150 tonnes of aid to the Rohingya refugees in Bangladesh, without making direct references to the Rohingyas as the recipient, which could be an effort to placate the Myanmar government.[39] Presently, China still acts as an active broker between China and Bangladesh in the Rohingya repatriation plan.[40]

In response to the 2021 military coup, in which General Min Aung Hlaing overtook power from the civilian government, it is relevant to this line of analysis since he was among those named in the 2018 report of the UN Fact-Finding Mission as responsible for crimes against humanity, war crimes and genocide committed against the Rohingyas.[41] In the initial response to the coup, China allowed a SC statement to advance, in which the SC expressed its concerns for the state of emergency imposed by the Tatmadaw and called upon the need to respect human rights and the rule of law.[42] It should be noted that the statement did not use the word coup and it is merely a statement and not a resolution, which is not legally binding. It was reported that China along with Russia was adamant on not using the word coup, which diplomatically protects Myanmar to an extent. Then in 2022, the SC adopted Resolution 2669 that called for an immediate cessation of violence and the release of all prisoners, to which China abstained.

Independently in 2022 and 2023, China pledged support to the Myanmar military 'no matter how to situation changes' and vowed to further deepen cooperation and exchanges between the two countries, respectively.[43]

Overall, once again, just as ASEAN and the majority of ASEAN States did in response to the Rohingya crisis, China stood in solidarity with Myanmar. Whilst some of its actions may seem as employing or endorsing Pillar I and II of R2P, no references were made; therefore, R2P had not been advanced as a guiding principle when it comes to responding to this crisis. Furthermore, a crucial factor that needs to be taken into account when it comes to analysing China's responses to this crisis is the fact that China also faces allegations of having committed crimes against humanity and possibly genocide against the Uyghurs and other predominately Muslim groups in Xinjiang, China.[44] Since China is in somewhat the same predicament as the Myanmar government, it would not strategically make sense if it were to call for stronger measures against the latter, or even invoke R2P as China could then be seen as a hypocrite. Similar to ASEAN States, Indonesia with the West Papua issues and other members with 'internal' sensitive issues cannot set a precedent for interference in its internal and regional affairs that would undoubtedly infringe upon its beloved sovereignties.

## 8.6 China and West Papua Crisis

As discussed in Chapter 7, West Papua crisis concerns treatments and policies enacted by the Indonesian government upon the Papuan since the territory was annexed into part of Indonesia in 1969. Since then, until the present day, there have been multiple reports and arguments by various scholars that crimes against humanity and genocide are being committed by the Indonesian security apparatus against the Papuans. Again, these are R2P crimes, which the international community and China have endorsed. Since Indonesia is the biggest member of ASEAN in terms of economy and population, there have been no reactions from ASEAN as an organisation or individual members, which can also be said for China. As discussed in Chapter 7, Section 7.4, there have been no reactions from the SC since 1969 regarding this crisis. Moreover, China has made neither a statement nor comments regarding this matter since it is being perceived as an internal matter of Indonesia and China is a staunch defender of the concept of non-interference. Notably not only that China has never reacted to the West Papuan crisis, but China is also even focused on deepening its cooperation with Indonesia through its Comprehensive Partnership, in an effort that is seen as competition with the US for hegemony in the Southeast Asia region.[45] On top of not referring to R2P, this crisis has not been and most likely will continue to not be on China's strategic radar.

## 8.7 Conclusion

Throughout this chapter, we have analysed China's positions on the concepts of sovereignty, non-interference, use of force and human rights, and the Pillars of R2P. Earlier in the chapter we categorised China as a wary supporter of R2P, which explains it's being supportive of Pillar I and II, but remaining wary of Pillar III. We then analysed China's reactions to the East Timor, Rohingya, and West Papua crises in order to see whether its *conceptual* endorsements of the two Pillars of R2P had been translated into action. To summarise China's *practical* engagements with R2P regarding these three case studies, we can be confident of saying that its commitment to R2P is weak, just as ASEAN and the ASEAN States. As discussed, whilst some efforts from China may be seen as implementation of the practice of R2P, no references were explicitly made to R2P. Whilst it may have been created with good intentions, R2P can easily be misused and employed as a 'Trojan horse' to advance the imperialistic agenda of other actors, such as in the case of NATO's intervention into Libya in 2011 which was discussed in Chapter 2. As such, it is natural for a State such as China that is protective of its sovereignty to be wary of a concept such as R2P. Furthermore, because China's positions on the *conceptual* and *practical* implementations of R2P mirror ASEAN and its member states, it acts as a formidable obstacle for R2P to become a guiding principle of international law when responding to humanitarian crises. As a result of this, it poses a serious challenge to the Western reconceptualised perception of sovereignty in that this concept is no longer viable in facing today's challenges. China, along with the ASEAN States acts as a reminder to the international community that respect for sovereignty and non-interference still supersedes other principles of international law, namely human rights, even when it comes to humanitarian crises.

### Notes

1 Pillar I refers to the responsibility of each State to protect its population against crimes against humanity, war crimes, ethnic cleansing and genocide. Pillar II refers to the responsibility of the international community to assist States in meeting their duty to protect. Finally, Pillar III refers to the responsibility that member states of the UN have to respond collectively to crises in a timely and decisive manner through the Security Council.
2 'The United States National Security Strategy' (October 2022), p. 8.
3 'Speech by Judge Xue Hanqin at the Chinese Observations on International Law at the International Criminal Law Network' (1 November 2006) <https://www.mfa.gov.cn/eng/wjb_663304/zwjg_665342/zwbd_665378/200612/t20061204_601878.html> accessed on 23 February 2024.
4 The principles included were sovereignty, equality, democracy, and self-determination; ibid.
5 Zhongqi Pan and Ping Du, 'The Logic of Contingency in China's Insistence on the Non-Interference Principle' [2015] 8 *Fudan Journal of Humanities and Social Sciences*, p. 600.
6 Mordechai Chaziza and Ogen S. Goldman, 'Revisiting China's Non-Interference Policy Towards Intrastate Wars' [2014] 7(1) *The Chinese Journal of International Politics*, p. 94.
7 The United Nations Charter, Article 39 and Article 51.
8 The *Panchsheel* Agreement or the Five Principles of Peaceful Coexistence (1954).

9 Constitution of the People's Republic of China (1982), Preamble.
10 National Report of China to the Human Rights Council as part of the Universal Periodic Review (2008), A/HRC/WG.6/4/CHN/1, Para 6.
11 'Wang Yi Attends the Opening Ceremony of the International Symposium Commemorating the 75th Anniversary of the Universal Declaration of Human Rights' (5 December 2023) <http://ki.china-embassy.gov.cn/eng/zgywx/202312/t20231211_11199389.htm> accessed on 23 February 2024.
12 The ASEAN Charter (2007), Article 2.
13 Mikelli Marzzini L.A. Ribeiro, et al., 'China's Engagement with R2P: Pluralist Shaper?' [2020] 12 *Global Responsibility to Protect*, p. 282.
14 'R2P Four Crimes Are Crimes Against Humanity, Ethnic Cleansing, War Crimes, and Genocide; Statement by the People's Republic of China at the Informal Interactive R2P Dialogue' (2005) <https://www.globalr2p.org/wp-content/uploads/2020/01/2014-IID-China.pdf> accessed on 24 February 2024.
15 Ibid.
16 'Statement by Ambassador Liu Zhenmin at the Plenary Session of the General Assembly on the Question of "Responsibility to Protect"' (2009) <https://www.globalr2p.org/resources/statement-by-china-at-the-2009-un-general-assembly-debate-on-r2p/> accessed on 24 February 2024.
17 'Statement by the People's Republic of China at the UN General Assembly Informal Interactive Dialogue on the Responsibility to Protect' (2011) <https://www.globalr2p.org/resources/statement-by-china-at-the-2011-un-general-assembly-informal-interactive-dialogue-on-the-responsibility-to-protect/> accessed on 24 February 2024.
18 'Statement by the People's Republic of China at the UN General Assembly Informal Interactive Dialogue on the Responsibility to Protect' (2013) <https://www.globalr2p.org/resources/statement-by-china-at-the-2013-un-general-assembly-informal-interactive-dialogue-on-the-responsibility-to-protect/> accessed on 24 February 2024.
19 'Statement by the People's Republic of China at the UN General Assembly Informal Interactive Dialogue on the Responsibility to Protect' (2014) <https://www.globalr2p.org/resources/statement-by-china-at-the-2014-un-general-assembly-informal-interactive-dialogue-on-the-responsibility-to-protect/> accessed on 24 February 2024.
20 'Statement by the People's Republic of China at the UN General Assembly Informal Interactive Dialogue on the Responsibility to Protect' (2015) <https://www.globalr2p.org/resources/statement-by-china-at-the-2015-un-general-assembly-informal-interactive-dialogue-on-the-responsibility-to-protect/> accessed on 24 February 2024.
21 'China's Statement at the 2016 UN General Assembly Thematic Panel Discussion, From Commitment to Implementation: Ten Years of Responsibility to Protect' (2016) <https://www.globalr2p.org/resources/statement-by-china-at-the-un-general-assembly-thematic-panel-discussion-from-commitment-to-implementation-ten-years-of-the-responsibility-to-protect-26-february-2016/> accessed on 24 February 2024.
22 'Statement by the People's Republic of China at the UN General Assembly Informal Interactive Dialogue on the Responsibility to Protect' (2017) <https://www.globalr2p.org/resources/statement-by-china-at-the-2017-un-general-assembly-informal-interactive-dialogue-on-the-responsibility-to-protect/> accessed on 24 February 2024.
23 'Spokesperson: Chinese Blue Helmets Become Vital Force in UN's Peacekeeping Efforts' (The State Council Information Office- The People's Republic of China, 31 May 2023) <http://english.scio.gov.cn/pressroom/2023–05/31/content_85949249.htm> accessed on 24 February 2024.
24 'How We Are Funded' (The United Nations Peacekeeping) <https://peacekeeping.un.org/en/how-we-are-funded#:~:text=The%20top%2010%20providers%20of,Japan%20(8.56%25)> accessed on 24 February 2024.
25 The United Nations Security Council Resolution 384, S/RES/384 (1975).
26 Katsumi Ishizuka, *The History of Peace-building in East Timor: The Issues of International Intervention* (Foundation Books, 2010) p. 14.

27 The United Nations Security Council Resolution 389, S/RES/389 (1976).
28 The United Nations Security Council Resolution 1236 (1999) S/RES/1236; and 1246 (1999), S/RES/1246.
29 Report of the Security Council Mission to Jakarta and Dili, 8–12 September 1999(S/1999/976) pp. 11–10.
30 The United Nations Security Council Resolution 1264 (1999), S/RES/1264, p. 2.
31 Marlise Simons and Hannah Beech, 'Aung San Suu Kyi Defends Myanmar Against Rohingya Genocide Accusations' (The New York Times, 23 January 2020) <https://www.nytimes.com/2019/12/11/world/asia/aung-san-suu-kyi-rohingya-myanmar-genocide-hague.html> accessed on 24 February 2024.
32 United Nations Human Rights Council, 'Report of the International Independent Fact-Finding Mission on Myanmar' (2018) A/HRC/39/64, Section VI.
33 Charlotte Gao, 'On Rohingya Issue, Both China and India Back Myanmar Government' (Reuters, 13 September 2017) <https://thediplomat.com/2017/09/on-rohingya-issue-both-china-and-india-back-myanmar-government/> accessed on 24 February 2024.
34 Statement by the President of the Security Council (2017) S/PRST/2017/22 <https://www.securitycouncilreport.org/atf/cf/%7B65BFCF9B-6D27-4E9C-8CD3-CF6E4FF96FF9%7D/s_prst_2017_22.pdf> accessed on 24 February 2024.
35 'China, Russia Block U.N Council Concern about Myanmar Violence' (Reuters, 17 March 2017) <https://www.reuters.com/article/us-myanmar-rohingya-un-idUSKBN16O2J6> accessed on 24 February 2024.
36 Tin Maung Maung Than, 'Myanmar and China: A Special Relationship?' [2003] *Southeast Asian Affairs*, pp. 198–200.
37 Shaun Cameron, 'Why Is Myanmar New Deep-Sea Port Such Hot Property?' (The Lowy Institute, 22 November 2023) <https://www.lowyinstitute.org/the-interpreter/why-myanmar-s-new-deep-sea-port-such-hot-property> accessed on 24 February 2024.
38 'China Proposed Three-Phase Plan for Rohingya Issue' (Reuters, 20 November 2017) <https://www.reuters.com/article/idUSKBN1DK07K/> accessed on 24 February 2024.
39 Charlotte Gao, 'China Aids Rohingya Refugees in Bangladesh While Backing Myanmar Government' (Reuters, 2 October 2017) <https://thediplomat.com/2017/10/china-aids-rohingya-refugees-in-bangladesh-while-backing-myanmar-government/> accessed on 24 February 2024.
40 'Myanmar Seeking to Repatriate Rohingya Refugees from Bangladesh' (Aljazeera, 31 October 2023) <https://www.aljazeera.com/news/2023/10/31/myanmar-176> accessed on 24 February 2024.
41 United Nations Human Rights Council, 'Report of the International Independent Fact-Finding Mission on Myanmar' (2018) A/HRC/39/64, Section VII (92).
42 Security Council Press Statement on Situation in Myanmar (4 February 2021) SC/14430.
43 Sebastian Strangio, 'China Pledges Support for Myanmar's Junta, "No Matter How the Situation Changes"' (The Diplomat, 4 April 2022) <https://thediplomat.com/2022/04/china-pledges-support-for-myanmars-junta-no-matter-how-the-situation-changes/> accessed on 24 February 2024; and Shi Jiangtao, 'China's Qin Gang Pledges Economic Help for Myanmar, Stops Short of Recognising Junta' (South China Morning Post, 3 May 2023) <https://www.scmp.com/news/china/diplomacy/article/3219288/chinas-qin-gang-pledges-economic-help-myanmar-stops-short-recognising-junta> accessed on 24 February 2024.
44 'China Committed Genocide Against Uyghurs, Independent Tribunal Rules' (BBC, 9 December 2021) <https://www.bbc.co.uk/news/world-asia-china-59595952> accessed on 24 February 2024; and The OHCHR Assessment of human rights concerns in Xinjiang Uyghurs Autonomous Region, People's Republic of China (2022).
45 'Joint Statement on Deepening Comprehensive Strategic Cooperation between the People's Republic of China and the Republic of Indonesia' (18 October 2023) <https://kemlu.go.id/portal/en/read/5393/siaran_pers/joint-statement-on-deepening-comprehensive-strategic-cooperation-between-the-peoples-republic-of-china-and-the-republic-of-indonesia-18-october-2023-beijing> accessed on 24 February 2024.

# 9 Conclusions

The humanitarian crises in Rwanda and Bosnia-Herzegovina represent two pertinent examples of intra-state conflicts leading to mass atrocity situations that shocked the international community. Today, there is a growing need to find the most appropriate response to these types of mass atrocities. Humanitarian intervention cannot represent the answer to these humanitarian crises. Legally, humanitarian intervention conflicts with two important provisions of the UN Charter, namely Article 2(4) and 2 (7), which prohibit, respectively, the use of force and intervention in the domestic affairs of a sovereign State. Politically, the vulnerability of humanitarian intervention lies in the fact that it can hide 'imperialistic' agendas. The controversial nature of humanitarian intervention was confirmed in the late 1990s when the North Atlantic Treaty Organization (NATO) intervened against the Federal Republic of Yugoslavia to stop the atrocities committed against the Kosovar Albanians. The Independent International Commission on Kosovo famously defined this intervention as legitimate and yet illegal under international law.

The international community's failure to protect innocent civilians in Rwanda and Bosnia-Herzegovina, on the one hand, and the controversial NATO intervention in Kosovo, on the other, revealed the urgent need for a different approach to mass atrocities in international law. The new approach emerged around the concept of the Responsibility to Protect (R2P). R2P was introduced as a political idea in 2001 by the International Commission on Intervention and State Sovereignty, which promoted a new interpretation of State sovereignty as a responsibility to protect one's population. In 2005, R2P was brought into the realm of international law by means of its inclusion in the United Nations World Summit Outcome. Later, an influential report by the UN Secretary-General formally defined the three-pillar structure of R2P. Pillar I refers to the responsibility of States to protect their populations against genocide, war crimes, crimes against humanity and ethnic cleansing. Pillar II refers to the responsibility of the international community to assist States in meeting their Pillar I duties. Finally, Pillar III refers to the responsibility of the international community, through the UN, to provide a decisive response to atrocity crimes situations should a State manifestly fail to protect its own population. The recent conflicts in Libya and Syria have highlighted a number of problems related to the interpretation and implementation of R2P. In Libya, NATO went beyond the mandate of Security Council Resolution 1973, contributing to the overthrow of

DOI: 10.4324/9781003436799-9

Gaddafi instead of focusing exclusively on the protection of civilians. In the case of Syria, the Security Council has been gridlocked due to geopolitical interests, preventing the invocation of R2P despite the gravity of the situation. Today, the precise meaning, scope, and implementation of R2P remain a subject of debate.

Other than through the UN, States can also cooperate through regional organisations to implement R2P. As discussed in Chapter 1 and briefly in Chapter 3, regional organisations can even be better suited than international ones to implement R2P measures. However, while regional organisations may offer an important avenue to tackle atrocity crimes situations, they may also further the problem of the lack of a universally agreed concept of R2P. Looking at R2P from a regional perspective may also contribute to highlighting the increasing importance of regional approaches to international law. As discussed in Chapter 1, international law is not as 'international' as it seems, given that different rules are being interpreted differently in different regions of the world.

This book has sought to contribute to the existing literature on R2P by looking precisely at the latter from the perspective of a regional organisation, that is, the Association of Southeast Asian Nations (ASEAN) and China. There are important reasons explaining the focus on this regional organisation and China. The organisation's growing significance in the international system is one: ASEAN has become a worldwide trading hub with official partnerships with the European Union, China, Japan, South Korea, and India and with an unofficial partnership with the United States. The combined economies of Southeast Asia countries are equivalent to the fourth biggest economy in the world, and the region is home to more than 700 million people, that is, more than the population of the European Union and the Middle East combined. On top of its increasing economic importance, Southeast Asia's geography is also of great importance due to its access to both the Indian and Pacific oceans. As noted in Chapter 1, whilst China is not a member of ASEAN, it wields incredible power in the international community especially as a Permanent member of the Security Council, making its similar perspectives to principles of international law and R2P to ASEAN States a crucial challenge to the usually dominant narratives of international law developed by Western States.

As discussed in Chapter 3, ASEAN operates under a specific set of rules and principles known as the 'ASEAN Way'. These include the highest respect for State sovereignty, strict adherence to the principle of non-interference, prohibition of the use of force in international relations and consensus decision-making. ASEAN has gradually developed into a rules-based organisation with a legal personality. It now includes an Intergovernmental Commission on Human Rights and has adopted a Human Rights Declaration to promote and protect human rights in the region. Despite looking promising, however, Chapter 3 suggests that these developments have not remedied ASEAN's main weaknesses, that is, the incapacity to operate independently from member states and an overly strict interpretation of the principle of non-interference. Evidently, these conservative attitudes are at odds with the central idea of R2P, which prioritises human rights over State sovereignty.

As noted before, a key element of the ASEAN Way is consensus decision-making, which ensures that ASEAN does not make any decision that is not supported by all its members. As there is no consensus among the ASEAN States on R2P, ASEAN as a collective organisation has not taken any direct position on this principle. However, Chapter 4 shows that, as part of their individual conduct, the vast majority of ASEAN States have supported R2P as a valuable guiding principle in international law in relation to humanitarian crises.

To understand the level of support that ASEAN States have for R2P, Chapter 4 analyses their official statements made during the UN General Assembly informal interactive dialogues on R2P held between 2012 and 2017. The chapter suggests that the conceptual endorsement of R2P varies among ASEAN members. Seven States can be described as Wary Supporters (Indonesia, Thailand, Malaysia, Singapore, the Philippines, Vietnam and Cambodia), two States can be described as R2P-neutral (Brunei and Laos) and one State can be described as Opposer (Myanmar). Wary Supporters tend to support Pillar I and II but remain sceptical of Pillar III. R2P-neutral States have neither rejected nor publicly supported any R2P Pillar. An Opposer State objects to R2P altogether.

Although Indonesia, Thailand, Malaysia, Singapore, the Philippines, Vietnam and Cambodia have endorsed Pillars I and II, none of them showed support for Pillar III. The fundamental reason for this hesitance is the fact that Pillar III clashes with the principles of the ASEAN Way that were mentioned earlier. In particular, Pillar III includes coercive measures such as sanctions, embargoes and ultimately military intervention which are taken without the consent of the State in question. This clashes with the principle of 'Westphalian Sovereignty' which, sitting at the centre of the ASEAN Way, affirms that States answer to no higher authority and have the prerogative to define and protect the rights of their people.[1] As discussed in Chapter 3, ASEAN States have embedded instruments into ASEAN's institutional architecture in order to protect their sovereignty since the organisation was formed in 1967. These instruments include the Bangkok Declaration, the Declaration on a Zone of Peace, Freedom and Neutrality, the Treaty of Amity and Cooperation, and the ASEAN Charter. These instruments have created an institutional framework to ensure that nothing can be done to infringe and/or interfere against a member's sovereignty and internal affairs.

Another central principle of the ASEAN Way which is incompatible with Pillar III is the principle of non-interference. ASEAN's perception of the concept of non-interference goes beyond the international law principle of non-intervention. As discussed in Chapter 3, in international law an intervention would only be deemed illegal if there is a coercive element attached to it. Instead, the concept of non-interference adopted by ASEAN does not require the presence of coercion as a defining element. Thus, merely criticising a State would amount to a violation of the principle of non-interference while not qualifying as an unlawful intervention in international law. It follows from the above that the implementation of the coercive measures of Pillar III would undoubtedly sabotage the beloved tenets of the ASEAN Way. The fact that Pillar III measures are not taken by individual States but are adopted by the Security Council collectively does not change things. The examination in Chapter 4 also showed that ASEAN States mistrust the Security Council, considering it unable to fairly implement R2P. On the other hand, Pillars I and II have received more support because they can be more easily reconciled with the ASEAN Way. ASEAN States have generally agreed that they have the primary responsibility to protect their population from atrocity crimes. The majority of them have also accepted the role that international and regional organisations can play in assisting States to meet their Pillar I responsibilities. Pillar II measures can range from preventive diplomacy and mediation dialogues to fact-finding missions and peacekeeping operations. Thus, the crucial feature of Pillar II is its consensual nature, which requires mutual commitment and active partnership from the State in question. Furthermore, three ASEAN States (Indonesia, Malaysia, and the Philippines) have explicitly expressed their preference for regional instead of international forms of assistance, as they feel more comfortable cooperating with a regional actor who has a more intimate understanding of the histories and cultures of the relevant State. However, although Indonesia, Thailand, Malaysia, Singapore, the Philippines, Vietnam, and Cambodia have shown general support for Pillars I and II of R2P, it would be inaccurate to say that they did so enthusiastically.

The second part of the book tested the effects of this general regional endorsement of R2P on both ASEAN and ASEAN States' practical position on atrocity crimes situations by focusing on three case studies, the 1999 East Timor crisis, which happened before the endorsement of R2P, the recent Rohingya crisis in Myanmar, and the current West Papua crisis, which happened after that. At the time of the East Timor crisis, the debates surrounding the need to do something to prevent and stop atrocity crimes had already reached a peak following NATO's intervention in Kosovo. Furthermore, the atrocities committed in East Timor after the 1999 referendum had reached the level of crimes against humanity and war crimes. Had R2P existed, it would have certainly been invoked by some parties. The crisis was triggered by the UN's mandated referendum for the East Timorese to choose between special autonomy within Indonesia or full independence. Once it was announced that the East Timorese had chosen full independence, mass atrocities were committed by pro-Indonesia militia sponsored by the Indonesian armed forces against pro-independence parties. The analysis in Chapter 5 showed that ASEAN stood in solidarity with Indonesia. When Indonesia invaded East Timor in 1975, ASEAN accepted Jakarta's justification for its action. Despite the intense activities at the international level about the possibility of holding a referendum, ASEAN did not refer to this situation and instead reaffirmed its commitment to the ASEAN Way.[2] Once the violence had escalated to the level of crimes against humanity, ASEAN still remained silent. In the same way, when later talks began about establishing a peacekeeping mission in East Timor, ASEAN did not urge Indonesia to consent to it and did not attempt to offer assistance or to promote any solution to the crisis.

The response by the ASEAN States was different. While Myanmar did not make any reference to Indonesia's duties, Cambodia, Laos, Vietnam, and Brunei recognised that it was Indonesia's primary responsibility to halt the atrocities committed against the East Timorese. Yet, they called for Indonesia's sovereignty to be respected by the international community. While these four States did not offer direct assistance to Jakarta, they explicitly stated that initiatives taken to resolve the crisis had to have the full consent of the Indonesian government. Thailand,

Malaysia, Singapore, and the Philippines did not criticise Indonesia for the events in East Timor nor did they make any reference to the fact that atrocity crimes had been committed. However, when pressure began to mount on Jakarta to accept a UN peacekeeping mission, they urged Indonesia to consent to UN assistance. As Indonesia did not have strong allies in the Security Council that could halt this course of action, it was essentially coerced into consenting to the peacekeeping mission. However, it was not Thailand, Malaysia, Singapore, and the Philippines that exercised decisive pressure, which instead came from the US, the World Bank and the International Monetary Fund. It can be said that the four ASEAN States acted in a non-confrontational way in order to respect Indonesia's sovereignty. Once the International Force East Timor was established, Thailand, Malaysia, Singapore, and the Philippines sent a significant number of personnel to the mission. However, it would be inaccurate to say that they were motivated by humanitarian concerns related to the widespread human rights violations against the East Timorese. Instead, they were more concerned about regional stability and limiting external interferences in the region.

The more recent Rohingya crisis in Myanmar, analysed in Chapter 6, confirmed much of ASEAN and ASEAN States' hesitations towards the principles underpinning R2P. This crisis reached its peak in 2016/2017 when the Tatmadaw launched military operations against the Rohingya allegedly in response to the violent terrorist attacks by the Arakan Rohingya Salvation Army. According to the 2018 Report of the Independent International Fact-Finding Mission on Myanmar set up by the UN Human Rights Council, in conducting these military operations the Tatmadaw committed war crimes, crimes against humanity and genocide. As it happened with respect to East Timor, ASEAN took no direct position on the crisis. Various ASEAN Summits and ASEAN Foreign Ministerial Meetings statements between 2017 and 2020 supported Myanmar's efforts to bring peace and stability to Rakhine State without referring to the atrocity crimes that the Tatmadaw had committed against the Rohingya.

The analysis of Chapter 6 showed that the introduction of R2P has not impacted ASEAN behaviour, despite the support for the principle shown by many ASEAN States. ASEAN's response to the Rohingya crisis mirrored its response to the East Timor crisis in that ASEAN essentially showed solidarity with both Indonesia and Myanmar. ASEAN did not show any humanitarian concern over the atrocities committed against the Rohingya, it did not use any R2P-based language and did not take any concrete action on the matter.

There is, however, one difference between ASEAN's reaction to the two crises that needs to be highlighted, namely the fact that in 2017 the ASEAN's Chairman released a statement on the situation in Rakhine State.[3] This was the first time that ASEAN released a statement addressing specifically a member's internal affairs. However, as discussed in Chapter 6, this statement misrepresented the reality. First, in an attempt to appease the Myanmar government, it did not refer to the Rohingya by name. Second, the statement referred to the situation as a 'complex inter-communal issue' rather than a victim-aggressor situation. On paper, this could be seen as the beginning of ASEAN's attempt to respond to a humanitarian crisis.

However, in reality, this statement is rather meaningless, since it lacks the power to force Myanmar to halt the atrocities and solve the root causes of the crisis.

On the other hand, individual responses from the ASEAN States varied dramatically. Although Chapter 4 suggests that the majority of ASEAN States have conceptually endorsed the fundamentals of R2P, Chapter 6 shows that these oral commitments did not actually translate into action. Thailand, Singapore, the Philippines, Laos, Vietnam, and Cambodia have been supportive of Myanmar, as they did with Indonesia during the East Timor crisis. They echoed the ASEAN Chairman's statement (mentioned earlier) by referring to the situation as 'a complex inter-communal issue'; they repeatedly stated that this 'issue' falls within Myanmar's internal affairs; and called for the international community to respect the sovereignty of the latter. Cambodia, the Philippines, Vietnam, and Laos also voted against a number of UN General Assembly resolutions condemning the Tatmadaw. Thailand and Singapore, instead, abstained. The Philippines also expressed a preference for regional assistance in situations of crisis. However, it did not take any initiative to get ASEAN involved in this crisis. It can, therefore, be concluded that these six States were not willing to challenge the sovereignty of Myanmar and did not apply the basic principles of R2P. This clashes with their position on R2P as discussed in Chapter 4, where Thailand, Singapore, the Philippines, Vietnam and Cambodia were described as wary supporters of the principle.[4] One possible explanation for this gap is that they showed support for R2P in order to increase their international legitimacy. In addition, they may have sought to show support for consensual forms of external assistance (Pillar II) in order to weaken the importance of coercive measures (Pillar III), and, ultimately, protect their sovereignty.

Brunei, Indonesia, and Malaysia responded quite differently from the six States mentioned earlier. While Brunei did not take a vocal position, it still voted in favour of the UN General Assembly resolutions condemning the Tatmadaw. This is also important considering that during the East Timor crisis Brunei remained rather neutral. Indonesia and Malaysia, instead, were more vocal. Indonesia criticised Myanmar's treatment of the Rohingya. In doing so, however, it chose to employ what can be described as a policy of 'quiet diplomacy'. It voted for the UN General Assembly resolutions condemning the Tatmadaw, but at the same time, it did not expressly condemn Myanmar. This could be due to two reasons. First, Indonesia might have had some sympathy for Myanmar since it found itself in a similar situation facing public international condemnation over the East Timor and West Papua crises (to an extent). Second, throughout the East Timor crisis Myanmar did not condemn Indonesia and called for respect of its sovereignty. It is important to note that in its efforts to resolve this crisis, Indonesia did implement measures of Pillar II but without explicitly invoking the doctrine of R2P. As discussed in Chapter 6, right after the violence escalated in 2017, the Indonesian foreign minister met with Aung San Suu Kyi personally to offer Indonesia's assistance to resolve the crisis. In its effort, Indonesia also presented Myanmar with a proposal (4+1 Formula) with steps to take in order to stop and address the crisis. Indonesia also launched the Indonesian Humanitarian Assistance for Myanmar programme to provide aid to Rakhine State.

The one ASEAN State that stands out the most in its reaction to the Rohingya crisis is Malaysia. Malaysia is the only ASEAN State to have referred to this situation as genocide. In an unprecedented move, it also called upon the international community to urgently take action given Myanmar's unwillingness to halt the atrocities. This was the first time in ASEAN history that a member called openly for some form of external intervention in the internal affairs of another member. Again, in an unconventional move, Malaysia publicly distanced itself from the 2017 ASEAN Chairman's statement on Rakhine State mentioned earlier. This reaction of Malaysia drastically departs from its reaction to the East Timor crisis. While Malaysia was one of the first State within ASEAN to urge Indonesia to consent to a peacekeeping mission and was willing to offer personnel contribution, it was done in a friendly way without infringing upon Indonesia's sovereignty. Malaysia was willing to assist, but its motivation was to preserve regional peace and stability and to protect the ASEAN Way. However, although Malaysia has been extremely critical of Myanmar in this crisis and has urged ASEAN to resolve this crisis, unlike Indonesia, Malaysia has not provided concrete solutions or assistance in halting the atrocities against the Rohingya.

Following the trend discussed in Chapter 6, which concluded that ASEAN member states' conceptual endorsements of R2P did not translate into action regarding the Rohingya crisis, the same conclusion can be reached for the West Papua crisis. Whilst there were several and occasional nuances in the ASEAN States' reactions to the Rohingya crisis, they have been quite synchronised in their silence on the matter. As a result of this, since ASEAN operates on a consensus basis, no reaction was ever recorded from the organisation either. It is rather telling that *realpolitik* considerations still play a crucial role when it comes to decision-making for ASEAN States, even when faced with a humanitarian crisis in its own region.

The combined examination of ASEAN and ASEAN States' responses to the East Timor, Rohingya, and West Papua crises highlighted a number of important points. First, through all these crises, ASEAN has abided by the principles of the ASEAN Way, respecting its members' sovereignty and refraining from interfering in their internal affairs. This means that, although the majority of ASEAN States have endorsed Pillar I and II of R2P, this has not had an influence on ASEAN collective behaviour. The fact that ASEAN States have different positions on the specific meaning of R2P makes it even more difficult for ASEAN to respond to atrocity crimes in R2P terms.

Second, in terms of individual members, the endorsement of Pillar I and II of R2P by Thailand, Singapore, the Philippines, Vietnam, and Cambodia did not translate into action in the Rohingya crisis. As discussed in Chapter 5, Thailand, Singapore, and the Philippines had urged Indonesia to accept UN assistance during the East Timor crisis. However, since Myanmar has opposed any form of external interference, these three States have respected its sovereignty, thereby fully upholding the principles of the ASEAN WAY over those of R2P.

Third, Indonesia and Malaysia applied, contrary to the States mentioned earlier, the principles of R2P in the Rohingya crisis, albeit without explicitly referring to R2P. For example, Indonesia implemented Pillar II by offering its assistance to

Myanmar and making a concrete proposal to address the crisis. Malaysia called for intervention by the international community given Myanmar's unwillingness to protect its population. However, one crucial element that needs to be taken into account here is that it is of no coincidence that the predominantly Muslim States within ASEAN are the ones who were most critical of Myanmar. This would explain why, for example, Malaysia did not respond so vehemently to the East Timor crisis. These inconsistencies in responding to atrocity crimes based on who the victims are pose a great challenge to the foundations of R2P. This is so because the implementation of the latter is meant to be impartial and not selective. The examination in Chapter 6 has also shown that personal relationships between States also play a big role in engagements in atrocity situations. As stated earlier, the motive behind Indonesia's 'quiet diplomacy' most likely stemmed from Indonesia's personal history with Myanmar, namely the fact that the latter respected Indonesia's sovereignty and did not interfere at all in its internal affairs at the time of the East Timor crisis.

As discussed in the last section of Chapter 6, the Myanmar Junta in February 2021 seized control through a coup from democratically elected officials. In response to this, citizens rallied to protest nationwide calling for democracy. The Junta has responded with forceful measures that, at the time of writing, have resulted in the deaths of more than 700 protestors.[5] ASEAN responded through an informal Foreign Ministers' Meeting, expressing its concern for the situation. However, it did not refer to the human rights violations committed by the Junta.[6] More recently, in its first unprecedented mediation effort, ASEAN held an emergency summit in order to discuss the situation and reached an agreement on the 'Five-point Consensus'.[7] This proposal called for the immediate cessation of violence and for dialogue and established a special ASEAN envoy to facilitate mediation. It also established that ASEAN will provide humanitarian assistance to Myanmar. At first glance, it would seem that, by doing the above, ASEAN has softened its position on the principle of non-interference in the internal affairs of States and has applied R2P Pillar II measures. A closer examination, however, paints a different picture. First, Myanmar agreed to call the ASEAN emergency summit. Second, the 'Five-point Consensus' only represents a step towards the right direction on paper. ASEAN has carefully crafted the language used in the proposal to ensure that it does not infringe upon Myanmar's sovereignty. Also, this proposal lacks enforcement power. In fact, while Myanmar verbally agreed to the proposal, military abuses have continued all around the country.[8] It could be argued, then, that Myanmar has agreed to these ASEAN mediation efforts to protect itself from harsher external interferences from the West, making itself appear to be cooperating with ASEAN in resolving the crisis. The second unprecedented move by ASEAN towards this crisis was the fact that the Myanmar Junta was barred from attending the ASEAN Summit since 2021 and its chairmanship of the organisation has been passed on to the Philippines in 2026. This is seen as an effort by ASEAN to navigate an issue of this magnitude within the scope of its ASEAN Way and ASEAN Charter.

At the same, it should not be forgotten that several ASEAN States, namely Thailand, Vietnam, Cambodia, Laos, and the Philippines, individually are still supporting the Junta. Only Indonesia, Malaysia, and Singapore have publicly deplored the lethal force used against the civilian population. These three States have been proactive in calling on the Junta to resolve this crisis peacefully and were the ones that called for the emergency ASEAN Summit to address this issue. The motivations behind the effort from Indonesia, Malaysia, and Singapore could be linked with an effort to protect the region from external international interference. Any action by ASEAN no matter how timid, could deter criticism and prevent additional interference from the international community. It also seems that Malaysia was more critical of the Junta's conduct against the Rohingya than it has been of the Junta's violent response to the civilians protesting on the streets.

Overall, this book has shown that the practical commitment to R2P in Southeast Asia is weak. First, ASEAN has no capacity to act independently from its members. Any collective position must mirror a collective agreement among members. Second, even after the introduction of R2P and several ASEAN States' *conceptual* endorsement of the principle, when faced with an actual atrocity situation ASEAN States have not *practically* engaged with R2P. In the Rohingya and West Papua crises, the vast majority of ASEAN States (with the exception of Malaysia) mirrored their reaction to the East Timor crisis, showing unwillingness to go against the principles of the ASEAN Way and to challenge the sovereignty of Myanmar.

A number of factors that generally shape ASEAN States' approach to R2P can be singled out here. The first factor, as discussed in Chapter 2, is the history of ASEAN States, which, in turn, contributes to explaining the creation of ASEAN and its commitment to the ASEAN Way. All ASEAN States (with the exception of Thailand) had been colonised by Western powers at one point in their histories. After becoming independent, these States have been understandably concerned about protecting their independence, leading to the adoption of a predominantly realist stance on issues of sovereignty, non-interference, and human rights. This realist stance is reflected in the way in which ASEAN States approach R2P. In particular, they reject Pillar III because of its non-consensual nature, since the measures taken under this Pillar would infringe upon the sovereignty of the affected States. A related theme is ASEAN States' lingering fear of neo-colonialism. Thus, when faced with atrocity crimes situations in the region, ASEAN States are very wary of Western States' interferences to avoid new forms of colonialism.

The second factor that contributes to shaping ASEAN States' approach to R2P is culture. ASEAN States prefer methods of quiet and non-confrontational diplomacy over more coercive forms of intervention, including the use or threat of force. Since the creation of ASEAN, ASEAN States have unanimously agreed upon a specific working culture among its members. This applies also to decision-making in that the ASEAN States prefer a consensus style over the Western's formal rigid voting style. This was purposely implemented into the ASEAN culture in order to protect members' sovereignty and ensure that no action interfering with members' internal affairs could be taken.

The third factor that contributes to shaping ASEAN States' approach to R2P is the concept of national interest. Speaking in realist terms, a sovereign State would only adopt a foreign policy that fits with its national ambitions and interests, be it economic, political, or military. The same applies to R2P scenarios. ASEAN States tend to engage with R2P when and if doing so aligns with their interests. For example, the majority of ASEAN States have conceptually endorsed Pillars I and II because this would, among other things, increase their perceived legitimacy within the international community. At the same time, rejecting Pillar III is in line with the ASEAN States' commitment to protect their sovereignty.

The fourth factor that affects how ASEAN States approach R2P is their individual relationship with the State in whose territory atrocity crimes are committed. Thus, if a given State has a close relationship with a State that is currently dealing with a mass atrocities crisis (even if the State in question is the perpetrator), the former is more likely to tread carefully and ensure that it does not act in any way that could be seen as disrespectful or infringing on the sovereignty of the latter. On the other hand, the lack of a close relationship between two States would allow one State to be more vocal and direct in dealing with the situation in the other State. This might also, on occasion, lead to calls for coercive measures under Pillar III in light of special circumstances (e.g. the case of Malaysia and Myanmar).

The fifth factor that contributes to shaping ASEAN States' approach to R2P is a State's relationships with the P-5 of the United Nations Security Council. Pillar III measures need to be authorised by the Security Council. As such, the P-5 hold significant power when it comes to implementing the coercive dimension of R2P. As a result of this, individual relationships between ASEAN States and the P-5 are important, especially when the State in question is the perpetrator of mass atrocities. If a State has a good relationship with any members of the P-5, it can essentially be shielded from all forms of Pillar III measures mandated by the Security Council. On the other hand, if the State in question does not, then it does not have the luxury of being protected from any form of coercive measures. In particular, for this region and the ASEAN States, the crucial P-5 actor is China. As China shares a similar culture and set of preferences in the realm of international law, it holds significant influence in the region. As such, before approaching an R2P situation in another member state, most ASEAN States will most likely take into account China's stance on the issue before responding.

All considered, ASEAN's approach to R2P is rather conservative. This is not surprising. The idea of R2P implies that sovereignty can no longer protect States which are unable or unwilling to protect their populations from mass atrocities. As such, R2P opens up the concrete possibility of eroding the principle of State sovereignty. Yet, ASEAN States abide by the ASEAN Way precisely because it places high value on the principle of sovereignty and protects the region from external interference. To these concerns one should also add that ASEAN States' fear that R2P interventions could be used by Western States to pursue imperialistic agendas, as confirmed by the 2011 NATO's intervention in Libya. This conservative approach to R2P, however, is neither the only nor the best way to protect the region from external interference because a lack of regional action is likely to lead to external action. Thus, it is my opinion that ASEAN should take a more active role in the implementation of R2P. This is especially true with regard to Pillar II. As discussed in the book, the idea of promoting a more flexible approach to sovereignty and non-interference in the context of atrocity crimes is not new in the region. In 1999, Thailand sought to introduce the concept of 'Flexible Engagement' within ASEAN by encouraging ASEAN and ASEAN States to openly discuss matters related to humanitarian crises that are both transnational and can have a spill-over effect in the region. Thailand suggested that when faced with matters that could pose a threat to regional security, the rigid interpretation of the concept of non-interference should be relaxed and that other member states should be welcome to express their opinions if the matter affects them without being accused of interfering in another member's internal affairs. If this approach were adopted by other ASEAN States, harsher forms of external interference in the region could be prevented. However, until some foundational changes are made to ASEAN's structure (in terms of institutional framework, *modus operandi* and guiding principles), its potential to take R2P action is far-fetched.

As discussed in Chapter 2, R2P also has a preventive dimension. Since ASEAN has not been capable/willing to take action in response to mass atrocities, one might wonder whether it could play a more significant role in relation to early prevention. As highlighted in Chapter 3, regional human rights mechanisms can contribute to the latter by means of early monitoring and reporting activities before a crisis escalates. While ASEAN has an Intergovernmental Commission on Human Rights, the latter cannot act independently from the ASEAN States. In order for this Commission to play a constructive role in preventing atrocities from occurring in the region, it should be given independent capacity to monitor and report on member states' activities. Furthermore, for its recommendations to be taken seriously, it should have the power to impose sanctions and/or suspend members in the event of grave violations and non-compliance.

More important changes, by contrast, could be seen in the future within individual States. The Rohingya crisis showed that Indonesia has implemented Pillar II measures even if it did not expressly invoke them, while Malaysia was even prepared to support coercive forms of intervention. The recent coup showed that Indonesia, Malaysia, and Singapore have been actively willing to assist Myanmar in resolving the crisis, thereby showing again an indirect endorsement and implementation of Pillar II of R2P. However, as already noted earlier, these States' progressive actions cannot be said to be exclusively inspired by R2P ideals.

At a broader level, this book has also highlighted that the gap between how the West and the East approach the concepts of sovereignty and non-intervention is not set to narrow in the near future. Chapter 8 dedicates to examining China's perception and implementation of the principles of international law and R2P in order to examine the correlation with ASEAN States in detail. As emphasised throughout this book, the fact that China's approach to humanitarian crises and R2P resembles ASEAN member states, both being wary supporters of the concept, and the crucial fact that its strict perceptions of the concepts of sovereignty, non-interference, and use of force resemble the ASEAN Way, its importance cannot be overstated. China wields significant power, diplomatically (P-5) and economically in the region and essentially the world, rivalling the US's hegemony. As a result of this, China, along with the ASEAN States' interpretation of the aforementioned principles of R2P, challenges the Western-dominated status quo, acting as a formidable obstacle for R2P to become a leading legal guiding principle responding to mass atrocities.

## Notes

1 Robert Gilpin, *War and Change in World Politics* (Cambridge University Press, 1981) p. 17.
2 Joint Communiqué of the 32nd ASEAN Ministerial Meeting (1999) <https://asean.org/?static_post=joint-communique-the-32nd-asean-ministerial-meeting-amm-singapore-23-24-july-1999> accessed on 22 April 2021.
3 'ASEAN Chairman's Statement on the Humanitarian Situation in Rakhine State' (2017) <https://asean.org/wp-content/uploads/2017/09/1.ASEAN-Chairmans-Statement-on-the-Rakhine.pdf> accessed on 18 April 2021.
4 Laos was defined as R2P neutral.
5 'Myanmar Coup: The People Shot Dead Since the Protests Began' (BBC, 13 April 2021) <https://www.bbc.co.uk/news/world-asia-56636345> accessed on 23 April 2021.
6 Chair's Statement on the Informal Ministerial Meeting (IAMM) (2021) <http://www.asean2021.bn/Theme/news/iamm-02.03.21.aspx> accessed on 23 April 2021.
7 Chairman's Statement on the ASEAN Leaders' Meeting (2021) pp. 3–4 <https://asean.org/storage/Chairmans-Statement-on-ALM-Five-Point-Consensus-24-April-2021-FINAL-a-1.pdf> accessed on 26 April 2021.
8 'Despite ASEAN Consensus, Military Abuses Continue Around the Country' (Myanmar Now, 30 April 2021) <https://www.myanmar-now.org/en/news/despite-asean-consensus-military-abuses-continue-around-the-country> accessed on 3 May 2021.

# Bibliography

## Books and Journal Articles


Abass, A., *Regional Organisations and the Development of Collective Security: Beyond Chapter VIII of the UN Charter* (Hart Publishing, 2004).

Acharya, A., 'Regional Military-Security Cooperation in the Third World: A Conceptual Analysis of the Relevance and Limitations of ASEAN' [1992] 29(1) *Journal of Peace Research*, pp. 7–21.

———, 'A Regional Security Community in Southeast Asia?' [1995] 18(3) *The Journal of Strategic Studies*, pp. 175–200.

———, 'Culture, Security, Multilateralism: The "ASEAN Way" and Regional Order' [1998] 19(1) *Contemporary Security Studies*, pp. 55–84.

———, *Whose Ideas Matter? Agency and Power in Asian Regionalism* (Cornell University Press, 2011).

———,*Constructing a Security Community in Southeast Asia: ASEAN and the Problem of Regional Order* (3rd edition, Routledge, 2014).

Acharya, A. and Johnston, A.I., *Crafting Cooperation: Regional International Institutions in Comparative Perspective* (Cambridge University Press, 2007).

Adediran, B., 'Implementing R2P: Towards a Regional Solution?' [2017] 9 *Global Responsibility to Protect*, pp. 459–488.

Alam, J., 'The Current Rohingya Crisis in Myanmar in Historical Perspective' [2019] 39(1) *Journal of Muslim Minority Affairs*, pp. 1–25.

Alatas, A., *The Pebble in the Shoe: The Diplomatic Struggle for East Timor* (Aksara Karunia, 2006).

Alexandra, L.A., 'The Incipient Development of ASEAN: A Chance for Mutual Learning' [2013] *Instituto Affari Internazionali*, pp. 65–70.

Anderson, K., 'Colonialism and Cold Genocide: The Case of West Papua' [2015] 9(2) *Genocide Studies and Prevention: An International Journal*, pp. 9–25.

Annan, K., 'Two Concepts of Sovereignty' [1999] 352(8137) *The Economist*, pp. 49–50.

Aris, S. and Wenger, A., *Regional Organisations and Security: Conceptions and Practices* (Routledge, 2014).

Bachman, J.S., *Cultural Genocide: Law, Politics, and Global Manifestations* (Routledge, 2021).

Barelli, M., 'Preventing and Responding to Atrocity Crimes: China, Sovereignty and the Responsibility to Protect' [2018] 23() *Journal of Conflict & Security Law*, pp. 173–201.

Barr, M.D., 'Lee Kuan Yew and the other "Asian values" Debates' [2000] 24(3) *Asian Studies Review*, pp. 309–334.

Bar-Tal, D., *Intractable Conflicts: Socio-Psychological Foundations and Dynamics* (Cambridge University Press, 2013).

Bellamy, A.J., 'Libya and the Responsibility to Protect: The Exception and the Norm' [2011] 25(3) *Ethics and International Affairs*, pp. 263–269.

Bellamy, A.J. and Beeson, M., 'The Responsibility to Protect in Southeast Asia: Can ASEAN Reconcile Humanitarianism and Sovereignty?' [2010] 6(3) *Asian Security*, pp. 262–279.
Bellamy, A.J. and Dunne, T., *The Oxford Handbook of the Responsibility to Protect* (1st edition 2006, Oxford University Press, 2016).
Betts, A. and Orchard, P., *Implementation and World Politics: How International Norms Change Practice* (Oxford University Press, 2014).
Blades, J., *West Papua: The Issue That Won't Go Away for Melanesia* (Lowy Institute Analysis, 2020).
Bone, Jr, R.C., *The Dynamics of the Western New Guinea (Irian Barat) Problem* (Cornell University, 1958).
Bozdaglioglu, Y., 'Constructivism and Identity Formation: An Interactive Approach' [2007] 3(11) *Review of International Law and Politics*, pp. 121–144.
Brundige, E., et al., 'Indonesian Human Rights Abuses in West Papua: Application of the Law of Genocide to the History of Indonesian Control' [2004] *The Allard K. Lowenstein International Human Rights Clinic Yale Law School*, pp. 1–75.
Buchan, R. and Tsagourias, N., 'The Crisis in Crimea and the Principle of Non-Intervention' [2017] 19(2–3) *International Community Law Review*, pp. 165–193.
Budiawan, 'How Do Indonesians Remember *Konfrontasi?* Indonesia-Malaysia Relations and the Popular Memory of "Confrontation" after the Fall of Suharto' [2017] 18(3) *Inter-Asia Cultural Studies*, pp. 364–375.
Burchill, R., 'The ICJ Decision in the Case Concerning East Timor: The Illegal Use of Force Validated' [1997] 2(1) *Journal of Conflict and Security Law*, pp. 1–22.
———, 'Regional Approaches to International Humanitarian Law' [2010] 41() *University of Wellington Law Review*, pp. 205–234.
Cai, C., 'New Great Powers and International Law in the 21st Century' [2013] 24(3) *European Journal of International Law*, pp. 755–795.
———, *The Rise of China and International Law: Taking Chinese Exceptionalism Seriously* (Oxford University Press, 2019).
Cassese, A., 'Ex Iniuria Ius Oritur: Are We Moving Towards International Legitimation of Forcible Humanitarian Countermeasures in the World Community?' [1999] 10(1) *European Journal of International Law*, pp. 23–30.
———, *International Law* (2nd edition, Oxford University Press, 2005).
Chairullah, E., *Indonesia's Failure in Papua: The Role of Elites in Designing, Implementing and Undermining Special Autonomy* (Routledge, 2022).
Chaziza, M. and Goldman, O.S., 'Revisiting China's Non-Interference Policy Towards Intrastate Wars' [2014] 7(1) *The Chinese Journal of International Politics*, pp. 89–115.
Cheesman, N., 'How in Myanmar "National Races" Came to Surpass Citizenship and Exclude Rohingya' [2017] 47(3) *Journal of Contemporary Asia*, pp. 461–483.
Chimni, B.S., 'Third World Approaches to International Law: A Manifesto' [2006] 8(3) *International Community Review*, pp. 3–27.
———, *International Law and World Order: A Critique of Contemporary Approaches* (Cambridge University Press, 2017).
Chinkin, C., 'East Timor: A Failure of Decolonisation' [1999] 20 *Australian Year Book of International Law*, pp. 35–54.
Chiou, Y., 'Unravelling the Logic of ASEAN's Decision-Making: Theoretical Analysis and Case Examination' [2010] 2(3) *Asian Politics & Policy*, pp. 371–393.
Ciorciari, J.D., 'Institutionalizing Human Rights in Southeast Asia' [2012] 34(3) *Human Rights Quarterly*, pp. 695–725.
Claes, J., 'Protecting Civilians from Mass Atrocities: Meeting the Challenge of R2P Rejectionism' [2012] 4(1) *Global Responsibility to Protect*, pp. 67–97.
Clark, R.S., 'Decolonization of East Timor and the United Nations Norms on Self-Determination and Aggression' [1980] 7(2) *The Yale Journal of World Public Order*, pp. 2–44.

———, 'East Timor and International Law' [1984] 2 *Mennesker og Rettigheter*, pp. 32–34.

Clarke, G., 'The Evolving ASEAN Human Rights System: The ASEAN Human Rights Declaration of 2012' [2012] 11(1) *Northwestern University Journal of International Human Rights*, pp. 1–27.

Coe, B, 'Regional Human Rights Institutions and R2P: The Role of State Monitoring in Atrocity Prevention' [2017] 9(3) *Global Responsibility to Protect*, pp. 294–317.

Cogan, J.K., Hurd, I. and Johnstone, I., *The Oxford Handbook of International Organizations* (Oxford University Press, 2016).

Collins, A., 'From Commitment to Compliance: ASEAN Human Rights Regression?' [2019] 32(2) *The Pacific Review*, pp. 365–394.

Corthay, E., 'The ASEAN Doctrine of Non-Interference in Light of the Fundamental Principle of Non-Intervention' [2015] 17() *Asian-Pacific Law & Policy Journal*, pp. 2–41.

Cryer, R., Herver, T., Sokhi-Bulley, B. and Bohm, A., *Research Methodologies in EU and International Law* (Hart Publishing, 2011).

Davies, M., 'The ASEAN Synthesis: Human Rights, Non-Intervention, and the ASEAN Human Rights Declaration' [2013] 14(2) *Georgetown Journal of International Affairs*, pp. 51–58.

———, 'Explaining the Vientiane Action Programme: ASEAN and the Institutionalisation of Human Rights' [2013] 24(4) *The Pacific Review*, pp. 385–406.

Doyle, N., 'The ASEAN Human Rights Declarations and the Implications of Recent Southeast Asian Initiatives in Human Rights Institution-Building and Standard-Setting' [2014] 63(1) *International and Comparative Law Quarterly*, pp. 67–101.

Dunn, L., Nyers, P. and Stubbs, R., 'Western Interventionism Versus East Asian Non-Interference: Competing "Global" Norms in the Asian Century' [2010] 23(3) *The Pacific Review*, pp. 295–312.

Dunne, T. and Gelber, K., 'Arguing Matters: The Responsibility to Protect and the Case of Libya' [2014] 6 *Global Responsibility to Protect*, pp. 326–349.

Dupont, A., 'ASEAN's Response to the East Timor Crisis' [2000] 54(2) *Australian Journal of International Affairs*, pp. 163–170.

Elmslie, J., *Economic and Social Indicators in West Papua* (Pacific Institute of Public Policy, 2013).

Evans, M.D., *International Law* (4th edition, Oxford University Press, 2014).

Feraru, A.S., 'ASEAN Decision-Making Process: Before and After the ASEAN Charter' [2015] 4(1) *Asian Development Policy Review*, pp. 26–41.

Forsythe, D.P., *Human Rights in International Relations* (3rd edition, Cambridge University Press, 2012).

Gallagher, A., 'The Promise of Pillar II: Analyzing International Assistance Under the Responsibility to Protect' [2015] 91(6) *International Affairs*, pp.1259–1275.

Gentry, M.E., 'Consensus as a Form of Decision-Making' [1982] 9 *Journal of Sociology & Social Welfare*, pp. 233–244.

Gifkins, J., 'The UN Security Council Divided: Syria in Crisis' [2012] 4 *Global Responsibility to Protect*, pp. 377–393.

Gilpin, R., *War and Change in World Politics* (Cambridge University Press, 1981).

Goldsmith, J., 'Sovereignty, International Relations Theory, and International Law' [2000] 52 *Stanford Law Review*, pp. 959–986.

Gray, C., *International Law and the Use of Force* (3rd edition, Oxford University Press, 2008).

Greenwood, C., 'International Law and the NATO Intervention in Kosovo' [2000] 49(4) *The International and Comparative*, pp. 926–934.

Gutherie, C. and Quinlan, M., *Just War: The Just War Tradition: Ethics in Modern Warfare* (Bloomsbury, 2007).

Haacke, J., 'ASEAN's Diplomatic and Security Culture: A Constructivist Assessment' [2003] 3 *International Relations of the Asia-Pacific Volume*, pp. 57–87.

———, 'The Nature and Management of Myanmar's Alignment with China: The SLORC/SPDC Years' [2011] 30(2) *Journal of Current Southeast Asian Affairs*, pp. 105–140.

Hanquin, X., 'Chinese Observations on International Law' [2007] 6(1) *Chinese Journal of International Law*, pp. 83–93.

———, *Comparative International Law* (Oxford University Press, 2018).

Haque, M.M., 'Rohingya Ethnic Muslim Minority and the 1982 Citizenship Law in Burma' [2017] 37(4) *Journal of Muslim Minority Affairs*, pp. 454–469.

Hatta, M., 'Indonesia between the Power Blocs' [1958] 36 *Foreign Affairs*, pp. 480–490.

Hehir, A., *Humanitarian Intervention: An Introduction* (Palgrave Macmillan, 2010).

Hehir, A. and Murray, R., *Libya: The Responsibility to Protect and the Future of Humanitarian Intervention* (Palgrave Macmillan, 2013).

Holzgrefe, J.L. and Keohane, R. (eds), *Humanitarian Intervention: Ethical, Legal and Political Dilemmas* (Cambridge University Press, 2005).

Ishizuka, K., *The History of Peace-building in East Timor: The Issues of International Intervention* (Foundation Books, 2010).

Jackson, R., *Sovereignty at the Millennium* (Blackwell Publishing, 1999).

Jago, M., 'InterFet: An Account of Intervention with Consent in East Timor' [2010] 17(3) *International Peacekeeping*, pp. 377–394.

Jilani, A.F.K., *A Cultural History of Rohingya* (Ahmed Jilani, 2001).

Joliffe, J., *East Timor: Nationalism and Colonialism* (University of Queensland Press, 1978).

Jones, D.M. and Jenne, N., 'Weak States' Regionalism: ASEAN and the Limits of Security Cooperation in Pacific Asia' [2016] 16(2) *International Relations of the Asia-Pacific*, pp. 209–240.

Jones, L., 'ASEAN's Unchanged Melody? The Theory and Practice of "Non-Interference" in Southeast Asia' [2010] 23(4) *The Pacific Review*, pp. 479–502.

———, *ASEAN, Sovereignty and Intervention in Southeast Asia* (Palgrave Macmillan, 2012).

Joshua, W. and Gilberd, S., *Arms for the Third World: Soviet Military Aid and Diplomacy* (John Hopkins Press, 1969).

Katsumata, H., 'Reconstruction of Diplomatic Norms in Southeast Asia: The Case for Strict Adherence to the "ASEAN Way"' [2003] 25(1) *Contemporary Southeast Asia*, pp. 104–121.

———, 'ASEAN and Human Rights: Resisting Western Pressure or Emulating the West' [2009] 22(5) *The Pacific Review*, pp. 619–637.

Katuoka, S. and Cepinskyte, A., 'Response to Large-Scale Atrocities: Humanitarian Intervention and the Responsibility to Protect' [2010] 3(121) *Jurisprudencija*, pp. 157–175.

Keling, M.F., Md. Som, H., Saludin, M.N., Shuib, M.S. and Ajis, M.N., 'The Development of ASEAN from Historical Approach' [2011] 7(7) *Asian Social Science*, pp.169–189.

Kelly, R.E., 'Security Theory in the "New Regionalism"' [2007] 9() *International Studies Review*, pp. 197–229.

Koga, K., 'Institutional Transformation of ASEAN: ZOPFAN, TAC, and the Bali Concord I in 1968–1976' [2014] 27(5) *The Pacific Review*, pp. 729–753.

Koops, A.J., et al., *The Oxford Handbook of Peace Operations* (Oxford University Press, 2015).

Krasner, S., *Problematic Sovereignty* (Columbia University Press, 2001).

Landweer, M.L. and Unseth, P., 'An Introduction to Language Use in Melanesia' [2012] 214 *International Journal of the Sociology of Language*, pp. 1–3.

Long, L., 'The Srebrenica Massacre' [2006] 15() *The Forensic Examiner*, pp. 43–45.

Lowe, V., et al., *The United Nations Security Council and War: The Evolution of Thought and Practice since 1945* (Oxford University Press, 2008).

Malksoo, L., *Russian Approaches to International Law* (Oxford University Press, 2015).

———, 'Civilizational Diversity as Challenge to the (False) Universality of International Law' [2019] 9 *Asian Journal of International Law*, pp. 155–164.

Marker, J., *East Timor: A Memoir of the Negotiations for Independence* (McFarland, 2003).

Marks, S.P. and Cooper, N., 'The Responsibility to Protect: Watershed or Old Wine in a New Bottle?' [2010] 2(1) *Jindal Global Law Review*, pp. 86–130.

Martin, I. and Mayer-Rieckh, A., 'The United Nations and East Timor: From Self-Determination to State-Building' [2005] 12(1) *International Peacekeeping*, pp. 125–145.

Martinkus, J., *The Road: Uprising in West Papua* (Black Inc, 2020).

May, B., *Indonesian Tragedy* (Routledge & Kegan Paul Ltd, 2001).

May, R.J., 'Fifty Years after the "Act of Free Choice": The West Papua Issue in a Regional Context' [2021] *The Department of Pacific Affairs*, pp. 1–23.

Mayersen, D. and Pohlman, A., *Genocide and Mass Atrocities in Asia: Legacies and Prevention* (Routledge, 2013).

Menon, P.R., 'The Legal Personality of International Organizations' [1992] 4 *Sri Lanka Journal of International Law*, pp. 79–97.

Mohamad, M., 'Towards a Human Rights Regime in Southeast Asia: Charting the Course of State Commitment' [2002] 24() *Contemporary Southeast Asia*, pp. 230–250.

Mohamed, S., 'Syria, the United Nations, and the Responsibility to Protect' [2012] 106 *American Society of International Law*, pp. 223–226.

Morada, N.M., 'The ASEAN Charter and the Promotion of R2P in Southeast Asia: Challenges and Constraints' [2009] 1 *Global Responsibility to Protect*, pp. 185–207.

Mulaj, K., 'Resisting an Oppressive Regime: The Case of Kosovo Liberation Army' [2008] 31(12) *Studies in Conflicts & Terrorism*, pp. 1103–1119.

Muller, W., 'China: An Illiberal, Non-Western States in a West-centric, Liberal Order?' [2014] *Baltic Yearbook of International Law*, pp. 1–19.

Munro, J., 'Why States Create International Human Rights Mechanisms: The ASEAN Intergovernmental Commission on Human Rights and Democratic Lock-in Theory' [2009] 10(1) *Asia-Pacific Journal on Human Rights and The Law*, pp. 1–26.

Naidu, G.V.C., 'The East Timor Crisis' [1999] 23(9) *Strategic Analysis*, pp. 1467–1480.

Narine, S., 'ASEAN and the Management of Regional Security' [1998] 71() *Pacific Affairs*, pp. 195–214.

———, 'State Sovereignty, Political Legitimacy and Regional Institutionalism in the Asia-Pacific' [2004] 17(3) *The Pacific Review*, pp. 423–450.

———, 'Humanitarian Intervention and the Question of Sovereignty: The Case of ASEAN' [2005] 4(3–4) *Perspectives on Global Development and Technology*, pp. 465–485.

———, 'Human Rights Norms and the Evolution of ASEAN: Moving Without Moving in a Changing Regional Environment' [2012] 34(3) *Contemporary Southeast Asia: A Journal of International and Strategic Affairs*, pp. 365–388.

Nasu, H., 'Revisiting the Principle of Non-Intervention: A Structural Principle of International Law or a Political Obstacle to Regional Security in Asia?' [2013] 3 *Asian Journal of International Law*, pp. 25–50.

Nesadurai, H.E.S., 'The Association of Southeast Asian Nations (ASEAN)' [2008] 13() *New Political Economy*, pp. 225–239.

Nishikawa, Y., 'The "ASEAN Way" and Asian Regional Security' [2007] 35(1) *Politics and Policy*, pp. 42–56.

Nye, J., *International Regionalism* (Little, Brown & Co, 1968).

Öberg, M.D., 'The Legal Effects of Resolutions of the UN Security Council and General Assembly in the Jurisprudence of the ICJ' [2006] 16(5) *The European Journal of International Law*, pp. 879–906.

Ortuoste, M., 'Timor-Leste and ASEAN: Shaping Region and State in Southeast Asia' [2011] 19(1) *Asian Journal of Political Science*, pp. 1–24.

Pan, Z. and Du, P., 'The Logic of Contingency in China's Insistence on the Non-Interference Principle' [2015] 8 *Fudan Journal of Humanities and Social Sciences*, pp. 505–520.

Pattharapong, R., 'Leadership in ASEAN: The Role of Indonesia Considered' [2014] 22() *Asian Journal of Political Science*, pp. 113–127.

Pattison, J., *Humanitarian Intervention and the Responsibility to Protect: Who Should Intervene?* (Oxford University Press, 2010).

———, 'The Ethics of "Responsibility While Protecting": BRAZIL, The Responsibility to Protect, and Guidelines for Humanitarian Intervention' [2013] *Human Rights and Welfare Working Paper 71*, pp. 1–26.

Paulker, G.J., 'The Soviet Challenge in Indonesia' [1962] 40(40) *Foreign Affairs*, pp. 612–626.

Pekkanen, S., Ravenhill, J. and Foot, R., *The Oxford Handbook of the International Relations of Asia* (Oxford University Press, 2014).

Piris, J. and Woon, W., *Towards a Rules-Based Community: An ASEAN Legal Service* (Cambridge University Press, 2015).

Quinton-Brown, P., 'Mapping Dissent: The Responsibility to Protect and Its State Critics' [2013] 5 *Global Responsibility to Protect*, pp. 260–282.

Ramcharan, R., 'ASEAN and Non-Interference: A Principle Maintained' [2000] 22(1) *Contemporary Southeast Asia*, pp. 60–88.

Rattanasavee, R., 'Leadership in ASEAN: The Role of Indonesia Reconsidered' [2014] 22(2) *Asian Journal of Political Science*, pp. 113–127.

Ribeiro, M.M.L.A., et al., 'China's Engagement with R2P: Pluralist Shaper?' [2020] 12 *Global Responsibility to Protect*, pp. 271–298.

Roberts, A., *Is International Law International?* (Oxford University Press, 2017).

Roberts, A., et al., *Comparative International Law* (Oxford University Press, 2018).

Robinson, G., 'People's War: Militias in East Timor and Indonesia' [2001] 9(3) *South East Asia Research*, pp. 271–318.

Rosyidin, M., 'Reconciling State's Sovereignty with Global Norms: Indonesia's Quite Diplomacy in Myanmar and the Feasibility of the Implementation of Responsibility to Protect (R2P) in Southeast Asia' [2020] 12(1) (Special Issue) *Global Responsibility to Protect*, pp. 11–36.

Ryan, A., 'Primary Responsibilities and Primary Risks' Australian Defence Force Participation International Force East Timor' [2000] 304 *Land Warfare Studies Centre*, pp. 1–136.

Ryngaert, C. and Schrijver, N, 'Lessons Learned from the Srebrenica Massacre: From UN Peacekeeping Reform to Legal Responsibility' [2015] 62() *Netherlands International Law Review*, pp. 219–227.

Ryu, Y. and Ortuoste, M., 'Democratization, Regional Integration, and Human Rights: The Case of the ASEAN Intergovernmental Commission on Human Rights' [2014] 27(3) *The Pacific Review*, pp. 357–382.

Salihu, MA.A., 'NATO Intervention in Kosovo in Light of Security Council Actions and International Law' [2013] 3(2) *ILIRIA International Review*, pp. 285–303.

Sani, M.A.D., 'Mahathir Mohamad as a Cultural Relativist: Mahathirism on Human Rights' [2008] *Universiti Utara Malaysia*, pp. 1–17.

Saul, B., 'Was the Conflict in East Timor "Genocide" and Why Does It Matter?' [2001] 2(2) *Melbourne Journal of International Law*, pp. 477–522.

Schulze, K.E., 'The East Timor Referendum Crisis and Its Impact on Indonesian Politics' [2001] 24(1) *Studies in Conflict and Terrorism*, pp. 77–82.

Seah, D., 'The ASEAN Charter' [2009] 58(1) *International and Comparative Law Quarterly*, pp. 197–212.

Sheid, D.E., *The Ethics of Armed Humanitarian Intervention* (Cambridge University Press, 2014).

Simma, B., 'NATO, the UN and the Use of Force: Legal Aspects' [1999] 10(1) *European Journal of International Law*, pp. 1–22.

Simpson, B., '"Illegally and Beautifully", The United States, the Indonesian Invasion of East Timor and the International Community, 1974–1976' [2005] 5(3) *Cold War History*, pp. 281–315.

Singh, B., *Papua: Geopolitics and the Quest for Nationhood* (Routledge, 2017).

Sohn, L.B., 'Introduction: United Nations Decision-Making: Confrontation or Consensus?' [1974] 15 *Harvard International Law Journal*, pp. 438–445.

Southgate, L., *ASEAN Resistance to Sovereignty Violation: Interests, Balancing and the Role of the Vanguard State* (Bristol University Press, 2019).

Stahn, C., 'Responsibility to Protect: Political Rhetoric or Emerging Legal Norm?' [2007] 101(1) *The American Journal of International Law*, pp. 99–120.

Stephan, P.B., 'Symmetry and Selectivity: What Happens in International Law When the World Changes' [2009] 10(1) *Chicago Journal of International Law*, pp. 91–123.

Stockwell, A.J, 'Malaysia: The Making of a Neo-Colony?' [1998] 26(2) *The Journal of Imperial and Commonwealth History*, pp. 138–156.

Strating, R., *The Post-Colonial Security Dilemma: Timor-Leste and the International Community* (ISEAS-Yusof Ishak Institute, 2018).

Subritzky, J., 'Britain, Konfrontasi, and the End of Empire in Southeast Asia, 1961–1965' [2000] 28(3) *The Journal of Imperial and Commonwealth History*, pp. 209–227.

Tan, H., *The ASEAN Intergovernmental Commission on Human Rights: Institutionalising Human Rights in Southeast Asia* (Cambridge University Press, 2011).

Thakur, R. and Maley, W., *Theorising the Responsibility to Protect* (Cambridge University Press, 2015).

Than, T.M.M., 'Myanmar and China: A Special Relationship?' [2003] *Southeast Asian Affairs*, pp. 189–210.

Trajano, J.C.I., 'Ethnic Nationalism and Separatism in West Papua, Indonesia' [2010] 16 *Journal of Peace, Conflict and Development*, pp. 12–35.

Wang, Y.W., 'Contextualizing Universal Human Rights: An Integrated Human Rights Framework for ASEAN' [2015] 25(3) *Duke Journal of Comparative & International Law*, pp. 385–426.

Ware, A. and Laoutides, C., *Myanmar's 'Rohingya Conflict'* (Hurst & Company, 2018).

———, 'Myanmar's "Rohingya" Conflict: Misconceptions and Complexity' [2019] 50(1) *Asian Affairs*, pp. 60–79.

Weissberg, G., *The International Status of the United Nations* (Oceana Publications, 1961).

Weller, M., *The Oxford Handbook of the Use of Force in International Law* (Oxford University Press, 2015).

Welsh, J.M., *Humanitarian Intervention and International Relations* (Oxford University Press, 2003).

Wheeler, N.J., *Saving Strangers: Humanitarian Intervention in International Society* (Oxford University Press, 2000).

White, N.D., 'The Legality of Bombing in the Name of Humanity' [2000] 5(1) *Journal of Conflict and Security Law*, pp. 27–43.

William, B.-W.W., 'Power Shifts in International Law: Structural Realignment and Substantive Pluralism' [2015] 56(1) *Harvard International Law Journal*, pp. 1–80.

Williams, P.D. and Bellamy, A.J., 'Principles, Politics and Prudence: Libya, the Responsibility to Protect, and the Use of Military Force' [2012] 18(3) *Global Governance*, pp. 273–297.

Wing, J. and King, P., *Genocide in West Papua? The Role of Indonesian State Apparatus and a Current Needs Assessment of the Papuan People* (The Centre for Peace and Conflict Studies, 2005).

Woon, W., 'The ASEAN Charter Ten Years On' [2017] 39() *Contemporary Southeast Asia: A Journal of International and Strategic Affairs*, pp. 245–251.

Wu, L., 'East Asia and the Principle of Non-Intervention: Policies and Practices' [2000] 5(160) *Maryland Series in Contemporary Asian Studies*, pp. 1–35.

Yasuaki, O., *A Transcivilization Perspective on International Law* (Hague Academy of International Law, 2010).

———, *International Law in a Transcivilizational World* (Cambridge University Press, 2017).

Zehfuss, M., *Constructivism in International Relations: The Politics of Reality* (Cambridge University Press, 2002).

## Websites

Adams, S., 'Myanmar's Deadly Coup and the Responsibility to Protect' (Global Centre for the Responsibility to Protect, 25 March 2021) <https://www.globalr2p.org/publications/myanmars-deadly-coup-and-the-responsibility-to-protect/> accessed on 10 April 2021.

Adetunji, J., Beaumont, B. and Chulov, M., 'Libya Protests: More Than 100 Killed as Army Fires on Unarmed Demonstrators' (The Guardian, 20 February 2011) <https://www.theguardian.com/world/2011/feb/20/libya-protests-benghazi-muammar-gaddafi> accessed on 20 January 2017.

Aghayev, E., 'Analysis and Background of the "Arab Spring" in Libya' (The Independent International Political Research Center, 20 August 2014) <http://www.iiprc.org/analysis-and-background-of-the-arab-spring-in-libya.html> accessed on 15 January 2017.

Aglionby, J. and Gittings, J., 'Timor Vote Sparks Brutal Militia Attack' (The Guardian, 5 September1999)<https://www.theguardian.com/world/1999/sep/05/indonesia.easttimor1> accessed on 10 January 2020.

'ASEAN Demands "Immediate Cessation of Violence" in Myanmar' (Aljazeera, 24 April 2021) <https://www.aljazeera.com/news/2021/4/24/myanmar-coup-leader-in-jakarta-for-southeast-asian-summit> accessed on 26 April 2021.

'ASEAN Summit Begins Without Myanmar After Top General Barred' (Aljazeera, 26 October 2021) <https://www.aljazeera.com/news/2021/10/26/asean-summit-begins-without-myanmar-after-top-generals-exclusion#:~:text=Myanmar%20not%20at%20ASEAN%20summit,end%20violence%20in%20the%20country.&text=Southeast%20Asian%20leaders-%20have%20begun,exclusion%20of%20its%20top%20general.> accessed on 27 February 2024.

Bemma, A., 'Rohingya Refugee Voices Amplify Across Southeast Asia' (The Jakarta Post, 8 July 2019) <https://www.thejakartapost.com/life/2019/07/08/rohingya-refugee-voices-amplify-across-southeast-asia.html> accessed 5 June 2020.

'Benny Wenda: Genocide Is Happening in West Papua' (United Liberation Movement for West Papua, 17 November 2023) <https://www.ulmwp.org/benny-wenda-genocide-is-happening-in-west-papua#:~:text=Over%2060%20years%20of%20genocidal,been%20killed%20by%20Indonesian%20forces.> accessed on 11 February 2024.

Bequelin, N., 'Behind China's Attempt to East the Rohingya Crisis' (The New York Times, 5 December 2017) <https://www.nytimes.com/2017/12/05/opinion/china-rohingya-crisis.html> accessed on 18 March 2021.

Blair, D., 'Syria War Crimes Investigators Amass Strongest Evidence "Since Nuremberg" Against Bashar al-Assad' (The Telegraph, 12 April 2016) <http://www.telegraph.co.uk/news/2016/04/12/syria-war-crimes-investigators-amass-strongest-evidence-since-nu/> accessed on 20 February 2017.

Bonner, R. and Perlez, J., 'Inquiry Sought on Mining Company' (The New York Times, 29 January 2006) <https://www.nytimes.com/2006/01/29/world/asia/inquiry-sought-on-mining-company.html> accessed on 7 February 2024.

'Brunei Calls for ASEAN Meeting to Discuss Myanmar Situation' (VOA News, 5 April2021)<https://www.voanews.com/east-asia-pacific/brunei-calls-asean-meeting-discuss-myanmar-situation> accessed on 5 April 2021.

Cabato, R., 'Duterte Highlights ASEAN Principle of Non-Interference' (CNN Philippines, 29 April 2017) <http://nine.cnnphilippines.com/news/2017/04/29/Duterte-ASEAN-speech-non-interference.html> accessed on 30 May 2019.

'Cambodia Leader Hun Sen Terms Myanmar Coup "Internal Affairs"' (VOA Cambodia, 1 February 2021) <https://www.voacambodia.com/a/cambodian-leader-hun-sen-terms-myanmar-coup-internal-affairs-/5759503.html> accessed on 5 April 2021.

Cambodia PM Hun Sen's Visit with Myanmar Military Chief Sparks Protest' (The Guardian, 8 January 2022) <https://www.theguardian.com/world/2022/jan/08/cambodian-pm-hun-sens-visit-with-myanmar-military-chief-sparks-protests> accessed on 27 February 2024.

Cameron, S., 'Why Is Myanmar New Deep-Sea Port Such Hot Property?' (The Lowy Institute, 22 November 2023) <https://www.lowyinstitute.org/the-interpreter/why-myanmar-s-new-deep-sea-port-such-hot-property> accessed on 24 February 2024.

'CARAT Indonesia 2022 Kicks Off with Indonesia and U.S. Navy and Marine Corps' (The United States Navy, 7 December 2022) <https://www.navy.mil/Press-Office/News-Stories/Article/3238091/carat-indonesia-2022-kicks-off-with-indonesian-and-us-navy-and-marine-corps/> accessed on 13 February 2024.

'China Committed Genocide Against Uyghurs, Independent Tribunal Rules' (BBC, 9 December 2021) <https://www.bbc.co.uk/news/world-asia-china-59595952> accessed on 24 February 2024.

'China Proposed Three-Phase Plan for Rohingya Issue' (Reuters, 20 November 2017) <https://www.reuters.com/article/idUSKBN1DK07K/> accessed on 24 February 2024.

'China, Russia Block U.N. Council Concern about Myanmar Violence' (Reuters, 17 March 2017) <https://www.reuters.com/article/us-myanmar-rohingya-un-idUSKBN16O2J6> accessed on 2 April 2021.

'Comment by UN Human Rights Office Spokesperson Ravina Shamdasani on Papua and West Papua, Indonesia' (Office of the High Commissioner for Human Rights Press Release, 30 November 2020) <https://www.ohchr.org/en/statements/2020/11/comment-un-human-rights-office-spokesperson-ravina-shamdasani-papua-and-west?LangID=E&NewsID=26551> accessed on 13 February 2024.

Doherty, B. and Lamb, K., 'West Papua Independence Petition Is Rebuffed at the UN' (The Guardian, 30 September 2017) <https://www.theguardian.com/world/2017/sep/30/west-papua-independence-petition-is-rebuffed-at-un> accessed on 13 February 2024.

Ellis-Petersen, H., 'Thailand Military-Backed PM Voted after Junta Created Loose Coalition' (The Guardian, 5 June 2019) <https://www.theguardian.com/world/2019/jun/05/thailand-military-backed-pm-prayuth-chan-ocha-voted-in-after-junta-creates-loose-coalition> accessed on 9 March 2021.

Evans, G., 'The Responsibility to Protect the People of Myanmar' (Australian Institute of International Affairs, 8 April 2021) <https://www.internationalaffairs.org.au/australianoutlook/the-responsibility-to-protect-the-people-of-myanmar/> accessed on 10 April 2021.

'The Fate of East Timor; In Clinton's Words: East Timor, Waco, Clemency Offer, and Other Issue' (The New York Times, 10 September 1999) <https://www.nytimes.com/1999/09/10/world/fate-east-timor-clinton-s-words-east-timor-waco-clemency-offer-other-issues.html> accessed on 15 January 2020.

'Fiery Debate Over West Papua at UN General Assembly' (RNZ, 27 September 2017) <https://www.rnz.co.nz/international/programmes/datelinepacific/audio/201860156/fiery-debate-over-west-papua-at-un-general-assembly> accessed on 13 February 2024.

'Fifty Years of Corporate Exploitation: The Story of US Mining Giant Freeport & Papua's Stolen Sovereignty (Part One)' (Corporate Accountability Law, 28 February 2022) <https://corpaccountabilitylab.org/calblog/2022/2/28/fifty-years-of-corporate-exploitation-the-story-of-us-mining-giant-freeport-amp-papuas-stolen-sovereignty-part-i> accessed on 4 February 2024.

FlorCruz, J.A., 'Russia, China and Partners Call for Non-Intervention in Syria and Iran' (CNN, 7 June 2012) <https://edition.cnn.com/2012/06/07/world/asia/china-russia-syria/index.html/> accessed 20 February 2017.

'Freeport-McMoran Profit Plunges on Reduced Production' (Mining Technology, 24 April 2023) <https://www.mining-technology.com/news/freeport-mcmoran-profit-plunges/?cf-view> accessed on 7 February 2024.

'Freeport Mining and Its Environment Impacts on the Riverine Ecosystem' (Lembaga Peduli Masyarakat Wilaya Mimika Timur Jau, 24 June 2022), p. 3 <https://www.ohchr.org/sites/default/files/2022-06/Solidarity%20for%20Indigenous%20Papuans1.pdf> accessed on 7 February 2024.

Gao, C., 'On Rohingya Issue, Both China and India Back Myanmar Government' (Reuters, 13 September 2017) <https://thediplomat.com/2017/09/on-rohingya-issue-both-china-and-india-back-myanmar-government/> accessed on 24 February 2024.

———, 'China Aids Rohingya Refugees in Bangladesh While Backing Myanmar Government' (Reuters, 2 October 2017) <https://thediplomat.com/2017/10/china-aids-rohingya-refugees-in-bangladesh-while-backing-myanmar-government/> accessed on 24 February 2024.

Gardner, F., 'Syria Blasts Signal Dangerous Escalation of Violence' (BBC, 10 May 2012) <http://www.bbc.co.uk/news/world-middle-east-18023668> accessed on 20 February 2017.

'"Genocide": Malaysian PM Mahathir Urges International Community to Act on Rohingya Issue' (Channel News Asia, 25 September 2019) <https://www.channelnewsasia.com/news/asia/malaysia-mahathir-rohingya-urges-world-to-act-united-nations-11940210> accessed on 18 March 2021.

'Global Condemnation Follows Bloodiest Day Since Myanmar Coup' (Bangkok Post, 28 March 2021) <https://www.bangkokpost.com/world/2090927/global-condemnation-follows-bloodiest-day-since-myanmar-coup> accessed on 5 April 2021.

Goldstein, E., 'Before the Arab Spring, the Unseen Thaw' (Human Rights Watch, 2012) <https://www.hrw.org/world-report/2012/country-chapters/global-middle-east/north-africa> accessed on 20 January 2017.

Gyo, M., 'East Timor and Burmese Democracy' [1999] 7(8) *The Irrawaddy* <https://www2.irrawaddy.com/article.php?art_id=1653&page=1> accessed on 30 March 2021.

'Hearing in Dutch Parliament Calls for UN Visit to West Papua' (United Liberation Movement for West Papua, 29 February 2024) <https://www.ulmwp.org/hearing-in-dutch-parliament-calls-for-un-visit-to-west-papua> accessed on 5 March 2024.

'History of West Papua' <https://www.freepapuamovement.org/about-us/> accessed on 4 February 2024.

'How We Are Funded' (The United Nations Peacekeeping) <https://peacekeeping.un.org/en/how-we-are-funded#:~:text=The%20top%2010%20providers%20of,Japan%20(8.56%25)> accessed on 24 February 2024.

Human Rights Watch, 'East Timor' (2001) <https://www.hrw.org/legacy/wr2k1/asia/etimor.html> accessed on 22 March 2021.

———, 'Human Rights in Papua: An Overview' (Watch Indonesia, 4–5 June 2003) <https://www.watchindonesia.de/6878/human-rights-overview-papua?lang=en> accessed on 4 February 2024.

———, 'Burma: Government Forces Targeting Rohingya Muslims' (Human Rights Watch, 31 July 2012) <https://www.hrw.org/news/2012/07/31/burma-government-forces-targeting-rohingya-muslims> accessed on 22 March 2021.

———, 'Southeast Asia: Accounts from Rohingya Boat People' (Human Rights Watch, 27 May 2015) <https://www.hrw.org/news/2015/05/27/southeast-asia-accounts-rohingya-boat-people> accessed on 22 March 2021.

———, 'Questions and Answers on Gambia's Genocide Case Against Myanmar before the International Court of Justice' (Human Rights Watch, 5 December 2019) <https://www.hrw.org/news/2019/12/05/questions-and-answers-gambias-genocide-case-against-myanmar-international-court> accessed on 18 March 2021.

'"Hundreds of Rohingyas" Killed in Myanmar Crackdown' (Al Jazeera, 3 February 2017) <https://www.aljazeera.com/news/2017/02/rohingyas-killed-myanmar-crackdown-170203101817841.html> accessed on 18 March 2021.

'In Dialogue with Indonesia, Experts of the Human Rights Committee Commend Measures Promoting Women's Political Participation, Raise Questions on Air Pollution and Water Pollution, and on Excessive Use of Force against Indigenous Papuans' (Office of the High Commissioner for Human Rights Press Release, 12 March 2024) <https://www.ohchr.org/en/news/2024/03/dialogue-indonesia-experts-human-rights-committee-commend-measures-promoting-womens> accessed on 12 March 2024.

'The Indigenous World 2022: West Papua' (International Work Group for Indigenous Affairs, 2022) <https://iwgia.org/en/indonesia/4660-iw-2022-west-papua.html?highlight=WyJ3ZXN0Iiwid2VzdCdzdXdldCdlbiIsInBhcHVhIiwicGFwdWEncyIsInBhcHVhJyIsIndlc3QgcGFwdWEiXQ==> accessed on 6 February 2024.

'Indonesia Dismisses U.N Experts' Call to Probe Alleged Abuses in Papua' (Reuters, 2 March 2022) <https://www.reuters.com/world/asia-pacific/indonesia-dismisses-un-experts-call-probe-alleged-abuses-papua-2022-03-02/> accessed on 13 February 2024.

'Indonesia, Malaysia Seeking ASEAN Meeting on Myanmar after Coup' (Bangkok Post, 5 February 2021) <https://www.bangkokpost.com/world/2063259/indonesia-malaysia-seeking-asean-meeting-on-myanmar-after-coup> accessed on 4 April 2021.

'Indonesian Minister to Raise Rohingya Plight with Suu Kyi' (AP News, 3 September 2017) <https://apnews.com/article/e9c79d7ae7ce4e7ab102dedf8e26e4ae> accessed on 18 March 2021.

'Indonesia Says "Positive" Signs from Myanmar's Warring Camp on Dialogue Effort' (Reuters, 24 November 2023) <https://www.reuters.com/world/asia-pacific/indonesia-says-positive-signs-myanmars-warring-camps-dialogue-effort-2023-11-24/> accessed on 27 February 2024.

'Indonesia: UN Experts Sound Alarm on Serious Papua Abuses, Call for Urgent Aid' (United Nations Human Rights Office of the High Commission Press Release, 1 March 2022) <https://www.ohchr.org/en/press-releases/2022/03/indonesia-un-experts-sound-alarm-serious-papua-abuses-call-urgent-aid> accessed on 12 February 2024.

'Indonesian, US Troops Begin "Super Garuda Shield" Joint Drills' (The Jakarta Post, 31 August 2023) <https://www.thejakartapost.com/indonesia/2023/08/31/indonesian-us-troops-begin-super-garuda-shield-joint-drills.html> accessed on 13 February 2024.

Jamasmie, C., 'Strike Hits Freeport's Grasberg Mine in Indonesia' (Mining, 3 October 2016) <https://www.mining.com/strike-hits-freeports-grasberg-mine-in-indonesia/> accessed on 10 February 2024.

James, R., '"We Are Living in a War Zone": Violence Flares in West Papua as Villagers Forced to Flee' (The Guardian, 11 May 2021) <https://www.theguardian.com/world/2021/may/11/we-are-living-in-a-war-zone-violence-flares-in-west-papua-as-villagers-forced-to-flee> accessed on 10 February 2024.

Jayadi, A., 'With a Seat on the UN Security Council, What Can Key ASEAN Member Indonesia Do to Solve the Rohingya Crisis?' (The Conversation, 24 September 2018) <https://theconversation.com/with-a-seat-on-the-un-security-council-what-can-key-asean-member-indonesia-do-to-solve-the-rohingya-crisis-102915> accessed on 18 March 2021.

Jiangtao, S., 'China's Qin Gang Pledges Economic Help for Myanmar, Stops Short of Recognising Junta' (South China Morning Post, 3 May 2023) <https://www.scmp.com/news/china/diplomacy/article/3219288/chinas-qin-gang-pledges-economic-help-myanmar-stops-short-recognising-junta> accessed on 24 February 2024.

Johnson, K. and Thepgumpanat, P., 'Analysis: Myanmar's Neighbour Thailand Unlikely to Toughen Stance on Coup' (Reuters, 2 April 2021) <https://www.reuters.com/article/us-myanmar-politics-thailand-analysis-idUSKBN2BP0LN> accessed on 5 April 2021.

'Joint Statement on Deepening Comprehensive Strategic Cooperation between the People's Republic of China and the Republic of Indonesia' (18 October 2023) <https://kemlu.go.id/portal/en/read/5393/siaran_pers/joint-statement-on-deepening-comprehensive-strategic-cooperation-between-the-peoples-republic-of-china-and-the-republic-of-indonesia-18-october-2023-beijing> accessed on 24 February 2024.

'Jokowi Urged to Resolve Freeport Worker Strike Amid Share Talks with CEOs' (West Papua Daily, 17 November 2023) <https://en.jubi.id/jokowi-urged-to-resolve-freeport-worker-strike-amid-share-talks-with-ceos/> accessed on 10 February 2024.

Karmini, N., 'ASEAN Leaders Tell Myanmar Coup General to End Killings' (AP News, 25 April 2021) <https://apnews.com/article/aung-san-suu-kyi-global-trade-indonesia-myanmar-singapore-2959338f61cbe0b0b7c6dd7599ee6e2c> accessed on 26 April 2021.

Krause-Jackson, F. and Kate, D.T., 'Myanmar Rape-Murder Sparks Outrage Over Abuse of Muslims' (Bloomberg, 31 August 2012) <https://www.bloomberg.com/news/articles/2012-08-31/myanmar-rape-murder-sparks-outrage-over-abuse-of-muslims> accessed on 2 April 2021.

Lam, L., 'Singapore Pledges $100,000 in Humanitarian Aid to Help in Myanmar's Rakhine Crisis' (The Straits Times, 19 October 2017) <https://www.straitstimes.com/singapore/singapore-pledges-100000-in-humanitarian-aid-to-help-in-myanmars-rakhine-crisis> accessed on 18 March 2021.

Lamb, K., 'West Papua Protests: Indonesia Deploys 1,000 Soldiers to Quell Unrest, Cuts Internet' (The Guardian, 22 August 2019) <https://www.theguardian.com/world/2019/aug/22/west-papua-protests-indonesia-deploys-1000-soldiers-to-quell-unrest> accessed on 10 February 2024.

'Malaysia PM Backs Indonesia's Call for ASEAN Summit on Myanmar' (Bangkok Post, 20 March 2021) <https://www.bangkokpost.com/world/2086847/malaysia-pm-backs-indonesias-call-for-asean-summit-on-myanmar> accessed on 4 April 2021.

'Malaysian PM Urges World to Act Against "Genocide" of Myanmar's Rohingya' (The Guardian, 4 December 2016) <https://www.theguardian.com/world/2016/dec/04/malaysia-pm-urges-world-to-act-against-genocide-of-myanmars-rohingya> accessed on 18 March 2021.

'Malaysia's Dissent on Myanmar Statement Reveals Cracks in ASEAN Façade' (Reuters, 25 September 2017) <https://www.reuters.com/article/us-myanmar-rohingya-malaysia-idUSKCN1C0124> accessed on 18 March 2021.

Mälksoo, L., 'Russia and China Challenge the Western Hegemony in the Interpretation of International Law' (Blog of the European Journal of International Law, 15 July 2016) <https://www.ejiltalk.org/russia-and-china-challenge-the-western-hegemony-in-the-interpretation-of-international-law/> accessed on 11 May 2021.

'Meeting in European Parliament Demands UN Visit to West Papua' (United Liberation Movement for West Papua, 22 January 2024) <https://www.ulmwp.org/meeting-in-european-parliament-demands-un-visit-to-west-papua> accessed on 13 February 2024.

Menon, R., 'Malaysia PM Opens Thorny Debate in Accusing Myanmar of Genocide' (Reuters, 9 December 2016) <https://www.reuters.com/article/us-myanmar-rohingya-malaysia/malaysia-pm-opens-thorny-debate-in-accusing-myanmar-of-genocide-idUSKBN13Y0IY> accessed on 18 March 2021.

Mufson, S. and Graham, B., 'U.S. and IMF Move to Isolate Indonesia' (Washington Post, 10 September 1999) <https://www.washingtonpost.com/wp-srv/inatl/daily/sept99/ustimor10.htm?> accessed on 15 January 2020.

'Myanmar Army Chief Says "No Right to Intervene" as U.N Weighs Rohingya Crisis' (Reuters, 24 September 2018) <https://uk.reuters.com/article/uk-myanmar-rohingya/myanmar-army-chief-says-no-right-to-interfere-as-u-n-weighs-rohingya-crisis-idUKKCN1M41KA> accessed on 5 June 2019.

'Myanmar: Army General Behind Coup "Agrees Violence Must Stop" after Regional Leaders Summit' (Sky News, 24 April 2021) <https://news.sky.com/story/general-behind-myanmar-coup-agrees-violence-must-stop-after-regional-leaders-summit-12285766> accessed on 26 April 2021.

'Myanmar Coup: Aung San Suu Kyi Detailed as Military Seizes Control' (BBC, 1 February 2021) <https://www.bbc.co.uk/news/world-asia-55882489> accessed on 4 April 2021.

'Myanmar Coup Leader Defends Action Amid Mass Protests' (BBC, 8 February 2021) <https://www.bbc.co.uk/news/world-asia-55975746> accessed on 5 April 2021.

'Myanmar Coup: The People Shot Dead Since the Protests Began' (BBC, 13 April 2021) <https://www.bbc.co.uk/news/world-asia-56636345> accessed on 17 April 2021.

'Myanmar Rebuffs Malaysia for Organizing OIC Meeting on Rohingya' (Reuters, 21 January 2017) <https://www.reuters.com/article/us-myanmar-rohingya/myanmar-rebuffs-malaysia-for-organizing-oic-meeting-on-rohingya-idUSKBN15508H> accessed on 18 March 2021.

'Myanmar Rohingya: UN Says Military Leaders Must Face Genocide Charges' (BBC, 27 August 2018) <https://www.bbc.co.uk/news/world-asia-45318982> accessed on 3 April 2019.

'Myanmar Seeking to Repatriate Rohingya Refugees from Bangladesh' (Aljazeera, 31 October 2023) <https://www.aljazeera.com/news/2023/10/31/myanmar-176> accessed on 24 February 2024.

'Myanmar Solidarity with Indonesia "Brothers"' (AFP, 13 September 1999) <https://www.burmalibrary.org/reg.burma/archives/199909/msg00559.html> accessed on 30 March 2021.

'Myanmar Will Not Be Allowed ASEAN Leadership in 2026' (Aljazeera, 5 September 2023) <https://www.aljazeera.com/news/2023/9/5/myanmar-will-not-be-allowed-asean-leadership-in-2026> accessed on 27 February 2024.

Narim, K., 'Cambodia, Myanmar Discuss Rohingya Refugees' (Khmer Times, 11 September 2019) <https://www.khmertimeskh.com/642106/cambodia-myanmar-discuss-rohingya-refugees/> accessed on 18 March 2021.

'New Zealand Calls for Pilot to Be Freed a Year after Papua Kidnapping' (The Jakarta Post, 5 February 2024) <https://www.thejakartapost.com/world/2024/02/05/new-zealand-calls-for-pilot-to-be-freed-a-year-after-papua-kidnapping.html> accessed on 10 February 2024.

Nichols, M., 'U.N Security Council Mulls Myanmar Action; Russia, China Boycott Talks' (Reuters, 17 December 2019) <https://uk.reuters.com/article/uk-myanmar-rohingya-un/u-n-security-council-mulls-myanmar-action-russia-china-boycott-talks-idUKKBN1OG2CH> accessed on 18 March 2021.

———, 'U.N. Security Council Wrestles with Threat of Action Over Myanmar Coup' (Reuters, 10 March 2021) <https://www.reuters.com/article/us-myanmar-politics-un-idUSKBN2B209S> accessed on 5 April 2021.

Osborne, S., 'US Criticises Russia's "Red Carpet Welcome" for Syrian President Assad' (The Independent, 22 October 2015) <https://www.independent.co.uk/news/world/americas/us-criticises-russias-red-carpet-welcome-for-syrian-president-bashar-al-assad-a6703951.html> accessed on 2 April 2019.

Peter Walker, 'Thai Military Claims Control after Coup' (The Guardian, 19 September 2006) <https://www.theguardian.com/world/2006/sep/19/thailand> accessed on 9 March 2021.

'Philippines' Duterte Cites "Genocide" in Myanmar, Says Will Take Refugee' (The Straits Time, 5 April 2018) <https://www.straitstimes.com/asia/se-asia/philippines-duterte-cites-genocide-in-myanmar-says-will-take-refugees> accessed on 18 March 2021.

'Philippines' Marcos Says Myanmar a Difficult Problem for ASEAN' (The Straits Times, 20 November 2023) <https://www.straitstimes.com/asia/se-asia/philippines-marcos-says-myanmar-a-difficult-problem-for-asean> accessed on 27 February 2024.

'Philippines President Duterte Tells Myanmar's Aung San Suu Kyi to Ignore "Noisy" Activists Over Rohingya Crisis' (The Independent, 27 January 2018) <https://www.independent.co.uk/news/world/asia/rohingya-refugee-crisis-myanmar-burma-bangladesh-asia-rodrigo-duterte-aung-san-suu-kyi-latest-a8180971.html> accessed on 18 March 2021.

'Pillay Concerned about Persistent Violence and Abuses in Papua (Indonesia)' (Office of the High Commissioner for Human Rights Press Release, 2 May 2013) <https://www.ohchr.org/en/press-releases/2013/05/pillay-concerned-about-persistent-violence-and-abuses-papua-indonesia?LangID=E&NewsID=13287> accessed on 13 February 2024.

'Protestor Killed in Indonesia Mine Strike' (The Guardian, 10 October 2011) <https://www.theguardian.com/world/2011/oct/10/indonesian-forces-striking-mine-workers> accessed on 10 February 2024.

Rahman, S., 'Myanmar's "Rohingya" vs "Bengali" Hate Speech Debate' (The Diplomat, 21 December 2019) <https://thediplomat.com/2019/12/myanmars-rohingya-vs-bengali-hate-speech-debate/> accessed on 2 April 2021.

'Remarks by Ms. Alice Wairimu Nderitu, Under Secretary-General, Special Advisor to the Secretary-General on the Prevention of Genocide' (United Nations Press Release, 4 July 2023) <https://www.un.org/en/genocideprevention/documents/Remarks_Alice%20Wairimu%20Nderitu_Special%20Adviser_53rd_Session_HRC_Interactive_dialogue%20.pdf> accessed on 13 February 2024.

'Remarks by President Obama at Opening Session of US-ASEAN Summit' (15 February 2016) <https://obamawhitehouse.archives.gov/the-press-office/2016/02/15/remarks-president-obama-opening-session-us-asean-summit> accessed on 7 December 2020.

'Resistance Leader Rejects East Timor Offer' (The BBC, 9 June 1998) <http://news.bbc.co.uk/1/hi/events/indonesia/latest_news/109595.stm> accessed on 21 February 2020.

Rodgers, L., et al., 'Syria: The Story of Conflict' (BBC, 11 March 2016) <http://www.bbc.co.uk/news/world-middle-east-26116868> accessed 20 February 2017.

'Rwandan Genocide: 100 Days of Slaughter' (BBC, 7 April 2014) <http://www.bbc.co.uk/news/world-africa-26875506> accessed on 14 December 2020.

'Seven Countries Support West Papua at the UN General Assembly!' (Free West Papua Campaign, 27 September 2016) <https://www.freewestpapua.org/2016/09/27/seven-countries-support-west-papua-at-the-un-general-assembly/> accessed on 13 February 2024.

Simons, M. and Beech, H., 'Aung San Suu Kyi Defends Myanmar Against Rohingya Genocide Accusations' (The New York Times, 23 January 2020) <https://www.nytimes.com/2019/12/11/world/asia/aung-san-suu-kyi-rohingya-myanmar-genocide-hague.html> accessed on 18 March 2021.

Shofa, J.N., 'Indonesia Says No One Brings Up Papua Issue at Recent UNGA Forum' (Jakarta Globe, 29 September 2023) <https://jakartaglobe.id/news/indonesia-says-no-one-brings-up-papua-issue-at-recent-unga-forum> accessed on 13 February 2024.

'Singapore Urges Calm from All Sides in Myanmar Conflict, Offers to Work with ASEAN to Provide Humanitarian Aid' (The Straits Times, 8 September 2017) <https://www.straitstimes.com/singapore/singapore-says-ready-to-work-with-myanmar-to-restore-peace-and-stability-in-rakhine-state> accessed on 18 March 2021.

Smith, M., 'The Muslim Rohingya of Burma' [1995] *Conference Paper at the Burma Centrum Netherlands*, p. 5 <http://www.netipr.org/policy/downloads/19951211-Rohingyas-of-Burma-by-Martin-Smith.pdf> accessed on 2 April 2021.

Sokhean, B., 'Another Shot: Mr Hun Sen Will to Hold Talks with Myanmar Junta Again' (Khmer Times, 12 October 2023) <https://www.khmertimeskh.com/501375066/another-shot-mr-hun-sen-willing-to-hold-talks-with-myanmar-junta-again/> accessed on 27 February 2024.

'Southeast Asian Leaders Struggle with Myanmar Crisis at Summit' (Aljazeera, 11 November2022)<https://www.aljazeera.com/news/2022/11/11/southeast-asia-leaders-struggle-with-myanmar-crisis-at-summit> accessed on 27 February 2024.

'Special Committee on Decolonization' (United Nations) <https://www.un.org/dppa/decolonization/en/c24/about> accessed on 13 February 2024.

'Speech by Judge Xue Hanqin at the Chinese Observations on International Law at the International Criminal Law Network' (1 November 2006) <https://www.mfa.gov.cn/eng/wjb_663304/zwjg_665342/zwbd_665378/200612/t20061204_601878.html> accessed on 23 February 2024.

Spencer, R., 'France Supplying Weapons to Libyan Rebels' (The Telegraph, 29 June 2011) <http://www.telegraph.co.uk/news/worldnews/africaandindianocean/libya/8606541/France-supplying-weapons-to-Libyan-rebels.html> accessed on 20 March 2021.

'Spokesperson: Chinese Blue Helmets Become Vital Force in UN's Peacekeeping Efforts' (The State Council Information Office- The People's Republic of China, 31 May 2023) <http://english.scio.gov.cn/pressroom/2023-05/31/content_85949249.htm> accessed on 24 February 2024.

Sterling, J., 'Daraa: The Spark That Lit the Syrian Flame' (CNN, 1 March 2012) <http://edition.cnn.com/2012/03/01/world/meast/syria-crisis-beginnings/> accessed on 20 February 2017.

Strangio, S., 'ASEAN Foreign Ministers Meet to Discuss Myanmar Crisis' (The Diplomate, 3 March 2021) <https://thediplomat.com/2021/03/asean-foreign-ministers-meet-to-discuss-myanmar-crisis/> accessed on 4 April 2021.

———, 'Singapore Joins Calls for Emergency ASEAN Summit on Myanmar' (The Diplomat, 26 March 2021) <https://thediplomat.com/2021/03/singapore-joins-calls-for-emergency-asean-summit-on-myanmar/> accessed on 5 April 2021.

———, 'China Pledges Support for Myanmar's Junta, "No Matter How the Situation Changes"' (The Diplomat, 4 April 2022) <https://thediplomat.com/2022/04/china-pledges-support-for-myanmars-junta-no-matter-how-the-situation-changes/> accessed on 24 February 2024.

'Strike Prolonged in Controversial Papuan Mine' (Aljazeera, 9 November 2011) <https://www.aljazeera.com/economy/2011/11/9/strike-prolonged-in-controversial-papuan-mine> accessed on 10 February 2024.

Supriatma, M., 'The Second Amendment to Papua's Special Autonomy Law and the Recentralization of Power to Jakarta' (ISEAS Perspective, 2021) <https://www.iseas.edu.sg/articles-commentaries/iseas-perspective/2021-123-the-second-amendment-to-papuas-special-autonomy-law-and-the-recentralization-of-power-to-jakarta-by-made-supriatma/> accessed on 10 February 2024.

'Thailand "Run Against Dictatorship" Draws Thousands' (The BBC, 12 January 2020) <https://www.bbc.co.uk/news/world-asia-51082419> accessed on 18 March 2021.

'Thailand Says Closely Watching Myanmar Crisis, Ready to Provide Aid' (Reuters, 1 October 2017) <https://www.reuters.com/article/us-thailand-myanmar-rohingya/thailand-says-closely-watching-myanmar-crisis-ready-to-provide-aid-idUSKCN1C60XN> accessed on 18 March 2021.

Tien, N., 'Vietnam Calls for End of Violence to End in Myanmar' (Vietnam Express International, 17 November 2023) <https://e.vnexpress.net/news/news/vietnam-calls-for-end-of-violence-in-myanmar-4582791.html> accessed on 27 February 2024.

Tisnadibrata, I.L., 'Jakarta Sends More Humanitarian Aid Relief for Rohingya' (Arab News, 21 September 2017) <https://www.arabnews.com/node/1164771/world> accessed on 18 March 2021.

Tobing, D.H., 'Will Indonesia Bring the Rohingya Issue to UN Security Council? Jakarta Post Contributor' (The Strait Times, 25 June 2018) <https://www.straitstimes.com/asia/se-asia/will-indonesia-bring-the-rohingya-issue-to-un-security-council-jakarta-post-contributor> accessed on 18 March 2021.

Tong, G.C., 'ASEAN Is "At a Loss for Ideas" on How to Address Myanmar Crisis, Says Indonesia; Sex Foreign Minister' (CNBC, 5 September 2023) <https://www.cnbc.com/2023/09/05/asean-at-a-loss-for-ideas-on-myanmar-crisis-ex-indonesian-minister.html> accessed on 27 February 2024.

'UN Fails to Take Action on Order Against Myanmar on Rohingya' (Aljazeera, 5 February 2020) <https://www.aljazeera.com/news/2020/2/5/un-fails-to-take-action-on-order-against-myanmar-on-rohingya> accessed on 5 April 2021.

'U.S Congress Maintains Restrictions on Military Assistance for Indonesia' (East Timor & Indonesia Action Network, 21 November 2004) <https://www.etan.org/news/2004/11appr.htm> accessed on 13 February 2024.

'Vietnam Calls on World Community to Help Myanmar Prevent Violence' (VN Explorer, 10 April 2021) <https://vnexplorer.net/vietnam-calls-on-world-community-to-help-myanmar-prevent-violence-a2021146179.html> accessed on 10 April 2021.

'Wang Yi Attends the Opening Ceremony of the International Symposium Commemorating the 75th Anniversary of the Universal Declaration of Human Rights' (5 December 2023) <http://ki.china-embassy.gov.cn/eng/zgywx/202312/t20231211_11199389.htm>accessed on 23 February 2024.

'West Papuans Jailed for Raising Banned Morning Star Flag' (RNZ, 2 September 2022) <https://www.rnz.co.nz/international/pacific-news/473973/west-papuans-jailed-for-raising-banned-morning-star-flag> accessed on 10 February 2024.

'The West Papua Report: March 2004' (East Timor & Indonesia Action Network, 2004) <https://www.etan.org/issues/wpapua/rfk2/0403wpap.htm> accessed on 13 February 2024.

'Why Russia Is Standing by Syria's Assad' (BBC, 15 June 2012) <http://www.bbc.co.uk/news/world-europe-18462813> accessed on 20 March 2021.

Withnall, A., 'Burma: 21,000 Rohingya Muslims Flee to Bangladesh Amid "Attempted Genocide"' (The Independent, 6 December 2016) <https://www.independent.co.uk/news/world/asia/burma-21000-rohingya-muslims-flee-bangladesh-attempted-genocide-a7458091.html> accessed on 22 March 2021.

Young, H.A., 'Intrastate Conflicts: Refocus on the Intractable' (MPSA, 12 September 2017) <https://blog.mpsanet.org/2017/09/12/intrastate-conflicts-refocus-on-the-intractable/> accessed on 7 December 2020.

Zhang, R., 'Beating the Odds: How ASEAN Helped Southeast Asia Succeed' (Harvard Political Review, 15 March 2020) <https://harvardpolitics.com/asean-beats-the-odds/> accessed on 7 December 2020.

Zhou, L., '"Let's Build a Digital Silk Road": Xi Jinping Looks to Cement China's Ties with ASEAN' (South China Morning Post, 27 November 2020) <https://www.scmp.com/news/china/diplomacy/article/3111612/lets-build-digital-silk-road-president-xi-promises-ways-china> accessed on 7 December 2020.

# Index